D1797134

Borders and Boundaries

This book examines the making and remaking of borders and boundaries primarily relating to Ireland.

Borders and Boundaries features selected papers from the 33rd Irish Conference of Historians held by the University of Galway in May 2021 on the theme of 'Borders and Boundaries'. It covers the medieval to the contemporary, allowing a long view to be taken of the north-west border of Ireland, the borders of the early modern state, the impact of the partition of Ireland and social boundaries in the late twentieth century. It aims to stimulate debate and highlight how borders can be written out of history while remaining essential to comprehending the making and remaking of our worlds.

This volume will be of value for those interested in border studies, Irish history and modern history.

Tomás Finn is Lecturer in History at the University of Galway. He has published a book and articles on the role of intellectuals and the influence of ideas in the modernisation of Ireland. These include his monograph *Tuairim, Intellectual Debate and Policy Formulation: Rethinking Ireland, 1954–75*.

Kieran Hoare works as an archivist at University of Galway Library. His research interests cover urban studies in later medieval Ireland.

Routledge Studies in Modern History

Genocide and Fascism
The eliminationist drive in Fascist Europe
Aristotle Kallis

Scientific Research in World War II
What scientists did in the War
Edited by Ad Maas and Hans Hooijmaijers

Restoration and History
The search for a useable environmental past
Edited by Marcus Hall

Foundations of Modernity
Human agency and the imperial state
By Isa Blumi

Transpacific Revolutionaries
The Chinese Revolution in Latin America
By Matthew D. Rothwell

First World War Nursing
New perspectives
Edited by Alison S. Fell and Christine E. Hallett

Borders and Boundaries
Historical Perspectives
Edited by Tomás Finn and Kieran Hoare

For more information about this series, please visit: https://www.routledge.com/Routledge-Studies-in-Modern-History/book-series/MODHIST

Borders and Boundaries

Historical Perspectives

Edited by Tomás Finn and Kieran Hoare

Routledge
Taylor & Francis Group

LONDON AND NEW YORK

First published 2026
by Routledge
4 Park Square, Milton Park, Abingdon, Oxon OX14 4RN

and by Routledge
605 Third Avenue, New York, NY 10158

Routledge is an imprint of the Taylor & Francis Group, an informa business

© 2026 selection and editorial matter, Tomás Finn and Kieran Hoare; individual chapters, the contributors

The right of Tomás Finn and Kieran Hoare to be identified as the authors of the editorial material, and of the authors for their individual chapters, has been asserted in accordance with sections 77 and 78 of the Copyright, Designs and Patents Act 1988.

All rights reserved. No part of this book may be reprinted or reproduced or utilised in any form or by any electronic, mechanical, or other means, now known or hereafter invented, including photocopying and recording, or in any information storage or retrieval system, without permission in writing from the publishers.

Trademark notice: Product or corporate names may be trademarks or registered trademarks, and are used only for identification and explanation without intent to infringe.

British Library Cataloguing-in-Publication Data
A catalogue record for this book is available from the British Library

ISBN: 978-1-032-69186-2 (hbk)
ISBN: 978-1-032-69187-9 (pbk)
ISBN: 978-1-032-69188-6 (ebk)

DOI: 10.4324/9781032691886

Typeset in Sabon
by Apex CoVantage, LLC

Contents

Figures

Maps

Contributors

Ian d'Alton, FRHistS, FRNS, is a visiting research fellow at the Centre for Contemporary Irish History, Trinity College Dublin. He has recently published *Southern Irish Protestants – Histories, Lives & Literatures* (Dublin, 2024).

Steven Ellis, MA, PhD, DLitt, MRIA, FRHistS, taught history in English and Irish at the University of Galway for forty years until his retirement in 2015 as Established Professor of History and Head of the School of Humanities. His latest book is *Ireland's English Pale, 1470–1550: The Making of a Tudor Region* (Woodbridge, 2021).

Raingard Esser is Professor of Early Modern History at the University of Groningen. She is a specialist in early modern migration, border studies and cultures of memory in Western Europe. Her recent publications include *Borders, Bordering Practices and Mobility in Early Modern Europe* (edited with Steven G. Ellis, Hannover, 2025). She currently works on the international cross-border project "Grenzgänger" together with colleagues from the Universities of Groningen and Oldenburg.

Gerard Hanley is a research fellow in the School of History and Geography at Dublin City University. He holds a PhD in history from Dublin City University. He has recently published *Workers, Politics and Labour Relations in Independent Ireland, 1922–46* (Dublin, 2024).

Leslie Herman has a BS in architecture from the University of Virginia, an MS in historic preservation and a PhD in architectural history and theory from Columbia University, where she was awarded the Ali Jawad Malik Memorial History/Theory Award.

Seán Ó Hoireabhárd is currently postdoctoral fellow on the 'Power and Patronage: Clonard from the sixth to twelfth centuries' project at Maynooth University, and a former John O'Donovan Scholar at the Dublin Institute for Advanced Studies (2022–5) and Irish Research Council Government of Ireland Postgraduate Scholar (2017–21). He has recently published 'The Medieval Irish kings and the English Invasion' (2024) with Liverpool University Press.

Barry Keane is an independent scholar. His books include *Massacre in West Cork* (Cork, 2014) and *Cork's Revolutionary Dead* (Cork, 2017).

Stephen Kelly is Head of the School of Humanities and Professor of Modern Irish History and British-Irish Relations at Liverpool Hope University. He has recently published *Gerald Boland: A Life* (Dublin, 2024).

Christopher Maginn, PhD, FRHistS, is Professor of History at Fordham University. His publications include, with Steven Ellis, *The Tudor Discovery of Ireland* (Dublin, 2015).

Ciara Molloy is Lecturer in Criminology in the School of Law, University of Sheffield. Recent publications include 'Images of Youth Deviance in the Irish Republic: The Case of the Bugsy Malones', *Irish Probation Journal*, 20 (2023), pp. 38–55.

Cormac Moore holds a PhD in history from De Montfort University, Leicester, and an MA in Modern Irish History from University College Dublin. He is Historian in Residence for Dublin South East and the author of *The Root of All Evil: The Irish Boundary Commission* (2025), *Laois: The Irish Revolution, 1912–23* (2025), *Birth of the Border: The Impact of Partition in Ireland* (2019), *The Irish Soccer Split* (2015), and *The GAA V Douglas Hyde: The Removal of Ireland's First President as GAA Patron* (2012). He is a columnist with the *Irish News* and editor of its daily 'On This Day' segment. He also co-presents the history podcast series The Irish History Boys with Tim McGarry.

Neil Murphy is Associate Professor of History at Northumbria University. His publications include *The Tudor Occupation of Boulogne: Conquest, Colonisation and Imperial Monarchy, 1544–1550* (Cambridge, 2019).

Barry Sheppard is an independent researcher. He completed his PhD thesis at Queen's University Belfast. His PhD thesis focused on the Irish priest and rural leader, John Hayes, and the transnational connections his organisation, Muintir na Tire made in the mid 20th-century. Barry was the presenter of the History Now television show on Belfast's Northern Visions Television. He was an Associate Fellow of the Institute of Irish Studies at Queen's University and a previous recipient of the Robert Dudley Edwards History Prize (2012).

Catherine Swift is Lecturer in History at Mary Immaculate College, University of Limerick. Her most recent publication is, as coeditor, *Limestone and River: Essays on Thomond History in Honour of Liam Irwin* (Dublin, 2024).

1 Introduction

The Making and Re-making of Borders

Tomás Finn and Kieran Hoare

The chapters in this volume are a selection of those read at the 33rd biennial Irish Conference of Historians held online by the University of Galway on 21–22 May 2021 under the aegis of the Irish Committee of Historical Sciences (the representative body for national historical societies throughout the island of Ireland).

The biennial conference has been the principal general meeting of academic historians in Ireland and, from the earliest conferences in the 1950s, the programme has traditionally included a number of distinguished historians from outside Ireland and is broadly based. 'Borders and Boundaries', the theme for this conference, has likewise been interpreted in the widest sense for this publication, to include a range of papers from the medieval, early modern and modern eras.

As conference organisers, we are especially grateful for financial and other assistance to Prof Enrico dal Lago, head of the School of History and Philosophy at the University of Galway, Prof Daniel Carey, director of the Moore Institute, and John Cox, University Librarian. Holding the conference online in the midst of a global pandemic posed its own unique set of problems, and we wish to thank Cormac Staunton of Stauntonmedia whose professionalism and technical expertise proved invaluable. The publication of these proceedings has been made possible through generous grants from the Galway2020 fund of University of Galway, and from the Irish Committee of Historical Sciences.

In this era of neo-liberal globalisation and the various authoritarian responses to it, the political discourse around borders and boundaries has taken on new meaning. Whether in Trump's America, Brexit Britain, or – more recently – the re-igniting of the Cold War and invasion of the Ukraine. Nationalist and Regionalist responses to political, economic and social trends tend to reinforce and remake borders. The late-twentieth-century impulse towards loosening legal and social restrictions around a range of class, gender and other personal boundaries within society has also elicited a range of responses. This does not happen in a vacuum; historical perspectives are vital to our understanding of these trends, as is the historical accuracy necessary to combat against the phenomenon of 'fake news'.

DOI: 10.4324/9781032691886-1

The papers in this volume look at the making and remaking of borders and boundaries primarily, but not exclusively, relating to Ireland. It ranges in time from early medieval to contemporary. The first group of papers look at borders and boundaries as identity markers in religious, political and economic spheres in the Middle Ages. A second group of papers examine the state formation process in the early modern period. They also examine border creation, interaction within border communities and reaction to the sharpening religious and political divides at this time.

A further group of papers deal with border formation on the island of Ireland in the twentieth century, with a number of articles on the impact, reaction to and aftermath of partition. There are studies of southern protestant identity, political discourse and the everyday lives of people living along the newly created border.

Finally, the last group of papers focus on a range of societal and political questions that have challenged and responded to various divisions in Irish society from the 1930s onwards. They deal with the trade union movement, Muintir na Tíre, political parties, the teddy boy sub-culture and British responses to the Irish Border under Margaret Thatcher's premiership.

The historiographical setting for medieval and early modern borders highlights the concept of the frontier which was first established at the end of the nineteenth century in relation to the American west.[1] Archibald Lewis adapted many of the ideas put forward by F. J. Turner in his work on medieval Spain. This in turn influenced the work of historians such as Charles Julian Biishko, Robert I. Burns and Angus Mackay.[2] The work of Robert Bartlett and others highlights not only the role of the European 'core' in defining Latin Christendom in the late Middle Ages but also the role of the periphery in interacting to various degrees with the core lands.[3] The march, as a society 'organized for war' to quote Elena Lourie's memorable phrase, has been studied extensively.[4] David Abulafia and Nora Berend's edited volume on medieval frontiers explores the vagueness of the term and examines it as an imaginary construct, highlighting the role of religious and cultural assumptions rather than a 'hard' border. Indeed, David Abulafia asserts that medieval frontiers were not so much a 'hard fact' as 'an identifiable tool' for historians to make sense of social and political developments in the periphery.

When one looks at the themes around medieval frontiers, many of them are applicable to Ireland. While it excites David Abulafia's considerable ire that 'celtic lands' and northern Europe rather than the Mediterranean zone have dominated case studies of medieval frontiers, most of the themes identified in his methodological approach have been illustrated in Irish historiography. Certainly, the military nature of the frontier and the border society it generated in the late Middle Ages has been closely studied.[5]

The concept of core and periphery, as outlined by Immanuel Wallerstein's world systems theory, describes the relationship between dominant and subordinate regions within a larger economic system.[6] In this model, the core represents the dominant regions, which control the most advanced technologies and the highest levels of capital accumulation. The periphery consists of the subordinate regions, which tend to be more dependent on the core for economic support. This framework can be applied to medieval Europe, where powerful empires like the Holy Roman Empire, Byzantine Empire, and the Islamic Caliphates can be seen as the core. Smaller states and kingdoms on the periphery like Ireland, Scotland, and Wales were often marginalised and subject to external influence. In the high Middle Ages, concepts of otherness began to appear, with groups like the Moors, Jews and Romani people being cast as outsiders within European society. This language of otherness anticipated many of the theories of race and power that would come to the fore in the early modern and modern eras.[7]

In the context of Ireland, the country has long been viewed as England's first colony, with English control of the island dating back to the Norman invasion in the twelfth century. This colonial relationship has shaped how we view pre-Norman Ireland, as well as the interaction between English and Gaelic lords in the late Middle Ages and their interaction with royal government. Nationalist and unionist traditions have further shaped our understanding of Irish history.[8] Overall, the trope of core and periphery and the language of otherness have played a significant role in shaping our understanding of medieval European history and the ongoing impact of colonialism on contemporary societies.

This has shaped our view of the economic relationship Ireland had – primarily with England – and its role in providing land for settlers, as well as natural resources for core areas; for example, wool was exported to Coventry and wool and hides to the Flemish ports and fish to Bristol and Chester. It also provided a ready, if small, market for manufactured and imported goods from these ports.[9] In terms of the political context, the impact of border conditions in medieval Ireland on what were essentially English institutions, and the interaction between royal government and lordship society, has been well studied.[10] The impact of this frontier society on perceptions of the other has been another strand of historiography which has yielded some excellent scholarship.[11]

The military nature of medieval frontiers has also been to the fore in the European historiography,[12] perhaps best typified in later medieval Ireland by the English Pale.[13] While notions of a frontier have been tied into early modern state formation, there can be little doubt that political, religious and economic identity in later medieval Europe played a role in frontier development. The myriad of borders and boundaries which formed across medieval Europe also existed in Ireland. These include monastic and diocesan boundaries, jurisdictional boundaries such as liberties, boroughs and other micro-frontiers, lordship boundaries and within the lordship different cadet branches contesting for power. People may have had multiple identifiers, and could move over frontiers to take on new roles. The three medieval papers in this volume reflect this fluidity and show the complexity of borders and boundaries in the lives of people. They also highlight that these issues were as much to the fore in pre-Norman Ireland as they were in the late Middle Ages. Catherine Swift's snapshot of Limerick city and its immediate hinterland in 1200, a Hiberno-Norse town under O Briain control, coming to terms with the new order and reconstituted as a royal borough, highlights the range of borders and boundaries in a small area. Seán Ó Hoireabhárd's study of the contested territory of Cairpre Dromma Cliabh in present-day County Sligo examines not only the regional and local implications of this frontier zone but also offers a trenchant criticism of the historiographical boundary between pre-Norman and Anglo-Norman studies. The final paper in this section examines the notion of urban decline in later medieval Ireland showing that the imperative for defence provided opportunities for urban civic elites, and that their experience needs to be placed in the wider context of the borderlands of the English polity.

It is clear that the concept of frontiers and boundaries played a significant role in the development of political, religious and economic identity in medieval Ireland. These frontiers were not static, but rather constantly in flux as different groups vied for power and influence. Religious and jurisdictional boundaries such as monastic and diocesan boundaries, shires, liberties and boroughs, and lordship boundaries all contributed to the complexity of these frontier zones. People in medieval Ireland often had multiple identities and could move freely across these borders to take on new roles.

If the concepts surrounding borders and boundaries remain vague and multi-faceted in medieval Europe, thoughts begin to crystalise in the early modern era. This process can be framed in terms of discovery, reform and hardening borders. Information and administrative processes begin to take centre stage with the ready availability of paper, a level of literacy, and the widening exploration of the world by Europeans. The transmission of requests, reports and analysis of issues becomes more commonplace in the sixteenth century. With the 'age of paper' rulers and their proxies issue instructions, supervise administrators in far-flung corners and influence local elites.[14]

While it could be argued that later medieval Ireland was always known to royal administrators in London through petitions, oral reports from messengers and indeed the attendance at court by Irish aristocrats and administrators, the 'reformation of Ireland' treatises of the late fifteenth and sixteenth centuries represents an altogether different level of information gathering, both in terms of the range of information and attempts to influence royal policy.[15] In a similar vein, the mapping projects of the later sixteenth and seventeenth centuries allowed for the visualisation of geographic knowledge, as well as the definition of political borders, natural boundaries, and all manner of sub-divisions.[16] All of this impacted the administration of Ireland and how it interacted with the court in London.[17]

This availability of information fed into the process of state formation in early modern Europe, and the subsequent impetus for political and religious reform. With state formation, political borders become more defined, and there are many contested spaces where various political and religious reforms are enthusiastically adopted or strenuously resisted. For border areas, state formation often accelerated core/periphery interaction in the borderlands. It is also true to say that what did and did not constitute a citizen of the state influences one's agency in a socio-economic, political and cultural setting. Across Europe, this led to political and confessional conflict. The exercise of authority and interaction with government led to a change in expectations for both rulers and ruled.[18] Living at the frontier or border shaped identity under these new power structures, and much of the political milieu is informed by attempts to reconcile or resolve the conflicts which inevitably arose from this change. In an Irish setting, this was probably most evident in the religious and political changes which occurred.[19] It is also evident in terms of the various plantations and introduction of the New English settlers through the course of the later sixteenth and seventeenth centuries,[20] as well as the reaction of the Gaelic and Old English communities.[21] Ireland's location in the early modern Atlantic world also played a part in forming identity, whether it was links with the Irish Catholic émigré community in Europe or with the trading network built on access to the Atlantic throughout the early modern period.[22]

All of these historiographical strands influence or are influenced by questions around borders and boundaries. If borders and boundaries in the medieval period were identified broadly by lordship, in the early modern era, identity is tied up more with state allegiance, religion and socio-economic considerations. Physical boundaries, rather than allegiance of people, become a key signifier, and there is ultimately little room for deviation, as markers of language, law and custom become more uniform.

The chapters in this volume reflect these issues, either in case studies or through detailed study of the historiography surrounding borders and boundaries. Neil Murphy's study of the Laws of Guines offers us a blueprint for other Tudor plantations in Ireland and ultimately across the Atlantic world. Steven Ellis contends that a boundary such as the English Pale around Dublin were as much points of interaction as they were points of separation. In re-visiting the border of north-west Ireland in the later sixteenth century, Christopher Maginn draws together many of the practical difficulties facing government policy at this time, and how the absence of a loyal Irish or planted English community necessitated costly military garrisons which were financially unsustainable, and ultimately led to the Nine Years War. Raingard Esser's paper on the issuing of *saovegardes* offers insights into not only the impact of borders and boundaries on wider historiographical questions but also how we must guard against missing hidden communities who traverse and live across boundaries as this time and can as a result get written out of history. Although technically not an early modern paper, Leslie Herman's paper deals with one such group, Irish architects working in colonial America and how later historians' perceptions of civility and race conceal their identity from public knowledge.

If the first half of this volume deals with the making of borders and boundaries, and that liminal area between shifting loyalties and expectations, the second half deals with the impact of questions around borders and boundaries on twentieth-century Ireland. More generally globalisation and the nation state have been brought into sharp focus in recent research, and border studies have taken up the challenge of understanding the various processes at work in the relationship between the two.[23] Ireland and Northern Ireland have been well-served by general histories in the last forty years,[24] and indeed the border as it now exists has been the subject of some excellent studies.[25] Historians have grappled with the wider historiographical issues of nationalist history, globalisation, so-called New British history, and the 'Europeanisation' of Irish history.[26] Public history has also had an impact on how we write history. Most notably but not exclusively around the recent 'Decade of Commemorations' – which, being Ireland, runs from the Covenant to the Irish Boundary Commission 2012 to 2025! As the space formerly held by academic historians becomes more populated with funding bodies, trusts, activism, populist commentary, broadcasters and so on, is there a place in society for historical professionalism and expertise?[27] Equally, is academic history equipped to meet the demands for representing equality and diversity in the twenty-first century?

The papers in this section reflect both the impact of partition and its continuing ramifications, but also the impact of boundaries on other aspects of Irish society. There are three papers within this book that deal with the impact of partition; Barry Keane's study of Protestant demography from 1911–1926, Cormac Moore's survey of the day-to-day effects of partition, and Ian D'Alton's paper on the creation of a Protestant Free State within the Irish Free State. Gerard Hanley's examination of the schism in the trade union movement after independence and Barry Sheppard's paper on rural activism both highlight some of the social boundaries existent in 1930s Ireland and attempts to overcome them. Another social boundary, that of the responses of youth to post–Second World War Irish society, is explored in two papers, Ciara Malloy's evocation of the Teddy Boy sub-culture and Tomás Finn's study of the youth wing of Ireland's political parties at the time. Stephen Kelly's paper on Margaret Thatcher's view of the border reflects a regime bereft of political ideas in dealing with the Troubles, but also dealing with the real security concerns posed by the border.

In his lengthy afterword for *In Defence of History* published three years after the initial publication, Richard J. Evans ended by stating 'stimulating debate was one of the book's principal aims; it was never intended to close down discussion (nor would that have been a feasible aim in any case)'.[28] In our own case, we can but hope that this volume will stimulate debate around the many facets of borders and boundaries. It is important that the questions raised by the study of borders and boundaries are brought into the wider historiographical debate. A second aim was to show borders and boundaries can be written out of history, and to show how overarching historiographical tropes can stymie research. It is hoped this collection of papers helps to challenge received notions of 'our' history, and will allow new techniques and fields of research to develop around the question of borders and boundaries in history. Ultimately, it reflects the diversity of our past.

Notes

1 F.J. Turner, 'The Significance of the Frontier in American History', in F.J. Turner (ed.), *The Frontier in American History* (New York, 1920), pp. 1–38; L. Febvre, 'The Problem of Frontiers and the Natural Bounds of States', in *A Geographical Introduction to History* E.G. Mountford and J.H. Paxton (trans.) (London, 1932), pp. 296–314; L. Febvre, '*Frontière*: The Word and the Concept', in P. Burke (ed.), *A New Kind of History: From the Writings of Lucien Febvre*, K. Folca (trans.) (London, 1973), pp. 208–218; Owen Lattimore, *Studies in Frontier History* (London, 1962); A.L. Hartado, 'Parkmanizing the Spanish Borderlands: Bolton, Turner and the Historians' World', *Western Historical Quarterly* 26 (1995), pp. 149–167.

2 Archibald Lewis, 'The Closing of the Medieval Frontier, 1250–1350', *Speculum* 33 (1958), pp. 475–483; Charles Julian Bishko, 'The Castilian as Plainsman: The Medieval Ranching Frontier in La Mancha and Extremadura', in Archibald R. Lewis and Thomas F. McGann (eds.), *The New World Looks at its History* (Austin TX, 1963), pp. 47–69; Robert I. Burns, 'The Significance of the Frontier in the Middle Ages', in Robert Bartlett and Angus McKay (eds.), *Medieval Frontier Societies* (Oxford, 1989), pp. 307–330; Angus MacKay, *Spain in the Middle Ages: From Frontier to Empire, 1000–1500* (London, 1977).

3 Robert Bartlett, *The Making of Europe: Conquest, Colonization and Cultural Change, 950–1350* (Princeton, NJ, 1994).

4 E. Lourie, 'A Society Organised for War: Medieval Spain', *Past & Present* 35 (1966), pp. 54–76; on the military nature of medieval frontiers see the articles in D.J. Power and N. Standen (eds.), *Frontiers in Question: Eurasian Borderlands, 700–1700* (Basingstoke, 1999); on this concept in the British Isles, see A. Goodman, 'The Anglo-Scottish Marches in the Fifteenth Century: A Frontier Society?', in R.A. Mason (ed.), *Scotland and England, 1286–1815* (Edinburgh, 1987), pp. 18–33; Steven G. Ellis, 'The English State and its Frontiers in the British Isles, 1300–1600', in Power and Standen (eds.), *Frontiers in Question*, pp. 153–181; M. Liebermann, *The Medieval March of Wales: The Creation and Perception of a Frontier, 1066–1283* (Cambridge, 2010).

5 James F. Lydon, 'The Problem of the Frontier in Medieval Ireland', *Topic* 13 (1967), pp. 5–22; James Muldoon, *Identity on the Medieval Irish Frontier: Degenerate Englishmen, Wild Irishmen, Noble Nations* (Gainesville, FL, 2003); James Muldoon (ed.), *The North Atlantic Frontier in Medieval Europe* (Farnham, 2009); Brendan Smith, 'Beyond Reform and Revival: English Government in Late Medieval Ireland', in Christopher Maginn and Gerald Power (eds.), *Frontiers, States and Identity in Early Modern Ireland and Beyond: Essays in Honour of Steven G. Ellis* (Dublin, 2016), pp. 21–35; Cathy Swift, 'A Frontier Town in Europe's Wild West', *Archaeology Ireland* 33(3) (2019), pp. 14–17.

6 Immanuel Wallerstein, *The Modern World Systems*, vol. 1: Capitalist Agriculture and the Origins of the European World Economy in the Sixteenth Century (London, 1974). For the application of the ideas of core and periphery in medieval Europe see John Hudson, 'The Making of Europe: A Brief Summary', in John

Hudson and Sally Crumplin (eds.), *The Making of Europe: Essays in Honour of Robert Bartlett* (London, 2016), pp. 5–10.

7 Steven Epstein, *Purity Lost: Transgressing Boundaries in the Eastern Mediterranean, 1000–1400* (Baltimore, 2007); Geraldine Heng, *The Invention of Race in the European Middle Ages* (Cambridge, 2018). On the concept of colony as it applies to medieval Ireland, see now Peter Crooks, 'Colony', in Jackson W. Armstrong, Peter Crooks, and Andrea Ruddick (eds.), *Using Concepts in Medieval History: Perspectives on Britain and Ireland, 1100–1500* (Cham, 2022), pp. 55–72.

8 Kieran Hoare, 'From Region to Nation: The Development of Irish Nationalist Historiography 1880–1920', in S.G. Ellis et al. (eds.), *Frontiers, Regions and Identities in Europe* (Pisa, 2009), pp. 205–221; Ciarán Brady, *James Anthony Froude: an Intellectual Biography of a Victorian Prophet* (Oxford, 2013); Owen Dudley Edwards, 'Victorian Historical Consciousness: Carlyle, Macauley, Froude and Lecky: A Review Essay', *Carlyle Studies Journal* 29 (2013), pp. 115–136; Nicholas Canny, *Judging Ireland's Pasts: Early Modern Ireland through the Centuries* (Oxford, 2021).

9 Timothy O'Neill, *Merchants and Mariners in Medieval Ireland* (Dublin, 1987); Wendy Childs and Timothy O'Neill, 'Overseas Trade', in Art Cosgrove (ed.), *A New History of Ireland*, vol. 2: Medieval Ireland 1169–1534 (Oxford, 1987), pp. 492–524; Kevin Down, 'Colonial Society and Economy in the High Middle Ages', in Cosgrove (ed.), *A New History of Ireland*, vol. 2, pp. 439–491; Margaret Murphy, 'The Economy', in Brendan Smith (ed.), *The Cambridge History of Ireland*, vol. I, 600–1550 (Cambridge, 2018), pp. 385–414; Susan Flavin, *Consumption and Culture in Sixteenth-century Ireland: Saffron, Stockings and Silk* (Woodbridge, 2014).

10 Robin Frame, 'The "Failure" of the First English Invasion of Ireland', in Robin Frame (ed.), *Ireland and Britain, 1170–1450* (London, 1998), pp. 1–14; Robin Frame, 'Exporting State and Nation: English Institutions and English Identity in Medieval Ireland', in Len Scales and Oliver Zimmer (eds.), *Power and the Nation in European History* (Cambridge, 2005), pp. 143–165; Peter Crooks, 'Representation and Dissent: 'Parliamentarianism' and the Structure of Politics in Colonial Ireland, c. 1370–1420', *English Historical Review* 125 (2010), pp. 1–34; Peter Crooks, 'The Structure of Politics in Theory and Practice, 1210–1541', in Smith (ed.), *The Cambridge History of Ireland*, pp. 441–468; Simon Egan, 'The Resurgence of Gaelic Power in Ireland and Scotland and Its Wider Impact, c. 1350–1513' (Unpublished PhD thesis, UCC, 2016).

11 John Gillingham, 'Normanizing the English Invaders of Ireland', in Huw Pryce and John Lovett Watts (eds.), *Power and Identity in the Middle Ages: Essays in Memory of Rees Davies* (Oxford, 2007), pp. 84–97; John Gillingham, 'The Beginnings of English Imperialism', in James Muldoon (ed.), *The North Atlantic Frontier of Medieval Europe* (Farnham, 2009), pp. 71–88; Caoimhe Whelan, 'The Transmission of the Expugnatio Hibernica in Fifteenth-century Ireland', in Georgia Henley and Joseph McMullen (eds.), *Gerald of Wales: New Perspectives on a Medieval Writer and Critic* (Cardiff, 2018), pp. 243–258; Brendan Kane, 'Did the Tudors Read Giraldus? Gerald of Wales and Early Modern Polemical Historiography', in Henley and McMullen (eds.), *Gerald of Wales*, pp. 259–287; Steven G. Ellis, "Reducing Their Barbarous Wildness . . . Unto Civility": England and "the Celtic Fringe", 1415–1625', in Brendan Smith (ed.), *Ireland and the English World in the Late Middle Ages: Essays in Honour of Robin Frame* (Basingstoke, 2009), pp. 176–192; Deidre Fennell, *A Tudor Viceroy: Sir William Fitzwilliam of Milton, 1560–1575: The Reluctant Lord* Deputy (Hannover, 2020); Carla Lessing, *Promoting 'English Civility' in Tudor Ireland: Ideology and the Rhetoric of Difference* (Hannover, 2021).

12 Daniel Power and Naomi Standen (eds.), *Frontiers in Question: Eurasian Border-lands, 700–1700* (Houndmills, 1999).

13 Steven G. Ellis, *Defending English Ground: War and Peace in Meath and North-umberland, 1460–1542* (Oxford, 2015); Steven G. Ellis, 'The English State and It's Frontiers in the British Isles, 1300–1600', in Daniel Power and Naomi Standen (eds.), *Frontiers in Question: Eurasian Borderlands, 700–1700* (Hound-mills, 1999), pp. 153–181; Christopher Maginn, 'Gaelic Ireland's English Fron-tiers in the Late Middle Ages', *Proceedings of the Royal Irish Academy* 110C (2010), pp. 173–190; Gerald Power, *A European Frontier Elite: The Nobility of the English Pale in Tudor Ireland, 1496–1566* (Hannover, 2012); Gerald Power, 'English-born men in Ireland, c. 1450–1530', in Christopher Maginn and Ger-ald Power (eds.), *Frontiers, States and Identity in Early Modern Ireland and beyond: Essays in Honour of Steven G. Ellis* (Dublin, 2016), pp. 36–54; Sparky Booker, *Cultural Exchange and Identity in Late Medieval Ireland* (Cambridge, 2018).

14 Elizabeth Eisenstein, *The Printing Press as an Agent of Change: Communications and Cultural Transformations in Early Modern Europe* (Cambridge, 2021); Paul M. Dover, *The Information Revolution in Early Modern Europe* (Cambridge, 2021); on the process of scientific discovery see James D. Fleming, *The Invention of Discovery 1500–1700* (Farnham, 2011).

15 Caoimhe Whelan, 'James Yonge and the Writing of History in Late Medieval Dublin', in Seán Duffy (ed.), *Medieval Dublin XIII* (Dublin, 2013), pp. 163–195; Aisling Byrne, 'The Earls of Kildare and Their Books at the End of the Middle Ages', *The Library* 14 (2013), pp. 129–153; Aisling Byrne, 'Family, Locality and Nationality: Vernacular Adaptations of the Expubnatio Hibernica in Late Medi-eval Ireland', *Medium Aevum* 82 (2013), pp. 101–118; Christopher Maginn and Steven G. Ellis, *The Tudor Discovery of Ireland* (Dublin, 2015); David Heffernan, *Reform Treatises on Tudor Ireland, 1537–1599* (Dublin, 2016); David Heffernan, 'Patrick Finglas's A Breviat of the Conquest of Ireland and of the Decay of the Same, c. 1535, and the Tudor Conquest of Ireland' *Sixteenth Century Journal* 49 (2018), pp. 369–388.

16 David Buisseret (ed.), *Monarchs, Ministers and Maps: The Emergence of Car-tography as a Tool of Government in Early Modern Europe* (Chicago, IL, 1992); Jeremy Black, 'Mapping Early Modern Europe', *European History Quarterly* 25 (1995), pp. 431–442; David Turnbull, 'Cartography and Science in Early Mod-ern Europe: Mapping the Construction of Knowledge Spaces', *Imago Mundi* 48 (1996), pp. 5–24; Annleigh Margery, 'The Emergence of Londonderry c. 1600–1625: Evidence from the Surveys and Maps', in Brian G. Scott (ed.), *Walls 400: Studies to Mark the 400th Anniversary of the Founding of the Walls of Lon-donderry* (Derry, 2015), pp. 57–75; Annaleigh Margery, 'Plantation Towns: Ban-don, Derry-Londonderry and Armagh', in Howard B. Clarke and Sarah Gearty (eds.), *More Maps and Texts: Sources and the Irish Historic Towns Atlas* (Dublin, 2018), pp. 199–219.

17 See, for example, Christopher Maginn, *William Cecil, Ireland, and the Tudor State* (Oxford, 2012).

18 Nicholas Canny, *The Elizabethan Conquest of Ireland: A Pattern Established* (Hassocks, 1976); Nicholas Canny, *Making Ireland British, 1650–1650* (Oxford, 2001); Christopher Maginn and Stephen G. Ellis, *The Making of the British Isles: The State of Britain and Ireland, 1450–1660* (London, 2013); Raingard Esser and Steven G. Ellis (eds.), *Frontier and Border Regions in Early Modern Europe* (Hannover, 2013); Pádraig Lenihan, *Consolidating Conquest: Ireland 1603–1727* (London, 2013); Jane Ohlmeyer, 'Introduction: Ireland in the Early Modern World', in Jane Ohlmeyer (ed.), *The Cambridge History of Ireland*, vol. 2, 1550–1730 (Cambridge, 2018), pp. 1–22.

19 Alan Ford, *The Protestant Reformation in Ireland, 1590–1641* (Dublin, 1997); James Murray, *Enforcing the English Reformation in Ireland: Clerical Resistance and Political Conflict in the Diocese of Dublin, 1534–1590* (Cambridge, 2009); Elizabethanne Boran and Crawford Gribben (eds.), *Enforcing Reformation in Ireland and Scotland, 1550–1700* (Aldershot, 2006); Tadhg Ó hAnnracháin, 'Counter-Reformation: The Catholic Church, 1550–1641', in Jane Ohlmeyer (ed.), *The Cambridge History of Ireland*, vol. 2, 1550–1730 (Cambridge, 2018), pp. 171–195; Colm Lennon, 'Protestant Reformations, 1550–1641', in Jane Ohlmeyer (ed.), *The Cambridge History of Ireland*, vol. 2, 1550–1730 (Cambridge, 2018), pp. 196–219.

20 Michael MacCarthy-Morrogh, *The Munster Plantation: English Migration in Southern Ireland, 1583–1641* (Oxford, 1986); Éamonn Ó Ciardha and Micheál Ó Siochrú (eds.), *The Ulster Plantation: Ideology and Practice* (Manchester, 2013); Diarmuid Wheeler, 'From Gaelic Lordships to English Counties: The Tudor Transition in Leix and Offaly, c. 1547–1603' (Unpublished PhD thesis, NUI Galway, 2018); Brendan Scott (ed.), *Society and Administration in the Ulster Plantation Towns, 1610–89* (Dublin, 2019); R.J. Hunter, with John Morrill, *Ulster Transformed: Plantation in Early Modern Ireland, c. 1590–1641* (Belfast, 2020); Gerard Farrell, 'The Irish and the Economy of Plantation Ulster', *PRIA* 122C (2022), pp. 169–202. For an excellent overview of plantations in Ireland, see now Annaleigh Margey, 'Plantations, 1550–1641', in Jane Ohlmeyer (ed.), *The Cambridge History of Ireland*, vol. 2, 1550–1730 (Cambridge, 2018), pp. 555–583.

21 Aidan Clarke, *The Old English in Ireland, 1624-42* (London, 1966); Nicholas Canny, *The Formation of the Old English Elite in Ireland* (Dublin, 1975); Ciaran Brady and Raymond Gillespie (eds.), *Natives and Newcomers: Essays on the Making of Irish Colonial Society, 1534–1641* (Dublin, 1986); Patrick J. Duffy, David Edwards and Elizabeth Fitzpatrick (eds.), *Gaelic Ireland, c. 1250-c. 1650: Land, Lordship and Settlement* (Dublin, 2001); David Edwards, Pádraig Lenihan, and Clodagh Tait (eds.), *Age of Atrocity: Violence and Political Conflict in Early Modern Ireland* (Dublin, 2007); Joseph Mannion, 'Landownership and Anglicisation in Tudor Connaught: The Lordships of Clanricard and Hy-Many, 1500–1590' (Unpublished PhD thesis, NUI Galway, 2010); John Cunningham, *Conquest and Land in Ireland: The Transplantation of Connacht 1649–1680* (London, 2011).

22 Nicholas Canny and Anthony Pagden (eds.), *Colonial Identity in the Atlantic World, 1500–1800* (Princeton, 1987); Thomas O'Connor and Mary Ann Lyons (eds.), *Irish Communities in Early Modern Europe* (Dublin, 2006); Orla Power, 'Friend, Foe or Family? Catholic Creoles, French Hugenots, Scottish Dissenters', in Niall Whelehan (ed.), *Transnational Perspectives on Modern Irish History* (New York, 2014), pp. 24–49.

23 Ian Lustick, *Unsettled States, Disputed Lands: Britain and Ireland, France and Algeria, Israel and the West Bank*-Gaza (Ithaca, NY, 1993); Donald Horowitz, 'Self-Determination: Politics, Philosophy and Law', in Margaret Moore (ed.), *National Self-Determination and Secession* (Oxford, 1998), pp. 181–214; Brendan O'Leary, Ian Lustick, and Thomas Callaghy (eds.), *Right-Sizing the State: The Politics of Moving Borders* (Oxford, 2001); Allen Buchanan and Margaret Moore (eds.), *States, Nations and Borders: The Ethics of Making Boundaries* (Cambridge, 2008).

24 J.J. Lee, *Ireland, 1912–85: Politics and Society* (Cambridge, 1989); Jonathan Bardon, *A History of Ulster* (Belfast, 1992); Diarmaid Ferriter, *The Transformation of Ireland, 1900–2000* (London, 2004); Paul Bew, *Ireland: The Politics of Enmity, 1789–2006* (Oxford, 2007); Gearóid Ó Tuathaigh, 'Ireland 1880–2016: Negotiating Sovereignty and Freedom', in Tom Bartlett (ed.), *The Cambridge History of Ireland*, vol. 4: 1880 to the Present (Cambridge, 2018), pp. 1–33.

25 Eamonn Phoenix, *Northern Nationalism, Nationalist Politics, Partition and the Catholic Minority in Northern Ireland 1890–1940* (Belfast, 1994); Susan McKay, *Northern Protestants: An Unsettled People* (Belfast, 2008); Cormac Moore, *Birth of the Border: The Impact of Partition in Ireland* (Dublin, 2019); Diarmaid Ferriter, *The Border: The Legacy of a Century of Anglo-Irish Politics* (London, 2019).

26 Recent debates on these topics include Enda Delaney, 'Our Island Story? Towards a Transnational History of Late Modern Ireland', *Irish Historical Studies* 37 (2011), pp. 599–621; Michael Gehler, '"Europe", Europeanizations and Their Meaning for European Integration Historiography', *Journal of European Integration History* 22 (2016), pp. 141–174; Enda Delaney and Fearghal McGarry, 'Introduction: A Global History of the Irish Revolution', *Irish Historical Studies* 44 (2020), pp. 1–10; Ben Tonra, 'Irish Diplomacy in a Time of Crisis and the Evolution of a "European" Diplomatic Service', *Irish Studies in International Affairs* 28 (2017), pp. 117–131.

27 Thomas Cauvin and Ciaran O'Neill, 'Negotiating Public History in the Republic of Ireland: Collaborative, Applied and Usable Practices for the Profession', *Historical Research* 90 (2017), pp. 810–828.

28 Richard J. Evans, *In Defence of History* (London, repr. 2000), p. 316.

2 Limerick c. AD 1200

A Frontier City in Europe's Wild West

Catherine Swift

The annalists of Loch Cé opened their account of AD 1193 with a notable death:

> *Domnall Ó Briain locrand solusda siddha ocus cogta ocus rella adhanta einich Leithe Modha ocus na Muimhnech do dhul déc.* 'Domnall Ó Briain died: shining lamp of peace and war and burning star of the honour of the southern half of Ireland and the men of Munster'.

In Mac Carthaigh's Book, Domnall's death is followed by a statement that his son Muirchertach took the kingdom of Thomond.[1] At the time, Thomond was a much smaller unit than the wider Dál Cais over-kingdom which included territories as far east as the Kilkenny borders and as far south as Clonmel, but it was still the major power in north Munster. By 1212, however, this larger Dál Cais over-kingdom had disappeared and the building of a royal Angevin castle at Domnall's city of Limerick had commenced. In short, around AD 1200, the mid-west region ceased to belong to one of the major Irish kingdoms and became absorbed into the western frontier zone of the Norman world.

The city of Limerick is located beside an important geographical boundary. The twice daily tidal ebb can lower the depth of the Shannon by up to 5.5 m and this allows for the first crossing point of the river after entering the estuary nearly a hundred kilometres away. The political importance of this crossing point is indicated by the fact that the Angevin castle was located, not on the highest ground on King's Island, the core of the Ostman city, but instead by the head of this fording spot while the monies allocated for the Angevin castle included the creation of a major bridge.[2]

The tidal surge extends east of the city but the rocky and shallow nature of the river-bed beneath means that the stretch of river between Limerick and Killaloe is impossible to navigate for boats of any size. Doonass is some five kilometres upriver from Limerick and the mid-seventeenth-century Down Survey states that 'near the Castle of Dunasse there is a greate fal by which only obstruction shipps are hinddred their further passage on

DOI: 10.4324/9781032691886-2

the said river into the very bowells of this Dominion'. At Killaloe, William Goode wrote in 1610:

> There stands a rock in the mid channel of the river Shannon, from which the water rushes down a main with a great fall and noise, and by standing thus in the way as a bar hinders the river that it can carry vessels no further.[3]

Thus, Limerick is located not only by the first fording point of the Shannon but also at the last point of easy access for shipping for some twenty-four kilometres above the city. Vessels arriving from the Atlantic estuary had to moor in the deeper water west of the city at what was known in the twelfth century as *Linn Luimnigh* or the 'Pool of Limerick' and on modern Admiralty charts simply as the Pool.[4] Between there and Lough Derg, transport was either by small boats, known locally today as gandelows, or by land.

The value of this impassable stretch of shallow waters was appreciated by earlier Uí Bhriain kings. In 1124, an attack by Toirdelbach Ua Conchobair of Connacht resulted in his fleet having to be dragged past Doonass and amassed again at the deep-water harbour of Foynes. The *Annals of the Four Masters* add that Toirdelbach built a *longphort* or fortification (possibly for ships) at *Áth Caille* 'Woodford', where an earlier Ua Briain king had built a bridge in 1071.[5] Along with those of Athlone and Dublin, this is identified in the *Triads of Ireland* as one of the three great fords of Ireland.[6] It does not survive as a modern place-name, but in the twelfth-century *Mórthimchell Éirenn*, the army of Muirchertach travelled from *Áth Caille* to Cratloe indicating a location in the Limerick hinterland. Modern Athlunkard or *Áth Longphoirt* 'ford of the fortified place', immediately east of the city, seems a plausible location, especially as Viking silver weights have been found in the vicinity of Athlunkard bridge.[7] While the river zone between Limerick and Killaloe was impassable for shipping, it did provide fording points for those who, for whatever reason, wanted to avoid the city itself.

One particular Uí Bhriain dynasty is linked to this section of the river. They were known as the *Muinter Chonaing* and are described as descendants of Conaing son of Donn Chuan, Brian Boru's first cousin.[8] Conaing is Brian's most frequently mentioned relative outside the immediate family in *Cogadh Gaedhel re Gallaibh*, the saga of Clontarf. Conaing was playing chess with Brian's eldest son when Máel Morda of Leinster made his ill-fated visit to Brian at *Cenn Coradh*; he is identified as one of three men most valued by Brian; he and Máel Morda killed each other at Clontarf and he is remembered in the *Annals of Ulster* as one of the small élite buried with Brian at Armagh.[9] His name was attached to *Caisleán Uí Chonaing* or Castleconnell, a pre-Norman castle occupied by Uí Bhriain leaders in 1175:

> Diarmait son of Tadhg Uí Bhriain and Mathgamain son of Tairdelbach Uí Bhriain were blinded by Domnall Ua Briain in *Caislen Uí Chonaing*

in the middle of his own house. The son of Gille Leithderg Ó Concobhair was killed by Domnall Ua Briain on the same day.[10]

Domnall Mór Ua Briain began his career as king of Thomond in 1168 before acquiring *ríge Dál Cais uile* 'the kingdom of the entire Dál Cais' with the defeat of his brother Brian, lord of *Ur-Muman* 'eastern Munster or Ormond' in northern Tipperary.[11] The blindings at *Caislén Uí Chonaing* represented the removal of some of Domnall's other rivals as well as their Ua Conchobair ally from north Kerry. A description of *Caislén Uí Chonaing* in 1651 says that, at that time, it held a bridge 'with an old castle' at one end while the overland route from there to Killaloe and to Limerick was almost (but not quite) impassable due to surrounding bogs.[12] In creating a defensive settlement described by the new Anglo-French term *castél,*[13] the Uí Bhriain leadership clearly valued the natural defences provided by this location.

West of Limerick city, *Carraig Ó gCoinneall* is identified in *Mac Carthaigh's Book* as a manor given to Donnchadh Cairbreach Ó Briain by King John in 1210. *Mac Carthaigh's Book* is a fifteenth-century manuscript and it is thought that this spelling is a modernisation of *Carrac Uí Chonaing.*[14] The existence of both these placenames and the fact that both refer to fortifications strongly suggest that the Uí Chonaing controlled the impassable river zone.

Giolla na Naomh Ó hUidhrín's fourteenth-century *Tuilleadh feasa ar Éirinn óigh* describes this river section as *Túath Luimnigh* and state that the territory was marked by two estuaries, presumably the rivers Mulkear and Maigue which enter the Shannon on either side of the city. This territorial base help to explain the political importance of the Uí Chonaing in twelfth-century records culminating in 1185 when Ruaidrí Ó Conaing was a leader in Domnall Mór's army at *Tibraid-Fachtna* or Tibberaghny on the southern border of Kilkenny.[15]

Such control gave the Uí Chonaing powers to impede if not control Limerick city's access to Ireland's interior as well as an ability to by-pass the city's fording point. Whether this territorial unit first developed in the era of Brian Boru or was a more ancient phenomenon is unknown. The multi-period *Bethu Phátraic* refers to the men of Thomond travelling south in boats to Donaghmore and contains a detailed origin legend of St Patrick baptising Carthenn son of Cas and his son Eochu Ballderg on the hill of Singland (both located within the Southern Liberties of Limerick City).[16]

Brian Boru's direct ancestry descended from Blait son of Cas. Only minor differences exist between the twelfth-century copies of Dál Cais genealogies in the *Book of Leinster* and the manuscript Rawlinson B. 502. The exception is a section inserted into Rawlinson which introduces yet another son of Cas, named Óengus. Four generations later, this line produced a king Ferdomnach:

> It is he, that particular Ferdomnach, who gave *Inis Sibtonn* to Mainchíne of Limerick and to Crónán and Mainchíne gave a blessing of pre-eminence on Ferdomnach.[17]

Inis Sibtonn is King's Island, the core of Ostman Limerick. Mainchíne or St Munchin is the city's patron saint and bishop, while Crónán was patron of Tuamgraney in Clare and Roscrea in *Ur-Muman*. Combined with the evidence for Carthenn's descendants, it is evident that there were a number of Uí Bhriain families living in and around the Ostman city by the time these genealogies were compiled. While the descendants of Brian Boru and his cousin Conaing were the most powerful of these, there were other Dál Cais families whose membership of the wider grouping was based on a much older and considerably weaker ancestry.

Our records do not allow the tracing of the early phases of the political and territorial interrelationships of these families in detail prior to Brian Boru. Towards the end of the twelfth century, on the other hand, there is some evidence for two other important Uí Briain families apart from those of Domnall Mór and the Uí Chonaing. The first are the descendants of Domnall's great uncle, Conchobar Slapar Salach, who was a son of Diarmait, brother and co-ruler of the late eleventh-century king of Ireland, Muirchertach Mór. After the deaths of Muirchertach and Diarmait in AD 1119 and 1118, respectively, Conchobar emerged as the strongest of the Uí Bhriain of his generation and is identified in the Book of Leinster as king of Thomond.[18] In 1130, he is said to have captured a thief who took relics from Clonmacnoise whom he hanged at *Cluain Briain* in the parish of Athlacca. Later Uí Bhriain genealogies identify this as part of the holdings of Conchobar's family in south Limerick and north Cork.[19] An Uí Bhriain poem of the 1080s refers to *flaith Luimnigh a Liathmuine* – the chieftain of Limerick from *Liathmuine*[20] where *Liathmuine* is Cloghleafin in the same north Cork area, suggesting that the Uí Bhriain connection may stretch further back than the era of Conchobar himself.

After the death of Domnall Mór's father Toirdelbach in 1167, a grandson belonging to this south Limerick branch was involved in the jockeying for the overall headship:

> Muirchertach [of *Dún na Sgiath* – Fort of the Shields] son of Taird-
> elbach Ua Briain, was slain by Conchobar grandson of Conchobar
> [*Slapar Salach*] and that same
>   Conchobar was slain on the third day after that by Ua Faeláin. And
> much slaughter was inflicted by the men of Thomond on one another.[21]

Other annals add that this Muirchertach of Donaskeagh, County Tipperary was also identified by some as lord of Thomond or king of the Dál Cais.[22] Through his mother, he was a step-brother of the contemporary king of Connacht, Ruairi Ua Conchobair. A feature of the internecine wars between dynastic rivals was the search for powerful external patrons who could support them in their ambitions and in many cases, as here, the Connacht over-king fulfilled this role. In the year before his murder, Muirchertach had accompanied Ruairi on a major expedition to Tyrone, involving twenty battalions of foot soldiers and cavalry, together with a fleet from Donegal.[23] Returning to the Ua Conchobair base at Tuam, the high-king had then given

Muirchertach his father's drinking horn as *tuarastal* – the word for gifts given by superiors to aristocratic subordinates to reward loyalty. Ruairi is then said to have ridden with the *Meic Carthaigh* ruler south to *Cnoc Áine*. Perhaps Mac Carthaigh dropped poison in the high-king's ear about his north Munster rival or perhaps it was the death of Muirchertach's father in the interim which changed the political imperatives but for whatever reason, the alliance between Thomond and Connacht then broke down to the point that some locals believed that the Connacht ruler instigated Muirchertach's murder.[24]

Cnoc Áine or Knockainey in County Limerick is identified in *Cogadh Gaedhel re Gallaibh* as the home of the Uí Enna whose name survives in the later Norman cantred of *Huhene*.[25] The later king Cormac mac Meic Carthaigh is identified with *Rath Áine* in the immediate vicinity of the rock, in 1121.[26] In the Book of Leinster genealogies, the Uí Enna traced their ancestry to the father of the first king in the Cashel king-list, a man also claimed as a Meic Carthaigh progenitor.[27] The *Annals of the Four Masters* state that *Cnoc Áine* was the location for the division of Munster between the Uí Bhriain and the Meic Carthaigh in 1168 but the sources are not entirely consistent – the Armagh annalist, in contrast, states that this assembly took place at *Grian-Cliach* in a region fought over by both the Meic Carthaigh and the Uí Bhriain lords of Coonagh.[28] This last was an Uí Bhriain family which had faded from view in the later twelfth-century annals, but it is impossible to believe that they did not form part of the contemporary political scene. They were descendants of Donnchad, son of Brian Boru, a man who survived the battle of Clontarf and retained his position as Uí Bhriain leader for almost fifty years until his death in 1064. In his more successful phases, he was credited with the title of both king of Munster (*ardríg Muman*) and king of Ireland.[29] His son Murchad was active in the 1050s and 1060s until his death in Longford in 1068 while his grandson, Brian, was present in the battle of Glenmire in Cork in 1127/28.[30] A further annal in 1158 refers to this Brian's grandson, through his son Donnchad while later genealogies state that Donnchad and his brother held Uí Bhriain lordships in Coonagh and Aherlow, respectively.[31]

The politics and powers of these twelfth-century feuding Uí Bhriain families are difficult and confusing to disentangle and it cannot be said that the picture is entirely clear. What is apparent is that dynasties emerging from known figures of Brian Boru's era and later were taking over territories and establishing bases in what is known today as County Limerick. To judge by *Caislén* and *Carrac Uí Chonaing*, some were then fortifying these holdings, using the best contemporary techniques available. It is in this context that we have to evaluate unique information gathered for the eighteenth-century bishop of Cloyne, John O'Brien, which states that the manor of *Caislen Uí Chonaing* was bestowed by King John on William de Burgo in 1201.[32] Goddard Orpen accepted the validity of this in his mammoth work, *Ireland under the Normans*, and has been followed by modern scholars – even if the precise phraseology used seems somewhat implausibly discursive in nature.[33] Better (because contemporary) records exist for *Castello Ocunig que fuit terra Willelmi de Burgo* which is recorded in 1212, and it was one of the richest of de Burgo Munster manors at the death of William's son, Richard in 1242.[34] This poses a question: how and why did Domnall Mór, who in 1175 had his own house at *Caislén Uí Chonaing*, lose control of this major resource?

This was not the only land unit which, having been under the authority of the Uí Bhriain, was transferred to William de Burgo. The territory surrounding *Carrac Uí Chonaing* or Carrigogunnel today is the civil parish of Kilkeedy. A fifteenth-century rental in the Norman chartulary known as *the Black Book of Limerick* equates this with a church of Esclon: '*Ecclesia de Escluana alias Kylkyde cuius rector est prior de Athissell, taxa 12 marca*'.[35] The Irish equivalent, *Aes Cluana*, was the territory of famous Uí Bhriain churchmen known as the Uí Enna[36] and the genealogists identified their particular ancestor as the brother of the Cairthenn baptised by St Patrick.[37] (It is noteworthy how, as one works through them, all of these twelfth-century Limerick families can be divided between those tracing their ancestry to Brian Boru's era and those who are only linked to the very remote original sons of Cas himself.)

The Irish Pipe Roll 14 John confirms the fortification of *castel de Esclon* (presumably that known in Irish as *Carrac Uí Chonaing*) by 1212.[38] Amongst early material in the *Black Book* is a charter recording a gift of two ploughlands *de feodo meo de Esclone* 'from my manor of Esclon' by William de Burgo.[39] In July 1215, the *castrum de Askelon* was restored to William's son, Richard, and in 1242, along with *Castlén Uí Chonaing*, it was listed as two of Richard's chief manors in Limerick.[40] William de Burgo may well have been, as Adrian Empey long ago described him, a man of 'extraordinary vitality' and one 'with a forceful military mind verging on genius',[41] but his ability to acquire key Uí Bhriain holdings, located in what later armies termed almost impassable terrain, remains noteworthy.

The explanation may be that William married Domnall Mór's daughter and thus did not necessarily acquire these lands as a result of military conquest. Fifteenth-century genealogies record the marriage[42] while the principle that hired Norman mercenaries needed to be bribed with royal women as well as land had been firmly established with Strongbow's marriage to Aífe. Contemporary annals, moreover, tell of William fighting alongside Domnall Mór's sons against Uí Bhriain enemies. In 1201, for example, William and his Gaill 'Foreigners', together with Muirchertach, Conchobor Ruad and Donnchad Cairbreach, fought the Ua Donnabáin king of the central Limerick kingdom as well as the *Múscraige Mittaine* (around Macroom and Ballyvourney). The overall aim of this expedition was to attack the Meic Carthaigh and their city of Cork. The following year William led a second hosting back into southern Munster and brought *braigdi ocus chís ocus cáin* (hostages and renders and taxes) back to Limerick. Again, 'accompanied by the great men of Munster', he then raided Connacht to such effect that he was able to install a new king, Cathal Crobderg, who, like himself, was married to a daughter of Domnall Mór.

With three adult sons of Domnall Mór already in situ, however, simply becoming their brother-in-law is not enough to explain William's success in acquiring Uí Bhriain assets. His army of Gaill may have given the Uí Bhriain military advantages, but other, more politically complex, explanations are also possible. The widespread Dál Cais over-kingdom had been difficult to control for all the twelfth-century Uí Bhriain kings and the various Uí Bhriain families frequently found themselves re-structuring their allegiances, depending on political and military necessities. These processes are presented in the annals from the leaders' standpoint, often as the sub-division of defeated territories and the insertion of new dynasts who, it was hoped, would act as loyal subordinates and territorial representatives for their over-king. *Caislén* and *Carrac Uí Chonaing* may have been handed over to de Burgo in exactly the same way and William's Uí Bhriain marriage may have been as much the consequence of, as the motivation for, his adoption as an Uí Bhriain dynast. The story of the first Irish generation of Norman colonists has been almost entirely told from the perspective of the incomers and the political thinking of Irish dynasties who engaged with them has yet to be examined in any detail. We know, however, that, as early as 1177, Domnall Mór had allied himself with Miles de Cogan and Fitzstephen in raids on the Meic Carthaigh and he allowed a Norman castle to be built at Bruis in Aherlow in 1193.[43] This last provides a concrete example of his willingness to provide the incomers with assets taken from rival Uí Bhriain families.

The suggestion that William de Burgo might have been seen as a useful ally by various Uí Bhriain rivals has the merit of contextualising his rapid acquisition of important territorial and military assets. The Tipperary manor of Kilfeakle, for example, which William had acquired by 1203, includes Coonagh where the descendants of Donnchad mac Briain had settled.[44] The territory of Fonn Timchell included the deanery of Aherlow where the Norman castle of Bruis was built; William de Burgh was granted lands there by King John in 1199. The charter for *Fonn Timchell* is the only surviving contemporary legal description of land-transfers to William de Burgo in Limerick. It uses Norman legal formulae including lands held *de nobis et heredibus nostris* 'from us and our heirs'.[45]

We know that Domnall Mór had declared homage to King Henry II on the banks of the Suir in 1171 *firmissimis subieccionis vinculis* 'by the very strongest bonds of submission' and this expression of feudal homage was confirmed in the Treaty of Windsor in 1175 which stated that 'those who are now in possession of their lands and rights shall hold them in peace as long as they remain in the fealty of the king of England'. In 1185, however, Domnall was one of the three kings whom Giraldus describes as determined in their opposition to John and he attacked the royal army at Ardfinnan close to the Limerick/Cork border where he killed John's foster-brother.[46] We do not know whether Domnall's son Muirchertach or his Uí Bhriain rivals swore fealty to John in the years immediately after Domnall's death. Military campaigns by de Courcy and de Lacy against *Gaill Laighen ocus Muman*, as well as attacks by Cathal Crobderg which destroyed *caisléin ocus baileda* 'castles and settlements', show how various lords sought to benefit from Domnall's death. The statement in Mac Carthaigh's book that Cathal was expected to ally himself with the *Síl Briain* implies that they and the *Gaill Mumhan* were on opposite sides on this occasion.[47]

However John's 1197 charter for Limerick city as well as that for the Uí Bhriain foundation of Monasternenagh, signed in November 1200, confirming gifts to that institution by *reges vel principes Hyberniensium et Francorum* suggests that relations between John and the Uí Bhriain had improved.[48] A letter from John to the justiciar, bailiffs and barons of Ireland refers to the bishop Donatus Ua Briain of Limerick as *fidelis meus in proteccionem et custodiam meam* and states that *pro honore et amore meo et negociis meis laboravit* – for the honour and love of King John, he had worked on various matters for him. This letter was signed at Rouen which fell to Philip Augustus in 1204 and the letter may therefore date, as postulated by the editor, to AD 1199–1203.[49] A situation where at least one Uí Bhriain leader was prepared to work not just with William de Burgo but also with King John's claims as his feudal overlord would explain why gifts of Uí Bhriain land at *Caistlén* and *Carrac Uí Chonaing* are linked to King John's name even if the relevant Norman charters do not survive.

In this interpretation, William emerges as a classically liminal border magnate keeping two very different masters happy. Such a situation could not last long. In fairly rapid order, the 1201 alliance between William and Domnall Mór's sons broke down and normal Uí Bhriain rivalries re-emerged. A list of church lands belonging to Limerick's cathedral was drawn up under William's aegis but while witnesses guaranteeing this document included the archdeacon and the Uí Bhriain bishop of Killaloe, the bishop of Ross and the abbot of Scattery Island, the only secular Uí Bhriain supporter was Conchobor Ruad Uí Bhriain.[50] Shortly, afterwards, however, William took Conchobor prisoner and sent him to Limerick where he was rescued by a supporter, Aed Ua hAichir, from the Killaloe area.[51] Once free, Conchobar then attacked his brother Muirchertach but was killed.

In the same year and for reasons which, since Orpen's day, have frequently been put down to John's 'usual capriciousness', John reversed his previous approach of small-scale land grants to a variety of lords and instead made his favourite William de Braose lord of the honour of Limerick with only de Burgo retaining his lands.[52] A charge of 'capriciousness' ignores any local rationale for a change of political policy. It is not hard to imagine that, once the unified Uí Bhriain leadership had again fissured into rival groups, John may well have felt that a strong and most importantly, an external leader was now required in north Munster.

The decision of King John's justiciar, Meiler Fitz Henry, together with a great army of 'the Foreigners of Ireland' to attack Limerick at this point reinforces the idea that royal officers, at least, were now perturbed about events in Limerick. The short annual records do not allow us to detect the sequence of events but a Connacht contingent under Cathal Crobderg as well as Muirchertach and the men of Thomond all turned against William at the same time. All three Irish leaders were duly defeated by Meiler. Since there are subsequent references to William's sons 'and other hostages' under Angevin control, it looks as if the annalist's phrase, *ducsadar sain uli a mbraigdi don Iustís* 'they all surrendered their hostages to the Justiciar', included William's half-Irish son Richard who was subsequently brought up in England.[53] Meiler wrote to the king, warning about William's activities but his complaints were referred to the king's justices who apparently ruled that William's various *castris et castella* be returned to him in 1204. Notwithstanding this, the king brought William out of Ireland to Normandy and his Irish career appears to have effectively come to an end.[54]

William died in 1206 while his sons were still minors and it was only under Henry III that their uncle's patronage brought the two boys, Richard and Hubert, back to Limerick. Hubert became bishop of Limerick while his brother Richard was given the seneschalship of Munster, made royal bailiff and keeper of the Angevin castle of Limerick and given control over his father's lands.[55] What this means, in effect, is that in the period of construction of the first phases of the royal Angevin castle in Limerick, control of the city's immediate hinterland was in the hands of John himself.

The Irish Pipe Roll shows that during Richard's minority, the revenue from the various de Burgo lands in Limerick and Tipperary were collected by the royal sheriff of Munster, Geoffrey de Marisco, for John's benefit.[56] Whether such assets were transferred in any meaningful way to the Irish treasury or were simply offset against local expenses in building the castle at Limerick is not known although the latter seems likely. No geological study has been done on the early castle stonework but strong local control can only have had a beneficial effect on quarrying and transport costs as well as providing added security for those undertaking the actual building.

By making William's half-Irish son Richard subsequently responsible for the castle, a weak Henry III effectively transferred power over both the royal city and its eastern hinterland back to dynasts with the strongest of local connections in an era when Limerick was the only major port serving Ireland's Atlantic coast. It is perhaps not surprising then that a bardic poem written in honour of Richard, sometime in the first half of the thirteenth century, describes him in the following terms:

Créd agaibh aoidhigh a gcéin / a ghiolla gusan ngaillsgéimh/ a dhream ghaoidhealta
ghallda / maoidheanta shenag shaorchlannda?
Whence comes it that you have guests from afar, O youth of foreign beauty, O ye

who are become Gaelic, yet foreign, young, graceful and highborn?
Thine is the castle named *Caislén Uí Chonuing.*
A house wherein there are more golden jewels, a house wherein were
more serving men, a house wherein were more spencers of noble
birth – that has not been and will not be built![57]

Notes

1 W.M. Hennessy (ed.), *The Annals of Loch Cé: A Chronicle of Irish Affairs, 1014–1590*, 2 vols (London, 1871), i, p. 186; Seamus Ó hInnse (ed.), *Miscellaneous Irish Annals (AD 1114–1437)* (Dublin, 1947), p. 74.

2 Dan Tietzsch-Tyler 'King John's Castle: Staged Development, Imperfect Realisation', *North Munster Antiquarian Journal* 53 (2013), pp. 135–170, 160.

3 Down survey of Ireland, downsurvey.tcd.ie/down-survey-maps.php#bm=Clanwilliam&c= Limerick (accessed 10 January 2022); William Goode, 'Account of County Clare Taken from William Camden's Britannia 1586', in Brian Ó Dálaigh (ed.), *The Stranger's Gaze: Travels in Co. Clare 1534–1950* (Ennis, 1998), p. 10.

4 J. Carmichael Watson (ed.), *Mesca Ulad* (Medieval and Modern Series, 13, Dublin, 1941), p. 13.

5 Gearóid Mac Niocaill (ed.), *Annals of Tigernach* (2010), https://celt.ucc.ie/published/T100002A/index.html (accessed 10 July 2022), *s.a.* 1124; John O'Donovan (ed.), *Annála Ríoghachta Éireann: Annals of the Kingdom of Ireland by the Four Masters* (Dublin, 1848–51), *s.a.* 1124; Seán Mac Airt (ed.), *The Annals of Inisfallen* (Dublin, 1944), *s.a.* 1071.

6 Kuno Meyer (ed.), *The Triads of Ireland* (Todd Lecture series, 13, London, 1906), p. 6.

7 *ATig s.a.* 1171, *AFM s.a.* 1171; John O'Donovan, 'The Circuit of Ireland by Muirchertach mac Néill, Prince of Aileach', John O'Donovan (ed.), *Tracts Relating to Ireland Volume 1* (Irish Archaeological Society, Dublin, 1841), pp. 24–58, 46–47; H. Morris, 'The Circuit of Ireland by Muirchertach na gCochall gCroiceann', *Journal of Royal Society of Antiquaries of Ireland* 6 (1936), pp. 9–31, 22–23; Eamonn P. Kelly and Edmund O'Donovan, 'A Viking Longphort Near Athlunkard', *Archaeology Ireland* 12(4) (1988), pp. 13–16.

8 M.A. O'Brien (ed.), *Corpus Genealogiarum Hiberniae* (Dublin, 1962), p. 238.

9 James Henthorn Todd, *Cogadh Gaedhel re Gallaibh: The War of the Gaedhil with the Gaill* (London, 1867), pp. 144, 166, 184; Seán Mac Airt and Gearóid Mac Niocaill (eds.), *The Annals of Ulster* (Dublin, 1983), p. 449.

10 *ATig, s.a.* 1175; *ALC s.a.* 1175.

11 *ATig,* s.a. 1168.

12 Edmund Ludlow, 'The War in County Clare, 1651', in Ó Dalaigh (ed.), *The Stranger's Gaze,* p. 34.

13 R.A. Breatnach, 'IA < Ē in Early Modern Irish Loan-words', *Celtica,* 13 (1980), pp. 109–114, 110; Tadhg O'Keeffe, *Ireland Encastellated AD 950–1550* (Dublin, 2021), pp. 36–41.

14 Gearóid Mac Spelan, *Cathair Luimnighe Cuid I 432–1691* (Dublin, 1948), p. 196.

15 *AI, s.a.* 1185; *ALC* i, *s.a.* 1185 *ATig, s.a.* 1185.

16 Kathleen Mulchrone (ed.), *Bethu Phátraic* (Dublin 1939), p. 123.

17 *Corp. Gen. Hib.,* p. 240.

18 Anne O'Sullivan (ed.), *Book of Leinster, Formerly Lebar na Núachongbála* (Dublin, 1983), p. 1472.
19 Tadhg Ó Donnchadha (ed.), *An Leabhar Muimhneach* (Dublin, 1940), p. 234.
20 Myles Dillon (ed.), *Lebor na Cert* (Irish Texts Society, 46, Dublin, 1962), pp. 140–141.
21 *Misc. Ir.Annals, s.a.* 1167.
22 *AFM*, ii, *s.a.* 1164, 1167; *AI, s.a.* 1167; *ATig, s.a.* 1167.
23 *ATig, s.a.* 1167; *AFM*, ii, *s.a.* 1167.
24 *AFM* ii, *s.a.* 1168.
25 *Cog.GG*, p. 83; Paul McCotter, *Medieval Ireland: Territorial, Political and Economic Divisions* (Dublin, 2008), pp. 189–190.
26 Paul McCotter, 'The Rise of Meic Carthaigh and the Political Geography of Desmumu', *Journal of Cork Archaeological and Historical Society* 111 (2006), pp. 59–76, 66.
27 *Book of Leinster VI*, pp. 1375, 1472.
28 *AFM*, ii, *s.a.* 1170; Annala Uladh; W.M. Hennessy and B. Mac Carthy (eds.), *Annals of Ulster Otherwise Annals of Senat*, 4 vols (Dublin, 1887–1901), ii, pp. 158–160; MacCotter, *Medieval Ireland*, p. 190, MacCotter, 'Rise of Meic Carthaig', pp. 69–70.
29 *ALC*, i, *s.a.* 1164; *ATig, s.a.* 1164; Pádraig Ó Riain, 'The Shrine of the Stowe Missal Redated', *PRIA* 91C (1991), pp. 285–296, pp. 293–294.
30 *ALC*, i, *s.a. 1128; ATig, s.a. 1128; AU, s.a. 1128; AFM*, ii, *s.a. 1128; Misc. Ir. Annals, s.a.* 1128; W.M. Hennessy (ed.), *Chronicon Scottorum* (London 1866), p. 272.
31 Ó Donnchadha, *Leabhar Muimhneach*, pp. 235, 299, 354–356; *Misc. Ir.Annals, s.a.* 1058.
32 Meidbhín Ní Urdáil, 'Some Observations on the Dublin Annals of Inisfallen', *Ériu*, 57 (2007), pp. 133–153.
33 Goddard Henry Orpen, *Ireland under the Normans 1169–1216*, 6 vols (Oxford, 1911–1920), ii, p. 167.
34 Oliver Davies and David B. Quinn (eds.), 'The Irish Pipe Roll of 14 John, 1211–12', *Ulster Journal of Archaeology*, 3rd series, 4 (1941), pp. 1–76, 70; Paul Dryburgh and Brendan Smith (eds.), *Inquisitions and Extents of Medieval Ireland* (List and Index Society cccxx, Kew, 2007), pp. 1–3.
35 James McCaffrey (ed.), *The Black Book of Limerick* (Dublin, 1907), p. 146.
36 Donnchadh Ó Corrain, 'Dál Cais Church and Dynasty', *Ériu* 24 (1973), pp. 52–63, 53.
37 O'Brien, *Corpus Gen. Hib.*, pp. 242, 245. The *Aes Cluana* territory appears to have included lands on the north bank of the Shannon where they were identified with the wider Dál Cais (through the Uí Caissin) rather than the Uí Bhriain.
38 Davies and Quinn, 'The Irish Pipe Roll', p. 70.
39 *The Black Book of Limerick*, pp. 110–111.
40 H.S. Sweetman (ed.), *Calendar of Document Relating to Ireland Preserved in the Public Record Office*, 5 vols (London, 1875–1886), i, pp. 91, 94; Dryburgh and Smith, *Inquisitions*, p. 1.
41 Adrian Empey, 'The Settlement of the Kingdom of Limerick', in James Lydon (ed.), *England and Ireland in the Late Middle Ages: Essays in Honour of Jocelyn Otway-Ruthven* (Dublin, 1981), pp. 1–25, 8.
42 John O'Donovan (ed.), *The Tribes and Customs of Hy Many, Commonly Called O'Kelly's Country* (Irish Archaeological Society, Dublin, 1843), pp. 44–45.
43 *ATig*, p. 300; *AI*, p. 318; *Misc. Ir.Annals*, p. 74.
44 MacCotter, *Medieval Ireland*, p. 189; *Cal.Doc. Ire. 1172–1251*, p. 95.

45 Thomas Duffus Hardy (ed.), *Rotuli chartarum in turri Londinensi asservati*, vol. 1, part 1 (London 1837), p. 19.
46 A.B. Scott and F.X. Martin (eds.), Giraldus Cambrensis, *Expugnatio Hibernica – the Conquest of Ireland* (Dublin, 1978), pp. 93, 235, 241; *ALC*, i, 144, 170; Edmund Curtis and R.B. McDowell (eds.), *Irish Historical Documents 1172–1922* (London, 1943), pp. 22–24.
47 *ALC* i, p. 190; *Misc. Ir.Annals*, p. 74.
48 *Chartae, priviliegia et immunitates: Being Transcripts of Charters and Privileges to Cities, Towns and Other Bodies Corporate 1171–1395* (Irish Record Commission, Dublin, 1889), p. 36; Gearóid Mac Niocaill, *Na Buirgéisí*, 2 vols (Dublin, 1964), i, 236–237; Hardy, *Rotuli chartarum*, p. 78.
49 MacCaffrey, *Black Book*, p. 38, 173; Paul Webster, *King John and Rouen: Royal Itineration, Kingship and the Norman 'capital' c. 1199–1204* (Cardiff Historical Papers, 2008), p. 2.
50 McCaffrey, *Black Book*, pp. 27–29.
51 *AI*, pp. 330–332; *Leabhar Muimhneach* pp. 307, 308.
52 Orpen, *Normans*, ii p. 172; Colin Veach, 'King John and Royal Control in Ireland: Why William de Briouze had to Be Destroyed', *English Historical Review* 129 (2014), pp. 1051–1078.
53 *Cal.Doc.Ire. 1172–1251*, i, 29; Brendan Smith, 'Burgh, Richard de', in *Oxford Dictionary of National Biography*, https://doi.org/10.1093/ref:odnb/3994 (accessed 15 January 2022).
54 Thomas Duffus Hardy, *Rotuli patentium in turri Londinensi asservati*, vol. 1, part 1 (London, 1835), p. 39.
55 *Cal.Doc.Ire 1172–1251*, pp. 91, 94 170, 191.
56 Davies and Quinn, *Irish Pipe Roll*, pp. 69–74.
57 Osborn Bergin, *Irish Bardic Poetry* (Dublin, 1970).

3 Historical Boundaries and Historic Borders

The Case of Cairpre Dromma Clíabh

Seán Ó Hoireabhárd

Modern Divisions

One of the complicating factors in the crisis that followed Brexit, itself the inspiration for this collection's theme, 'borders', was and is the nature of the polities involved. Both the European Union and UK are unions of multiple peoples or nations, and as collectives, they sometimes pursue policies contrary to the will and detrimental to the interests of one or more of their constituent groups. Scotland, for example, voted against Brexit, and through its assembly has continuously upheld the desire to remain a part of the trading bloc or to return to it by the pursuit of independence from the UK. The idea of placing a border in the Irish Sea and separating Northern Ireland from the rest of the UK also inspired anger in Unionist circles, notwithstanding the fact that Northern Ireland voted against Brexit too.

Just as dividing lines or borders carry implications for the nature of modern polities and their operations, so too do they for medieval equivalents. Consideration of such demarcations demands some precision about the nature of the political units on each side of the line and what they were trying to achieve strategically. Regrettably, the medieval Irish context has been poorly served in this regard. This is especially true of the Irish kingdoms in the immediate post-invasion period.

The problem lies at least partly in the fact that 1169, the year of the English invasion, is the most significant dividing line in Irish historiography. Traditionally, scholars either ended or began their treatment of Irish history at this point. A corollary was that those interested in Gaelic Ireland tended towards pre-invasion studies and their counterparts in Anglo-Irish studies avoided straying into that field. All historiographical boundaries are arbitrary but adding cultural to temporal separation reinforces a perception of immediate transformation. It compounds an offence against the reader in this regard, because nothing was inevitable, in many regards, change was gradual, and individuals and groups which were, in medieval Ireland, neighbours and intimates (and not just as enemies) have been treated by modern historians as if they belonged to entirely different worlds.

DOI: 10.4324/9781032691886-3

The problem has been widely recognised. As early as 1981, Robin Frame called for an assessment of the impact of the English invasion on Gaelic Ireland, something he suggested was needed 'more urgently' than further studies of the Anglo-Irish colony.[1] Similarly, Seán Duffy, whose own book, *Ireland in the Middle Ages* (1997), was remarkable for placing 1169 in the middle of the narrative, wrote, 'Irish politics did not begin in 1169. Therefore, one must guard against the assumption that everything which occurred after that date is a product of the new age'.[2] He suggested:

> With this generation of scholars the earlier barrier between Anglo-Ireland and Gaelic Ireland may with confidence be said to be breaking down. It is no longer acceptable to treat the affairs of one in a vacuum. Both natives and newcomers in medieval Ireland mingled in their daily lives; they must mingle too on the pages of history.[3]

Nevertheless, a dismissive attitude has remained prevalent. To take one example, in her review of the second volume of *A new history of Ireland*, Lisa Bitel noted that nineteen of the twenty-nine articles were play-by-play accounts of Anglo-Norman and Anglo-Irish gains and setbacks.[4] She saw this as a natural outcome of the fact that 'native politics were, if possible, even more confusing than relations among the Anglo-Irish themselves and with the kings across the Irish Sea. When the authors do mention Gaelic territories and leaders, they try to explain away the political disorganisation for which the medieval Irish are historically famous, without promoting the charge of tribalism (to which Irish historians are sensitive)'.[5]

Notwithstanding her observation that the book was overwhelmingly focussed on the colony, she therefore implicitly endorsed the flawed structure of *N.H.I.* and its underlying methodology, while also laying the charge of sensitivity at the feet of those who justifiably pointed out its inadequacy. The grounds for this endorsement, the supposed political 'disorganization' of Gaelic Ireland, is an impression that results from Anglocentricity rather than a justification of the same. It has led writers to avoid close scrutiny of the strategic aims of Gaelic polities, and the idea that 'tribalism' is now avoided simply because Irish historians are 'sensitive' can only be regarded as further evidence that serious engagement is often lacking.

Other examples can be given from the very text Bitel reviewed (as well as from elsewhere). J.A. Watt, tasked with writing an assessment of 'Gaelic polity and cultural identity', argued:

> The detail of the incessant, intense, localised, and usually indecisive warfare, with all its complex shifts and changes of allegiance, is suffocatingly tedious. Those who compiled annals recording this detail made no attempt to stand back from the turmoil of their times to make an overall national assessment of the situation.[6]

F.X. Martin asserted that between 1152 and 1166, Tigernán Úa Rúairc and Diarmait Mac Murchada 'changed allies and partners with no apparent consistency or high policy', something he presumably took to be true of other Irish kings as well.[7]

Gaelic history has not been universally neglected, and great progress has been made in certain quarters. We may note the pioneering work of historical geographer Paul MacCotter here; his publications have helped to locate Irish kingdoms and dynasties within more precise boundaries, something of central importance to the present discussion.[8] Additionally, Katharine Simms and Máire Ní Mhaonaigh have added to their extensive contributions in recent years; Simms published the authoritative *Gaelic Ulster in the Middle Ages* in 2020, while Ní Mhaonaigh co-authored the impressive *Norse–Gaelic contacts in a viking world* with Colmán Etchingham, Jón Viðar Sigurðsson and Elizabeth Ashman Rowe in 2019.

Simms' *Gaelic Ulster* was described by Brendan Smith as a 'wonderful book' that succeeded in tying together 'diverse threads' of political and cultural development into a coherent account of Ulster's development over a millennium.[9] Here, as in few other works, focus stayed with the Gaelic peoples even after they were overtaken by invasions, conquests, and other disasters. Such an approach restores the agency of those who are normally reduced to the role of passive victims and, I suggest, for this reason, it must serve as a template for future writers.

The 'scholarly brilliance' of *Norse-Gaelic contacts* has also been commented upon.[10] This book presented a series of literary case studies with historical context, emphasising the possibility of hitherto overlooked links between Ireland, the Isles, and Scandinavia. The omission of mainland Scotland was notable but, as with *Gaelic Ulster*, a sustained examination of Gaelic and Norse viewpoints offered the reader a chance to see the subject in a new light.

Sadly, despite the works of MacCotter, Simms, Ní Mhaonaigh, Etchingham, Kenneth Nicholls and others, the issue has not been entirely rectified and much remains to be done. Quite often, writers pay lip service to concepts like cultural interaction while remaining conservative in their views and approaches. We lack a dedicated history of the Irish kingdoms across the 1169 divide, which itself has the implication that Irish individuals can never be included in a narrative on equal terms with their English contemporaries. With very few exceptions, modern accounts of this period attribute agency principally to English lords and magnates, with Gaelic kings and subjects reduced to passive by-standers. This depiction of the past is, it seems, one of the most enduring legacies of colonisation.

More might be said about the damaging effects that dismissive comments can have in the wider field, but the aim of this paper is to illustrate how an inclusive approach to Anglo-Gaelic politics can prove profitable for historians interested in either culture. As such, it is appropriate to examine a moment immediately after the invasion when, for the first time, representatives of both cultures were in prolonged contact in Ireland and began to have mutually incompatible territorial claims. In this instance, multiple incompatible suzerains may also have been implied. Our case study, Cairpre Dromma Clíabh or Carbury Drumcliff, underlines how military strategy and geography were shared concerns for Gaelic Irish kings and English colonists alike.

Medieval Borders

Cairpre Dromma Clíabh, corresponding to the modern barony of Drumcliff, County Sligo, was a contested territory throughout the Middle Ages. As descendants of Cairpre mac Néill, the occupying nobility claimed kinship with other Uí Néill branches, but they often fell under the lordship of different groups. This genealogical connection itself was a sore point in some quarters; a thirteenth-century poem in the Book of Fenagh notes that 'the seed of mild Cairbre have Druim-Cliabh, though the Connacians like it not'.[11] We shall see now why such feeling was heightened in the thirteenth century.

In his obituary of 1029, Áed Úa Rúairc was referred to as 'king of Cairpre', and indeed he was killed in an attack on that area.[12] He did not belong to the Cairpre but rather to a Connacht dynasty beginning to style itself 'Uí Briúin Bréifne' in imitation of the province's most successful group, Uí Briúin Aí.[13] Áed was not the head of his dynasty but rather of a junior branch, and one associated with the sub-division of Uí Rúairc holdings known as Dartraige (Co. Leitrim). His title to Cairpre seems to represent a territorial expansion of that area; the confused reference to the death(s) of 'the king of Cairbre and the king of Dartraige' in the corresponding entry in Chronicon Scottorum may belie the recency of the change, and this was not corrected in the Annals of the Four Masters.[14]

Uí Rúairc seizure of Cairpre Dromma Clíabh constituted just one element of a period of growth and expansion for the dynasty. While they directed their burgeoning resources towards the kingship of Connacht for a time, they were nonetheless eclipsed in that arena by the Uí Chonchobair family of Síl Muiredaig and Uí Briúin Aí. Through frustration and ambition, they began to expand eastward at the expense of the Uí Máel Sechlainn kings of Meath. So doing, they carved out a territory large enough to constitute a provincial kingdom and it became universally recognised as such. 'King of Uí Briúin' in twelfth-century annals was an alias of 'king of Bréifne', and not a reference to other Uí Briúin dynasties, as it had once been.

This provincial kingdom reached its greatest extent under Tigernán Úa Rúairc, who reigned *c.* 1124–72. In one of the *notitiae* preserved in the Book of Kells, his territory was delimited at 'Magh Tlachta' in the east, and 'Trácht Eothaile' in the west.[15] 'Magh Tlachta' represents the plain of the Hill of Ward, near Athboy in modern County Meath, while 'Trácht Eothaile' equates with Trawohelly on Ballysadare Bay in County Sligo. This strand, part of which is now submerged, is known today as Beltra and is on the south side of Ballysadare Bay.[16] It seems to have been considered a southern border of

Cairpre Dromma Clíabh on at least some occasions, so its use by Úa Rúairc may be a shorthand for the entire territory.[17] Tlachta also represented the southern boundary of Úa Rúairc's kingdom, not the northern.

It became something of an accepted fact that Bréifne, properly constituted, ran from this part of the west coast the whole way across the island. In 1258, for instance, Áedh Ó Conchobhair took the hostages of 'all the Ui Briuin from Kells to Drumcliff', notwithstanding the fact that both points had long since been conquered by different parties.[18] The formulation 'from Ath-Droichit [Drogheda] to Sligo' as a delineation of Bréifne also appears several times in the Book of Fenagh.[19]

At an unknown point between 1172 (Tigernán Úa Rúairc's death) and 1181, Cairpre Dromma Clíabh was annexed from Uí Briúin Bréifne by Connacht. This becomes suddenly apparent when the annals record, under 1181, 'the Battle of the territory of Carbury', fought between various Connacht princes and Flaithbertach Úa Máel Doraid, king of Cenél Conaill.[20] The battle was a decisive victory for the Cenél Conaill, giving control of Cairpre Dromma Clíabh to Úa Máel Doraid and Cenél Conaill, but further contention soon followed on the new frontier.

As regards Connacht's own seizure of the territory from Uí Briúin Bréifne, there is a telling remark in *A.L.C.*: 'Donnchadh, son of Domhnall Midhech O'Conchobhair, it was that brought Flaithbhertach O'Maeldoraidh, to defend the territory of Cairpre for himself'.[21] From other evidence, it seems that Donnchad mac Domnaill Midigh's claim on Cairpre was founded on inheriting his father's (i.e. Domnall Midech's) position. Neither Donnchad nor Domnall, it should be noted, ever held the kingship of Connacht.

Upon his death in 1176, Domnall Midech himself was called 'lord of the north of Connaught'.[22] He was also buried in Maigh Eó, rather than Clonmacnoise, which was the more typical burial place of major Uí Chonchobair dynasts.[23] More importantly still, he was styled 'Tanist of Bréifne' in fifteenth-century genealogies.[24] As such, it seems Bart Jaski was correct to suggest that this title was linked to the Cairpre Dromma Clíabh region.[25]

The annexation of Cairpre by Connacht can therefore be dated with some confidence to the period between the deaths of Tigernán Úa Rúairc (1172) and Domnall Midech Úa Conchobair (1176). It is difficult to say whether it was Domnall Midech himself who conquered the region, or whether it was appropriated diplomatically by his superior, the king of Connacht; the latter occurred in the case of Tír Túathail, a smaller territory which was also incorporated into Connacht at the expense of Uí Briúin Bréifne.[26]

The battle of 1181 itself was fought between Donnchad mac Domnaill Midigh and Flaithbertach Úa Máel Doraid on one side, and the rest of the named princes of Connacht on the other. The slain reportedly included sixteen sons of kings, along with many others.[27] The dead of the Uí Chonchobair dynasty alone included Brian Luignech and Magnus, both sons of Toirdelbach Úa Conchobair, as well as Máel Sechlainn, Muiredach, and

Muirchertach, three sons of Áed mac Toirdelbaigh. It was clearly a massive affair, and it even received a notice in *Ann. Inisf.*, a collection which, at this time, typically only recorded the most important events outside Munster: 'A battle between the Connachta and the Cenél Conaill, in which many nobles of the Connachta fell'.[28]

The most curious aspect of the affair is the absence of the king of Connacht, Rúaidrí Úa Conchobair. The size of the battle suggests some preparation, and Rúaidrí was not noted to have been active elsewhere. In 1182, he endeavoured to reverse the effects of the defeat, showing that by then at least he recognised its importance. Alongside his son, Conchobar Maenmaige, he inflicted a defeat on Úa Máel Doraid, who still had Donnchad mac Domnaill Midigh Uí Chonchobair as an ally.[29]

Nonetheless, it was Flaithbertach Úa Máel Doraid's victory and not Rúaidrí Úa Conchobair's that had the lasting effect. Due largely to the contests that were about to erupt for the kingship of Connacht, as well as the killing of Donnchad mac Domnaill Midigh, Úa Máel Doraid was able to retain control of Cairpre Dromma Clíabh.[30] As Cenél Conaill territory, it would be regularly targeted by their enemies and those of the Northern Uí Néill more generally.

In 1193, the English magnate Gilbert de Angulo, accompanied by the sons of Conchobar Maenmaige and his own entourage, made a raid upon Inis Clothrann, a location where important hostages were often kept.[31] This was de Angulo's first noted participation in a campaign in Connacht, though he may have been active west of the Shannon for some time. His base in Ireland was in Meath, where he held land from the de Lacys. The fact that he supported Conchobar Maenmaige's sons in 1193 could hint at a link with the dead king, since in the latter's obituary of 1189, he is called 'king of all Connaught, both English and Irish'.[32] Despite occasionally attacking English castles, Conchobar Maenmaige was also prepared to employ English mercenaries.[33] This could have led to the settlement of such freelancers in Connacht, including, perhaps, de Angulo.

Interestingly, by 1195, de Angulo had switched sides in the conflict for the kingship of Connacht and become a supporter of Cathal Crobderg. We know that in *c.* 1197, he was deemed to be the holder of Cairpre Dromma Clíabh by Prince John, who was confiscating his territory on that occasion.[34] We also know that in 1194, he led an unsuccessful attack to Assaroe against the Cenél Conaill.[35] It is therefore reasonable to speculate that it was through an arrangement concerning Cairpre Dromma Clíabh that Cathal Crobderg brought Gilbert into his entourage; this is the Irish grant hypothesised here.

If this supposition is correct, the grant by Cathal Crobderg was remarkably like those made by Henry II; a speculative grant of lands not yet conquered. It is also evident that de Angulo endeavoured to square the circle of dual loyalties by agreeing to hold the territory of Cairpre Dromma Clíabh from John as lord of Ireland. In his award of Cairpre to Walter de Lacy, whom he intended to replace de Angulo, John stipulated that de Lacy was to hold it on the same (unspecified) terms as de Angulo.[36] At no point in this sequence of events did either Gilbert de Angulo or Walter de Lacy hold Cairpre in reality; it continued to belong to the Cenél Conaill, who had taken possession *c.* 1181, as was discussed above.

It was as a direct result of his association with Cathal Crobderg that Gilbert found himself outlawed by John. He participated in the king of Connacht's attack on English castles in Munster in 1195,[37] and may even have been captured.[38] He was outlawed the following year and his remaining lands in Meath were seized by the justiciar on John's instructions.[39] There is no further record of him until 1200, when he appears once again in the entourage of Cathal Crobderg,[40] but it is still possible that he led the 'company of bowmen' better translated as 'mercenaries', who were sent by Úa Conchobair to support Desmond against the English in 1196.[41]

In 1207, John offered his peace to de Angulo and made a 'further grant that Gilbert have the cantred of Momeniach which the King of Connaught delivered to him'.[42] 'Momeniach', an Anglicisation of Maenmag, was in Uí Maine. It was the place from which Conchobar Maenmaige derived his sobriquet, evidently because of his fosterage there.

This shift of de Angulo's land holdings within Connacht from north to south corresponds with a change of focus to Munster on the part of Cathal Crobderg. William de Burgh's support for Cathal Carrach at the beginning of the thirteenth century represented a significant threat to Cathal Crobderg from the Munster direction, and it is in this context that Cathal Crobderg's decision to situate de Angulo in Maenmag ought to be understood.

Notwithstanding his new holdings in Maenmag or failure to make headway in Cairpre Dromma Clíabh, de Angulo did not abandon his claim in the north – even after he had officially lost seisin to Walter de Lacy. Walter's brother Hugh rebelled against John in 1210 and when the former became embroiled, he was dispossessed by the king of England. This meant Cairpre Dromma Clíabh was again a prize for the taking as far as de Angulo was concerned.

De Angulo was further encouraged by a dispute between John and Áed Méith Úa Néill, king of the Northern Uí Néill, which occurred when John visited Ireland in 1210. In the wake of that incident the Irish justiciary was instructed to attack Úa Néill's kingdom, which included Cenél Conaill and therefore Cairpre Dromma Clíabh.

De Angulo's name does not appear in the record of the first subsequent attack on Cairpre, in 1211, but he may well have been present.[43] This effort was directed against a place called 'Cael-uisce' or 'Narrow-water',[44] and was repulsed by Áed Úa Néill.[45] Cael-uisce was targeted again in 1212 by the justiciary, and this time de Angulo was certainly present. They built a castle at the site, and it is likely enough that it was intended to be just the first of several castles guarding that part of the River Erne most closely adjacent to Assaroe.[46]

In 1213, Úa hÉignigh of Fir Manach, a subordinate of Áed Úa Néill, attacked and demolished the castle of Cael-uisce. He also killed Gilbert de Angulo, who was among its defenders.[47] In so doing, Úa hÉignigh cut short an interesting experiment on both the English and Irish sides. De Angulo's service in Connacht certainly constituted a form of English infiltration, as shown by the fact that he tried to hold his lands from the king of England as well as the king of Connacht, but it was also illustrative of Irish attempts to adapt.

It is difficult to say what relationship Cathal Crobderg expected to have with Gilbert's Cairpre Dromma Clíabh, should it have been successfully taken from the Cenél Conaill. Clearly, in the 1190s, a tenurial relationship with the English lordship of Ireland had been envisioned; the involvement of the justiciar in 1212 would indicate that something similar was intended on the second occasion.

We also do not know whether service to Cathal Crobderg was a condition of the award of Cairpre Dromma Clíabh. Similarly, Maenmag was granted on unknown terms. It is generally repeated that the latter was 'given' to de Angulo,[48] from the statement in the close rolls that the cantred of Maenmag was originally 'delivered' by Cathal Crobderg to de Angulo, but it may be that Cathal Crobderg granted the lands on terms like those by which Henry II had annexed several Irish provinces.[49]

De Angulo, for his part, was prepared to risk or even sacrifice holdings in Meath to take service in Connacht. In doing so he displayed confidence that the kings of Connacht both desired English military assistance over an extended period and that they were prepared to richly reward someone who would provide it. To observers at the time, including the kings of Connacht, the eventuality of permanently alienating any territory awarded in this way must have been a consideration. Nevertheless, Cathal Crobderg, and perhaps Conchobar Maenmaige before him, made the grants such was the value they placed on de Angulo's service.

The de Angulo claim on Cairpre Dromma Clíabh evidently passed to Gilbert's brother Philip, for we hear under 1214 that 'the territory of Carbury, the possession of Philip Mac Costello [alias de Angulo], was preyed by Ualgarg O'Rourke, who carried off a number of cows'.[50] The Uí Rúairc had previously shown an interest in reviving their claim to the territory in 1187, only to be met with severe retaliation by Úa Máel Doraid of Cenél Conaill.[51] No immediate reaction was recorded for the 1214 raid, either by de Angulo or Úa Máel Doraid, so it is difficult to judge the former's progress. All the same, if Philip ever did establish himself in Cairpre, his success was fleeting. In 1239, the justiciary attacked Úa Domnaill, 'and they plundered Carbury', showing Cenél Conaill were still in possession.[52] When the same man died in 1240, *A.U.* styled him 'king of Tir-Conaill and Fir-Manach and Cairpri and Airghialla from the Plain downwards'.[53]

The importance of Cairpre Dromma Clíabh lay in the fact that it guarded access into 'the North' (understood as the three kingdoms of Northern Uí

Néill, Airgíalla, and Ulaid). Along with an eastern route, which approached Armagh through what is now County Louth, the route through Caipre Dromma Clíabh was the only other path considered militarily appropriate by successive generations of invading kings.

The pathway is best defined by *Cogadh Gaedhel re Gaillaib*'s description of Brian Bóraime's 1005 campaign:

> His route was through Ireland, the middle of Connacht, and into Magh-n-Ai [of Uí Briúin Aí], over the Coirr Shliabh [Curlew Mountains], and into Tir Ailella [of Uí Ailella]; and into the country of Cairpre [Cairpre Dromma Clíabh], and beyond Sligech [Sligo], and keeping his left hand to the sea, and his right hand to the land and to Beinn Gulban [Benbulbin], over Dubh [Duff River] and over Drobhaois [River Drowes], and into Magh-n-Eine [between the Drowes and Erne],[54] and over Ath Seanaigh [Ballyshannon] at Easruaidh [Assaroe]; and into Tir Aedha [Cenél nÁeda of Cenél Conaill], and over Bearnas Mor [Barnesmore], and over Fearsad [perhaps Farsetmore], and into Tir Eoghain, and into Dal Riada, and into Dal Araidhe, and into Ulaidh, until about Lammas [1 August] he halted at Belach Duin [Castlekieran].[55]

While at least some of this was meant to link Brian to the *Slige Midlúachra*, an ancient road associated with the kings of Ireland, the path through Connacht into Cenél Conaill is undoubtedly described accurately. It was probably the same in 1011, when there was 'a great hosting by Brian to Cenél Conaill both by land and sea'.[56] The same was true of Muirchertach Úa Briain in 1100 and 1101, when he too had fleets support the armies he conducted personally.

The conquest of Cairpre Dromma Clíabh by Cenél Conaill pushed their border with Connacht forty kilometres south. Before its acquisition, the key crossing point was at Assaroe; afterwards, at Ballysadare. Herein lies the explanation for the relative importance of both locations at different times, well attested by our sources, and this also shows how certain locations were used pointedly by the authors of our sources.

Consider the description of John de Courcy's invasion of Connacht in 1188:

> The English set fire to some of the churches of the country as they passed along, but made no delay until they reached Eas-dara (Ballysadare), with the intention of passing into Tirconnell, because the Connacians would not suffer them to tarry any longer in their country. As soon as O'Muldory (Flaherty) had received intelligence of this, he assembled the Kinel-Conell, and marched to Drumcliff to oppose them. When the English heard of this movement, they burned the entire of Ballysadare, and returned back, passing by the Curlieu mountains, where they were attacked by the Connacians and Momonians.[57]

Similarly, when Áed Úa Néill marched south in 1201, it was at Ballysdare that he was deemed to have entered Connacht – and at Ballysadare that he was prevented from leaving the province.[58] In 1235, a conquering English army 'proceeded, by regular marches, to Easdara [Ballysadare], where they took a prey from O'Donnell',[59] and in 1239, 'a great depredation was committed on O'Domhnaill by the Foreigners of Erinn, who plundered Cairbre; and the Justiciary himself was at Es-dara, awaiting them, his scouts having gone as far as Druim-cliabh'.[60]

By contrast, Assaroe represented the border before the conquest of Cairpre Dromma Clíabh. When the forces of the Northern Uí Néill invaded Connacht in 1131, for example, they crossed into the province at Assaroe. After their defeat, they were escorted home across the same border.[61] Following violence in 1137, one annalist reported that 'Connacht, then, was laid waste from Assaroe to the Shannon'.[62] Just as significantly, when Gilbert de Angulo tried to wrest control of Cairpre Dromma Clíabh from Cenél Conaill, he hoped to restore the old boundary at Assaroe. In 1194, his action was described as 'a hosting by Gilbert Mac Goisdealbh to Es-Ruaidh; and he returned from Es-Ruaidh without having obtained much profit on this hosting'.[63] It was just the same in the more concerted effort of 1212, when there was 'a hosting by the Connachtmen, at the command of the Foreign Bishop and Gillibert Mac Goisdelbh, to Es-Ruaidh, when the castle of Cael-uisce was erected by them'.[64] Failure on both occasions confirmed Ballysadare as the new border.

Conclusion

Instead of assuming that Irish kings operated with 'no high policy', we should apply ourselves to understanding the dynamics that underlay their actions.[65] In this endeavour, the value of Cairpre Dromma Clíabh as a case study is extensive. Here we have a place of longstanding strategic interest that preoccupied Irish kings on the opposite sides of the border, because it was through here that attacking armies could safely be led into rival provinces (and then extracted).

Cairpre Dromma Clíabh is of further interest because it seems to have been granted speculatively by an Irish king to an English magnate, perhaps in the hope that he would re-conquer it and hold it as a vassal. The complex relationships of the immediate post-invasion period are highlighted by Gilbert de Angulo's attempt to hold the territory from John, lord of Ireland, as well as from Cathal Crobderg, king of Connacht. It also shows that the English policy of granting land speculatively was used (or at least attempted) by some Irish kings.

Accounts that do not characterise English grants and grantees as intimately concerned with the course of Gaelic politics fail to do justice to their subject. It is, in fact, deeply surprising that a view as narrow as that contained in the existing historiography has been sustained so long. Nevertheless, there are signs that the problem has been recognised and is being dealt with. If this is to happen, English lordships in Ireland need to be understood as successor states of the Irish kingdoms they supplanted. This will require a fundamental shift in the way the history of this period has been approached, and a move away from 1169 as a division between two historiographical camps. This must be done carefully, of course, as innovation does not guarantee success – Gilbert de Angulo found this out to his cost in 1213.

Notes

1 Robin Frame, *Colonial Ireland, 1169–1329* (Dublin, 1981), vi.
    A treatment of this topic in its wider context, inclusive of material appearing here, has been published in Seán Ó Hoireabhárd, *The Medieval Irish kings and the English invasion* (Liverpool, 2024), alongside a more developed consideration of the historiography. See especially pp. 19–39, 92–102.
2 Duffy, *Ireland in the Middle Ages* (London, 1997), p. 2.
3 Duffy, *Ireland in the Middle Ages*, p. 6.
4 Lisa M. Bitel, 'Review: A New History of Ireland, 2: Medieval Ireland, 1169–1534', *Speculum* lxix(4) (October 1994), pp. 1147–1149 at 1147.
5 Bitel, 'Review: A New History of Ireland, 2: Medieval Ireland, 1169–1534', p. 1148.
6 J.A. Watt, 'Gaelic Polity and Cultural Identity', in Cosgrave (ed.), *N.H.I. II – Medieval Ireland 1169–1534*, pp. 314–351 at 325.
7 F.X. Martin, 'Diarmait Mac Murchada and the Coming of the Anglo-Normans', in Art Cosgrave (ed.), *N.H.I. II – Medieval Ireland 1169–1534* (Oxford, 1987), pp. 43–66 at 50.
8 See for example, MacCotter, *Medieval Ireland*; Paul MacCotter, 'The Early History and Sub-divisions of the Kingdom of Bréifne', in J. Cherry and B. Scott (eds.), *Cavan: History and Society* (Dublin, 2014), pp. 12–35; Paul MacCotter, 'Dál Cais after Clontarf', in Duffy (ed.), *Medieval Dublin XVI* (Dublin, 2017), pp. 210–217.
9 Brendan Smith, 'Review: Katharine Simms, Gaelic Ulster in the Middle Ages: History, Culture, and Society', *Peritia* xxxiii (2022), pp. 344–346.
10 Duffy, 'Review: Norse–Gaelic Contacts in a Viking World by Colmán Etchingham, Jón Viðar Sigurðsson, Máire Ní Mhaonaigh and Elizabeth Ashman Rowe', *History Ireland* xxvii(6) (November/December 2019), pp. 61–62 at 61.
11 W.M. Hennessy (ed.) and D.H. Kelly (trans.), *The Book of Fenagh* (Dublin, 1875), pp. 398–399: '*Druim chliab ac síl Cairbre chain gen gur miad le Connachtaib*'.
12 Ann. Tig. 1029.2: '*rí Cairpre*'; CS 1029.2; AFM 1029.5.
13 See Eoghan Ó Mórdha, 'The Uí Briúin Bréifni Genealogies and the Origins of Bréifne', *Peritia* xvi (2002), pp. 444–450.
14 C.S. 1029.2; A.F.M. 1029.5.
15 Gearóid Mac Niocaill, 'The Irish "Charters"', in Peter Fox (ed.), *The Book of Kells, MS 58 Trinity College Library Dublin: Commentary* (Luzern 1990), pp. 153–165 at pp. 160–161.
16 Henry Morris, 'The First Battle of Magh Turedh', *The Journal of the Royal Society of Antiquaries of Ireland*, sixth series, xviii(2) (December 1928), pp. 111–127 at p. 113 & n. 6.
17 A.U. 1012.2; AFM 1011.8.
18 A.C. 1258.9: '*O mBriuin uli o Chenannus co Druim Cliab*'.
19 Hennessy (ed.) and Kelly (trans.), *The Book of Fenagh*, pp. 80–81, 122–123, 134–135.
20 A.F.M. 1181.4; A.U. 1181.2; A.L.C. 1181.1; Ann. Inisf. 1181.4.
21 A.L.C. 1181.2: '*Donnchad mac Domnaill Midhigh h-I Conchobair ro thairring Flaithbertach. H. Moel Doraidh do chosnum criche Cairpri dhó feisin*'.

22 *A.F.M.* 1176.12: '*Domhnall mac Toirdealbhaigh Uí Concobhair ticcherna thuais-cceirt Connacht*'.
23 *A.F.M.* 1176.12; *Ann. Tig.* 1176.9.
24 'The Book of Lecan' R.I.A. MS 23 P 2, folio 64 verso: '*tanusti na breifne*'.
25 Bart Jaski, *Early Irish Kingship and Succession* (Dublin, 2000), p. 265.
26 See *A.L.C.* 1186.9: 'Conchobhar Maenmhaighe Came to Mucart, and Aedh O'Ruairc Went into His House, and Gave Hostages to Conchobhar, and Gave Tir-Thuathail to the Connachtmen', from the Irish '*Conchobar Maon Maige do techt co Mucart, 7 Aodh.H. Ruairc do techt ina tech, 7 braighde do thaphairt do Conchobar, 7 Tír Tuathail do taphairt do Connachtuiph*'.
27 *A.F.M.* 1181.4.
28 *Ann. Inisf.* 1181.4: '*Cath eter Chonnacta & Chenél Conaill in quo multi nobiles Connachtorum ceciderunt*'.
29 *A.U.* 1182.4; *A.L.C.* 1182.6; *Misc. Ir.Annals* 1183.2.
30 *A.U.* 1183.3.
31 *A.F.M.* 1193.10.
32 *A.F.M.* 1189.8: '*airdri Connacht eittir Gallaibh & Ghaoidealaibh*'.
33 See for example, *A.F.M.* 1185.9: 'The English came as far as Roscommon with the son of Roderic [Ruaidrí – i.e. Conchobar Maenmaige], who gave them three thousand cows as wages', from the Irish '*Na Goill feisne do theacht leis co Ross Commain, 7 mac Ruaidhri do thabhairt tri míle do bhuaibh dóibh i t-tuarastal*'.
34 *Gormanston Reg.*, pp. 7, 179.
35 *A.F.M.* 1194.5; *A.U.* 1194.4; *A.L.C.* 1194.6.
36 *Gormanston Reg.*, pp. 7, 179.
37 *A.F.M.* 1195.8, 1195.9; *A.L.C.* 1195.6, 1195.8.
38 *A.L.C.* 1195.5: '*Mac Goisdelb do ghab[áil]*'.
39 Dublin Annals of Inisfallen, Trinity College Dublin MS. 1281, sub anno 1196; *A.F.M.*, iii, p. 107 n. l.
40 *A.L.C.* 1200.2.
41 *Ann. Inisf.* 1196.6: '*rúta sersenach*'.
42 *Cal.doc.Ire.*, *1171–1251*, p. 46, no. 311; *Rot. litt. claus.*, *1204–24*, p. 78: '*Et cōcedim quod habeat cantredū de Momeniach quod Rex Connac ei liberavit*'.
43 *A.U.* 1211.1.
44 This location has been subject to different identifications. John O'Donovan identi-fied it as Belleek, east of Ballyshannon (*A.F.M.*, iii, p. 368 n. k.). P.J. Ó Gallachair argued for a location much further eastward, Corrakeel in Inishmacsaint parish. See Ó Gallachair, 'The Erne forts of Cael Uisce and Belleek', *Clogher Record* vi(1) (1966), pp. 104–118 at 107.
45 *A.U.* 1211.1.
46 *A.L.C.* 1212.1; *A.U.* 1212.5; *A.F.M.* 1211.4.
47 *A.L.C.* 1213.2; *A.U.* 1213.7; *A.F.M.* 1212.3.
48 See for example, Orpen, *Normans*, ii, p. 155; Hellen Walton, 'The English in Con-nacht 1171–1333' (PhD thesis, T.C.D., 1980), pp. 24–25.
49 *Rot. litt. claus.*, *1204–24*, p. 78: '*ei liberavid*'.
50 *A.F.M.* 1214.7: '*Creach criche Cairpre do dhenamh la h-Ualgarcc Ua Ruairc ar Philip Mac Goisdelbhaigh co rucc bú iomdha lais*'.
51 *A.F.M.* 1187.8; *A.U.* 1187.3; *A.L.C.* 1187.2.
52 *A.F.M.* 1239.5: '*ró airgset Cairpri*'.
53 *A.U.* 1241.1: '*ri Thire Connaill 7 Fer Manach 7 Cairpri 7 Airghiall o chlar anuas*'.
54 Diarmaid Ó Murchadha, 'Mag Cetne and Mag Ene', *Éigse* xxvii (1993), pp. 35–46.
55 *Cog. Gaedhel*, pp. 134–135: '*Ised do cóidh tré lár Connact, ocus hi Mag nAí isin Coirrsliab, ocus hi ttir Ailella, ocus hi ccrich Cairpre, ocus tar Slicceach, ocus lám clé le muir, ocus lám des le tir, ocus le Beinn Gulban, tar duib, ocus tar drobaois, ocus i Maigh nEine, ocus tar At Senaig ag Eassruaid ocus i ttír nAeda,*

ocus tar Bernas Mór, ocus tar Fersaid, ocus i ttír Eogain, ocus i nDail Riada, ocus i nDail Araide, ocus i nUltaib gur gabastair fo lugnasadh i mBealac Dúin'; A.F.M. 1005.8.

56 *Ann. Inisf.* 1011.5.

57 A.F.M. 1188.8, 1188.9: *'Loiscit na Goill araill do cheallaibh na tire rempa. Ni ro leiccit sccaoileadh doibh co rangattar Eas Dara. Ba do theacht i t-Tir Conaill ón, uair na ro leiccsiott Connachtaigh nias sia dia t-tír iad. Iar b-fios sccél do Ua Maol Doraidh do Fhlaithbertach, teaglomaidh-sídhe Cenel Conaill 'na c-coinne co Druim Chliabh. O 'd-cualadar na Goill sin ro loisccsed Eas Dara co leir. Soaid tar a n-aiss. Tiaghaid isin Coirrshliabh. Do-beartsad Connachtaigh 7 Fir Mumhan ammus forra'.*

58 A.L.C. 1201.5; A.U. 1201.4; A.F.M. 1199.9.

59 A.L.C. 1235.6: *'Do-chuadar assidhe i n-a n-uidhedhaibh imtheachta co h-Ess Dara co n-dearnadar creich ar Ua n-Domhnaill'.*

60 A.L.C. 1239.5: *'Crech mor do ghenum do ghalloib Erenn ar.H. nDomnall, gur aircset Cairpre, go raibhe an Giúsdís fein a nEss dara gá nurnaidhe, 7 condechadar a sirthi co Druim chliabh'.*

61 *Ann. Tig.* 1131.3.

62 *Ann. Tig.* 1137.9: *'Condachta didiu do fasugud o Eas Ruaidh co Sinaind'.*

63 A.L.C. 1194.6: *'Sluaiged le Gilli Pert mac Goisdealbh co h-Ess Ruaidh, 7 ro impó ó Ess Ruaidh gan rotharbha dont sluaiged sin'.*

64 A.L.C. 1212.1: *'Sluaighedh la Connachta tré thoghairm in ghaill espuic 7 Gilli Bert mic Goisdelb, co h-Ess Ruaidh, co n-dernad Caisslen Cháil Usce leó'.*

65 Martin, 'Diarmait Mac Murchada and the Coming of the Anglo-Normans', p. 50.

4 Urban Oligarchies and Border Society in Later Medieval Ireland

Kieran Hoare

It is accepted generally that Irish towns in the late Middle Ages were in decline. Having achieved a modest level of economic development in the thirteenth century with the establishment of the English lordship or colony over large parts of the country with its manorial economy – so the orthodox view holds – decolonisation and urban decline take their toll on Irish towns from the late fourteenth to early sixteenth centuries until the lordship was rescued from oblivion by massive subventions of men and money from England from 1534 onwards. Indeed, it is something of a miracle that any town survived the pressures placed upon them at this time.[1] The objective of this chapter is to take one group within the political community of late medieval Ireland – the civic elites of the larger towns – to examine the impact of the decline of royal authority on this group and the challenges and opportunities they faced in the border society which emerged. In particular, it will look at how the imperative for defence shaped the relationship of the royal administration in Ireland with the urban civic elites, the role these civic elites themselves played in defence, and the impact this had on their role with a lordship political community struggling to survive the realities of a border society.

In terms of historiography, in an Irish setting, there have been great strides in understanding the dynamics of the political setting of late medieval Ireland from the work of Robin Frame and Steven Ellis on the workings of royal government within the lordship, the impact of county political communities on the lordship through the work of Brendan Smith, and the importance of factionalism in driving the political dynamic in the writings of Peter Crooks.[2] The economic imperative has been well-examined by Margaret Murphy in particular, and these works have been further augmented by a range of recent studies.[3] As a result of this work, inspired to some degree by the pioneering work in an English setting by G.L. Harris, Christine Carpenter and others towards a new constitutional history of the fifteenth century[4] and the 'Age of Transition' in socio-economic terms typified by the work of R.H. Britnell, Christopher Dyer, B.M.S. Campbell, we are now in a position to have a better understanding of the political context within which the lordship of Ireland operated.[5] The work of Christian Liddy, Lorraine Attreed and Eliza Hartrich

DOI: 10.4324/9781032691886-4

has highlighted the small but significant role played by towns in national and regional politics in England at this time, challenging the traditional paradigm of finance for patronage to present a more complex relationship.[6] This chapter seeks to apply these historiographical trends to an Irish setting.

Of all the politically active sections of the English of Ireland in the late Middle Ages, it was perhaps the merchant civic elites of the larger towns who sought to retain and maintain royal authority the most, even when border defence and factional politics ushered in a different political dynamic from the late fourteenth century. The families which made up the urban oligarchies in late medieval Irish towns came from diverse backgrounds. Some, such as the Ronaynes and Skiddys of Cork or the Creaghs of Limerick, traced their origins back to pre-Norman property-holding within the town.[7] In Dublin, it was claimed that Oxmanstown, a suburb to the north-west of the town, was where the hiberno-norse or Ostman residents of the town had been expelled to in the aftermath of the conquest in 1170; in reality, it was fully integrated into the city by the late fourteenth century, with prominent Dublin merchants holding property in the suburb.[8] There was a cohort of families who had connections with the towns from the early thirteenth century when English traders and artisans were attracted by the economic opportunities these centres offered, including the Rice family of Waterford, the Arthurs of Limerick and the Burnells of Dublin for example.[9] Another group of families came in from the hinterland in the course of the fourteenth century, escaping the harsh economic and political conditions imposed by border society while retaining trading links there. The Blakes and Butlers of Galway, the Tyrrys, Lombards and Sarsfields of Cork, the Wyse family of Waterford and a number of families of Dublin and Drogheda included among them.[10] The economic dislocation around the Irish Sea following the Black Death saw a number of urban families also set up branches in England, the Mays and Lincoln families of Waterford and Bristol for example, or the Symcockes of Drogheda and Chester.[11] Finally, a small number of Gaelic merchant families found their way from the rural hinterland into the towns for much the same reasons, anglicised their names and were integrated into the civic elites of the town through marriage and commercial activity. The Kirwans and Darcys of Galway, the Sexten, Noonan and Creagh families in Limerick are of this trend.[12]

Whatever their origins, a number of merchant families in the larger Irish towns came to dominate municipal government in those towns, utilising their wealth through property and commercial activities, intermarriage and administrative and judicial activities acquired through royal patronage, along with charitable works and ecclesiastical donations, to cement their status as the leading families of the town. These and indeed all the townspeople were direct subjects of the crown in the towns of Dublin, Limerick, Waterford and Cork, enjoying their considerable liberties and privileges by royal charter.[13] Towns such as Drogheda, Kilkenny and Galway also enjoyed considerable royal favour through grants of privileges from the Crown, even though their initial borough charters would have been granted by a local lord.[14] It was in the interests of these families to have a well-run lordship, both in terms of the internal trading network and the flow of goods through their market to supply overseas demand for Irish goods and the importing of goods back into the hinterland in turn. The less stable border society which emerged in the fourteenth century provided economic and demographic dislocation, increased financial burden and the dangers of military service. This was true not only for those towns situated in what was known as the land of war, the march lands of the lordship, but also as we shall see for towns in the more settled parts of the lordship, the south-east of the country and the area which later formed the Pale around Dublin and Drogheda. While the structure of municipal government was English, local circumstances shaped the composition and actions of the urban civic elites who controlled that government.

From the late thirteenth century to the mid-fifteenth century, revenue collected by the Irish exchequer dropped from c.£5,000 to a little over £1000.[15] This fall in income reflected the weakness of royal authority over large swathes of the lordship, the economic and demographic decline of the lordship and the rise of local lords in the defence of their own areas. Subventions of men and money from the English exchequer were sent to Ireland on a grand scale in the mid-fourteenth century in a bid to reverse this process and to stabilise the economy. Through Parliament, the townspeople along with the aristocracy, clerics and gentry sought crown intervention in Ireland to restore good government. English-born governors received large scale subventions from the English exchequer. The royal expeditions of 1394 and 1399 were perhaps the last of these large-scale interventions, and in the long-term they did not achieve a lasting solution.[16] Under Lancastrian rule, a smaller force of between 300 and 500 archers would support a governor charged to the English exchequer, along with what could be garnered from the Irish Exchequer.[17] Under the Yorkists, the financial support for the chief governor decreased even further. The Earl of Desmond received £500 in 1463 and £100 annually thereafter and the respective Earls of Kildare received very little support from the English exchequer through their governorships.[18]

This meant that the day-to-day financial support for the Irish lordship effectively fell on the lordship itself. Consequently, as the administrative reach of the lordship contracted, the proportion of the financial burden placed on the townspeople increased. The fee-farms of the various towns (essentially a fixed amount paid from the town's liberties and privileges) was notionally at 590 marks per annum. It could be commuted for murage grants for example, or annuities to various officers in the administration, or offset to meet other exchequer charges. So, for example, James Earl of Ormond was appointed justiciar in July 1376 at a fee of £500 a year, but by February 1379, this was £369 8s. in arrears, and the sum of 1,100 marks was assigned to him from the fee-farms of Dublin, Limerick and Waterford.[19] Throughout the fifteenth century, Cork and Limerick made very sporadic proffers to the Irish exchequer for their fee-farm, citing murage grants and inability to pay on most occasions.[20] Waterford continued to pay its fee-farm, but by 1474, there were so many charges on it that it was exonerated from accounting at the exchequer in Dublin. There were also local subsidies paid to neighbouring lords for defence which were charged on the fee-farm, so for example the Earls of Desmond received £20 per annum from both Cork and Limerick, a similar amount to the Burkes of Clanricard was payable by the town of Galway. Even in the land of peace, the allowances for murage in Dublin and Drogheda crept up from £19.6.8 and £13.6.8 in 1467 to £69.6.8 and £33.6.8 by 1494.[21]

There were other means of taxing the towns. They were subject, as indeed all those represented in Parliament were, to parliamentary subsidy. For example, William of Windsor persuaded a parliament in Kilkenny in 1371 to give him a grant of £3,000, followed by another subsidy of £2,000. In reality, these two subsidies realised £2,855 for Windsor. This was after a range of new customs had been placed on goods coming into towns, and townspeople from Drogheda and Dublin had been subjected to fines and other demands for payments. As Peter Crooks has shown, these demands provoked sustained and determined opposition to the Windsor administration from Dublin and Drogheda as it was seen as being too much taxation.[22] Similar parliamentary subsidies were granted at regular intervals throughout the fifteenth century, although the extent and value of the subsidy varied as the needs changed. Another source of revenue came from customs and cocket, based on goods coming into the ports. For 1485, it was estimated at 100 marks each for Dublin, Cork, Limerick, Galway and Waterford, £40 for Drogheda and lesser amounts for smaller ports, amounting to £426.6.8 – again how much of that was gathered in a year varied. Tunnage doesn't appear to have been applied in Ireland, perhaps because of the hereditary (and much contested) right of the Earls of Ormond, as chief butler of Ireland, to take a cask of wine from each cargo of wine landed. However, there is evidence of poundage, an *ad valorium* proportional toll on all imported and exported goods. This toll was integrated into customs collection by 1493.[23] While there is no evidence of merchant loans to the royal administration on the scale of Bristol or York, or indeed the earlier activities of Italian Merchant Bankers in Ireland, there are lots of examples of payments to merchants in different towns who supplied the governor's household and his troops with the necessities of life, sometimes a long time after the goods had been provided.

As well as the financial support garnered from the towns, townspeople acted as royal officials in many roles in local administration, often at a cost to themselves. For example, Robert Lyncoll of Waterford was one of the Justices appointed to hear cases in Munster and south Leinster on 26 February 1432.[24] John Miagh (or Meade) of Cork was appointed as keeper of customs in Cork in 1414, a royal justice in 1420, and appointed coroner for

County Cork in 1423.[25] In 1450, the mayor and bailiffs of Dublin received the right in Parliament to appoint deputies to hear the pleas of the city when they are absent on the King's business.[26]

While some of the royal services performed could be profitable, such as judicial, land transfers or the farming of lands or offices in the hands of the crown, it is also clear that many royal services could be onerous. There are many examples of merchants seeking exemptions from royal service. In 1386, William Symcockes of Drogheda seeks an exemption from royal service so that he can trade overseas.[27] Similarly William Lyncoll of Waterford in 1452 sought exemption by reason of age.[28] It is also true to say that the towns themselves were expected to be centres of royal administration when required. From time to time, councils or parliaments would be held in particular towns, which were expected to provide venues, host retinues and provide an audience for proceedings. In December 1381 with the sudden death of Edmund Mortimer, Earl of March and Chief Governor at Cork, a hastily convened Council consisted of representatives from that city. At various stages Kilkenny, Limerick and Drogheda played a similar role, with Dublin providing something of a permanent base for royal administration. They were also centres for the day-to-day running of royal administration, most notably in Dublin, but townspeople in Ireland appear as collectors, receivers, coroners, gaolers and in other roles.

In terms of what the towns wanted in return for the financial support they gave to the Irish administration, it is clear that good government figures strongly in their petitions through the various parliaments and councils to the Crown. The townspeople wanted strong aristocratic leadership in the lordship, and gave their support for the Irish comital houses in particular to hold the office of chief governor. They saw themselves as part of a wider political community that needed strong leadership to defend the lordship from "Irish enemies and English rebels". The rule of law and stable trade were also a constant theme coming from the towns, and we find towns like Cork in 1406 writing to the Earl of Rutland requesting 'some English captains with twenty Englishmen, that may be captains over us all, and we will rise with them, to redress these enormities, all at our own costs'.[29] Limerick in 1455 seeks to have royal justices visit the town so that malefactors will be wary of the rule of law.[30] Much of what the towns wanted from royal government came down to defence, be it against Gaelic raids into the lordship, the destabilising effects of factionalism in their hinterlands, or the constant threat of piracy off their shores. We also finds towns seeking to ring-fence crown monies from the towns, either fee-farm or customs duties, for murage grants to strengthen their town walls or to pay the local lord to take a leading part in the defence of the town and hinterland.

With the exception of Limerick in 1376, no Irish town was overrun by Gaelic lords in the late Middle Ages. Given the degree of disorder in the countryside, this was due in no small part to the maintenance of town walls.

The importance of town walls can be seen in raids which came up to the walls of the towns at various times, with reports of the unwalled suburbs and surrounding countryside being laid waste. It is certainly true that these walls would have been used as a means of identifying the town and townspeople, as a boundary with external jurisdictions and a physical expression of the separateness of the town. In an Irish setting they also served a serious military purpose. Large-scale walling programmes were undertaken in Kilkenny at the turn of the fifteenth century, and the Irishtown of Limerick in the early fifteenth century. However, every town expended great sums to repair and maintain their walls, with their mural towers and gatehouses, as a means to defend the town and maintain order.[31]

In tandem with this most towns maintained a local watch, often at the expense of the burgesses, and maintained a civic militia. In 1457, for example, the Dublin Assembly granted that 8 men be appointed to a Night Watch to cover from curfew time to five o'clock.[32] In 1462, in Waterford, it was ordained that the toll exacted for the measuring of salt and corn in the town would go towards maintaining the watch.[33] We also know that the watch operated in other towns and was maintained by the mayor and bailiffs. Many municipal ordinances dealt with training citizens in the use of the English bow in particular, as well as other martial pursuits. In 1527 in Galway, for example, throwing quoits and stones was forbidden among the townspeople, but they were encouraged to use the long bow, short cross-bow and the throwing of darts and spears.[34] The merchants, viewed as among the wealthier citizens, were also expected to have a jenkin or armour for protection, and we have the example of John Foyle, citizen of Dublin, dividing his weapons and armour up among his four sons in his will.[35] Clearly, this training and furnishing of weaponry among citizens was important. The Statute obliging merchants to bring in a certain number of bows and sheafs of arrows as part of their cargo was part of this rearming of the civic militia which took place. Of the £20 a year given to the bailiffs of Dublin for defence, half was to be used on repairing the town walls, half on procuring bows and arrows for the town. The short-lived Guild of St. Edmund was set up to ensure this happened. The Guild of St. George, established in the Pale in 1473, also had a significant presence in it of the men of Dublin.[36] The training and arming of these civic militias was no idle exercise. For Dublin alone, for example, in October 1467, no Assembly was held in Dublin as the mayor, bailiffs and commons were in O'Byrne's country with John Tiptoft, the Lord Deputy. Again, in May 1468, they were 'engaged in a hostile incursion upon O'Conor's country', and in May 1470, under Gerald, earl of Kildare again in O'Byrne's country.[37]

The merchant oligarchies of fifteenth-century Irish towns had a range of opportunities allowing them to climb the social ladder into the lesser gentry. Indeed in both English and Irish historiography, merchants are portrayed as wishing to escape town life into the county gentry. It should be pointed out, however, that in the marcher conditions of late medieval Ireland, many lesser gentry families found their way into towns. Scion branches of the fitzEustace and Tyrell families, for example, become established as office-holders in Dublin. The Sarsfield family go from being gentry in Glanmire, to merchants in Cork, and later are found as mercers in Bodmin. It should also be noted that merchants often held property both within the town, suburbs and immediate hinterland of the town, operated as merchants and as a part of municipal government, while carrying out a range of administrative and judicial roles for royal government at local level, both within and outside the town. The Lombard family of Cork were descended from Cambino Donati, who served as sheriff of Cork and Limerick and finally as a justice of gaol delivery. He acquired the manor of Rahanisky (to the north of the city), which was added to by his heir John Lombard, receiving a royal grant of the castle of Gynes (Cloughroe, County Cork) and 30 carucates of land lately occupied by Dermot MacDermot MacCarthy. This same John had to defend his rights of denizenship against the bailiffs of Cork in 1388.[38]

An example of how border conditions could benefit individuals can be seen in the case of John Drake. He was appointed bailiff of Dublin in 1383, and served as mayor on five occasions, 1401, 1402, 1404–5 and again in 1411. He held property in Kinsele and Clougheran in County Dublin, as well as property in St. Francis St. in the suburbs of Dublin. He also had an extensive trading network, transporting wheat to Bordeaux in 1389, and in 1401, he getting Flemish goods held by the Constable of Dover Castle after his ship sunk off Dungennaise when it was bound for Ireland. He won renown in Summer 1402 for having led a force of Dubliners against the O'Byrnes and their O'Meaghair allies near Bray, killing, it is stated, around 490 of them. He was rewarded with an annuity of 5 marks per annum for life from the Exchequer and Dublin received its great civic sword in recognition of this feat of arms. Although Randolph Jones has argued that he was not knighted as he was only a lowly merchant, it may have had more to do with his rather troubled relationship with the Dublin ecclesiastical authorities, having tangled legally and militarily at times with the Abbey of St. Thomas, the Priory of Kilmainham and the Archbishop of Dublin. He was probably protected to some degree by his close alignment to the Ormond faction in lordship politics.[39]

Other Dublin office-holders were from the ranks of the lower gentry. Sir Walter Tyrell, mayor 1424–5 was probably a knight by blood.[40] Sir Nicholas Woder, who served as bailiff in 1444, as mayor 1445–6, 1448 and 1453, was knighted by Richard Duke of York on campaign against the O'Byrnes in 1449, after the battle at Symondeswode. Coming from a well-established civic elite family – his father, uncle and grand-father had served numerous times in civic office and built up extensive property in the town – Nicholas Woder also appears in numerous foundation charters in the city from this time, including the Guild of Holy Trinity (Merchants) in 1451, the Guild of Mary Magdalen (Barber-Surgeons) in 1450 and the Weaver's Guild. He was instrumental in royal moves against the Talbots in the 1440s, and it was probably for this rather than any military prowess that saw him knighted in 1449.[41] Alongside him was another civic office-holder, Sir Robert Burnell, again from a family with long connections to Dublin city, but who had moved to become lords of Castleknock in the 1380s through marriage and inheritance, who was with York in his role as sheriff of Dublin.[42] There can be little doubt, however, that it reflected Richard of York's attempts to build up a loyal faction in the lordship which led to these and other knighthoods among the Pale gentry.

It has been noted that in 1455, an act was passed in the Irish parliament prohibiting knights from holding the office of Mayor of Dublin and Drogheda. However, this act was repealed the following year, and we find office holders like Sir Thomas Newberry of Dublin (who served as mayor no less than ten times) and Sir James Dockery of Drogheda, who on 23 April 1468 as mayor with a force of 500 archers and 200 poleaxes from the town defeated Hugh O'Reilly of Brefney with 2,300 men at Malpas Bridge in County Louth, in recognition of which he was made constable of Carrickfergus Castle for life. There are many other examples of military action by the townspeople through the Kildare ascendency, most noticeably at the Battle of Knockdoe near Galway in 1504. Although towns outside of the Pale did not have this close association with royal government, civic elites were more than happy to grab opportunities when they arose, for example John Waters of Cork in his ill-fated support of Perkin Warbeck, but also the Sextens of Limerick and the Wyses of Waterford positioning themselves for royal favour in the court of Henry VIII. These examples show that border conditions, and the involvement of towns in their local and regional defences to a much greater extent than in England, for example, meant that they had opportunities open to them simply beyond finance or patronage, and participated fully in the martial society of late medieval Ireland.

In conclusion, the role of the urban civic elites in the fifteenth-century lordship of Ireland has not been examined sufficiently. The recent research into factionalism in lordship society and the connectivity of the Yorkist (and later Tudor) borderlands first highlighted by Steven Ellis, as well as the work of Brendan Smith on the Irish Sea Region, have all put the spotlight on aspects of late medieval political society where Irish civic elites played a small but significant role. More than most in Irish society they had a vested interest in royal authority, and had the resources to raise men and money not available to other groups. As in England, towns would not act alone militarily, but were willing to send out contingents for local defence as well as maintain strongholds for royal authority, finance for royal administration, and support local administration where possible. It is also true to say that in the marcher society of the fifteenth century, civic elites were able to strengthen their hold on corporations and municipal government, with any internal political conflict owing more to the lordship's factional politics rather than moves by craftsmen or other groups within the towns to achieve a level of governmental power. Ultimately, with their control of commerce, local government and property, these civic elites were well-placed to benefit from the modest but significant recovery evident in Yorkist and early Tudor Ireland.

Notes

1 Howard B. Clarke, 'Decolonisation and the Dynamics of Urban Decline in Ireland, 1300–1550', in T.R. Slater (ed.), *Towns in Decline, AD 100–1500* (Aldershot, 2000), pp. 157–192; John Bradley, 'The Irish Historic Towns Atlas as a Source for Urban History', in Howard B. Clarke, Jacinta Prunty, and Mark Hennessy (eds.), *Surveying Ireland's Past: Multi-disciplinary Essays in Honour of Anngret Simms* (Dublin, 2004), pp. 727–746; Brian Graham, 'Urbanisation in Ireland during the High Middle Ages, c. 1100-c. 1350', in James Muldoon (ed.), *The North Atlantic Frontier of Medieval Europe* (Ashgate, 2009), pp. 285–300; Brian Graham, 'Economy and Town in Anglo-Norman Ireland', in John Bradley (ed.), *Settlement and Society in Medieval Ireland: Studies Presented to F.X. Martin, OSA* (Kilkenny, 1998), pp. 241–260; John Bradley, 'The Definition and Classification of Medieval Irish Towns', *Irish Geography* 21 (1988), pp. 20–32. John Bradley, 'Towns in Medieval Ireland', in *Medieval Ireland: The Barryscourt Lectures I-X* (Carrigtwohill, 2004), pp. 289–310.
2 Robin Frame, 'The "failure" of the First English Conquest of Ireland', in Robin Frame, *Ireland and Britain, 1170–1450* (London, 1998), pp. 1–14; Robin Frame, 'Exporting State and Nation: English Institutions and English Identity in Medieval Ireland', in Len Scales and Oliver Zimmer (eds.), *Power and the Nation in European History* (Cambridge, 2005), pp. 143–165; Steven G. Ellis, *Reform and Revival: English Government in Ireland 1470–1534* (Woodbridge, 1986); Steven G. Ellis, *Defending English Ground: War and Peace in Meath and Northumberland, 1460–1542* (Oxford, 2015); Christopher Maginn and Steven G. Ellis, *The Tudor Discovery of Ireland* (Dublin, 2015); Brendan Smith, *Colonisation and Conquest in Medieval Ireland: The English in Louth, 1170–1330* (Cambridge, 1999); Brendan Smith, *Crisis and Survival in Late Medieval Ireland: The English of Louth and Their Neighbours, 1330–1450* (Oxford, 2013); Peter Crooks, 'Factions, Feuds and Noble Power in the Lordship of Ireland, c. 1356–1496', *Irish Historical Studies* 35 (2007), pp. 425–454; Peter Crooks, 'Representation and Dissent: "Parliamentarianism" and the Structure of Politics in Colonial Ireland, c. 1370–1420', *English Historical Review* 125 (2010), pp. 1–34; Peter Crooks, 'The Structure of Politics in Theory and Practice, 1210–1541', in Brendan Smith (ed.), *The Cambridge History of Ireland*, vol. 1, 600–1550 (Cambridge, 2018), pp. 441–468.
3 Margaret Murphy and Michael Potterton, *The Dublin Region in the Middle Ages: Settlement, Land Use and Economy* (Dublin, 2010); Margaret Murphy, 'Manorial Centres, Settlement and Agricultural Systems in Medieval Ireland, 1250–1350', in Margaret Murphy and Matthew Stout (eds.), *Agriculture and Settlement in Ireland* (Dublin, 2015), pp. 69–100; James A. Galloway, 'The Economic Hinterland of Drogheda in the Later Middle Ages', in Vicky McAlister and Tony Barry (eds.), *Space and Settlement in Medieval Ireland* (Dublin, 2015), pp. 167–185; Margaret Murphy, 'The Economy', in Brendan Smith (ed.), *The Cambridge History of Ireland*, vol. 1, 600–1550 (Cambridge, 2018), pp. 385–414.
4 G.L. Harriss, Political Society and the Growth of Government in Late Medieval England', *Past & Present* 138 (1993), pp. 28–57; G.L. Harriss, *Shaping the Nation: England 1360–1461* (Oxford, 2005); Christine Carpenter, 'Gentry

and Community in Medieval England', *Journal of British Studies* 33 (1994), pp. 340–380.

5 R.H. Britnell, *The Commercialisation of English Society, 1000–1500* (Manchester, repr. 1997); R.H. Britnell, *Britain and Ireland 1050–1530: Economy and Society* (Oxford, 2004); Christopher Dyer, *An Age of Transition? Economy and Society in England in the Later Middle Ages* (Oxford, 2005); B.M.S. Campbell, 'Benchmarking Medieval Economic Development: England, Wales, Scotland, and Ireland, c. 1290', *Economic History Review* 61 (2008), pp. 896–945.

6 Christian D. Liddy, *War, Politics and Finance in Late Medieval English Towns: Bristol, York and the Crown, 1350–1400* (Woodbridge, 2005); Christian D. Liddy, *Contesting the City: The Politics of Citizenship in English Towns, 1250–1530* (Oxford, 2017); Lorraine Attreed, *The King's Towns: Identity and Survival in Late Medieval English Boroughs* (Frankfurt-am-Main, 2001); Richard Goddard, *Credit and Trade in Later Medieval England, 1363–1532* (Basingstoke, 2016); Eliza Hartrich, *Politics and the Urban Sector in Fifteenth-Century England* (Oxford, 2019).

7 On 11 April 1465 Nicholas fitz Michael de Rupe grants to Maurice O'Ronane a property on the street of Stradyadornoke in Kinsale. The following year he is granted a property on the same street by John White and his wife Anastasia Lawless (Richard Caulfield, 'Original Documents Relating to the County and City of Cork', *Gentleman's Magazine* (1862), p. 562). Caulfield also posits that the Skiddys had Anglicised their name to Scudamore (Richard Caulfield, 'Chartae Tyrryanae Relating to Cork and It's Vicinity', *Topographer and Genealogist* 3 (1858), p. 117). M.F. Cusack, *The History of Cork* (Cork, 1875), p. 5 66; H.L. Tivy, 'Old Cork Celebrities', *Journal of the Cork Historical and Archaeological Society* 1 (1892), p. 29; T.F. Larnham, 'Skiddy's Castle', *Journal of the Cork Historical and Archaeological Society* 14 (1908), pp. 81–83; Anthony Candon, 'The Cork Suburb of Dungarvan', *Journal of the Cork Historical and Archaeological Society* 90 (1985), pp. 91–103. For the Creaghs of Limerick see Colm Lennon, *The Urban Patriciates of Early Modern Ireland: A Case-study of Limerick*, O'Donnell Lecture Series (Dublin, 1999); Colm Lennon, *An Irish Prisoner of Conscience in the Tudor Era: Archbishop Richard Creagh of Armagh, 1523–86* (Dublin, 2000).

8 On 22 October 1348, for example. William Foyll, who had extensive property rights throughout Dublin, granted his rents in Oxmantown to his eldest son Robert (M.J. McEnery and Ray Refaussé (eds.), *Christ Church Deeds* (Dublin, 2001), p. 83, no. 239). See also Emer Purcell, 'Land Use in Medieval Oxmantown', in Seán Duffy (ed.), *Medieval Dublin IV* (Dublin, 2003), pp. 193–228; Emer Purcell, 'The City and the Suburb: Medieval Dublin and Oxmantown', in Seán Duffy (ed.), *Medieval Dublin VI* (Dublin, 2005), pp. 188–223.

9 Edwin C. Rae, 'The Rice Monument in Waterford Cathedral', *PRIA* 69C (1970), pp. 217–228; Eamonn McEneaney, 'Politics and the Art of Devotion in Late Fifteenth Century Waterford', in Rachel Moss, Colmán Ó Clabaigh, and Salvador Ryan (eds.), *Art and Devotion in Late Medieval Ireland* (Dublin, 2006), pp. 33–50; Edward McLysaght and John Ainsworth, 'The Arthur Manuscript', *North Munster Antiquarian Journal* 6 (1949–52), pp. 29–49, 67–82; 7 (1953–7) pp. 168–182, 4–10; 8 (1958–9) pp. 2–19, 79–87; 9 (1962–3), pp. 51–59, 113–116, 153–164; Charles Smith, 'After the Tyrells: The Later Lords of Castleknock, co. Dublin', *JRSAI* 142–143 (2012–3), pp. 129–139.

10 Martin J. Blake, *Blake Family Records*, 2 vols (London, 1902–5); Edmund Curtis, 'The Pardon of Henry Blake of Galway in 1395', *Journal of the Galway Archaeological and Historical Society* 16 (1935), pp. 186–189; Edmund Curtis, 'Original Documents Relating to the Butler Lordship of Achill, Burrishoole and Aughrim. 1236–1640', *Journal of the Galway Archaeological and Historical Society* 15

(1931–3), pp. 121–128; Kevin Terry, *Terrys of Cork, 1180–1644: Merchant Gentry* (Andover, 2013); 'C.J.', 'Dr. Caulfield's Records of the Sarsfield Family of the County Cork', *Journal of the Cork Historical and Archaeological Society* 21 (1915), pp. 131–136; R. Lincoln, 'A List of the Mayors and Bailiffs of Waterford from 1365 to 1649', *Journal of the Royal Society of Antiquaries of Ireland* 5 (1935), pp. 313–319.

11 Brendan Smith, 'Late Medieval Ireland and the English Connection: Waterford and Bristol, ca. 1360–1460', *Journal of British Studies* 50 (2011), pp. 546–565; Chiara Buldorini, 'The Mayors, Provosts and Bailiffs of Drogheda in the Thirteenth Century', *Journal of the County Louth Archaeological and Historical Society* 27 (2009), pp. 26–38; James Galloway, 'The Economic Hinterland of Drogheda in the Later Middle Ages', in Vicky McAlister and Terry Barry (eds.), *Space and Settlement in Medieval Ireland* (Dublin, 2015), pp. 167–185.

12 Michael Kirwan, 'The Kirwans of the Galway City and County and of the County of Mayo', *The Irish Genealogist* 13 (2013), pp. 389–409; Brian Hodkinson, 'Edmund Sexten: the Irish Mayor of Limerick', in David Lee (ed.), *Remembering Limerick: Historical Essays Celebrating the 800th Anniversary of Limerick's First Charter Granted in 1197* (Limerick, 1997), pp. 107–111; Clodagh Tait, '"A Trusty and Wellbeloved Servant": The Career and Disinterment of Edmund Sexton of Limerick, d. 1554', *Archivium Hibernicum* 56 (2002), pp. 51–64; Colm Lennon, *Archbishop Richard Creagh of Armagh, 1525–1586: an Irish Prisoner of Conscience of the Tudor Era* (Dublin, 2000).

13 Gearóid Mac Niocaill, *Na Buirgéisí, XII-XV Aois*, 2 vols (Baile Átha Cliath, 1964); Howard B. Clarke, 'The 1192 Charter of the Liberties and the Beginnings of Dublin's Municipal Life', *Dublin Historical Record* 46 (1993), pp. 5–14; A.F. O'Brien, 'The Development of the Privileges, Liberties and Immunities of Medieval Cork and the Growth of an Urban Autonomy c. 1189 to 1500', *Journal of the Cork Historical and Archaeological Society* 90 (1985), pp. 46–64; Matthew Potter, *The Government and the People of Limerick: The History of Limerick Corporation/City Council, 1197-2006* (Limerick, 2006); Eamonn McEneaney, 'Mayors and Merchants in Medieval Waterford, 1169–1495', in William Nolan and Thomas Power (eds.), *Waterford: History and Society* (Dublin, 1992), pp. 147–176; Julian C. Walton, *The Royal Charters of Waterford* (Waterford, 1992).

14 Chiara Buldorini, 'Drogheda as a Case-study of an Anglo-Norman Town Foundation, 1188–1412' (Unpublished PhD thesis, Trinity College Dublin, 2009); John Bradley and Ben Murtagh, 'William Marshall's Charter to Kilkenny, 1207: Background, Dating and Witnesses', in John Bradley, Cóilín Ó Drisceoil, and Michael Potterton (eds.), *William Marshal and Ireland* (Dublin, 2017), pp. 201–248; John Bradley, *Treasures of Kilkenny: Charters and Civic Records of Kilkenny City* (Kilkenny, 2003); Gearóid Mac Niocaill, 'Medieval Galway: Its Origins and Charter', in Diarmuid Ó Cearbhaill (ed.), *Galway; Town and Gown 1484–1984* (Dublin, 1984), pp. 1–9.

15 J.F. Lydon, 'Three Exchequer Documents from the Reign of Henry III', *PRIA* 65C (1966), pp. 1–27; H.G. Richardson and G.O. Sayles, 'Irish Revenue, 1278–1384', *PRIA* 62 (1962), pp. 87–100; Steven Ellis, 'Ioncam na hÉireann', 1384–1534', *Studia Hibernica* 22/23 (1982/3), pp. 39–49.

16 J.A. Watt, 'The Anglo-Irish under Strain, 1327–99', in Art Cosgrove (ed.), *New History of Ireland*, ii, Medieval Ireland, 1169–1534 (Oxford, 1987), pp. 190–191. For earlier views on Richard II's reign in Ireland see Edmund Curtis *Richard II and Ireland* (Oxford, 1927); A.J. Otway-Ruthven, *Medieval Ireland* (London, 1968), especially chapter 10, 'Richard II and Ireland'; J.F. Lydon. 'Richard II's Expeditions to Ireland', *JRSAI* 92–93 (1962–3), pp. 135–149; Dorothy

Johnston, 'Richard II and the Submissions of the Lords of Gaelic Ireland', *IHS* 85 (1980), pp. 1–20; Dorothy Johnston, 'The Interim Years: Richard II and Ireland, 1395–1399', in J.F. Lydon (ed.), *England and Ireland in the Later Middle Ages* (Blackrock, 1981), pp. 175–195; Dorothy Johnston, 'The Draft Indenture of Thomas, Duke of Gloucester as Lieutenant of Ireland, 1391', *Journal of the Society of Archivists*, 7 (1982–5), pp. 173–195; Dorothy Johnston, 'Richard II's Departure from Ireland, July 1399', *English Historical Review* 98 (1983), pp. 785–805; Dorothy Johnston, 'Chief Governors and Treasurers of Ireland in the Reign of Richard II', in T.B. Barry, Robin Frame, and Katherine Simms (eds.), *Colony and Frontier in Medieval Ireland* (London, 1995), pp. 97–115; Anthony Tuck, 'Anglo-Irish Relations, 1382–1393', *PRIA* 69 C (1970), pp. 15–31; Peter Crooks, 'Factionalism and Noble Power in English Ireland, 1361–1423' (Unpublished PhD thesis, TCD, 2007); Peter Crooks, 'The "Calculus of Faction" and Richard II's Duchy of Ireland, c. 1382–1389', in Nigel Saul (ed.), *Fourteenth Century England V* (Woodbridge, 2008), pp. 94–115; Peter Crooks, 'Representation and Dissent: 'Parliamentarianism' and the Structure of Politics in Colonial Ireland, c. 1370–1420', *English Historical Review* 125 (2010), pp. 1–34.

17 E.A.E. Matthew, 'The Governing of the Lancastrian Lordship of Ireland in the Time of James Butler, Fourth Earl of Ormond' (Unpublished PhD, University of Durham, 1994); Brendan Smith, 'Before Reform and Revival: English Government in Late Medieval Ireland', in Christopher Maginn and Gerald Power (eds.), *Frontiers, States and Identity in Early Modern Ireland and beyond: Essays in Honour of Steven G. Ellis* (Dublin, 2016), pp. 21–35; Brendan Smith, 'Disaster and Opportunity: 1320–1450', in Smith, Brendan (ed.), *The Cambridge History of Ireland: Volume I. 600–1550* (Cambridge, 2018), pp. 244–271.

18 Steven G. Ellis, *Reform and Revival: English Government in Ireland 1470–1534* (Woodbridge, 1986); Christopher Maginn, 'Continuity and change: 1470–1550', in Brendan Smith (ed.), *The Cambridge History of Ireland*, vol. I, 600–1550 (Cambridge, 2018), pp. 300–328.

19 NAI: Calendar of Memoranda Rolls, 3 Richard II, pp. 4, 101, 114.

20 A.F. O'Brien, 'Irish Exchequer Records of Payments of the Fee Farm of the City of Cork in the Later Middle Ages', *Analecta Hibernica* 37 (1998), pp. 139–189.

21 James Graves (ed.), *A Roll of the Proceedings of the King's Council in Ireland, 1392–1393* (Rolls Series, London, 1877), pp. 120–121; Gearóid Mac Niocaill, 'Medieval Galway: Its Origin and Charter', in Diarmuid Ó Cearbhaill (ed.), *Galway: Town and Gown, 1484–1984* (Dublin, 1984), pp. 1–9.

22 Maud V. Clarke, 'William of Windsor in Ireland, 1369–1376', *PRIA* 41C (1932), pp. 117–118; Peter Crooks, 'Negotiating Authority in a Colonial Capital: Dublin and the Windsor Crisis, 1369–78', in Seán Duffy (ed.), *Medieval Dublin IX* (Dublin, 2007), pp. 150–151.

23 Steven G. Ellis, *Reform and Revival*, passim.

24 *Rotulorum patentium et clausorum Cancellariæ hiberniæ calendarium*, vol. 1, pt. 1, *Henry II – Henry VII* (hereafter RCH) John Tresham (ed.) (Dublin, 1828), p. 256, no. 141.

25 RCH, p. 204, no. 36; RCH p. 217, no. 18; Robin Frame, 'Commissions of the Peace in Ireland, 1302–1461', *Analecta Hibernica* 35 (1993), no 23.

26 H.F. Berry (ed.), *Statutes and Ordinances and Acts of Parliament of Ireland, 1427–1460* (Dublin, 1909), pp. 222–225.

27 RCH, p. 125, no. 138.

28 RCH, p. 266, no. 27.

29 Francis H. Tuckey, *Cork Remembrancer* (Cork, 1837), pp. 33–34.

30 Maurice Lenihan, *Limerick: It's History and Antiquities* (Dublin, 1866), pp. 68, 91; Matthew Potter, *The Government and the People of Limerick* (Limerick, 2006), pp. 82–87.

31 Avril Thomas, *The Walled Towns of Ireland*, 2 vols (Dublin, 1992); Paul Walsh, 'The Town Walls and Fortifications', in Elizabeth FitzPatrick, Madeline O'Brien, and Paul Walsh (eds.), *Archaeological Investigations in Galway City, 1987–1998* (Bray, 2004), pp. 309–336; O.H. Creighton and Robert Higham, *Medieval Town Walls: An Archaeology and Social History of Urban Defence* (Stroud, 2005); John Bradley, 'The Town Wall of Kilkenny Revisited: A Review Article', *Old Kilkenny Review* 58 (2006), pp. 185–195; Ian Johnston, 'Medieval Town Walls: Understanding the People within', *Decies* 62 (2006), pp. 67–87; Catríona Gleeson, 'A Social Archaeology of Anglo-Norman Cork' (Unpublished PhD thesis, University of Galway, 2015).
32 John T. Gilbert (ed.), *Calendar of Ancient Records of Dublin: In the Possession of the Municipal Corporation of That City* (hereafter CARD) (Dublin, 1889), i, p. 296.
33 'Archives of the Municipal Corporation of Waterford', John T. Gilbert (ed.), *Tenth Report of the Historical Manuscripts Commission,* Appendix, Part V, p. 286.
34 'Archives of the Town of Galway', John T. Gilbert (ed.), *Tenth Report of the Historical Manuscripts Commission,* Appendix, Part V, p. 402.
35 M.J. McEnery and Raymond Refaussé (eds.), *Christ Church Deeds* (Dublin, 2001), p. 83, no. 239.
36 Mary Clark and Gael Chenard, 'The Religious Guild of St George Martyr, Dublin', in Salvador Ryan and Clodagh Tait (eds.), *Religion and Politics in Urban Ireland, c. 1500–c. 1750: Essays in Honour of Colm Lennon* (Dublin, 2016), pp. 31–50.
37 CARD, i, pp. 327, 328, 357.
38 M.D. O'Sullivan, *Italian Merchant Bankers in Ireland in the Thirteenth Century* (Dublin, 1962); British Library: Additional Ms 4790, f.5, 61–62. *Cal Pat Rolls, 1354–8*, 370–371; TNA C47/10/19 (17).
39 For references to John Drake see CIRCLE, 10 Richard II, no. 62; NAI, Lodge MS 1, p. 46; RCH p. 138, no. 57; RCH p. 139, no. 99; RCH p. 142, no. 222; RCH p. 144, no. 112; RCH p. 150, no. 16; *Cal Pat Rolls, 1391–6*, p. 726; *Cal Close Rolls, 1392–6*, p. 508; *Cal Pat Rolls, 1396–9*, p. 209; *Cal Pat Rolls, 1399–1401*, p. 214; RCH p. 156, no. 56; *Cal Close Rolls, 1399–1402*, p. 341; RCH p. 168, no. 16; *Cal Pat Rolls 1401–5*, p. 183; RCH p. 176, no. 152; BL, Egerton MS 78, p. 26; *Cal Pat Rolls, 1401–5*, p. 183; RCH p. 177, no. 64; *Cal Close Rolls, 1402–5*, p. 353; NAI, RC 8/40, pp. 279–280; RCH p. 210, no. 26; John L. Robinson and E.C.R. Armstrong, 'On the Ancient Deeds of the Parish of St. John, Dublin, Preserved in the Library of Trinity College'. *Proceedings of the Royal Irish Academy* 33C (1916), pp. 195–197; RCH p. 210, no. 26; NAI, Lodge MS 17, pp. 151–152. See also Randolph Jones, 'Dublin's Great Civic Sword, Mayor John Drake and His Victory Near Bray in 1402', *Dublin Historical Record* 60 (2007), pp. 44–53.
40 Charles Smith, 'After the Tyrrells: The Later Lords of the Manor of Castleknock, Co. Dublin', *JRSAI* 142–143 (2012–2013), pp. 129–139; Eric St. John Brooks, 'The Grant of Castleknock to Hugh Tyrel', *JRSAI* 7th series, 3 (1933), pp. 206–220.
41 For Nicholas Woder, see *Cal Pat Rolls, 1441–6*, p. 288; Vincent Gorman, 'Richard, Duke of York, and the Development of an Irish Faction', *PRIA*, 85C (1985), pp. 169–179; H.F. Berry, 'The Records of the Dublin Gild of Merchants, Known as the Gild of the Holy Trinity, 1438–1671', *JRSAI* 10 (1900), p. 49; H.F. Berry, 'The Ancient Corporation of Barber-Surgeons, or Gild of St. Mary Magdalene, Dublin', *JRSAI* 33 (1903), p. 218; W.C. Stubbs, 'Weavers' Guild', *JRSAI* 9 (1919), p. 61; M.C. Griffith, 'The Talbot-Ormond Struggle for Control of the Anglo-Irish Government, 1414–47', *Irish Historical Studies* 2 (1941), p. 388; Edmund Curtis, 'Richard, Duke of York, as Viceroy of Ireland. 1447–1460; With Unpublished Materials for His Relations with Native Chiefs', *JRSAI* 2 (1932), p. 167.

42 RCH p. 262, no. 13; NAI, Lodge MS 1, pp. 54–55; BL, Egerton MS 75, p. 41; NAI, Lodge MS 17, p. 221; *Cal Pat Rolls, 1461–1467*, p. 201; *Statutes Ire, 1427–1460*, pp. 315, 403–405; Charles Smith, 'After the Tyrrells: the Later Lords of the Manor of Castleknock, Co. Dublin', *JRSAI* 142/143 (2012), p. 135; Frame, 'Commissions of the Peace in Ireland, 1302–1461', p. 13.

5 'Tudor England's French Frontier

The Laws of Guînes (1529) and the Defence of the Calais Pale'

Neil Murphy

In the early sixteenth century, England's most politically and strategically important frontier lay in France. While Lancastrian France collapsed in the mid-fifteenth century, the Calais Pale remained under English rule until 1558. Whereas English monarchs ruled the bulk of the lands they captured during the Hundred Years' War as the rightful king of France, Calais and its Pale became part of England. As well as forming England's principal gateway to the continent, the Calais Pale was the most militarised zone in the English monarch's dominions and vast amounts of state resources were poured into its defence. Even outside of periods of open warfare, the Pale saw regular skirmishing and raiding. Surrounded by powerful and frequently hostile powers, it was necessary to keep large numbers of soldiers in permanent garrison in the Calais Pale – a situation which placed considerable financial and logistical burdens on the English crown.

While historians have long studied English rule at Calais, they overwhelmingly focus on the town of Calais and say much less about the territories which formed the Pale, of which the county of Guînes (granted to Edward III in full sovereignty by the treaty of Brétigny in 1356) was the most significant.[1] By the sixteenth century, this county was governed by an English council based in Guînes, which sat on a militarised frontier with France and was a frontier town par excellence. The county's distinctive geopolitical situation meant that it bore the brunt of French attacks. Certainly, it suffered considerably during Henry VIII's war with France in the early 1520s, when, as the Guînes ordinances declare, the king's 'subiects, tenants and inhabitants' of the county of sustained many losses and suffered 'impoverishment'.[2]

To both improve the defence of the Pale and more firmly integrate this outlying region into the kingdom, on 29 August 1525 (the same month that an Anglo-French peace was sealed by the treaty of The More, bringing an end to the war which had begun in 1522), Henry VIII appointed a commission to Guînes to devise a new set of ordinances to overhaul the governance of the county – especially with regards to landholding practices – 'for [the] perpetuell record for the knowledge and generall instruction of all and every the kings tenants and subjects'.[3] The commission was composed of: William,

DOI: 10.4324/9781032691886-5

lord Sandes, an experienced soldier and administrator in the French Pale (and who would in 1530 be appointed captain of Guînes); Sir William Fitzwilliam, captain of Guînes, who like Sandes had considerable experience of frontier war and administration in France; Christopher Hales, solicitor-general; his cousin John Hales, baron of the exchequer and general surveyor of crown lands, and finally William Briswood, surveyor of the works at Calais.[4] The commissioners were instructed to first survey the county of Guînes to understand which lands it encompassed. This was an important task because the lack of a fixed frontier in this region (and only highly rudimentary means to delimit territory) meant that it was unclear precisely where the border of the Pale lay. It is likely that many residents of these lands gave their loyalty to the king of France (or oscillated between the two monarchs) when it suited them, especially as the region had the character of a march, rather than a solid frontier, where rulership was contested – a situation which the commission was empowered to halt. Once the commissioners had surveyed the lands, they were to devise and implement a set of new ordinances relating to landholding, which were designed to secure Henry's rule over this territory and ensure that all those who lived there gave their allegiance to the Tudor monarch alone. This was a major administrative undertaking and the text detailing these ordinances ('the boke of the new ordonnance, constitutions and decree for the towne and countie of Guisnes') was finally delivered to the bailly and freemen of Guînes in February 1529, though it is probable that they were in effective operation before this.

While the development of the Guînes laws marked a key episode in the Tudor monarchy's strategy to strengthen the kingdom's frontiers, they have been largely neglected. This probably a consequence of the lack of visibility of the text. In contrast to the well-studied reforming ordinance made at Calais in 1536, which was published in the *Statutes of the Realm* in the early nineteenth century, the earlier Guînes laws are only available as unpublished manuscripts.[5] While a contemporary manuscript copy of the 1529 laws is contained within *State Papers*, this important and substantial document receives only the briefest of mentions in *Letters and Papers* (the principal inventory of the government sources for Henry VIII's reign), which simply lists it as 'Ordinances for the town and county of Guisnes by the King's justices and commissioners' and provides few details about its contents beyond this general title.[6] Overall, this chapter provides a focused examination of these important but neglected laws and argues that they marked a key moment in the development of the early Tudor monarchy's concerns with the defence and administration of the frontiers of the realm.

After surveying the lands in the county of Guînes and 'Calling before them all and singuler men of the said subiects and tenants then inhabitinge and beinge within the said counyte', the commissioners prepared a new set of leases for farms in the region, which were to be granted through letters patent 'in fee simple used after the lawes of England'.[7] The Guînes ordinances abolished older landholding customs and replaced them with this standardised anglicised form. Although is unclear what forms of land tenure existed in this region prior to the formation of the Guînes ordinances, it is likely that there was a multiplicity of landholding rights and customs, some which may have been very old. It is possible too that the region had a status closer to that of one of the liberties found on other frontier regions of the kingdom, most notably in the north on the borders with Scotland.[8] Certainly, the commissioners noted that 'the moost ancient and substantiall men of the said Countie [of Guînes]. . . loth to transguesse and goo from the olde ordre and custumes of the said Countie' and that while some had tenants had come in and submitted to the king and received new charters confirming that they held their lands from the crown and setting out their obligations according to English law, others had not.[9] The actions of the Guînes commissioners in the 1520s perhaps also share some similarities to the policy of 'surrender and regrant' introduced into Ireland in the 1540s, whereby Gaelic chiefs who submitted to the king received a charter through which they held their lands (which were to be incorporated firmly within English systems of law, as happened as Guînes) from the crown.[10]

The comprehensive list of stipulations regulating landholding which accompanied these leases issued at Guînes were designed to realise the Tudor monarchy's vision for the best ordering of these borderlands. Leases for farms were to go to English farmers who – as well as asserting the Tudor monarch's claims to this territory by working the land – would produce foodstuffs, especially cereals, for the garrison at Guînes. This agricultural policy was intended to both strengthen the defence of the region and make it largely self-sufficient. The overall aim of the Guînes ordinances was to ensure that 'substantiall tenants and tenantries shalbe had within the said countie [of Guînes] soo that the inherent owners therof shall have in tyme comyng the more affection and appetitte to enhabite occupie and manure the same and tillage and husbondrye therby the better mayntened'.[11] The commissioners wanted to avoid granting leases to poor farmers, as they would be unable to provide a significant surplus for the garrisons. To this end, tenants had to meet a minimum 'yerely value of iiii^{xx} qz to let and set to ferme' in the county.[12] In other words, in order to be eligible to hold a lease in the county of Guînes, farmers needed to hold enough land to produce a minimum of eighty quarters of wheat per year (an amount sufficient to provide a surplus for the garrisons), which again underscores the emphasis the crown placed on arable farming in the county.

While this measure fell hard on less-substantial tenants, who now stood to lose their lands, the Guînes ordinances built in a range of mechanisms to help support those arable farmers who were able to meet the specifications of the leases. They were given tenancies with guaranteed possession of leases for 70 years, which could be passed on to heirs with no change in the terms.[13] As well as supporting tenants by giving them a good degree of security in their tenancies, this situation benefitted the crown by allowing it to develop a strong body of dependable farming families whose prosperity was tied to the county and who had a vested interest in maintaining Tudor rule over this region. Moreover, the land at Guînes was very fertile and amongst the best in the entire Pale – much of which was marshy and unsuitable to the production of crops – and was as good as the best arable farming land in southeastern England.[14]

As large farms could be expected to generate a greater surplus, the commissioners introduced a range of stipulations prohibiting the division of leases. In situations where a lease was currently held by multiple owners, the commissioners ruled that the person with the greatest share was permitted to buy out the others (unless co-leasers also met the yearly minimum level of grain production from their own share of the lands). Any person who refused to sell their portion of the lease under these circumstances would be compelled to do so.[15] To ensure that farms remained 'substantiall', the commissioners also prohibited the sub-leasing of lands and ruled that leases could not be left to multiple heirs.[16] Yet the ordinances included safeguards to offer redress against the unfair application of these measures, with compensation of one mesuage (a farmstead with a residential building) and twenty acres of land being given to person whose complaint about the allocation of leases was upheld.[17] The size of the farm perhaps gives an indication of the commissioners' conception of the minimum size of holding they envisaged to be able to produce the minimum yearly amount of grain for the garrison.

As part of the commission's efforts to encourage agricultural productivity, the Guînes ordinances included a series of stipulations designed to ensure that land was not left 'waste'. They ruled that all 'tenants within the countye of Guisnes shall not do ne suffer to be done any wast upon any platte of the lande' and that tenants were to 'kepe the necessarie reparations upon forfaiture of ther estates and interests and damage for wast'.[18] As cultivation played a key role in conferring ownership of a territory, by having his subjects work these lands the English monarch could assert his sovereignty over this disputed region (in Ireland, too, the 'plenished' land marked the effective frontiers of the Pale).[19] To better achieve this, the Guînes ordinances mandated that a minimum of one-third of all farms had to be put to arable use. The terms of the leases issued at Guînes were designed to ensure 'that the owners therof shall have in tyme coming the more affection and appetitte to enhabite, occupie and mansure the same and tillage husbondrye thereby the best mayntened'.[20] Manuring was important because it played a central role in arable farming and the improvement of lands, which provided a further justification for the occupation of 'waste' land.[21] Waste land was unworked land and thus not producing the grains which the garrisons required. Tenants were to undertake the 'bettering of landes' as part of which they would receive 'reasonable recompences for fallowing and composting of lande', which functioned as an additional incentive to improve the land.[22]

As part of their efforts to ensure that land was not left waste, the commissioners devised a series of regulations to ensure that farms were worked continually. They wanted to ensure the quick succession of a tenancy following the death of a leaseholder. Given that disputes over inheritance could slow down the transference of leases and thus hinder agricultural work, the Guînes ordinances stated that undue delays in the assigning of land – or problems arising because of fraudulent claims – would have to pay three times the value of the land to cover losses during the period when the lands lay 'wast'.[23] In cases where there was an unavoidable delay in the transfer of property (such as the forced confiscation of leases from people who did not meet the criteria laid down in the ordinances), disputed lands were to be placed under the direct administration of the council at Guînes, who presumably could organise to have the lands worked and any goods produced during this period to go directly to the garrisons.[24] Issues around inheritance were of particular concern to the commissioners. To maintain the integrity of farms, the Guînes ordinances prohibited the subdividing of lands amongst multiple children. Farms were to pass intact to the eldest male heir – and if there was no male then to the eldest female.[25] All bequests in wills also had to accord with the stipulations laid down by the new ordinances, and the mechanisms through which lands were passed on by inheritance was strictly monitored.[26] Upon the death of a leaseholder, those residents of the Pale seeking to stake a claim to land had to appear within two months before the exchequer at Calais and submit their petition to the comptroller.[27] If a claim for a tenancy at Guînes was subsequently found to be false, the lands were to be confiscated and let out to a new tenant.[28] In circumstances where there was a clear and undisputed heir, but that they were under the legal age to take up tenancies (sixteen for men, fourteen for women), the captain of Guînes was to place the lands of the tenancy under the guardianship of another resident of the Calais Pale. This solution was designed to encourage the continued working of the farm, especially as the guardian was permitted to draw a profit from these lands for the time they were under their care.[29] It was important that the guardian was resident in the Calais Pale to oversee the working of the land, as well as having first-hand experience of farming in the region. Aside from children, other types of persons were deemed to be incapable of running farms and were thus holding leases. Tenancies held by 'all natural folys, lunatyck parsons and madd parsons' were to be placed under the custody of a guardian, who was responsible for ensuring that the land was worked effectively. Beyond the incentive of making a profit, guardians were encouraged to ensure that the lands in their care were worked effectively by having to make restitution 'for wast done' to the lands during the time of their guardianship.[30]

Whether under the control of a tenant or a guardian, rent was to be paid annually either in coin or with 'wheat or other corne or grayne'. As the English administration ultimately wanted produce for the garrisons, having it paid in kind was preferred as it saved time and expense in having to buy goods and transport them to the garrison.[31] To this end, the leases encouraged the payment of rents with 'the rent corne of Guisnes'.[32] Payments were due on the feast day of St Michael the Archangel (29 September), which facilitated the focus on obtaining grains as it immediately followed harvest, when crops had been gathered and grains were at their most abundant. Any-one unable to make full payment by this date was given until the Feast of St. Andrew the Apostle (30 November) to pay the outstanding amount without incurring a penalty. Again, this was probably tied to farming considerations as a late harvest which extended into September would leave little time to prepare the grain to make the payment, with the late November date act-ing as a buffer against adverse environmental conditions. Should payments remain outstanding after the November deadline, officers at Guînes were empowered to take grain and animals up to the cost of the rent owed.[33] The names of all those who were late with their rents were to be read out in the church at Guînes, which served to publicly shame people into making pay-ments. Should debts continued to be unpaid beyond the confiscation of grain and livestock, tenancies would be forfeited to the crown and leased to some-one better able to draw a profit from them.[34]

Yet it was not in the crown's interest to resort to such heavy-handed actions, as it meant having to find new tenants and risked lands being left waste. Indeed, the commissioners included a range of measures to support farmers, including offering compensation for losses incurred through bor-der warfare. Farmers would be discharged for a year's rent if during 'tyme of warre with France or Flanders or otherwise . . . the tenants and other inhabituantes of the said countie shall happen to have ther houses burned, ther corne and catell dispoyled'. Arable farmers living on the frontiers of the kingdom faced considerable dangers. While animals could be killed or captured during enemy raids, raising livestock was a safer form of farming on borderlands because animals could be brought into the safety of a walled town or castle, whereas crops inevitably would be destroyed. The provisions contained in the laws of Guînes were designed to encourage farmers to till the land grounds by building in specific safeguards to ensure that tenants would not lose money should their crops be damaged. The commissioners noted that while many 'within the saide countie in tyme of the warres have tylled [and] manure[d] ther said lands', recurrent French raids meant that 'many of the kings tenants of the said Countie of Gusines have bene utterly leftid and disturbed to tak any profit' from their lands. As a consequence, farm-ers taking up leases here could obtain compensation for any loss of income incurred as a result of not being able to till the ground during time of war. They were to declare 'what parte of that land have not been tilled, sowen or manured at any tyme durin the said warres yf any such be and by what tyme and whiche part shalbe sowen or tilled or otherwise manured at any tyme during the warres'.[35]

As with the populations of other Tudor frontiers, residents of the county of Guînes were expected to take up arms in response to attacks on the region.[36] Yet while it was useful to have as many men in arms as possible, the situation in the Calais Pale was different to that in Ireland and in northern England, where there were only small numbers of soldiers in permanent garrison and the defensive responsibilities largely fell on the tenantry who were raised by local lords. In contrast, the Calais Pale was the most militarised region in the Tudor monarch's dominions and even in peace time there were large numbers of soldiers in permanent garrison based here. As such, the foodstuffs farmers in the county of Guînes could provide – rather than their active participation in arms – was the crucial aspect of their contribution to the defence of the region. To this end, in addition to the customary payments they were asked to make in the form of the 'rent corne of Guisnes', during times of war, each tenant was expected to provide for the defence of this territory by 'bring[ing] suche porcion of his cornes castell and other vitailles carte and other cariages as shalbe requisite for vitalling and defence of the saide Castell . . . and towne of Gusines'. Failure to do so incurred the punishment of the 'paine of forfeiture [of] ther tenures within the saide countie'.[37] The severity of the punishment highlights the importance the Tudor regime attached to the obligation to provide food for the garrison.

As well as overhauling land tenure and encouraging an agricultural policy pivoted around arable farming, concerns with the defence of the Pale in France led the Guînes commissioners to take a range of measures to anglicise these borderlands. This was an important development as the Pale had large numbers of French and Flemish farmers. To underscore that the county of Guînes was part of the kingdom of England, the commissioners mandated the exclusive use of English across all the official judicial and administrative systems which operated in the county. All legal cases were to be 'entered, afformyd, recorded and presented in englishe' in the court at Guînes 'within the realme of England by the commen lawes of the same realme'.[38] Common law was implemented through a series of special provisions which reflected the highly militarised character of these lands. Rather than use royal justices, the council of Guînes enforced the law and heard appeals. The Guînes regulations reinforced the fact that this territory was a part of England, with the laws repeatedly stating that the county was to be governed according to the 'lawes of England', while announcements made regarding the governing of the county was to be made in English.[39]

While intermarriage between English and French or Flemish was common in the Pale, the Guînes laws sought to restrict it. Henceforth, any person who wanted to take a 'husband or wife any alien borne' had to gain 'the kings special lycence under his greate seale . . . [on] payne of forfeiture of the possession and profitte of all the said lande'. The commissioners were particularly concerned about foreigners gaining control of farms in the Pale by marrying English women. Accordingly, those who issued the leases were given powers over women covert-baron to prevent lands and estates from coming under the control of any non-English husbands. Measures were put in place to ensure that lands or tenancies did not pass to the 'heir or heirs to any alien not being denizen'.[40] The laws also declared that 'all landes and tenants within the saide countie of Guisnes nowe being in the possession of any alien' were to be forfeited to the English monarch.[41] These measures went beyond the standard anti-alien measures introduced during times of war with France. Any aliens who held lands in Guînes and were not unable to obtain denizen status were to be 'expelled and put out from holds' from any of the lands or tenancies 'claymed by any of the saide aliens as his proper landes in hisowne right or in the right of his wife', and these lands were then to be leased out to those who met these ethnic stipulations.[42] These measures were not designed to completely remove all non-English people from the county of Guînes, but to exert close control over the process. As large farms (such as those the commissioners wanted to encourage for the county of Guînes) were dependent on labour, a French and Flemish workforce would be required (in the same way that Gaelic peasants worked the land in the Pale in Ireland) though they were not permitted to hold their own tenancy.[43]

These ethnic measures were taken in the interests of the defence, with the administrations in the Calais Pale increasingly seeing non-English residents of the king's lands as suspect and forming a potential fifth column. However, if aliens living in the county of Guînes were able to persuade the commission that their loyalty lay unquestionably to the Tudor monarch, they might be permitted to hold a tenancy. The ordinances stated that if three out of the five members of the commission agreed then they could grant a lease to 'person or persons being aliens borne'. Any such person had to be 'of longe tyme dwellinge within the said countye of Guînes or have married Englishe and have used themselves as the kings true subiects'.[44] Any non-English residents tenants of county who were permitted to remain were instructed to 'lerne the Englishe tong and shall use to speke Englishe'.[45] As we see, the overall intent was that in circumstances where French or Flemish were permitted to retain hold of their tenancy, they would have already proved their loyalty to the Tudor monarch and would become fully anglicised.

Similar measures were also replicated on other Tudor frontiers. The ethnic laws which the English monarch implemented in Ireland in 1537 following the suppression of the Kildare revolt, and then during the colonisation of Laois and Offaly of the 1550s – while resurging older practices in Ireland (codified in the 1366 Statute of Kilkenny) – also formed part of a much wider concern to anglicise the frontier lands of the kingdom under the Tudor monarchs, with similar measures being adopted in both France and Ireland. Eight years after the laws of Guînes bound all French residents of this territory to learn English, Henry VIII issued 'An Act for the English Ordr, Habit and Language', which ruled that the Irish 'shall use and speak commonly the English tongue and language'.[46] The reform ordinance issued for Calais in 1536 similarly ordered all 'the Englisshe language used within this Realme of England to be spoken and used in every one of his or their said Parisshes from tyme to tyme, aswell amonge the Householders and the servauntes, as the chylderne of their parochians and others resorting unto the same'.[47] Brendan Bradshaw saw the legislation introduced in the late 1530s prohibiting the use of the Irish language and controlling marriage between English and Irish as deriving from the anglicising measures included in the reforms devised for Calais in 1536.[48] Yet the ethnic legislation contained the Guînes laws pre-dated the Calais ordinance and it was concerns with border defence rather than the implementation of Cromwellian legislation in the 1530s which really drove the anglicisation of the frontiers during its formative period.[49]

The development of the 1525 laws of Guînes marked an important moment in the development of the Tudor monarchy's concern with the defence of the frontiers. While there had been some efforts to reform the Calais Pale to better secure its defence during the reign of Henry VII, the Guînes laws marked the first systematic attempt by the Tudor monarchy to reform entire landholding patterns and settlement structures to secure the borders of the kingdom. The Guînes laws also played an important role in the emerging colonialism of the early English empire from the 1540s. They provided the blueprint for the English settlement of the Boulonnais – which lay immediately adjacent to the county of Guînes – in the 1540s. Here Henry VIII conquered tens of thousands of acres of land and drove the indigenous population out with great violence, repopulating the territory with English settlers. The laws of Guînes were especially suitable because, as in the 1520s, the English monarch sought to attract commercial farmers who could sell goods to the garrisons. This model of colonialism for defensive purposes was employed on other Tudor frontiers, as seen with the actions of the earl of Kildare in Ireland and then with the establishment of garrisons in Laois and Offaly, with civilian populations producing goods for the soldiers.[50] On the border with Scotland, in the 1570s, Christopher Dacre proposed to build fortifications manned by permanent garrisons across the northern border, with the soldiers being provided for by civilian populations established in attendant farming settlements.[51] As we see, similar processes were at work across different border regions under the Tudors. While there has been some excellent work on the comparative history of England's frontiers during this period, much more needs to be done on to understand how concerns with defence, settlement and ethnicity determined the character of three land borders of the Tudor state.[52]

Notes

1 Mark Ormrod, *Edward III* (New Haven, 2011), p. 405. For the principal studies of Calais, see: David Grummitt, *The Calais Garrison: War and Military Service in England, 1436–1558* (Woodbridge, 2008); P.T.J. Morgan, 'The Government of Calais, 1485–1558' (DPhil thesis, University of Oxford, 1966); Susan Rose, *Calais: An English Town in France, 1347–1558* (Woodbridge, 2008); G.A.C. Sandeman, *Calais under English Rule* (Oxford, 1908).

2 The National Archives, Kew [hereafter TNA] SP 1/52, fol. 174r.

3 TNA SP 1/52, fol. 203v. Though it was the following summer before the commissioners began surveying the county of Guînes and their efforts continued into 1528: TNA SP 1/36, fol. 2r, 1/50, fol. 86r (J.S. Brewer, J. Gardiner, and R.H. Brodie (eds.), *Letters and Papers, Foreign and Domestic, of the Reign of Henry VIII*, 21 vols (London, 1862–1932) [hereafter *LP*], 4, nos. 1612, 4712.

4   TNA SP 1/52, fol. 174r.
5   *The Statutes of the Realm*, 10 vols (London, 1810–28) [hereafter *SR*], 3, pp. 632–650.
6   *LP*, 4, no. 5247. For the full document, see: TNA SP 1/52, fols. 174r-206v.
7   TNA SP 1/52, fols. 195r, 205v.
8   For these liberties, see: Michael Prestwich (ed.), *Liberties and Identities in the Medieval British Isles* (Woodbridge, 2008).
9   TNA SP 1/36, fol. 2r (*LP* 4, no. 1612).
10 For surrender and regrant, see: C. Maginn, '"Surrender and Regrant" in the Historiography of Sixteenth-Century Ireland', *Sixteenth-Century Studies* 38 (2007), pp. 955–974.
11 TNA SP 1/52, fol. 195r.
12 TNA SP 1/52, fol. 195r.
13 TNA SP 1/52, fol. 195r.
14 For the topography of the Calais Pale, see: Grummitt, *Calais Garrison,* pp. 6–8; H.A. Dillon, 'Calais and the Pale', *Archaeologia* 53 (1893), pp. 289–388.
15 TNA SP 1/52, fols. 195r-195v.
16 TNA SP 1/52, fol. 195r.
17 TNA SP 1/52, fol. 201v.
18 TNA SP 1/52, fol. 201v.
19 Ellis, *Ireland's English Pale*, p. 45.
20 TNA SP 1/52, fol. 201v.
21 John Patrick Montaño, *The Roots of English Colonialism in Ireland* (Cambridge, 2011), pp. 97, 101, 111.
22 TNA SP 1/52, fol. 201v.
23 TNA SP 1/52, fol. 198v.
24 TNA SP 1/52, fol. 195r.
25 TNA SP 1/52, fols. 194v-195r.
26 TNA SP 1/52, fol. 195r.
27 TNA SP 1/52, fol. 196v.
28 TNA SP 1/52, fol. 196v.
29 TNA SP 1/52, fol. 200v.
30 TNA SP 1/52, fol. 201v.
31 TNA SP 1/52, fol. 195r.
32 TNA SP 1/52, fol. 195r.
33 TNA SP 1/52, fol. 198v.
34 TNA SP 1/52, fol. 199r.
35 TNA SP 1/52, fol. 199v.
36 For military obligations of the populations in the Pale in Ireland and on the border with Scotland, see: Ellis, *Ireland's English Pale*, pp. 53–58; R.W. Hoyle, 'An Essay on Border Service', in C. Maginn and G. Power (eds.), *Frontiers, States and Identity in Early Modern Ireland and Beyond* (Dublin, 2016), pp. 109–129.
37 TNA SP 1/52, fol. 202r.
38 TNA SP 1/52, fol. 204r.
39 TNA SP 1/52, fol. 199r.
40 TNA SP 1/52, fol. 200r.
41 TNA SP 1/52, fol. 200r. Similar measures were introduced into Calais in 1536 as part of the reform of its administration, with the ordinance stating that 'for as moche as it is evydently knowen that there ben at this presente tyme many more Pycardes and Flemmynges inhabytynge within the said Towne and Marches of Caleys than Englysche men, which is ageynste the perfecte weake suertie and tuycion of the said Towne ad Marches', it was ordered that lands or properties of the king's demesne land were not to be let 'to any maner of person or persons beyng

or whiche herafter shalbe any Alyant borne . . . without the specyall lycence of the Kynges Highnes his heires or successours under the greate seale of this Realme of England': *SR*, 3, p. 643.

42 TNA SP 1/52, fol. 200r.
43 On this point for Ireland, see: Ellis, *Ireland's English Pale*, pp. 9–10.
44 TNA SP 1/52, fol. 200v.
45 TNA SP 1/52, fol. 199v.
46 *Irish History from Contemporary Sources (1509–1610)*, ed. C. Maxwell (London, 1923), p. 113; *The Statutes at Large, Passed at the Parliaments Held in Ireland*, 20 vols (1786–1804), vol. 1, pp. 119–122.
47 *SR*, 3, p. 648.
48 Brendan Bradshaw, *The Irish Constitutional Revolution of the Sixteenth Century* (Cambridge, 1979), p. 127.
49 For the 1536 act, see: A.J. Slavin, 'Cromwell, Cranmer and Lord Lisle: A Study in the Politics of Reform', *Albion* 9 (1977), pp. 316–336; David Grummitt, '"One of the Mooste Pryncpall Treasours Belonging to His Realme of Englande": Calais and the Crown, c. 1450–1559', in David Grummitt (ed.), *The English Experience in France, c. 1450–1558: War, Diplomacy and Cultural Exchange* (Aldershot, 2002), pp. 46–62; Rose, *Calais*, pp. 126–128.
50 Ellis, *Ireland's English Pale*, chapters 3 and 4; D.G. White, 'The Tudor Plantations in Ireland before 1571' (PhD thesis, Trinity College, Dublin, 1968).
51 Marcus Merriman, '"The Epystle to the Queen's Majestie" and Its "Platte"', *Architectural History* 27 (1984), pp. 25–32.
52 See especially: Steven Ellis, *Tudor Frontiers and Noble Power* (Oxford, 1995); Steven Ellis, *Defending English Ground: War & Peace in Meath and Northumberland, 1460–1542* (Oxford, 2015).

6 Conquest or Recovery

Enlarging the English Pale in Early Tudor Ireland

Steven Ellis

The creation of Ireland's English Pale marked a final attempt by medieval English kings to build a frontier to preserve the English character of the colonial parts, keeping Ireland's two medieval nations apart, and 'driving a cultural barrier between them'. Despite small armies sent for defence, and legislation proscribing Irish law and custom, the frontier's limits gradually contracted to the 'four obedient shires' around Dublin. Standing defences were then erected around what became the Pale to create a 'hard border', still partly visible in the many tower-houses, dikes and ditches across the region. Professor James Lydon's pioneering survey in 1967 nonetheless concluded that this frontier strategy culminating in the Pale was 'a complete failure', a futile attempt to reverse the contraction of English rule and preserve its English character. It was 'the Tudors who first faced up to the frontier problem' realistically, he argued, seeing a conquest as 'the only real answer'.[1]

Lydon's seminal paper summarized perceptively successive unavailing attempts to build a defensive frontier to halt the contraction of English rule. Of the English Pale's specific origins and development, however, Lydon offered only the briefest of sketches, leaving it to others to flesh out his survey, a task which remains ongoing. His theory of the shrinking Pale nonetheless captured the historical imagination, reappearing periodically in later studies of the Pale.[2] Most recently, Dr Sparky Booker's monograph and related articles on cultural exchange and identity in 'the four obedient shires' considered the Pale at some length, also identifying 'gaelicization' as central to its contraction.[3]

My view of Ireland's English Pale, first sketched in a study of English revival in 1986, since modified, was that it was broadly successful, its expanding frontiers screening it more effectively from Irish raids.[4] Rather than immediately confronting the Pale's difficult, apparently contradictory sources for a sequel to *Reform and revival*, however, I opted to write a comparative study of Tudor frontiers, conceptualizing the Pale in the framework of European frontier and border studies. The fresh insights into the Pale's character afforded by this approach and the additional evidence uncovered then laid the basis for a more rounded study of developments.[5] Yet, even a cursory glance at the early Tudor sources pointed to an expanding Pale and moving

DOI: 10.4324/9781032691886-6

frontier. Following its recovery from O'Kelly in 1537, Athlone castle was described as 'the defence of the English Pale thereto adjoining'. And in south Dublin, where the Kildare earls had recovered significant land from O'Toole and O'Byrne, a jury inquiring in 1545 whether Kiltiernan and Kilpole nearby were 'situated at or near the bounds of the English Pale' confirmed that lands in Kiltiernan 'touch the extreme parts of the English Pale, and lie near the O'Toles on the south'.[6] A survey of the Pale's landed additions suggests that they were chiefly of two kinds, by conquest and by restoration. Some lands were conquered from Irish chiefs, chiefly by successive earls of Kildare. Other additions were of lands where English lineages had clung on, despite contracting royal government, but over which English rule was now restored. This paper explores the themes of conquest and restoration. The role and responsibility of successive Kildare earls in developing the Pale is perhaps broadly familiar, but less so are the earls' promotion of tillage as a means of consolidating conquest. The resultant revival of English manorialism relied heavily on an influx of Irish labourers to work the land, sparking complaints in early Tudor reform literature about 'the increase of Irishmen'. Seemingly, this also lies behind modern accounts of the Pale's increasing 'gaelicization', but as is argued here, the earls' policies, far from promoting 'gaelicization', helped to consolidate English culture and identity in an expanding Pale.

The region's description as an 'English Pale' alluded to its new standing defences, from the 1450s erecting a military frontier around the four shires. Statutes required teams of labourers with spades and pickaxes to construct dikes and ditches, offered marcher landowners subsidies to build defensive towers ('the ten-pound castles'), and fortified bridges over the River Liffey to inhibit Irish raids north of Dublin.[7] The region's extent and limits were also more closely defined by statutes of 1477 and 1488, although these have wrongly been construed as creating impervious fixed boundaries. The 1488 Act of Marches and Maghery made it treason to impose coign and livery on English ground, except for landlords on their own tenants in the marches. To distinguish between the marches, where landowners could billet horsemen and kerne for defence, and the maghery where this was prohibited, a detailed statutory definition of this internal march-maghery boundary was included. This also regulated revised arrangements for hostings by a mobile force to supplement the Pale's standing defences: in the marches, 'everie gentleman . . . shall sende an horseman well appointed' for each ten marks yearly of land; in the maghery, landlords contributed one footman, usually an able archer, for every £20 yearly of landed income. South of Dublin, the march-maghery boundary followed the line of dikes and ditches; in Kildare, the great bend in the River Liffey marked the boundary; but in Meath and Louth the boundary remained largely undefended, its purpose chiefly administrative. The Pale had no agreed external 'border line', however, unlike the Tudors' extended frontier with Scotland, and historians' attempts to chart a static frontier are misconceived. If the 1488 internal boundary had marked its outer limits, it would have described a very truncated Pale.[8]

Map 6.1 The English Pale under the early Tudors.

Source: Author copyright.

These new frontier defences across 'the four obedient shires' were first described as an 'English Pale' in 1495 in legislation of Poynings' parliament. Professor Lydon had thought the Pale's origins lay much earlier, citing a document of 1446 later shown to be a mid-Tudor interpolation.[9] The new name highlighted the Pale's military character and was inspired by the Pale at Calais where Edward Poynings served as governor just before appointment as governor of Ireland. The statute's purpose was to strengthen 'the marches of the iiii shires' but was entitled 'diches to be made about the Inglishe pale'.[10] So, the 1488 boundary could hardly be the 'Pale ditch', seven years before its first naming. Dr Booker has since attempted to restore Lydon's vision of continuing contraction, claiming that the 'term "Pale", like maghery, described a smaller inner portion of the four shires', but these were alternative medieval and Tudor names for the region, as Lord Chancellor Alen later confirmed, and were often used interchangeably.[11] Already by 1495, however, the region included 'a parte of the coun[n]tie Catherlaghe, wch therle of Kyldare dyde conquere on Irishemen and but latelye inhabyted'. Carlow also contributed to the 120 kerne and 46½ horsemen (Baltinglass abbey sent three horsemen) due for militia service in the Pale's hostings from Kildare and Carlow.[12] The region's description as 'the four shires' became even less appropriate in 1542 when Meath's division by statute into two shires created Co. Westmeath as another shire with four new baronies on the lands of English marcher lineages. The 1495 statute marked the final stage in erecting this military frontier. It said nothing about the maghery or fixed boundaries, although its observation that, because the marches were 'open & not fe[n]sible in ffastnes of diches and castels', Irishmen did 'great hurts' there, implied that its standing defences had hitherto focused on the maghery. The statute sought instead to strengthen marcher defences, ordering a double ditch and rampart built there, plus further ditches 'in the wastes' beyond at 'such time and places' as the shire's commissioners overseeing these earthworks should appoint. The military value of ditches in uninhabited wastes was slight, but as the frontier was pushed out further, they consolidated control of more marchland. A statutory definition of boundaries for a moving frontier would have been pointless. Its limits were the furthest reach of English government.[13]

In Kildare, these limits clearly encompassed all fourteen baronies from which taxation was levied in 1481, including lands recently conquered by Kildare from Irish chiefs, despite claims that the Pale included 'only a small corner of north-eastern Kildare'.[14] The earls' conquests were notorious. That prolific composer of anti-Kildare reform tracts, Robert Cowley, supplied a partial list c. 1526. This included the 'banishing of the Tooles from Fercullen' east of Kildare, 'expulsed by force of the sword' and leaving 'the country in possession with the earl of Kildare and his brethren', likewise 'the "Fferture" taken from the Byrnes', and further south 'Clonmore, the Fassagh of Bantry and Old Ross taken from MacMurrough'. In the south-west, Carlow, Kilkea, and Athy were all

> taken from the Mores; Rathangan and Keshboyne taken from O'Connor, and now very late . . . the barony of Rebane taken from O'More where . . . Kildare hath built a manor called Woodstock. All the said lands have been long time in Irishmen's hands and by the earl of Kildare and his father by reason of the king's authority plucked and taken from the said Irishmen.

Cowley also claimed improbably that in 'Kildare, named one of the 4 obeisant shires in the English Pale, . . . may be heard [not] one word of English spoken but all Irish'. He also noted the 'increase of Irishmen', their 'Irish habit and tonsures . . . and Irish garments'.[15] Historians agree that Kildare was more heavily populated with Irish than other Pale shires, but this was evidence of the earls' success in restoring English manorialism and tillage on conquest lands, not of 'gaelicization'.[16] Tillage was more labour-intensive than pastoralism, but the Kildare earls addressed the shortage of English labourers by bringing in 'poor Irish earthtillers' (the description is significant) to work their rebuilt manors secure behind the Pale's extended defences. When crown officers surveyed ex-Kildare estates in 1540–41, Irish tenants were especially numerous on these recovered manors – along the River Barrow, and around the Leinster mountains.[17] As governor, Kildare could offer 'charters of English liberty' to 'poor earthtillers' providing the additional labour needed to extend cereal cultivation in the marches. Legally, this practice probably originated in legislation of 1465 affording Irishmen in the four shires the chance to become English by culture and identity. One statute, observing 'the great number of Irishmen who exceed greatly the English', required Irishmen aged between sixteen and sixty, dwelling with Englishmen and speaking English, to have English longbows in 'augmentation of the king's liege men'. Another ordered Irishmen dwelling among Englishmen to be sworn the king's liegeman before the governor within one year, wear English dress and take an English surname (town, colour, or occupation). Anticipating a strong response, an additional clause extended this 'swearing English' to those whom the governor 'will assign . . . for the multitude . . . to be sworn', perhaps Kildare's two resident ex-governors, Lords Kildare and Portlester. The legislation certainly answered the Kildare earls' needs, as ruling magnate, for Irish labour to rebuild their manors on this conquest land.[18]

A prime example of this was Rathangan manor, recovered by Kildare from O'Connor Faly, probably in 1459. Its subsequent development reflected the earls' policies for strengthening the Kildare marches. By 1515, 'every village and towne' across Kildare 'within 6 myles to the wylde Iryshe' was 'dycheyd and hegeyd strongly'. The 'cesse of the werkes' also required townships with a plough to provide a cart 'to cary stones to the castels on the borders' and a labourer 'to cast diches and fastnes upon the borders', each for a week, an axeman for two or four days 'to cutte passages upon the borders', with the country's gentlemen and horsemen on hand 'to defende them'.[19] By 1540, Rathangan boasted a dovecot, a garden, sixty acres of demesne land, and a watermill farmed in 1518 for an impressive 240 pecks of wheat and malt annually, so confirming the 9th earl's reputation as 'the gretest improver of his landis in this land'. Rathangan was dominated by a stone castle 'scitum in finibus patrie Anglicane . . . super limites patrie de Offalye ubi O Cconour . . . commorat', with supporting towerhouses in outlying townships at Ballinure and Caryk Everyly.[20] The land's quality was not, however, the only reason for Kildare's promotion of cereal cultivation. A well-populated landscape of manorial villages protected by defensive towers and longbowmen also strengthened the marches. The tenants were mostly Irish in 1540, but humble earthtillers apparently, not from politically influential clans like O'Connor. Some half-dozen were sufficiently established to serve as jurors on the extent jury, although a recent study of extent juries concluded that the 'presence of a major Kildare manor or castle' hardly 'made much difference to the status of the Irish in the region'.[21] With tillage greatly extended hereabouts, Offaly's baronial subsidy assessment had risen steeply from nine ploughlands in 1481 to 14¾ ploughlands by 1533. The subsidy collectors also included a sprinkling of Irishmen: Cowroll McDermot in 1520–21; Donogh McConoghor and Maurice Obeghan in 1533. Thus, in seventy years, successive earls had built up a thriving manor with a significant Irish population on unimproved wasteland recovered from O'Connor.[22]

In the nearby township of Keshboyne (alias Kishawanny), Cowley listed another parcel of conquest lands where the earl had built a tower c. 1480 on the banks of the Boyne dividing O'Connor's lordship of Offaly from Carbury and Berminghams' country. Berminghams' country was the shire's only example of a major Pale extension made chiefly by restoring English rule over the supposedly 'gaelicized' lordship of an English lineage, the Berminghams, although this practice was more prevalent in western Meath.[23] In 1540, the tenants were again mainly Irish in Keshboyne and surrounding west Carbury estates formerly held by Sir Walter Delahide, the 9th earl's steward, but in the heart of Berminghams' country the tenants were mostly English. English jurors were also prominent on the extent of Delahide's former manors of Carbury and Ballina. Otherwise, conditions resembled Rathangan, with tillage greatly extended across Carbury, and the barony's subsidy assessment increased from seven ploughlands in 1481 to twelve ploughlands by 1533. By the 1520s, some established Irish tenants around Carbury were also serving as subsidy collectors, including Conly Makkygan in 1520–1521, and Thady Okylleghan and Thady Ohonne in 1533. In 1534, however, the collector was none other than William Bermingham of Dunfierth, chief of his nation, to whom Henry VIII granted a peerage in 1541 as baron of Carbury.[24] The earlier inclusion of Carbury and Rathangan in an extended Pale was also confirmed when the council advised the king that nearby towers at Ballinure, Castlejordan, Kinnefad, and Kishawanny guarded 'the onely passages where [O'Connor] muste entier within your Pale': their refurbishment would 'keep hym and all the Yrishemen behind hym from invading your Pale with any horsemen'.[25]

Apart from Berminghams' country, the Pale's extended frontiers in Kildare were mainly conquest land, reflecting the earls' dominant position as ruling magnate and their estate management policies promoting tillage. Essentially, the earls expelled Irish chiefs from lands bordering the Pale, restored English rule and manorialism there, and brought in Irish labourers to work the land who were 'sworn English' and increasingly integrated into English local government. Although taken as evidence of widespread 'gaelicization', the scores of Irish tenants and jurors recorded in the 1540–1541 extents are only visible to us because the ongoing processes of English acculturation and naturalization underpinning their integration remained incomplete. In Kildare, however, Irishmen serving as subsidy collectors were much more widespread than elsewhere, pointing to their rising status and closer integration. Of sixteen collectors appointed for ten Kildare baronies in 1533, fourteen had Irish names, a far higher proportion than elsewhere. Of fourteen collectors appointed for 1534, twelve had Irish names.[26]

A similar pattern to Rathangan is apparent at Threecastles, east of the Great Earl's principal manor of Rathmore on the south Dublin-Kildare frontier with the O'Tooles, where the military dimension of Kildare's manor building was even more apparent. Kildare had built Threecastles manor on conquest lands stretching 'up to the high mounteyns' in O'Tooles' country. Three extents described ten towerhouses there defending twelve nearby townships (plus five more townships now deserted) with ninety-six tenants, but only five tenants clearly had English names. Under the Statute of Arms, husbandmen with goods worth £10 were required to have 'an Englishe Bowe & a Sheff of Arrowes'; but recently, the manor's husbandmen, left unsupported by horsemen after venturing into the mountains, were intercepted by O'Tooles' kerne who slew sixty and captured Threecastles tower.[27] Ironically, this reverse consolidated the rising status on the manor of one Fernand McGyoghoo, although leaving five townships untenanted. McGyoghoo now held 160 acres arable and 60 acres pasture with other tenants for £4 13s. 4d. annually plus services. As lead tenant in three townships there, with custody of Threecastles and Athgarrett towers, he also served as juror on extents in two shires at Ballymore Eustace, Co. Dublin (with six more Irish jurors, four English) and at Ballycutland, Co. Kildare. The recent claim that 'many, if not most' Irish extent jurors lacked 'access to English law' may suggest McGyoghoo's rising status was exceptional, but his juror description as 'per sacramentum . . . proborum et legalium hominum de viceneto' suggests otherwise.[28]

A second county seeing wholesale expansion was Meath, but here the main driver was not conquest but the reintegration of English lineages and lands in the far west. Dr. Booker again dismisses this expansion, suggesting that the Pale 'ended near Trim in 1495 and at nearby Dangan in 1515', leaving the shire's western marches entirely beyond the Pale.[29] The underlying causes of expansion were again unwittingly disclosed by Kildare's inveterate opponent, Robert Cowley, in another reform treatise of late 1533 discussing the *man-raed* of 'the iiij obedient shires, termed thEnglish Pale'. Cowley's discussion was premised on the established distinction between marches and maghery in militia service for hostings, for which the English lineages now supplied the shire's best troops. Cowley dismissed the combat value of maghery levies as

> no redy men of warr for the mor parte, neith[r] to spoile nor burne a contrey or to resist an invasion aft[r] the maner of the lande, but they be footmen . . . few in number & to small purpose.

The Pale's 'strength & in effect all', he argued, 'consisteth in the marches'. 'In the marches of Meath, when so euer the kinges depute had nede, Dalton, Dillon, Tirrell, Delamare, captaines of their contreys & nations . . . did come forth wth a band of horsemen & footmen', he elaborated, supporting the governor with 'diuerse oth[r] gentlemen & marchers', Bermingham, Walshmen, Harrold, 'captaines of those oth[r] marches, euery of them for defence of the contrey or oth[r] exploit', and 'all being togeth[r], made a goodly company'. Yet the present 'erle & his fath[r] beinge the kinges deputies' had since 'purchased the grete qualitie of the lands of those contreys & placed their sonnes, bretherne, . . . & follow[rs] there'. They had 'subdued & extinguished all the march captaines', he added, converting to themselves 'the obedienc & strength of those marches'.[30]

As Cowley's hostile account suggests, the earls had certainly bought up lands in districts held by march captains.[31] The key point, however, was that English lineages previously not amenable to royal government had since been brought back under English rule. This included Berminghams' country in Carbury, and Harolds' country and the Walshmen in south Dublin. In Meath, the captains were more numerous, held extensive lands, and now supplied most of the shire's *manraed*. Revealingly, the earls had recognized the march captains' land titles in this recovery, by contrast with their outright conquest of lands held by Irish chiefs. In 1511, Meath's sheriff listed eleven captains receiving writs to hostings, including Dalton, Delamare, Dillon, and Tyrrell. Earlier, taxation levied on western baronies adjoining their 'countries' had indicated the captains' partial reintegration into the Pale. At Michaelmas 1498, the exchequer appointed subsidy collectors for eighteen Meath baronies, including the western baronies of Moygoish, Corkaree, Magheradernon, and Moyashel. The collectors included Tyrrell of Portloman and Petit of Irishtown, both on the sheriff's list in 1511, as were others who, while answering writs for hostings, 'obey not the kinges lawe': Delamare of the Straid, and both 'Dalton of Glascan. with all West Meth' and 'Dillon w[t] all Maghir Corke' who were listed in Moygoish barony but resided further west towards Athlone. By then, the crown was also enforcing right of wardship over Tuit of Sonnagh, Moygoish's leading landowner and occasional subsidy collector, and over various other Tuits and Petits. Finally, in 1542, Maghirquirke became Kilkenny West, one of four new baronies erected on lands of English marcher lineages, so confirming their reintegration into the Pale in the newly created Co. Westmeath, with Robert Dillon appointed its first sheriff.[32]

The impact on tillage of the Pale's expansion in Meath also differed somewhat from Kildare. Screened from Irish raids by an extended march now defended by the English lineages, the Meath maghery saw a vast extension of tillage: subsidy assessments increased by 25%, from 236 ploughlands in 1479 to 295½ ploughlands in 1533. Individual baronial assessments now regularly exceeded thirty ploughlands, but in the marches tillage levels remained far lower, rising only slightly after 1508 and nowhere exceeding 7½ ploughlands per barony.[33] In the far west, English lineages remained on the land, with no Irish 'earthtillers' introduced, apparently, even on lands bought up by Kildare, and so little impact on tillage levels. Tillage increases in the maghery were also mostly achieved without the wholesale introduction of Irish 'earthtillers' on conquest lands as in Kildare. On the earl's recently improved manors of Moylagh, Moynalvy, and Portlester, Irish tenants were numerous in 1540, but fewer served on extent juries. Irish tenants and jurors were prominent elsewhere on Meath manors, but overall, Irish immigration was perhaps lighter and later in Meath than Kildare. The small numbers of Irish subsidy collectors (normally well-established tenants) appointed for Meath baronies also suggest this.[34]

The Kildare earls seldom sought to extend across the Pale's northern marches their strategy of promoting tillage to consolidate control of conquest lands. Following the king's grant in 1496 of Duke Richard's Ulster estates around Cooley and Carlingford, however, the Great Earl reintroduced tillage in the Cooley peninsular where the remnants of an English population had survived. This was reflected in Cooley barony's revived subsidy assessment in 1499, initially 11½ ploughlands, with Geoffrey White appointed subsidy collector. The following term, however, the importance which Kildare attached to the experiment was reflected in the exceptional appointment as collector 'in partibus de Coly' of a parliamentary peer, Kildare's brother-in-law, Christopher Fleming, Lord Slane. Despite this, no evidence survives of immigrant 'Irish earthtillers' in war-torn Cooley and cereal cultivation later declined, probably because Cooley lay too far from the earl's principal estates in the Pale's southern marches for him to organize adequate protection.[35]

Clearly, Ireland's English Pale was far from resolving all the problems of English rule, but this cheap solution in a minor theatre of Tudor operations nonetheless held many attractions for the crown, not least marking time pending a general reformation. As ruling magnate, successive Kildare earls built up a military frontier around 'the four shires', extending and transforming them into a larger, more viable Tudor region whose English culture and

identity long outlived in the popular memory its political and military significance. The early Tudor Pale initially enjoyed an unwonted measure of political stability, and its new-found military and financial self-sufficiency saved
the king some £3,000 a year, the basic cost of a governor and retinue from
England. So why, given this stability and political and economic expansion,
has the myth of the shrinking Pale proved so tenacious?

For the Pale's political community, the Kildare ascendancy was never
more than a temporary expedient, pending the long-expected royal visit and
resumption of forward policy to reduce Ireland to obedience. By 1515, Henry
VIII was regularly receiving distinctive reform treatises from his Irish officials outlining governmental shortcomings and urging reform of English rule.
Reform writers could hardly criticize royal policy directly, so Kildare increasingly attracted the blame, often from disenchanted officials lobbying for a
new governor. Polemical claims in reform treatises provided the king with
colourful but highly partisan accounts criticizing the earl's rule. They also
marginalized 'the lytle Englishe Pale withyn the counties of Dublyne, Mydthe
and Uryell whiche passed not xxx or xl myles in compace'.[36] And Kildare's
reputation disappeared entirely with the 1534 rebellion. The spread of Irish
immigrants, customs, law, and language across the Pale supposedly also demonstrated the 'complete failure' of its military frontiers. These accounts have
been extensively mined in modern studies highlighting the Pale's decline and
decay. Reducing the Pale area to that of the maghery placed all Kildare's
conquest lands beyond the Pale, discounting the integration in culture and
identity of Irish earthtillers there. Yet a careful examination of the regime's
more dispassionate administrative records, the court rolls and records which
chart the actual operation and reach of royal government, reveals a very different picture of the Pale's English culture, identity, and expansion, with an
effective system of defences.

The purpose of the military frontiers had never been to establish a sort of
Berlin Wall around the Pale, only to discourage habitual raiding by neighbouring Irish chiefs. Like other early modern frontiers, the Pale's frontiers
were otherwise porous and theatres of cultural exchange: elsewhere, this
unremarkable feature of frontiers scarcely attracts much historical comment.
There were established procedures whereby Irish earthtillers could cross the
Pale frontier, be 'sworn English', acquiring an English identity and be integrated into an English Pale ruled by English law and custom. The intru-
sion of this modern concept, 'gaelicization', misleadingly implies that the
reverse was true of the English lineages beyond the Pale. Professor Lydon
had used the contemporary Tudor term, describing the English lineages as
'degenerate'.[37] They declined or decayed from English civility, but no amount
of 'gaelicization' made them Gaelic by culture or identity. They were frequently castigated as 'English rebels', but not as 'Irish enemies', and viewed
from across the Pale's frontiers, they resolutely remained *Gaill*, not *Gaedhil*.
As the Pale's frontiers rolled westwards past Carbury and Kilkenny West

towards Athlone, it restored English rule over a supposedly 'gaelicized' William Bermingham or Robert Dillon, and also confirmed their English culture and identity.

Notes

1 James Lydon, 'The Problem of the Frontier in Medieval Ireland', republished in Peter Crooks (ed.), *Government, War and Society in Medieval Ireland: Essays by Edmund Curtis, A.J. Otway-Ruthven and James Lydon* (Dublin, 2008), pp. 317–331 (quotations, pp. 327, 330, 331).
2 Tadhg O'Keeffe, 'Medieval Frontiers and Fortification: The Pale and Its Evolution', in F.H.A. Aalen and Kevin Whelan (eds.), *Dublin City and County: From Prehistory to Present* (Dublin, 1992), pp. 57–77; Margaret Murphy and Michael Potterton, *The Dublin Region in the Middle Ages: Settlement, Land-use and Economy* (Dublin, 2010), ch. 8.
3 Sparky Booker, 'Intermarriage in Fifteenth-century Ireland: The English and Irish in the "Four Obedient Shires"', *PRIA* 113 (2013), pp. 219–250; Sparky Booker, 'The Geraldines and the Irish: Intermarriage, Ecclesiastical Patronage and Status', in Peter Crooks and Sean Duffy (eds.), *The Geraldines and Medieval Ireland: The Making of a Myth* (Dublin, 2016), pp. 292–324; Sparky Booker, *Cultural Exchange and Identity in Late medieval Ireland: The English and Irish of the Four Obedient Shires* (Cambridge, 2018).
4 S.G. Ellis, *Reform and Revival: English Government in Ireland, 1470–1534* (Woodbridge, 1986), pp. 50–66. In particular, the seeming equation of the Pale with the Maghery in one of the earliest reform treatises in 1515 convinced me that more research was first needed for a full study: *S.P. Hen. VIII*, ii, 22.
5 S.G. Ellis, *Tudor Frontiers and Noble Power: The Making of the British State* (Oxford, 1995); S.G. Ellis, *Defending English Ground: War and Peace in Meath and Northumberland, 1460–1542* (Oxford, 2015); S.G. Ellis, *Ireland's English Pale, 1470–1550: The Making of a Tudor Region* (Woodbridge, 2021).
6 *Calendar of ancient deeds . . . in the Pembroke Estate Office, Dublin* (Dublin, 1891), nos. 221–222; *S.P. Hen. VIII*, ii, 409–419.
7 Parliament rolls, 8 Henry VI cc 12–13, 32 Henry VI cc 47–50, 33 Henry VI c. 11, 34 Henry VI c. 37, 38 Henry VI c. 44, 15 and 16 Edward IV c. 84 (*Stat. Ire., Hen. VI*, pp. 32–36, 299, 314–315, 402–405, 756–759; *Stat. Ire., Edw. IV, 2*, 442–445); *Alen's reg.*, p. 250.
8 S.G. Ellis, 'Parliament and Great Councils, 1483–99: Addenda et corrigenda', *Analecta Hibernica* 30 (1980), pp. 104–105; *Alen's reg.*, pp. 250–251; Christopher Maginn and S.G. Ellis, *The Tudor Discovery of Ireland* (Dublin, 2015), pp. 100–101. For the 1488 boundary, Murphy and Potterton, *Dublin Region in the Middle Ages*, pp. 265–269.
9 S.G. Ellis, *Ireland in the Age of the Tudors 1447–1603: English Expansion and the End of Gaelic Rule* (London, 1998), p. 74; Lydon, 'Problem of the Frontier', p. 326.
10 Statute roll, 10 Hen. VII c. 34 (Agnes Conway, *Henry VII's Relations with Scotland and Ireland, 1485–1498* (Cambridge, 1932), pp. 215–216).
11 TNA, SP 60/11, ff 153–159; Booker, *Cultural Exchange*, p. 28.
12 Conway, *Henry VII's Relations*, pp. 215–216; Maginn and Ellis, *Tudor Discovery*, pp. 81, 101; Gearóid Mac Niocaill (ed.), *Crown Surveys of Lands 1540–41 with the Kildare Rental Begun in 1518* (Dublin, 1992), p. 351.
13 Conway, *Henry VII's Relations*, pp. 215–216; Ellis, *Defending English Ground*, pp. 130–133.
14 BL, Royal MS 18C, XIV, f. 107v; Booker, *Cultural Exchange*, p. 29.

15 David Heffernan (ed.), 'Robert Cowley's "A Discourse of the Cause of the Evil State of Ireland and of the Remedies Thereof", c. 1526', *Analecta Hibernica* 48 (2017), pp. 15, 23.
16 Booker, *Cultural Exchange*, pp. 59, 222; Ellis, *Ireland in the age of the Tudors*, p. 33.
17 Mac Niocaill (ed.), *Crown Surveys*, pp. 104–229.
18 Parliament roll, 5 Edward IV cc 16, 17 (*Stat. Ire., Edw. IV*, 1, 290–293).
19 Hore and Graves, *Southern & Eastern Counties*, pp. 161–162; Mac Niocaill (ed.), *Crown Surveys*, pp. 236, 278; *S.P. Hen. VIII*, 2, 20.
20 *S.P. Hen. VIII*, ii, 300; Mac Niocaill (ed.), *Crown Surveys*, pp. 156–160, 278; Ellis, *Tudor Frontiers*, pp. 110–115, 129.
21 Booker, 'Geraldines and the Irish', p. 312; Niocaill (ed.), *Crown Surveys*, pp. 156–160.
22 TNA, E 101/248, no. 21, SP 65/1, no. 2; BL, Royal MS 18C, XIV, f. 107v; Memoranda roll, 25 Henry VIII m. 26d (NAI, Ferguson coll., iv, f. 179).
23 Parliament roll, 19 & 20 Edward IV c. 35 (*Stat. Ire., Edw. IV*, 2, 764–765); Gerald Power, *A European Frontier Elite: The Nobility of the English Pale in Tudor Ireland, 1496–1566* (Hannover, 2012), pp. 85, 102–105. 130; K.W. Nicholls, *Gaelic and Gaelicized Ireland in the Middle Ages* (Dublin, 2003), pp. 207–210.
24 TNA, E 101/248, no. 21, SP 65/1, no. 2; BL, Royal MS 18C, XIV, f. 107v; Memoranda rolls, 25 Henry VIII m. 26d, 26 Henry VIII m. 10d (NAI, Ferguson coll., iv, ff 179, 184); Mac Niocaill (ed.), *Crown Surveys*, pp. 183–189; N.B. White (ed.), *Extents of Irish Monastic Possessions, 1540–41* (Dublin, 1943), pp. 161, 309; Power, *European Frontier Elite*, pp. 102–105.
25 *S.P. Hen. VIII*, 3, 241, 297.
26 Memoranda rolls, 25 Henry VIII m. 26d, 26 Henry VIII m. 10d (NAI, Ferguson coll., 4, ff 179, 184).
27 *S.P. Hen. VIII*, 3, pp. 16, 18–19, 27–28; NAI, Lodge MS 17, f. 221; Niocaill (ed.), *Crown Surveys*, pp. 206–210.
28 Niocaill (ed.), *Crown Surveys*, pp. 206–210; White (ed.), *Extents of Irish Monastic Possessions*, p. 22; Booker, *Cultural Exchange*, p. 56, n. 2.
29 Booker, *Cultural Exchange*, p. 29; Booker, 'Geraldines and the Irish', pp. 318–324.
30 TNA, SP 60/6, f. 119 (*L. & P. Hen. VIII*, xiii (i), no. 883).
31 Niocaill, *Crown Surveys*, pp. 62, 123–129, 211 313, 297–301; Ellis, *Defending English Ground*, p. 130.
32 Memoranda rolls, 14 Henry VII m. 2d (NAI, RC 8/43, pp. 91–93), 15 Henry VIII m. 17d (NAI, Ferguson coll., iv, f. 73); TCD, MSS 569 ff 33v-35, 594 f. 28v; *S.P. Hen. VIII*, ii, 7, 111; Ellis, *Defending English Ground*, pp. 93–94, 130–133.
33 Ellis, *Defending English Ground*, pp. 126–129.
34 Niocaill (ed.), *Crown Surveys*, pp. 108–129, 211–213, 293–302; White (ed.), *Extents of Irish Monastic Possessions*, pp. 250–322. Only one or two baronies had Irish collectors each year, e.g. Shane Mcmaghon, joint collector for Moygoish, 1498 (Memoranda roll, 14 Henry VII m. 2d, NAI, RC 8/43, pp. 91–93), John Obreckan, joint collector for Dunboyne, William Halpyn and Philip Mcgaghran, collectors for Slane, 1500 (Memoranda roll, 15 Henry VII m. 17d, NAI, RC 8/43, pp. 185–186), Magonius OTege, collector for Magheradernon, 1508 (Memoranda roll, 24 Henry VII m. 5d, NAI, RC 8/43, pp. 274–275).
35 Memoranda rolls, 14 Henry VII mm 1, 17d, 15 Henry VII mm 2d, 17d (NAI, RC 8/43, pp. 94, 135, 164–165, 187); *Cal. Pat. Rolls, 1494–1509*, pp. 62, 109, 443; Power, *European Frontier Elite*, pp. 58–60; TNA, SP 65/1, no. 2, E 101/248, no. 21.
36 Maginn and Ellis, *Tudor Discovery*, p. 73. Cf. David Heffernan (ed.), *'Reform' Treatises on Tudor Ireland* (Dublin, 2016).
37 Lydon, 'Problem of the Frontier', pp. 326–330.

7 The Final Tudor Frontier

The North-West of Ireland in the Late Sixteenth Century

Christopher Maginn

Within months of Queen Elizabeth's accession to the throne, she agreed, as a term of the Treaty of Cateau-Cambrésis, to the surrender of Calais to King Henry of France. Calais was the last of the English crown's Continental possessions. The young queen hoped, one day, to regain possession of this relic of her medieval inheritance. But time would show that the Tudor territories had in fact assumed their final form in 1559. The queen now ruled over two kingdoms: England, which included Wales, and Ireland. So far as Elizabeth and her government was concerned, her kingdoms were possessed of only one landed border: that which England shared with the kingdom of Scotland to the north. That border, historically the source of international conflict and chronic lawlessness, became less of a concern as Anglo-Scottish relations broadly improved over the course of Elizabeth's reign, especially following the conclusion in 1586 of the Treaty of Berwick with the king of Scots.[1] In Ireland, Elizabeth saw a kingdom of perfect territorial integrity: an island without landed borders.[2] Elizabeth and her ministers, however, understood perfectly well at the start of her reign that there were areas of Ireland which were beyond royal control. Indeed, for the next two and a half decades, her government pursued policies which sought to erase the *de facto* political, social and cultural borders which continued to exist within the island kingdom. Government efforts to this end were most concentrated in the west and north. For here, in a crescent running from the O'Flaherty lordship of Iar-Connacht, outside the royal town of Galway in the west, to the O'Cahan and O'Neill lordships in the north, powerful independent native lineages predominated and English structures of government and social organisation were almost entirely unknown. The introduction in this region by the mid-1580s of English county administration and the establishment of a strong provincial government for the western shires removed the kingdom's last political borders; cultural borders remained, but these, so the official thinking went, would soon wither as local English structures of government and law developed. This chapter will explore Ireland's north-west region as a liminal space which contained the final landed frontier of the Tudor territories. In so doing, it will highlight some of the complexity of interaction between crown

DOI: 10.4324/9781032691886-7

government and the region's native inhabitants. It will show, moreover, that despite the veneer of English government established by the 1580s, parts of the region remained outside the effective control of royal government. It will conclude by suggesting that the existence of an administrative border and a frontier society in the north-west of Ireland into the final decade of the reign of the last Tudor monarch helps to explain why this region became the heart of the final challenge to Tudor authority made by a confederacy of Irish lords in the mid-1590s.

Historians of the late medieval and early Tudor periods are accustomed to studying Ireland within the interpretative framework of borders and boundaries. Robin Frame memorably described the Ireland of the fourteenth century as a 'land of many marches'. Later, Steven Ellis characterised Ireland at the dawn of the Tudor age as 'a frontier society divided between the English and Gaelic worlds'.[3] The era of political expansion and territorial exchange in Ireland, first by English kings and their agents in the twelfth and thirteenth centuries and then by a multilateral Irish resurgence which arrested and turned back this English intervention in the fourteenth century, was replaced by what may be broadly regarded as a period of political and military stasis. By the mid-fifteenth century, Englishness and Irishness were more or less territorially fixed features of Ireland. Borders and frontiers were the points where the two cultures and their respective systems of government and socio-economic organisation met. Historians have been keen to explore these intersections for all the evidence of dissimilarity and hybridity, chauvinism and acculturation, accommodation and disharmony they generated.[4] This interpretative framework is much more difficult to sustain after 1541, however. It was then that Ireland was erected into a kingdom and Henry VIII was recognised as its king. Royal authority, in theory at least, now extended throughout the new realm, rendering its centuries-old legal and constitutional borders obsolete. Historians associate the later part of King Henry's reign with the commencement of a new period of English socio-political and territorial expansion often referred to as the Tudor conquest of Ireland. These were decades not of stasis, but of movement: in which Henry VIII, and afterward his children, made good on the letter of the Act for Kingly Title of 1541. So ingrained in the historiography of early modern Ireland is the Tudor conquest, so inexorable was Tudor expansion in the sixteenth century, that historians have generally overlooked the continued existence of frontiers in Ireland late into the reign of Elizabeth I.[5]

It is ironic that the Spanish Armada, which had the effect of transforming with its launch the southeast of England – the seat of English power and wealth – into an exposed frontier, should, by wrecking along Ireland's distant northwest coast, expose a more traditional area of England's weakness. The queen's councillors appreciated the danger which a foreign invasion of Ireland posed to England. Earlier in the decade, Elizabeth's councillor, Sir Christopher Hatton, wrote: 'this rule I hold in all certainty, that in Ireland

and Scotland the entries and ways to our destruction most aptly be found. If there we safely shut up the postern-gate we are sure to repulse the peril'. Hatton's correspondent was Sir Francis Walsingham, the secretary of state, who had introduced into their correspondence this notion of Scotland as the 'postern-gate'.[6] The northern point of access was by the end of the 1580s safely 'shut up', in Hatton's words; but the other 'postern-gate', in the remote parts of Ireland, remained, as it were, ajar. Indeed, it was little more than twenty years earlier that Sir Henry Sidney, then the lord deputy of Ireland, wrote to Elizabeth to explain how he found Galway 'to rather resemble a towne of warre fronteringe apon an enemye then a civill towne in a countre under one soveraigne'.[7]

In 1588, however, Elizabeth and her government could take solace in the fact that Spanish troops landed in a part of Ireland which, though far distant from centre of royal power at Dublin, had recently been made shire-ground. Along the Atlantic coast from counties Clare (Thomond) and Galway – shired in 1569 and 1570, respectively – north to counties Mayo and Sligo, both shired in 1576, through to counties Leitrim, Donegal and Coleraine, each shired in 1585, a framework for English government was in place for the first time.[8] With the exception of the latter two counties, which lay in the ancient Irish province of Ulster, the entire region, the province of Connaught, was subject to the authority of a provincial president based at Athlone. The sweeping judicial powers invested in the president of Connaught went some way towards making up for the fact that there were as yet no sheriffs carrying out their duties in the province's three most recently shired counties. Still, the Spaniards who escaped capture and made their way inland caused grave concern for the government.[9] The concern arose chiefly from the fear that the survivors might combine with some, or all, of the many native lineages, that had ruled the region for centuries. Most were Irish clans, like the O'Flaherties in Galway and the O'Rourkes in Leitrim; but there were also families of English extraction, such as the Joyces and the numerous MacWilliam Burkes, who dominated large swathes of Mayo. Apart from their surname, these English families, whose forebears had settled in the area centuries earlier, were politically and culturally indistinguishable from their Irish neighbours. The continued existence of alternate structures of political power and social influence in the region, for that was what these dozens of extended familial groupings each represented, showed the limitations of royal authority. Indeed many of these new shires had been superimposed onto what amounted to the boundaries of existing Irish lordships. Some, like the county of Leitrim, were essentially co-terminous with the existing O'Rourke lordship; others, like county Donegal, were, in effect, dominated by the O'Donnells, whose lordship of Tyrconnell was now located within the boundaries of the new-made county. The well-known diary account of the Armada survivor, Captain Francisco de Cuellar, who spent months in the north-west on the run from English authorities, offers a remarkably vivid description of the region. Captain Cuellar described what was a liminal space, where royal power was capable of penetrating most anywhere, but where the local lords that Cuellar encountered, like O'Rourke and MacClancy, lived beyond the regular exercise of the new English institutions of government. At the news of the coming of the governor of Ireland with an army to his territory, the latter chief, according to Cuellar, 'decided to fly to the mountains, which was his only remedy'. The remote mountains, in Cuellar's telling, were the only area truly safe from Queen Elizabeth's power.[10]

One might dismiss Captain Cuellar's observations as exaggerated or misplaced – those of a stranger in a strange land. But an analysis of the writings of locally-based royal officials and soldiers not only supports de Cuellar's description of the region as an area in transition, it reveals that these men carried out their service to the queen conscious of the fact that they had to navigate borders. In a letter to the queen's chief advisor, Lord Burghley, written several years after the Armada, Sir Richard Bingham, the president of Connaught, identified two borders that were a feature of his government. The O'Rourkes' country posed particular difficulty, he explained, because it lay

> not . . . in the harte of the same as the inner countries of Galwaie, Thomond and other p[ar]tes doth but upon the most worste *fruntuer* of all the province, bourdered on by sundrie countries and septes of people subiecte to noo lawe and owt of my goverm[en]t.[11]

This last reference to 'owt of my goverm[en]t' referred to a border of Elizabeth's own making: the creation some twenty years earlier of the presidency of Connaught itself. The new provincial government broadly adhered to the boundaries of what had been Ireland's western province, or *cúige*, literally 'a fifth' of Ireland's ancient territorial divisions. It was an administrative border that separated out the Irish families of the province of Ulster from Bingham's jurisdiction. It was a border which Bingham was not prepared to transgress. In late 1592, Brian Oge O'Rourke, the banished lord of Leitrim, raided in Connaught and then crossed back into Ulster, 'whither', Bingham reminded Burghley, 'I may not prosecute him without the lord deputy's commission', the region being 'owt of the bourders of Connaughte'.[12] This administrative border need not have posed much of a problem had Ulster also been subjected to the authority of a provincial president. But such an administration, though mooted many times over the years, was never established there.[13] True, all of Ulster, like Connaught, was now shire-ground, but the most powerful Irish lineages were resisting the introduction of sheriffs and the apparatus of English government that came with them.[14] This explains Bingham's remark that the 'septes of people' dwelling on the borders of Connaught were 'subiecte to noo lawe'. Ulster was thus technically the responsibility of the lord deputy of Ireland who was normally resident in Dublin.

The other border identified by Bingham was an internal one. He makes a clear distinction between the 'inner' and, by implication, the outer shires within his jurisdiction. Counties Mayo, Sligo and Leitrim – Bingham revealingly continued to call the last 'O'Rourke's country' – clearly belonged among the latter. We may include in this outer border area those parts of

Cos. Galway and Roscommon bordering the outer shires. The coming of the Armada had sparked a cycle of rebellion in this part of the province, centring on the MacWilliam Burkes of Mayo. Already chaffing under Bingham's heavy-handed government, the appearance of Spaniards emboldened dissident elements in the region to resist the agents of royal authority. The MacWilliam Burkes had murdered the sheriff of Mayo, along with his under-sheriff and twenty of their men in early 1589.[15] Shortly thereafter, Captain Edward Bermingham was besieged at his castle at Milltown along the Mayo-Galway border by several hundred men led by the O'Flaherties. Bermingham reported that the rebels 'came to the borders where I dwell' where he beat them back.[16] Later, President Bingham described another attack on a crown official deep in Co. Mayo. In 1591, The MacWilliam Burkes at the head of 400 men ambushed the president's brother, John, the sheriff of Mayo, and a contingent of English soldiers. John Bingham was trying to establish himself at Castlebar ['Castle Barry'] so as to bridle the MacWilliam Burkes whose strength was concentrated in the area. President Bingham recognised the importance of the location: 'a stronge garrison placed in this castell . . . will much restraine them [the Burkes] from theire accustomed insolencies and outrages, and bringe and tye them to a more stricte dutie of obedience to Her Highnes and her lawes'.[17] Even with inferior numbers, Sheriff Bingham repulsed the attack. Yet, what is most remarkable about this encounter was Bingham's casual reference to the fact that the Burkes had cloaked their gathering together of hundreds of men in the occasion of a man-to-man combat which was to be fought between one William Burke, of Tirawley, and Alexander MacHugh Boy MacDonnell, a gallowglass captain. Evidently, such an occurrence, perhaps a kind of trial by combat, and the large audience it attracted, was sufficiently common as to provoke no undue notice.[18] The combat would appear to have been to the death: the Irish annalists recorded that Alexander, whom they described as a follower of William Burke, killed his master that year.[19] This extra-legal episode captures something of the lawless frontier quality of this part of Co. Mayo in these years. More broadly, the continued ability of lineages to assemble so many men capable of violence into the early 1590s speaks to the difficulty of the task of transforming this region into something resembling a collection of English shires.

Both borders identified by Bingham found expression in a map of Connaught sent over to Lord Burghley in 1591.[20] Burghley, whose interest in Ireland and its physical and political geography is now well attested, had earlier in 1589 requested that Bingham prepare him a 'plot' of the province.[21] At one level, the map can be interpreted as the visual representation of the arrival of Tudor rule in the west. The province was at last brought under the rule of a president whose government was financially and politically underpinned by a transformative 'composition' which had been imposed on the inhabitants of Connaught in 1585.[22] The map set out in detail the boundaries of the province and the counties and baronies which now comprised it. Yet Burghley's request for the map did not arise out of his wish to gaze contentedly upon the administrative divisions which had been created. Rather, he sought through this visual representation a more exact understanding of a region whose northern borders were chronically troubled and which was recently the scene of a Spanish landing. Burghley, as was his wont to do, annotated the map, placing in the appropriate places the names of lineages some of which continued to resist Bingham's authority. In Mayo, for example, he sketched a brief genealogy of the MacWilliam Burkes. The O'Rourkes, whose 'countrie' was already identified on the map, rather than the county into which it had been subsumed, had long been a source of trouble. Burghley would seem to have misinterpreted Bingham's recently prepared written discourse on O'Rourke's country for the promise of a more specific 'plot', or map, of the same. Bingham apologised to Burghley for the confusion, but explained that he could not 'take the plott of Orourkes countrie myself, w[i]thout the force of the p[ro]vince to gward me, that countrie being so bordered upon by Mc Qwire, O Donnell and others, the worste men of all the northe'.[23] From the vantage of Athlone and Whitehall alike, there was acknowledgement that internal and external borders continued to exist in the north-west.

But President Bingham was bent on eliminating the internal border within his jurisdiction. The office of president was only a thin official exterior placed on Bingham the soldier, whose reputation for using violence and intimidation to establish his authority was already well known. He had routed an invading army of Scots mercenaries in a pitched battle in 1586, hunted down Spanish soldiers and crushed multiple rebellions in the west.[24] He had, in the words of the last Irish annalist writing in Connaught, 'made a bare, polished, garment of the province'.[25] And that was all before 1590. Bingham's bellicosity troubled both the lord deputy and council in Dublin and the queen herself, who had earlier sought to temper his excesses.[26] On the ground, however, Bingham continued to tighten his grip within his jurisdiction. By summer 1592, he was concentrating his efforts on the remaining pocket of resistance in the mountains south and west of Castlebar.[27] In June, the Burkes attacked Bingham who was in the area holding sessions and making preparations to see Castlebar re-edified and garrisoned. The Burkes fled into the mountains where they interspersed themselves among several upland lineages, notably the Joyces, 'a people', in Bingham's estimation, 'that lie in the greatest fastness . . . within all Ireland'.[28] In August, President Bingham had them pinned down: 'not a Burke of them has once offered to come out of the mountaynes . . . but do kepe w[th]in as in a prison'.[29] Bingham then campaigned into the mountains. It was a carefully coordinated expedition backed by naval support, which shadowed the president's movements by sea and denied any rebels the refuge of the hundreds of islands in Clew Bay. In little more than a week, the Burkes submitted along with nearly half a dozen other lineages. The importance of Bingham's success in the mountains was not lost on the Irish annalists who observed how

the Governor dispatched heavy troops of English and Irish soldiers to search for the Burkes, who were in rebellion and engaged in plundering, on the rugged mountain-tops, and in the bushy dense and intricate

woods. They the soldiers had not been long in this search, when they
returned to the Governor with many preys and spoil, with prisoners,
both women and men, and with many cows and horses. After this, all
the Burkes . . . came and submitted to the award of the Governor; upon
which the Governor, by authority of the Sovereign, took the castles of
the country into his own possession, and left John Bingham and companies of his own soldiers to guard them.[30]

Bingham's victory was a triumph over the terrain as much as it was a triumph over the Burkes. The mountains of western Connaught were no longer
beyond royal power. Bingham said as much when he remarked: 'this journey
has made me now a guide all Connacht over'.[31] Shortly thereafter, Sir Ralph
Lane, the muster-master general, travelled through parts of Connaught with
Bingham. He told Burghley that he was 'an eye witness of the peaceablenes'
of the province 'whereof (God be thanked) was no lesse, than enye p[ar]te of
Englande, that is quietest'.[32]

However Connaught's northern border with the 'virtual' shires of Ulster
remained. It was here, beyond the nominal boundaries of Co. Leitrim, where
those 'septes of people subiecte to noo lawe' resided. Chief among them were
the Maguires, led by Hugh Maguire, lord of Fermanagh. Maguire was the
focal point of resistance to the introduction of English county government in
his lordship. By early 1593, the threat which they posed to Connaught was
sharply escalating. Maguire was an ally of Red Hugh O'Donnell whom he
had welcomed into his inaccessible and lake-dotted lordship in early 1592 as
a fugitive from Dublin Castle whence he had escaped. O'Donnell was elected
chief in April.[33] The appearance on the scene of a dynamic and recalcitrant
O'Donnell was especially problematic because the O'Donnells had traditionally exercised great political influence in Lower (northern) Connaught,
which now lay within Bingham's presidential jurisdiction. O'Donnell also
possessed the ability to import large numbers of mercenaries from Scotland,
'Redshanks', through the influence of his formidable mother, Ineen Duff (*née*
MacDonnell). Maguire and O'Donnell opened up their lordships as a refuge
to dissident elements, like Richard Burke of Mayo, known as the 'Devil's
Hook', who had refused to submit to Bingham, and to O'Rourke, who was
allowed to cross at will the border that was such an impediment to Bingham.
But, as Bingham and Burghley had become aware by early 1593, the northern border concealed a far more serious threat.[34] The Catholic archbishop of
Armagh, Edmund Magauran, lately returned to Ireland from the Continent,
moved freely between O'Donnell's and Maguire's lordships. Magauran carried a promise of military support from Philip II of Spain in the event of an
Irish rebellion against Elizabeth. Maguire, O'Donnell and O'Rourke formed
the nucleus of a confederation that evidently included, though at this point
secretly, Hugh O'Neill, the earl of Tyrone, and stretched to the isles of Scotland and reached all the way to Spain and even to Rome, where letters from

O'Donnell and Magauran were directed.[35] By then, Walsingham and Hatton were dead, but the fear they had articulated the decade before was manifesting itself along the final Tudor frontier in Ireland's north-west.

Emboldened by the prospect of foreign military assistance, the confederates began over the next few months to test Connaught's borders. In March, they moved against Belleek in Co. Fermanagh, which was held by O'Donnell's enemy, Hugh Duff O'Donnell. Belleek, by dint of its castle's position between the western shore of Lough Erne and the sea, commanded the most northerly entrance into Connaught but lay outside of Bingham's jurisdiction. Lane referred to Belleek as one of the 'kaies of that frontier'. He hoped to be granted it, and the neighbouring castle of Ballyshannon, along with the 'guard of the fron[n]tiere'.[36] In early summer, the confederates crossed into Connaught from the north-east through O'Rourke's country: O'Rourke attacked Ballymote, in Co. Sligo, where George Bingham was stationed; then Maguire, 'keeping Lough Allen to his left', marched south into Roscommon, where President Bingham himself engaged the rebels, killing Archbishop Magauran in the mêlée.[37] The limits of Bingham's presidential authority were underlined in these months as Lord Deputy Fitzwilliam sought to defuse the mounting tensions by employing the earl of Tyrone to treat with Maguire. Better to reclaim Maguire, Fitzwilliam reasoned, than to incite a wider rebellion by permitting Bingham to revenge himself. Fitzwilliam, for his part, was pressing for his recall to England and wanted nothing more than to return home able to point to the tranquillity of Ireland. Unable to pursue the confederates beyond the boundaries of Connaught, Bingham could only assume a defensive position. But in July Elizabeth herself weighed in. Bingham, as Burghley indicated to Fitzwilliam, would seem to have alerted the queen's influential favourite, Robert Devereux, earl of Essex, to his predicament.[38] The queen was absolutely furious to learn that Bingham had been prohibited by the deputy from pursuing the rebels across the administrative border. She wrote directly to Bingham licensing him to go on the offensive. The same day she wrote a stinging letter to Fitzwilliam and the council to express their 'greate fault' in having restrained Bingham.[39] However, such was the perceived military capacity of the confederacy, and such was the inaccessibility of Maguire's lordship, that royal retaliation came in the form of a campaign towards the end of the year organised by the government at Dublin and led by Marshal Bagenal.

Still, these incursions into Connaught are revealing. Connaught's borders were not a frontier zone in the traditional sense – like what had developed over time around the English Pale around Dublin, or elsewhere in the Tudor territories. There was nothing like a wide fortified march with dykes and ditches and tower-houses to deter raiding. Nor was there a resident peer or a population group, akin to the marcher lineages in south Dublin, or the border surnames between England and Scotland, to organise defence; chains of nucleated settlements boasting loyal and armed populations of

Englishmen were also absent.[40] Bingham's solution to the problem was a distinctly sixteenth-century one. He proposed the inhabiting of a town in Co. Roscommon with Englishmen backed by a garrison. In July 1593, he told Burghley, 'the countyes of Roscoman and Sligo will nev[r] be assured from the incursyons of the bordering tratoures till there be a towen at the Boile [Boyle] and a streighth for a garrison'.[41] He asked that he, or another gentleman, be leased Boyle and permitted to build a castle at the site of the decayed abbey there to protect the proposed town. The establishment of a town in this way would, in effect, create almost immediately what had taken decades, or centuries, to emerge elsewhere. The wards he had seen established – at Boyle, in Roscommon, Sligo, Ballymote and the New Fort at Ballinafad, the latter three in Co. Sligo – offered a measure of protection, being the only strongholds, he told Burghley, 'from the verie ffrontieres unto the towen of Galway'.[42] But these were far distant from each other and could not effectively prevent raids across an extended frontier. Bingham, moreover, had few English troops at his disposal – only 92 foot and 48 horse. As he often indicated, Bingham found Irish troops unreliable but had to rely upon the 'rising out' of the province, which totalled an additional 80 Irish horse, to help with the defence in summer 1593.[43] It was Bingham's concern for Connaught's borders which prevented him from joining Marshal Bagenal's plan to strike deeper into Ulster against O'Donnell following Bagenal's defeat of Maguire in October 1593.[44] While Bingham was gathering his forces near the border in support of Bagenal's attack on Fermanagh, Maguire had despatched 'The Devil's Hook' Burke home to Mayo to raise rebellion and distract the president thereby. Maguire's plan worked: Burke slipped through the frontier forcing Bingham to send half of his troops into Mayo 'to assure the inward p[ar]tes of the province'. Thereafter, Bingham placed all his forces 'upon the frontours', including the bands under the command of his brother, George, and Henry Street, which he placed in the barony of Carrickallen, Co. Leitrim, adjoining Maguire's country. He claimed that he could 'at all tymes on the sudden draw others together to annoy the tratoure [Maguire]'.[45] Bingham's offer to inhabit Boyle and to develop it into a defensive hub offered a more permanent protection for Connaught's borders, but the queen never agreed to it.

By then, such a commitment no longer seemed necessary. Maguire was, to all appearances, greatly diminished; the crisis contained. Captain John Dowdall, who had taken command of the queen's forces from Bagenal, had penetrated the heart of Maguire's lordship. In February 1594, he took Maguire's castle at Enniskillen and placed an English garrison there. Bingham and his Connaught forces had played a part in the campaign, cutting off support for the confederacy from dissident elements in the west and denying Maguire escape to the Connaught side of Lough Erne. The Dublin administration now looked to see garrisons placed in Cos. Donegal and Fermanagh.[46] By pushing out the frontier in this way, Connaught's borders would be made secure. In January, Lord Deputy Fitzwilliam could write that Ireland was 'in univ[er]sall quietnes', noting that, 'ev[er]y man maie travele w^thout touche of body or goodes into all the partes of this realme'. 'I think', he continued, 'I maie saie boldlie that for everie one that was ameaneable to lawe 6 yeres agoe there be nowe 6 insomuche as Her Maties writes of all natures are currant thoroughe out this realme'. However, he excepted 'the partes' of Ireland 'towardes Tireconell and those bordres where scattered ragges of this late rebellion' continued to lurk.[47] Geoffrey Fenton, the secretary of state, had the previous month expressed the danger in a manner Walsingham would have understood well: the north-west with Maguire at large remained 'a gapp . . . keepte open for the Spaniarde or other forreine ennemie to execute enie attempts against this realme'.[48] Bingham was much closer to the situation than either the deputy or the secretary. And he shared their view, though he expressed it through a provincial prism. Connaught was, according to Bingham, more tranquil than it had been in living memory. But what prevented the queen's subjects from living 'as quietly in Conaght as in the countye of Dublin', he claimed, was the threat posed by O'Donnell in particular: 'theire cannot be an ill man banished out of any p[ar]te of the realme but straight ways he flieth to Odonnell'. Bingham urged Burghley to move Elizabeth to secure Connaught's northern border by placing garrisons at Ballyshannon, Belleek and Bundrowes, the 'kaies of that frontier' earlier identified by Lane. This way, Bingham reasoned, O'Donnell might only 'make any roade' on his friends to the north and east of his lordship, deeper into Irish Ulster in other words, and would, in so doing, only hurt himself.[49]

Historians have cast Elizabethan government as negligent in its response to the danger posed by the confederacy whose nucleus lay beyond the borders of Connaught.[50] But they do so with the benefit of hindsight, with the knowing for a certainty that the earl of Tyrone would shortly throw in his lot with the confederacy and transform it into something approaching a national rebellion. In the circumstances of early 1594, however, royal government in England appreciated the danger in Ireland. The recent defeat of Maguire notwithstanding, the kingdom weighed on an aged and sick Burghley. He confessed in an unguarded letter to his son, Robert, 'how to remedy this misgovernme[n]t ther I know not, and yet it may not be left unattempted by one waye or other'.[51] When, probably sometime in early March 1594, Fitzwilliam's and Bingham's more favourable construction of the situation in Ireland reached him, Burghley did not overlook their shared concern about the north-west. He was with the queen at Hampton Court by mid-March. Not for the first time, his physical presence at court occasioned the discussion of 'Ireland matters' and resulted in the queen's letter to her lord deputy and council (which he helped to draft).[52] Elizabeth now resolved, in an effort to bridle the confederacy, to place wards at Belleek and Bundrowes, on the northern border of Leitrim. The queen was, in effect, following the strategy Bingham had set out and which was probably communicated to her by Burghley, with Robert Cecil and other like-minded councillors running support.[53] Burghley wrote Bingham a letter (now lost) seeking additional information on the state of Connaught the same day as the queen's letter to the lord deputy and council.[54] Indeed Bingham was to be central to the endeavour. Not only was he to provide the men for the new wards – out of the garrison at Sligo – he was chosen to become a lord justice – a temporary governor – should the ailing Fitzwilliam's health fail. Bingham's knowledge and experience of Ireland's final frontier had earned him a central role in the government's strategy to suppress the confederacy.[55]

In Bingham's paper on Connaught, drawn up in mid-April, he again drew Burghley's attention to the necessity of screening the province's borders. He claimed he had banished O'Rourke 'xx tymes out' only to see O'Donnell send him back the next week. This time, however, Bingham simplified his strategy: the government should focus its efforts on garrisoning Belleek (he now deemed Bundrowes 'inutile' owing to his own recent experience of circumventing it in the campaign against Maguire). Bingham identified other garrisons throughout the kingdom from which troops could be redeployed to Belleek. Burghley, whom Bingham urged to consult the map, or 'cart' he had sent him, duly scratched 'Belyck' in the margin.[56] Bingham's recommendation, that 'there is no one thinge more necessarye to be done than to have a ward putt' into Belleek, made its way into the Queen's instructions for Sir William Russell who was appointed to replace Fitzwilliam as governor in May 1594.[57] However the transfer of power from Fitzwilliam to Russell took months: the new governor did not take up the sword until August. In the meantime, all government intelligence now pointed to Tyrone's leadership of the rebellion in Ulster. Over the summer, the confederates boldly laid siege to Enniskillen. Fitzwilliam had neither the troops, the constitution, nor, in his last months in Ireland, the support of the governing establishment to mount an offensive. He looked to England for men and money. But English concern over the Spanish presence in Brittany trumped the deteriorating situation in Ireland. Spanish possession of Brittany would, in the words of the English commander there, be as 'prejudicial' as if they held Ireland.[58] Two thousand English troops were despatched to Brittany not to Enniskillen. It was a clear reminder that though the final landed frontier in the Tudor territories lay in Ireland, Queen Elizabeth also had to contend with the Channel which represented a 'border province' in its own right.[59]

Russell eventually relieved Enniskillen, in person, at the end of August. Bingham, who had earlier in the month attended a consultation at Dublin at which the new governor was acquainted with the state of the kingdom, accompanied him and some of the privy council on the hard journey through O'Rourke's country into Ulster. Russell hoped to ward Belleek, as he had been instructed, before he departed; but Bingham, he claimed, 'assured us, that yt was ruined in such sort as the expenses of £200 would not make yt gardeable, neither could it be repaired in short time'.[60] Only four months earlier, Bingham had reckoned that £100 would be sufficient to re-edify the castle at Belleek. But O'Donnell had 'defaced' the castle there, and the one at

Bundrowes, in an effort to prevent the establishment of additional garrisons nearer his lordship.[61] After Enniskillen, Bingham was not in a position to linger beyond the borders of Connaught to oversee work on Belleek: in his absence O'Rourke with some of O'Donnell's men had attacked Sligo. Following Russell's return to Dublin, however, Bingham wrote Ralph Lane seeking to learn the governor's attitude towards placing wards at Ballyshannon and Belleek.[62] Burghley in England had not given up on the strategy. In an October memorial for Ireland, he noted how Connaught was 'in good order', but that O'Donnell, 'borderyng uppo[n] them havy[n]g a passadg at y[e] ford nere Bellyck', remained a threat to the province. Bingham, Burghley continued, should secure Belleek and Bundrowes and use the fines from the county sessions in Connaught to pay for the re-edification of the two castles – the new wards should be supplied out of Sligo.[63]

Burghley's suggestions for the defence of Connaught's northern border were not immediately acted upon, however. Royal government was then engaged in what was essentially a policy of temporising with Tyrone. No one in government, from Bingham in Connaught, to Russell in Dublin to the queen in England, officially espoused such a policy, but in the absence of immediate military support from England to oppose the growing strength of the confederacy, policy it became. The earl continued to deny his involvement in the confederacy: this was sufficient grounds for officials to justify a policy which would bring Tyrone around through negotiation and thereby avoid a major rebellion in Ulster. Such a policy would also gain the queen time to strengthen her military strength in Ireland as English military operations in Brittany were coming to an end following the defeat of Spanish forces at Crozon, near Brest, in October–November 1594.[64] In the meantime, there was acceptance in Dublin of the existence of a border between rebel held areas of Ulster and the English Pale. Russell strengthened this border 'to prevent bodragges and nightly stealthes' as talks with Tyrone continued and a truce was established with the rebels.[65] In this, Russell could do what Bingham could not: order the Palesmen to take up their own defence. One of O'Donnell's demands communicated to the government was that those people expulsed from Connaught should be able 'to lyve in theyre countries w[th]out danger'.[66] On the other side of that border, however, the incursions from Ulster were escalating. By the end of the year, Bingham complained that O'Rourke, supported by O'Donnell, had wasted counties Sligo and Leitrim to the extent that he could no longer collect the queen's revenues in either shire. Bingham reiterated the importance of placing garrisons along the border at Belleek and Ballyshannon, so that Connaught 'shalbe impailed from Ulster'. He now also emphasised how these castles might also be used to 'breake' O'Donnell from the earl.[67]

The army of English veterans from Brittany which arrived in Ireland in March allowed the government at Dublin to remedy what the queen deemed its previous 'week proceedings' with Tyrone.[68] But it was already too late for Connaught: in spring 1595 O'Donnell personally led two hostings deep into the province. The first came in March. Bingham offered little in the way of detail in his report of the incursion, beyond the fact that O'Donnell's forces raided into Co. Roscommon.[69] However, the Irish annals tell of a major military undertaking by O'Donnell in which something of the changed military character of the Irish confederacy is revealed.[70] After O'Donnell crossed the Erne, he marched south deliberately and carefully, owing to the prevalence of English power throughout Connaught but especially in its 'guarded port towns and impregnable fortresses' [*ina portaibh airechais agus dunarusaibh diotoghlaighibh*]. Six locations were identified, which together amounted to the province's outer rim of defences: Roscommon; Boyle; Tulsk; Ballinafad, Ballymote; and Sligo. O'Donnell ordered his troops – which now included some of the disgruntled Connaught lineages – drawn out in array so he could review them. He then, after marching into the heart of Roscommon, divided up his forces into marauding parties to spoil the shire before reassembling them to convey their spoils across the Shannon into Leitrim. Bingham caught up to them there, killing some of those in the rear, but the damage had been done. O'Donnell had shown how difficult it was for Bingham effectively to defend such a long frontier from isolated garrisons.

O'Donnell returned the next month. He again crossed the Erne and again targeted Roscommon, plundering those areas he had not plundered the previous month. This time, however, O'Donnell attacked Cos. Longford and Cavan from Connaught. Bingham recognised the danger to the province by virtue of its 'openes . . . and o^r fronture above xl^{ti} miles in length wch we had to defende'. He asked Russell to send him three or four of the 'British' companies lately landed at Waterford and 50 horsemen. Connaught was, in Bingham's estimation, the key theatre: 'almost half the rebellion of Ulster lieth against this province', and he reckoned O'Donnell and Maguire's forces to be equal to that commanded by Tyrone.[71] Bingham hoped to capture Ballyshannon to prevent O'Donnell from crossing into Connaught for a third time in as many months. But in June Bingham's cousin George the commander of the ward at Sligo was murdered, by his ensign. The castle was seized and then handed over to O'Donnell. Sligo was, according to Bingham, 'the verie key of the province and passadge from Tereconnell' and was 'the worste newes that ever happened in Connaught in my tyme'.[72] That summer most of the counties of Sligo and Leitrim and the northern half of Co. Mayo were lost to the rebels. According to the Irish annalists: 'in the course of one month the greater part of the inhabitants of the district, from the western point of Erris and Umhall to Drowes, had unanimously confederated with O'Donnell; and there were not many castles or fortresses in those places, whether injured or perfect, that were not under his control'. By the end of the year, O'Donnell had destroyed Sligo castle and commanded sufficient influence in the province to revive the MacWilliam lordship, to which he had elected Theobald Burke.[73] With rumours of a Spanish invasion through the town of Galway, the lord deputy made a rare appearance in the west to fortify the medieval capital and heart of English Connaught.[74]

The spilling over into Connaught of the Ulster rebellion occurred not from royal government's failure to recognise the existence of a border running through Ireland's north-west. Officials like President Bingham and Ralph Lane repeatedly drew attention to the weakness of Connaught's borders and made recommendations to erect garrisons beyond them. Their suggestions made their way into the highest levels of royal policy-making for Ireland. But policy to strengthen the border was meaningless unless government officials could implement that policy consistently and promptly. It is easy to point to Elizabeth's chronic indecisiveness, or to her notorious aversion to committing money to Ireland, as the reasons behind the disconnect between policy and action. Certainly, the latter was a real hindrance: her servants in Ireland were already stretched too thin, and they were expected to stretch their limited resources still further to defend a long border. In the queen's defence, however, her forces were operating in multiples theatres at once. And as soon as her troops in Brittany could be spared, they were transferred to Ireland. A deeper problem was the nature of the border itself. Unlike in Munster, where an ambitious state-sponsored plantation scheme was being attempted, there were no plans to settle Connaught with Englishmen. In the absence of a resident population loyal to the crown, be they English or Irish, the border could only be defended by military garrisons. Not only were establishing individual garrisons costly, but also they were naturally populated with soldiers whose presence strained relations with the surrounding population. Speculating on the cause of George Bingham's murder by his ensign and the betrayal of Sligo, Secretary Fenton thought it 'grounded upon a pryvat revenge towards the Binghams, whose name is hated in the contrey'.[75] Indeed, much of the 'peaceabless' and supposed Englishness of the north-west that royal officials in Connaught trumpeted had roots which were very shallow. Titles like 'the MacWilliam' and 'the O'Rourke', and the lineage based society they stood for, still carried power: liminality, after all, was a two-way street. By the mid-1590s, it was clear that a military contest between the English crown and the Irish confederacy, led by O'Neill and O'Donnell, would decide whether Ireland was a kingdom without borders.

Notes

1 Susan Doran, 'James VI and the English Succession', in Ralph Houlbrooke (ed.), *James VI and I: Ideas, Authority, and Government* (Aldershot, 2006), pp. 25–42.
2 There can be no doubt that Elizabeth was possessed, at the very least, of a broad familiarity with the geography of her kingdoms. Completed after Mary I's death in 1558, the 'Queen Mary Atlas' clearly depicted the islands of Britain and Ireland in relation to France, Spain and Portugal. This map was presented to Elizabeth upon her accession. Legend holds that the young queen personally rubbed out the arms of her sister's husband, Philip II, which were emblazoned on the map: D.B. Quinn, *Explorers and Colonies: America, 1500–1625* (London, 1990), pp. 62–63.
3 Robin Frame, 'Power and Society in the Lordship of Ireland, 1272–1377', *Past & Present* 76 (1977), p. 32; S.G. Ellis, *Ireland in the age of the Tudors, 1447–1603: English Expansion and the End of Gaelic Rule* (London, 1998) (quotation from back cover).

4 For a listing of some of these works, see Christopher Maginn, 'Gaelic Ireland's English Frontiers in the Late Middle Ages', *Proceedings of the Royal Irish Academy* 110C (2010), note 2. The enduring attraction of Ireland's borderlands is evident in the more recent works by S.G. Ellis, *Defending English Ground: War and Peace in Meath and Northumberland, 1460–1542* (Oxford, 2015) and Sparky Booker, *Cultural Exchange and Identity in Late Medieval Ireland: The English and Irish of the Four Obedient Shires* (Cambridge, 2018).

5 An exception is Gerald Power's essay on the survival into the late sixteenth century of the English Pale as a distinct region in Ireland, and thus an area possessed of recognisable borders: 'The English Pale as a Region in Later Tudor Ireland, 1541–1603', in S.G. Ellis and Raingard Esser (eds.), *Frontiers and Regions in Early Modern Europe* (Hannover, 2013), pp. 77–96. See also the comment in Christopher Maginn, 'Beyond the Pale: Regional Government and the Tudor Conquest of Ireland', in S.G. Ellis and Raingard Esser (eds.), *Frontiers and Regions in Early Modern Europe* (Hannover, 2013), pp. 41–43.

6 *Memoirs of the Life and Times of Sir Christopher Hatton* (ed.), Harris Nicolas (London, 1847), pp. 67, 159.

7 Sidney to Elizabeth, 20 April 1567, TNA, SP 63/20/66, fo. 141.

8 Christopher Maginn, *William Cecil, Ireland, and the Tudor State* (Oxford, 2012), pp. 198, 200.

9 Christopher Maginn, 'After the Armada: Ireland's First Thanksgiving, 1589', *Historical Research* 93 (2020), pp. 23–37.

10 Hugh Allingham (ed.), *Captain Cuellar's Adventures in Connacht and Ulster, A.D. 1588* (London, 1897), p. 34.

11 Bingham to Burghley, 6 March 1592, TNA, SP 63/163/51. fo. 101 (my italics).

12 Bingham to Burghley, 17 December 1592, TNA, SP 63/167/38. ff. 144^v, 145^v.

13 For earlier suggestions to erect a provincial government in Ulster, see Maginn, 'Beyond the Pale', pp. 43–45, 47, 52, 55.

14 See, for example, the actions of the MacMahons and Maguires: Fitzwilliam and council to privy council, 31 March 1589, TNA, SP 63/142/57; Patrick Foxe to Walsingham, 31 March 1589, TNA, SP 63/142/61.

15 Fitzwilliam to Burghley, 31 March 1589, TNA, SP 63/142/58, fo. 127. For more on this, see Christopher Maginn, '"A True Report": A Journal Account of the Commissioners' Proceedings in Galway, 1589', *Analecta Hibernica* 51 (2020), pp. 1–50.

16 Bermingham to Lucas Dillon, 31 March 1589, TNA, SP 63/143/12(viii), fo. 34.

17 Bingham's notes on the Burkes, July 1592, TNA, SP 63/166/36, fo. 98^v.

18 Bingham's notes on the Burkes, July 1592, TNA, SP 63/166/36, fo. 98^v.

19 John O'Donovan (eds.), *Annála ríoghachta Éireann: Annals of the Kingdom of Ireland by the Four Masters from the Earliest Period to the Year 1616*, 7 vols (Dublin, 1851), *s.a.* 1591.

20 J.H. Andrews, 'Sir Richard Bingham and the Mapping of the West of Ireland', *Proceedings of the Royal Irish Academy* 103C (2003), pp. 61–95.

21 The map, by John Browne, now resides in Trinity College, Dublin: MS 1209, 68.

22 An analysis of the 'Composition of Connaught' and its implementation may be found in Bernadette Cunningham, *Clanricard and Thomond, 1540–1640: Provincial Politics and Society Transformed* (Dublin, 2012), esp. pp. 21–27.

23 Bingham to Burghley, 6 March 1592, TNA, SP 63/163/51, fo. 101^v.

24 Bernadette Cunningham, *s.v.* 'Richard Bingham', in *Oxford's Dictionary of National Biography* (Oxford, 2004).

25 W.M. Hennessy (ed.), *The Annals of Loch Cé. A Chronicle of Irish Affairs from A.D. 1014 to A.D. 1590*, 2 vols (London, 1871), ii, *s.a.* 1589.

26 Maginn, 'A True Report'.

27 Bingham to Burghley, 15 June 1592, TNA, SP 63/165/7.
28 Bingham to Burghley, 25 September 1592, TNA, SP 63/166/66.
29 Bingham to Fitzwilliam, 3 August 1592, TNA, SP 63/166/44(iii), fo. 124.
30 *AFM*, *s.a.* 1592. The annalists' reference to 'English and Irish soldiers' [*Gallda agus Gaoidhealcha*] would seem to refer, on account of their use of the term 'Gallda' [literally foreigners, but in effect Englishmen born in Ireland] rather than 'Sassanaigh' [Englishmen from England], to the fact that Bingham employed local troops from the province in this campaign. It was the earl of Clanrickard and Theobald Dillon, both *Gaill* in the traditional Irish reckoning of race, who furnished him with the men: Bingham to Burghley, 25 September 1592, TNA, SP 63/166/66.
31 Bingham to Fitzwilliam, 8 September 1592, TNA, SP 63/166/57(i).
32 Lane to Burghley, 14 January 1593, TNA, SP 63/168/4, fo. 7.
33 Judith Barry, *s.v.* 'Hugh Maguire' and Hiram Morgan, *s.v.* 'Hugh O'Donnell', in James Maguire (ed.), *Dictionary of Irish Biography* (Cambridge, 2008).
34 Bingham to Fitzwilliam, 6 March 1593, TNA, SP 63/168/68(i).
35 Micheline Kerney Walsh, 'Archbishop Magauran and His Return to Ireland, October 1592', *Seanchas Ardmhacha* 14 (1990), pp. 68–79; George Bingham to Richard Bingham, 3 January 1593, TNA, SP 63/168/8(xi).
36 Lane to Burghley, 25 March 1593, TNA, SP 63/168/77, fo. 257; Lane to Burghley, 17 April 1593, TNA, SP 63/169/19, fo. 88.
37 Fitzwilliam and council to privy council, 30 June 1593, TNA, SP 63/170/23; *AFM*, *s.a.* 1593.
38 Burghley to Fitzwilliam, 7 July 1593, TNA, SP 63/170/39, fo. 132.
39 Elizabeth to Bingham, 6 July 1593, TNA, 63/170/35, fo. 118; Elizabeth to lord deputy and council, 6/7 July 1593, TNA, SP 63/170/36, fo. 120 (quotation).
40 Ellis, *Defending English Ground*, p. 31.
41 Bingham to Burghley, 19 July 1593, TNA, SP 63/170/45, fo. 165 (quotation); *Calendar Salisbury MSS*, pp. 338–339.
42 Bingham to Burghley, 19 September 1593, TNA, SP 63/171/37, fo. 147.
43 Bingham to Fitzwilliam, 27 September 1593, TNA, SP 63/172/2(vii); Bingham to Fitzwilliam, 30 September 1593, TNA, SP 63/172/2(xiii).
44 James O'Neill, 'Death in the Lakelands: Tyrone's Proxy War, 1593–4', *History Ireland* 23 (2015), pp. 14–17.
45 Bingham to Burghley, 15 November 1593, TNA, SP 63/172/15, fo. 80 (quotations); Bingham to Lane, 23 December 1593, TNA, SP 63/172/38(i), fo 220.
46 Fitzwilliam to Burghley, 30 January 1594, TNA, SP 63/173/8; Lane to Burghley, 30 January 1594, TNA, SP 63/173/12, fo. 39.
47 Fitzwilliam to Burghley, 30 January 1594, TNA, SP 63/173/9, fo. 33.
48 Fenton to Burghley, 23 December 1593, TNA, SP 63/172/39, fo. 224.
49 Bingham to Burghley, 15 February 1594, TNA, SP 63/173/28, ff 91–1ᵛ.
50 Hiram Morgan, *Tyrone's Rebellion: The Outbreak of the Nine Years War in Tudor Ireland* (Woodbridge, 1993), p. 167.
51 Burghley to Cecil, 22 February 1594, TNA, SP 63/173/51, fo. 140.
52 Queen to lord deputy and council, 14 March 1594, TNA SP 63/173/85, fo. 225. Maginn, *William Cecil*, p. 103.
53 On the same day he wrote to Burghley, Bingham wrote similar, though less detailed, letters to Robert Cecil and John Puckering, the lord keeper: TNA, SP 63/173/29–30.
54 Bingham to Burghley, 14 April 1594, TNA, SP 63/174/15, fo. 36.
55 Rory Rapple, *Martial*, pp. 292–293.
56 Bingham to Burghley, 14 April 1594, TNA, SP 63/174/15, fo. 37.
57 Instructions for Russell, 3 May 1594, TNA, SP 63/174/35, fo. 98.

58 Penry Williams, *The Later Tudors: England, 1547–1603* (Oxford, 1995), p. 348.
59 J.S. Nolan, 'English Operations around Brest, 1594', *The Mariner's Mirror* 81 (1995), p. 259 (quotation).
60 Lord deputy and council to privy council, 12 September 1594, TNA, SP 63/176/11, fo. 19.
61 Burghley's memorial for Ireland, 24 October 1594, TNA, SP 63/176/64, fo. 188.
62 Bingham to Lane, 18 September 1594, TNA, SP 63/176/36(i), fo. 90.
63 Burghley's memorial for Ireland, 24 October 1594, TNA, SP 63/176/64, fo. 188.
64 Williams, *The Later Tudors*, p. 348.
65 Russell to Cecil, 8 November 1594, TNA, SP 63/177/6, fo. 23.
66 Tyrone to Edward Moore, 15 October 1594, TNA, SP 63/176/60(i), fo. 161.
67 Bingham to Burghley, 6 December 1594, TNA, SP 63/177/34, fo. 135.
68 Queen to lord deputy and council, 20 March 1595, TNA, SP 63/178/99, fo. 236.
69 Bingham to Burghley, 12 March 1595, TNA, SP 63/178/85, fo. 210.
70 *AFM, s.a.* 1595. On the newly-developed military sophistication of the confederacy, see James O'Neill, *The Nine Years War, 1593–1603: O'Neill, Mountjoy and the Military Revolution* (Dublin, 2017), pp. 202–212.
71 Bingham to Burghley? 26 April 1595, TNA, SP 63/179/51, fo. 116. To whom this letter was written is unknown. In it, Bingham referred to an earlier letter he had sent to the recipient in February outlining O'Donnell's invasion of Roscommon. But O'Donnell attacked in early March; Bingham wrote Burghley on 12 March (see above). It may be that Bingham had the month wrong and was referring to the earlier letter to Burghley.
72 Bingham to lord deputy, 6 June 1595, TNA, SP 63/180/22(ii), fo. 79.
73 *AFM, s.a.* 1595.
74 Christopher Maginn, 'Vice-regal Visits to Galway in the Age of the Tudors', *Journal of the Galway Archaeological and Historical Society* 71 (2019), pp. 60–61.
75 Fenton to Burghley, 7 June 1595, TNA, SP 63/180/17, fo. 62.

8 Early Modern Border Management and New Historiographical Approaches

Raingard Esser

A good fence helpeth to keep peace between neighbors, but let us take heed that we make not a high stone wall, to keepe us from meeting.[1]

The debates on borders and their management are not a modern phenomenon, harnessed to the rise of the nation state. As the letter by Reverend Ezekiel Rogers to John Winthrop in the epigraph indicates, the management of borders had already been carefully discussed and negotiated in early modern times. For today's world, observers have noticed that "borders are back".[2] After a period of seemingly vanishing borders in the 1990s, the difficulties around the Brexit-protocol for Northern Ireland between the EU and the UK have bought the relevance of borders once again into sharp relief. The protracted debates about territorial borderlines on the island of Ireland or, alternatively, in the Irish Sea, seem to indicate that territoriality is again a defining feature of political sovereignty and, by extension, social and economic regimes. However, a closer investigation into the positions concerning the border regime in Northern Ireland demonstrates that "territory plays tricks" with our concepts of sovereignty, as Lauren Benton has aptly phrased it for her research on law and geography in early modern Empires.[3] In earlier as well as in recent conflicts, it is less the territoriality itself which is contested, but the rights and regulations attached to a geographical and political entity. What seemed a particularly early modern understanding of European borders as a multifaceted and multilayered complex with sometimes overlapping, sometimes conflicting jurisdictions and extraterritorial rights involving different national, regional and local agents is, maybe, not so different to scenarios that we are witnessing today, and not only on the island of Ireland. At the same time, the role of borders for the management of migration and mobility of people has received an even greater urgency in European Union policies and their Schengen borders.

The purpose of this present article is not to draw oversimplified comparisons between current and early modern border management. It will outline, instead, recent trends in the historiography of early modern borders,

DOI: 10.4324/9781032691886-8

boundaries, and their management from a continental European perspective and with a particular focus on the early modern Low Countries and the Holy Roman Empire. Comparative studies undertaken in recent European research programmes and conducted with colleagues from continental Europe, Britain and Ireland have highlighted the similarities, but also the significant differences between European borders.[4] Steven Ellis has identified the fluid and shifting nature of the early modern Anglo-Irish border compared to the military nature of the Anglo-Scottish border, with warfare or the prevention of warfare as a defining feature of border management and border societies.[5] The no less bellicose realities in the early modern Low Countries and the Holy Roman Empire and other borders in early modern Europe have allowed for a more nuanced management of defence and collaboration, and the continuity of traditions across newly erected military frontlines and reorientations over time. This might be the result of another characteristic distinction between continental Europe and, certainly, the Anglo-Scottish border. While the latter was clearly defined by the Treaty of York in 1237 and remained thus fixed during the early modern period, the practice of partition (as well as acquisition) was a traditional dynastic policy of aristocratic families in medieval and (albeit decreasingly) in early modern Europe.[6] Changing borders along dynastic lines were the norm, rather than the exception. Moreover, partible inheritance was also a common practice in landholding societies on the Continent, particularly in the Holy Roman Empire (as well as in some parts of the British Isles), which also supported the idea that territories, both on regional and on local levels, were subject to geographical changes and rearrangements, which were not necessarily the outcome of conflicts.[7]

Three important strands have informed recent scholarship on early modern borders: firstly, the study of borders in the context of concepts of sovereignty, territoriality, and the law. Secondly, a praxeological approach to border management analysing the instruments and methods of bordering also in the context of changing spheres and practices of knowledge-production. Thirdly, the study of borders within the framework of migration and mobility studies. These approaches, which are sometimes addressed together in overlapping research, will be discussed in the following pages.[8]

The renewed interest in the early modern use and application of the law and legal frameworks beyond the learned sphere of universities and legal councillors at courts has also informed a new understanding of border regions and their inhabitants as agents, rather than as victims or mere recipients of centralised policies. The argument, which has been made very convincingly in Tamar Herzog's seminal study on "Frontiers of Possessions", refocuses our understanding of early modern borders and their management from the national to the regional and even local perspective.[9] Rather than reacting to state politics, it was often small, local conflicts over field boundaries, grazing rights and tax regimes that forced local and often only subsequently central authorities to act. In these conflicts, as Herzog has carefully outlined, references to legal codes, precedents and tradition played an important role, but their interpretation often changed subtly and sometimes not so subtly according to the changing context and agenda at hand as well as in accordance with changing discursive conventions of their times. Herzog also reminds us that it was not only members of the regional elites but also farmers and citizens, who could and did exercise (some) power in the management of borders and cross-border politics. For the contested border areas of the Holy Roman Empire, the Dutch Republic and the Spanish Netherlands, a region peppered with different jurisdictions and individual territorial overlords, it was local and regional concerns about marauding soldiers and their quartering, the management of retorsion, *sauvegardes*, toll and tax regulations, and, not least, confessional regimes that determined local and regional politics and allegiances in the bellicose sixteenth and seventeenth centuries.[10]

This focus on borderers and their agency has also been informed by the research agenda of Transregional History, and has led to an interest in transregional border families and their strategies both vis-a-vis their cross-border peers and the territorial rulers of their own territories.[11] Perhaps reflecting the perception of a seemingly "borderless world" of the late twentieth and early twenty-first century, and in response to a traditional historiography focussing on the nation states and its borders, scholars have emphasized the connections rather than the separations of early modern societies. While certainly members of the elite such as students and scholars, diplomats and merchants, or aristocratic families were not restricted by early modern borders, this was not the experience of the majority in early modern men and women.[12] At a regional level, the perceived vagueness of early modern territorial integrity has led to an assumption that borders should be interpreted as border zones whose political lines of separation remained porous and which served more as zones of contact and exchange rather than providing strict lines of inclusion and exclusion.[13]

Interdisciplinary approaches from geography, anthropology and cultural studies aim to re-conceptualize border research to the study of "borderscapes" advocating epistemological and ontological approaches to a multi-layered understanding of borders.[14] However, more recent scholarship on early modern borders has cautioned against an interpretation of borders and borderlines as cultural constructions which borderers could and did simply utilize to their own advantage. Moreover, scholars have wondered whether the focus on communality and reciprocity has not overshadowed the importance of categories such as the rule of law, and administrative and other institutional networks based on political power structures which were distinct on both sides of the border.[15] Researchers now caution against a trend in historiography which has de-bordered early modern societies and has emphasized global connections rather than regional limitations.[16] While the strategy of breaking with an anachronistic reliance on national borders is certainly welcome, this scholarship underestimates the role of borders denoting differences that existed between early modern political units and their economic, confessional and social make-up. The many interactions and connections in the early modern world took place not only in spite of borders but also by managing the political, economic or confessional distinctions and differences demarcated by a border.

How these concerns were dealt with is a topic that contributes to a second important strand in recent historiography, which analyses the practical management of borders – with its legal and administrative instruments, the *sauvegardes*, letters of safe conduct, passports, and *licenten* licencing trade in peace and war. Using the concept of "bordering" scholars have investigated the processes of drawing dividing lines of different territorial regimes in early modern times.[17] Luca Scholz and Andreas Rutz have recently contributed to this topic with important research monographs, which focus on the many politically and geographically diverse territories of the Holy Roman Empire.[18] Both scholars draw chronological lines which transgress the traditional markers of scholarship with Rutz incorporating studies on medieval border management and Scholz progressing his research to the end of the Old Reich in the early nineteenth century. They allow for a broader view of early modern borders and their management. Both scholars point out that border fortifications in early modern Europe, which played a prominent role in the Anglo-Scottish scenario, were not signposts of lines of demarcations, but were erected to fortify and to defend particular geographical passages, toll stations or prominent towns and other settlements. Only from the second half of the eighteenth century onwards did they become fortified border stations. Economic historians have identified a transition from a system of 'passage duties' (Passierzoll) or 'thoroughfare duties' (Verkehrslinienzoll) to a system of 'territorial duties' (Gebietszoll) or 'border duties' (Grenzzoll) for that period.[19] For the divided Duchy of Guelders in the early modern Low Countries, the most striking visualization, which gives testimony to this interpretation, is the rather over-ambitious Fossa Eugeniana, a canal connecting the Rhine and the Maas to undercut the Dutch Rhine and Schelde toll and defended by a string of twenty-two ramparts and two larger fortifications, as visualized in the map of Michel Faulte of 1627.[20]

The international project, which had been started in 1625, had been dreamed up by the Archdukes Albert and Isabella, then ruling the Southern Low Countries, and was promoted by, among others Ambrogio Spinola, the banker and head of the army in the Spanish Netherlands, as a major economic (as well as defensive) enterprise.[21] In this depiction of the territory of Upper Guelders, the southern part of the Duchy under Spanish Habsburg rule, the Fossa Eugeniana became and remained a defining feature of the visualization of the land as a borderland. It is still not clear how much of the canal and the fortification works had actually been completed. But it continued to capture the imagination of international mapmakers, who, like Michel Faulte, Hendrik Hondius or Joannes Blaeu, particularly featured the canal and its fortifications long after the construction work had been quietly abandoned

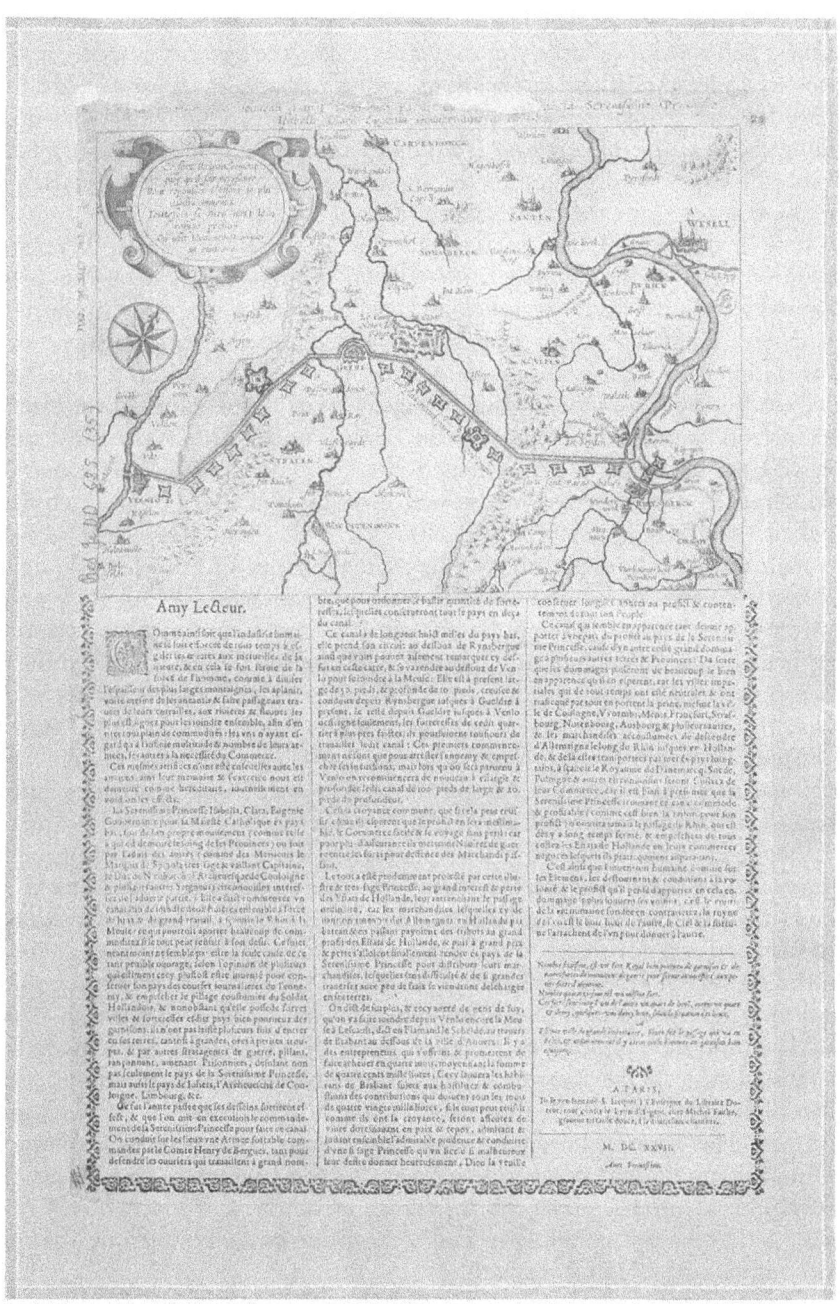

Map 8.1 Le vray pourtraict du nouveau canal commencé par le commandement de la sérénissime princesse Isabelle Clara Eugenia gouvernante des Pays-Bas, workshop Michel Faulte, 1628.

(*Source*: BNF)

due to spiralling costs. The fascination of cartographers with this ambitious project still remains a largely untold story.[22] For the current purpose, it suffices to understand their publications as inscriptions of Upper Guelders as a border area made visible by the (partly, if not largely imaginary) bastions lining the heart of the territory from its eastern border with Cleves and the Prince-Bishopric of Cologne to the main economic hub of the Quarter in Venlo, but not along the territorial borders of the Duchy.

It is in this period, and particularly during the Eighty Years' War, that the profession of the land-surveyor rose to prominence as a border agent commissioned by local, regional and only subsequently state authorities to define, mathematically, geographically and visually (on a map), what was within and what was outside a territory. There is still no comprehensive study of early modern land surveyors, but useful information can be taken from case studies focussing on English and North American examples.[23] Land surveyors often fashioned themselves as go-betweens facilitating the demands of local overlords in conversation, but more often in conflict with the resident population about the lie of the land. Their role as well as their self-descriptions embody the gradual change of knowledge systems of borders, initially focused on landmarks and confirmed by memory practices such as annual perambulations to what were marketed as accurate, mathematically calculated drawings of field boundaries and jurisdictions.[24] This process of "drawing boundaries" did not replace traditional forms of what Achim Landwehr has called "finding boundaries in the land"[transl. RE] until well into the eighteenth century.[25] A close look into, particularly, regional and local archives demonstrates that maps often provided information supplementing legal documents, oral testimonies, rituals and material markers in the land.[26] But land surveyors, indeed, became omnipresent employees in early modern Dutch towns. The continuous appointment of land surveyors by the city of Roermond (a border town in Upper Guelders), for instance, gives evidence of the day-to-day practice of border management in the region.[27] Jan van Ryckenroy's Kroniek of Roermond, a late sixteenth and early seventeenth-century town chronicle, mentions both the task of the surveyor and their limitations. In an entry for the year 1615, he recorded the perambulation of the Roermond magistrates together with the representatives of neighbouring Daelenbroeck along the borders between the two jurisdictions. This form of bordering was subsequently confirmed by a common meal. The traditional practice had been deemed necessary, and ultimately more decisive after a surveyor's results were contested as inaccurate.[28] And this "good fencing" certainly helped to keep the peace between neighbours without making a high stone wall.

The omnipresence of requests for and references to *sauvegardes*, letters of protection in early modern administrative documentation, particularly for border areas, is a telling example of the use that early modern borderers or other travellers made of instruments to manage and to negotiate these borders. José Javier Ruiz Ibáñez has labelled these documents, somewhat dismissively, as a 'resource of the weak', but these letters were not only sometimes more, sometimes less effective instruments of protection, they also allowed actions across the border and they were strategically used as such.[29] In the partitioned Duchy of Guelders, the mutual acceptance of *sauvegardes* issued by their respective overlords was a recurring feature of cross-border negotiations often dealing with travel to possessions and businesses now on the respective other side of the borders. They were also used to manage confessional divides. In 1626, the newly appointed Calvinist ministers working in Upper Guelders, the Southern Quarter of the partitioned Duchy under Spanish Habsburg rule, asked for the continuation of the *sauvegarde* that had been issued by Archduchess Clara Isabella Eugenia and her husband to their predecessors in the context of the Twelve Years' Truce (1609–1621). She gave a positive response to this new request upon condition that the same should apply to the Catholic priests operating in the three Northern quarters of the Duchy, which had taken the side of the United Provinces in the conflict.[30] In 1628, Archduchess Isabella encouraged the Roermond magistrates to request letters of *sauvegarde* from the "oproerige provintiën" (revolting provinces) for six months' duration in order to repair the dykes of the river Maas, then situated in enemy-occupied territory, which was a vital trade route for their city's merchants.[31] The strategy of mutual reciprocity in the issue of *sauvegardes* across the divided Duchy was a frequently used tactic, particularly in the Truce and immediate post-Truce years, when the political status of the Northern and Southern part of the Duchy remained undecided and residents of both sides of the border maintained their connections to those on the respective other territory.[32]

If the granting of *sauvegardes* in reciprocity was a recurring feature in regional administrative archives to manage the border, so were *licenten* (letters to facilitate trade) and passports (letters allowing travel), which were comparable to letters of *sauvegarde* and gradually emerged as preprinted documents which only needed to be personalized for the holder. They became widely used. For the early modern period, Bram de Ridder has unearthed twenty-six large volumes of passport registers in the archives of the Council of State in Brussels alone as well as several collections of "loose" material scattered in other archives in the Southern Low Countries.[33]

Sauvegardes or passports were not requested for the commonly recognized practice of *Auslaufen*, the possibility to maintain confessional homogeneity within a territory, through an acceptance that dissenting inhabitants could follow their religious obligations across the border. As Benjamin Kaplan has pointed out with respect to early modern confessional regimes, crossing a border to comply with confessional needs could function as a safety valve in times of tension. Allowing dissenting religious communities to worship in another territory facilitated internal stability and the maintenance of a status quo at home. When conflicts arose, they did not centre around the practice itself, but at the ostentatious display of the practice which was regarded as a provocation or an attempt at proselytizing.[34] At the same time, utilizing facilities outside the political boundaries of one's territory allowed borderers to claim agency, by referring cases of conflict to the neighbouring overlords, sometimes successfully playing them off against each other. For the Upper Guelders region bordering neighbouring territories under Calvinist confessional regimes, cases of *Auslaufen* could and did lead to conflicts, in which the regional and central powers were forced to react due to the actions of local dissenters, many of whom seemed to have known very well where to turn when claiming their rights and privileges.[35]

Whether passports or *sauvegardes* were necessary for the many local elite families, who had possessions in different territories, sometimes divided by war, depended partly on their status and reputation, partly on the actual situation on the ground. Partition, in any case, did not terminate cross-border acquisitions and business, and offered career opportunities as well as safe havens for borderers.[36]

The management of *sauvegardes* features prominently in Luca Scholz's already mentioned monograph "Borders and the Freedom of Movement in the Holy Roman Empire". It situates the practice within the broader discussion of migration and mobility regimes, which has been mentioned as the third research field, to which recent scholarship on early modern borders contributes. Scholz discusses their impact on the freedom of movement and long-distance, rather than neighbourhood migration, which had featured more prominently in earlier scholarship on border societies. Scholz's conclusion that early modern borders had a low impact on the channelling of migratory flows since they were "characterized by a low degree of boundary coincidence, with limited overlap between military, administrative, and other divisions", is based on the aforementioned premise that there existed no actual border line in the practice of early modern border management, which was focused on border passage points.[37] The interest in long-distance and (semi-) permanent migration rather than day-to-day neighbourhood migration has also informed the research of Jovan Pesalj, who has studied the, in many respects exceptional, Habsburg-Ottoman border, characterized by scholars as a "military frontier".[38] He has investigated the changes in border regimes after the Treaty of Karlowitz of 1699, which was regarded as a turning point in Habsburg-Ottoman relations. With the end of the perceived threat of an Ottoman invasion, the strict border arrangement facilitated by a series of strong fortifications of both sides turned from a military front line enforced in times of armed conflict into a permanent border officially described as a *cordon sanitaire* to prevent the spread of the plague and other infectious diseases, but in practice managing migration flows through mutually accepted administrative procedures. These standardized procedures kept the borders open for those who complied with the necessary paperwork, and still turned a blind eye to the day-to-day border crossing of the local populations on both sides who would utilize the gateways of a "green border" (to use a contemporary term). What ultimately mattered to the management of mobility and migration, so Pesalj argues, were membership regimes, namely residency and naturalization rights that regulated entry and long-term settlement of migrants in new political surroundings rather than border controls as such.[39]

What insights can historians of early modern borders take from this brief survey of recent strands of scholarship? Firstly, although this might be a truism, border research is as much embedded in wider historiographical trends and their agendas as any other research area in history. Secondly, if border management should be seen as a product of or a tool in state formation, it should not be interpreted as a linear process with increasing powers and pressure from the central authorities, but it developed in tandem with requirements from and agency of local and regional players. Thirdly, the act of crossing a border, while significant particularly in times of conflict, was less relevant as such when trying to understand migration and mobility patterns in early modern times. The permeability of borders had different meaning for different people or goods transported from across them. It is, therefore, unhelpful to understand border regimes in terms of an oversimplified dichotomy of "open" and "closed" borders when discussing mobility and migration, territoriality, and border management.

Notes

The writing of this chapter has profited much from the discussions during my Master Seminar "Good Fences make good Neighbours?" 2021/2022. I would particular like to thank Louisa Thomas and Jakub Mlynarski for their comments on the text. An extended version of this chapter entitled 'Early modern borders, bordering practices and mobility regimes: current historiographical approaches' has been published in: Raingard Esser and Steven G. Ellis (eds.), *Borders, Bordering Practices and Mobility in Early Modern Europe* (Hannover, 2025), pp. 15–36.

1 Letter of Reverend Ezekiel Rogers to John Winthrop, 31 August 1640, Winthrop Papers, vol. IV, 1633–1644 Massachusetts Historical Society online edition, https://www.masshist.org/publications/winthrop/index.php/view/PWF04d256#sn=4 (accessed 10 December 2021).
2 Thus the title of chapter one of Steffen Mau, *Sortiermaschinen. Die Neuerfindung der Grenze im 21. Jahrhundert* (Munich, 2021).
3 Lauren Benton, *A Search for Sovereignty. Law and Geography in European Empires, 1400–1900* (Cambridge and New York, 2010), p. 279.
4 See, for instance the publications of working group 5, Frontiers and Identities, CLIOHRES.net, Network of Excellence, European Commission, 6th Framework Programme: Steven G. Ellis, Raingard Esser (eds.), *Frontiers, Regions and Identities in Europe* (Pisa, 2009). See also: Steven Ellis and Raingard Esser (eds.), *Frontiers and the Writing of History, 1500–1850, The Formation of Europe*, vol. 1 (Hannover, 2006) and Raingard Esser and Steven Ellis (eds.), *Frontiers and Border Regions in Early Modern Europe, The Formation of Europe*, vol. 7 (Hannover, 2013).
5 Steven G. Ellis, *Defending English Ground. War and Peace in Meath and Northumberland, 1460–1542* (Oxford, 2015), Steven G. Ellis, 'Region and Frontier

in the English State: the English Far North, 1296–1603', in Esser et al., (eds.), *Frontiers, Regions and Identities in Europe,* pp. 77–100.

6 See, for instance, Matthew Romaniello and Charles Lipp (eds.), *Contested Spaces of Nobility in Early Modern Europe* (London, 2016). See also: Mario Müller, Karl-Heinz Spieß, and Uwe Tresp (eds.), *Erbeinungen und Erbverbrüderungen in Spätmittelalter und Früher Neuzeit: generationsübergreifende Verträge und Strategien im europäischen Vergleich* (Berlin, 2014).

7 David W. Sabean, *Kinship in Neckarshausen, 1700–1800* (Cambridge, 1998).

8 For a more general, interdisciplinary and cross-chronological discussion mapping the research agenda on borders, see: Suzanne Conklin Akbari et al., 'AHR Conversation. Walls, Borders, and Boundaries in World History', *American Historical Review* 122 (2017), pp. 1501–1553.

9 Tamar Herzog, *Frontiers of Possession, Spain and Portugal in Europe and the Americas* (Cambridge MA and London, 2015).

10 Important case studies are provided by Dániel Moerman. See his "A 'Scandal' in Aldekerk: a case study of persecution, litigation and negotiation in the (religiously contested border area of Upper Guelders, 1627–1628", in Raingard Esser and Steven G. Ellis (eds.), *Borders, Bordering Practices and Mobility in Early Modern Europe* (Hannover, 2025), pp. 141–161. See also his MA dissertation: 'Nobles at the Frontier Noble Politics and Diplomacy along the Border Regions of the Low Countries and the Holy Roman Empire during the Eighty and Thirty Years' Wars: A Transregional Approach' (MA, University of Groningen, 2019).

11 Bram de Ridder and Violet Soen, 'Transregional History. New Perspectives on Early Modern Borders and Borderlands in the Low Countries and the Habsburg World', in B. de Ridder, V. Soen, W. Thomas, and S. Verreyken (eds.), *Transregional Territories. Crossing Borders in the Early Modern Low Countries and beyond* (Turnhout, 2020). For an earlier discussion of transregional families see Christopher Jonson et al. (eds.), *Transregional and Transnational Families in Europe and beyond: Experiences Since the Middle Ages* (New York, 2011).

12 Examples for cross-border mobility of distinct societal groups include: Margaret C. Jacob, *Strangers Nowhere in the World. The Rise of Cosmopolitanism in Early Modern Europe* (Philadelphia, 2006); Mark Netzloff, *Agents beyond the State: The Writing of English Travellers, Soldiers, and Diplomats in Early Modern Europe* (Oxford, 2020); Violet Soen et al. (eds.), *Transregional Reformations. Crossing Borders in Early Modern Europe* (Göttingen, 2019).

13 The idea has been particularly developed in scholarly debates about the character of the American frontier in the 1990s. See, for instance, Richard White, *The Middle Ground. Indians Empires, and Republics in the Great Lake Region, 1650–1815* (Cambridge, 1991). For a critique of this approach see, for instance, Herman Wellenreuther, '"Enclave" and "exclave" on the North American Revolutionary Frontier: Schönbrunn and Welhik Thuppeck', in Steven Ellis and Raingard Esser (eds.), *Frontiers and the Writing of History, 1500–1850* (Hannover, 2006), pp. 245–274.

14 Chiara Brambilla, 'Exploring the Critical Potential of the Borderscapes Concept', *Geopolitics* 20 (2015), pp. 14–34.

15 A critique of this interpretation has been provided by Raingard Esser and Steven Ellis, 'Introduction', in Raingard Esser and Steven G. Ellis (eds.), *Frontier and Border Regions in Early Modern Europe*, pp. 7–18. See also Anna Groundwater, 'Renewing the Anglo-Scottish Frontier: Reassessing Early Modern Frontier Societies' in the same volume, pp. 19–38.

16 See, for instance, Bram de Ridder, 'Border Management during the Eighty Years' War. Passports for Persons Crossing the New Habsburg-Dutch Border 1568–1648', in B. De Ridder, V. Soen, W. Thomas, and S. Verreyken (eds.),

Transregional Territories, pp. 183–208. See also his 'Lawful Limits: Border Management and the Formation of the Habsburg-Dutch Boundary, ca. 1590–1665' (PhD, KU Leuven, 2016).

17 For a discussion of the concept of bordering from a contemporary perspective see most recently Henk J. van Houtum, 'Beyond "Borderism": Overcoming Discriminative B/Ordering and Othering', *Tijdschrift voor Economische en Sociale Geografie* 112 (2021), pp. 34–43.

18 Luca Scholz, *Borders and the Freedom of Movement in the Holy Roman Empire* (Oxford, 2020); Andreas Rutz, *Die Beschreibung des Raums. Territoriale Grenzziehungen im Heiligen Römischen Reich* (Cologne/Weimar/Vienna, 2018).

19 For a more detailed discussion of these concepts, see Otto Stolz, 'Zur Entwicklungsgeschichte des Zollwesens innerhalb des alten deutschen Reiches', *Vierteljahrschrift für Sozial-und Wirtschaftsgeschichte* 41 (1954), pp. 1–41, esp. pp. 26–31. See, moreover, Andrea Komlosy, 'Ein Land – viele Grenzen. Warenund Reiseverkehr zwischen den österreichischen und den böhmischen Ländern (1740–1918)', in Andrea Komlosy, Václav Bůžek, and František Svátek (eds.), *Kulturen an der Grenze: Waldviertel, Weinviertel, Südböhmen, Südmähren* (Vienna, 1995), pp. 59–72.

20 Michel Faulte, *Le vray pourtraict du nouveau canal commencé par le commandement de la sérénissime princesse Isabelle Clara Eugenia gouvernante des Pays-Bas* (Paris, 1627).

21 Further details on this project are provided by: Roel Zijlstra, *Troebele betrekkingen. Grens, scheepvaart en waterstaatskwesties in de Nederlanden tot 1800* (Hilversum, 2017), pp. 441ff.; Lina Schröder, *Der Rhein-(Maas-)Schelde-Kanal als geplante Infrastrukturzelle von 1946–1985* (Münster, 2017), pp. 85ff.

22 See, for instance, Hendrik Hondius, Amsterdam 1635 Fossa Eugeniana que a Rheno ad Mosam duci coepta est. See also Fossa Sancta Mariæ, quæ et Eugeniana dicitur vulgo De Nieuwe Grift (Canal of Saint Mary, also that of Eugenia, commonly called The New Canal [Fossa Eugeniana, historic canal in Germany]) from "Theatrum Orbis Terrarum, sive Atlas Novus in quo Tabulæ et Descriptiones Omnium Regionum, Editæ a Guiljel et Ioanne Blaeu" (Theater of the World, or a New Atlas of Maps and Representations of All Regions, Edited by Willem and Joan Blaeu), 1645.

23 See, for instance, Marcus Gallo, 'Land Surveying in Early Pennsylvania: A Case Study in a Global Context', *Journal of Early American History* 6 (2016), pp. 9–39; John Norden and Mark Netzloff, *John Norden's the Surveyor's Dialogue (1618)* (London, 2010). The PhD study by Desiree Krikken (University of Groningen) will close this gap for the Dutch Republic and the Holy Roman Empire.

24 For memory practices in early modern English rural society see the seminal: Andy Wood, *The Memory of the People: Custom and Popular Senses of the Past in Early Modern England* (Cambridge, 2013).

25 Achim Landwehr, *Die Erschaffung Venedigs. Raum, Bevölkerung, Mythos 1570–1750* (Paderborn, 2007), p. 88.

26 This process is extensively traced for territories of the Holy Roman Empire by Rutz, *Die Beschreibung des Raums*.

27 Th. W. Harmsen, 'De landmeetkundige in het gebied van de tegenwoordige Nederlandse provincie Limburg voor 1794', *Publications de la Société D'Archéologie dans le Duché de Limbourg* 94–95 (1958–1959), pp. 353–469.

28 Friedrich Nettesheim (ed.), *Kroniek der Stad Roermond van 1562–1638 [probably by Jan Ryckenroy]* (Roermond, 1876), pp. 302–303.

29 José Javier Ruiz Ibáñez, 'La guere, les princes, et les paysans: les pratiques de neutralisation et de sauvegarde dans les Pays-Bas et du nord de royaume de France', in Jean-François Chanet and Christian Windler (eds.), *Les ressources des faibles*

Neutralités, sauvegardes, accommodements en temps de guerre (XVIe-XVIIIe siè-cle) (Rennes, 2009), pp. 187–204; Bram de Ridder, 'Border Management during the Eighty Years' War. Passports for Persons Crossing the New Habsburg-Dutch Border 1568–1648', in De Ridder, Soen, Thomas, and Verreyken (eds.), *Transregional Territories*, pp. 183–208.

30 Jean Baptiste Sivré (ed.), *Inventaris van het Oud Archief der Gemeente Roermond*, vol. 2 (Roermond, 1869), 1626, 28 Januarij, p. 243.

31 Jean Baptiste Sivré (ed.), *Inventaris van het Oud Archief der Gemeente Roermond*, vol. 3 (Roermond, 1870), 1628, p. 124.

32 For the correspondence to negotiate mutual sauvegardes see: J.B. Sivré (ed.), *Inventaris van het Oud Archief der Gemeente Roermond*, vol. 2, 1621–1624. Briefwisseling tusschen de staten van het Zutfensche kwartier en het Overkwartier met betrekking tot het verkrijgen van wederzijdsche sauvegarde brieven.

   Orig. en minute, in omslag 13 N0 12. (p. 201); 1622–1623. Briefwisseling tus-schen de staten van liet Overkwartier en die van het kwartier van Nijmegen over het bekomen van wederzijdsche sauvegarde brieven, over executiën wegens con-tributiën, over retorsien en vorderingen door gemutineerden.

   Minuten en orig. in omslag 13 N0 2. (p. 201). The political situation of the Duchy remained unresolved even in the Treaties of Westphalia, where it was stated that the Southern part should be traded against an equivalent at a suitable moment.

33 Bram de Ridder, 'Border Management during the Eighty Years' War', in De Ridder, Soen, Thomas, and Verreyken (eds.), *Transregional Territories*, pp. 183–208.

34 Benjamin J. Kaplan, 'Religious Encounters in the borderlands of early modern Europe: the case of Vaals', *Dutch Crossing* 37 (2013), pp. 4–19. See also Benja-min Kaplan, *Cunegonde's Kidnapping. A Story of Religious Conflict in the Age of Enlightenment* (New Haven and Yale, 2014).

35 Examples are provided by Dániel Moerman, *Nobles at the Frontier*, pp. 85–100.

36 For examples from Upper Guelders see Raingard Esser, 'Upper Guelders' Four Points of the Compass: Historiography and Transregional Families in a Contested Border Region between the Empire, the Spanish Monarchy and the Dutch Repub-lic', in De Ridder, Soen, Thomas, and Verreyken (eds.), *Transregional Territories*, pp. 23–42.

37 Scholz, *Borders and the Freedom of Movement*, p. 230. For a critique of Scholz's study and its disregard of the wealth of early modern German juridical texts which clearly outlined borders between German territories see Axel Gotthard, 'Luca Scholz, Borders and Freedom of Movement in the Holy Roman Empire, Oxford 2020', *Bulletin of the German Historical Institute London* 43 (2021), pp. 108–113.

38 Jovan Pesalj, 'Monitoring Migrations: The Habsburg-Ottoman Border in the Eighteenth Century' (PhD, University of Leiden, 2019). An overview on the historiography of the Habsburg-Ottoman border is provided by: William O'Reilly, 'Border, Buffer and Bulwark. The Historiography of the Military Fron-tier 1521–1881', in Ellis and Esser (eds.), *Frontiers and the Writing of History*, pp. 229–244.

39 Pesalj, *Monitoring Migration*, pp. 319–320.

9 Building Narratives

Ireland and the Borders of Architectural History

Leslie Herman

Architectural historians have long linked early American architecture to the architecture of England, a trans-Atlantic tie that formed the foundation of architectural surveys for almost a century. Within this Anglo-centric framework, Ireland is entirely absent, the result of a confluence of causes that cast Ireland beyond boundaries both real and imagined. In the late nineteenth century, the idea of a distinctly "American" architecture became entangled with debates over national identity and efforts to define the United States by excluding particular populations. Due to these efforts, the United States, from its earliest foundations, was projected as a white, Anglo-Saxon, Protestant nation.[1] By the beginning of the twentieth century, early American architecture had become a field for scholarly study, its objects subjected to methodological and disciplinary traditions borrowed from art history, and simultaneously shaped by the internal debates of a newly credentialed architectural profession. The rise of architectural education at elite institutions such as MIT (1865), Columbia (1881), and Harvard (1893), helped to elevate architecture as a professional practice distinguishable from that of builders, thereby drawing class borders between them. Finally, by the 1920s, American architectural historians had issued a series of works that established the field's historiographical parameters, works that continue to have influence today.[2]

By the 1940s, the historiography of early American architecture was being synthesized and systematized. Frank Roos published his *Writings on Early American Architecture*, a bibliographical survey, in 1943, and attributed the increased interest in the subject among architectural historians and the general public to rising nationalism. Anticipating the future codification of "this area of American production and culture," Roos outlined a system of classification by style, dividing the colonial and early national periods with a line drawn at 1780 to denote independence from Britain.[3] The early national period was further divided into a series of historical revivals: Roman, Greek, and Renaissance. The Renaissance was then sub-divided into two types: English and French. The English Type was represented by two figures, James Hoban and James Gibbs, Gibbs being cited solely for his influence on church spires.[4] On closer examination, this was a curious classification, as Roos's

DOI: 10.4324/9781032691886-9

English Type was represented by an Irish Catholic who arrived in America from Dublin in 1785, and a London-based, Rome-trained, Scottish Catholic Jacobite who first achieved fame in the 1720s. That the English Type of American architecture was represented by two Catholics, neither one English, went unremarked. Furthermore, no reference was made to Ireland despite Roos's recognition of Hoban's Irish origins.[5]

Nine years later, the American architectural historian Hugh Morrison built on Roos's work, producing what was then the most extensive survey of the field.[6] Morrison's *Early American Architecture* opened with two charts. One delineated the history of Renaissance architecture as it travelled northward from fifteenth century Italy, through France and Spain, to England, then westward to America, arriving c. 1700 [figure 9.1].

The other, a "Chart of the chief periods and styles of American architecture to 1860," was temporally bounded by the founding of the first permanent English settlement at Jamestown in 1607 and the outbreak of the American Civil War c. 1860 [figure 9.2].

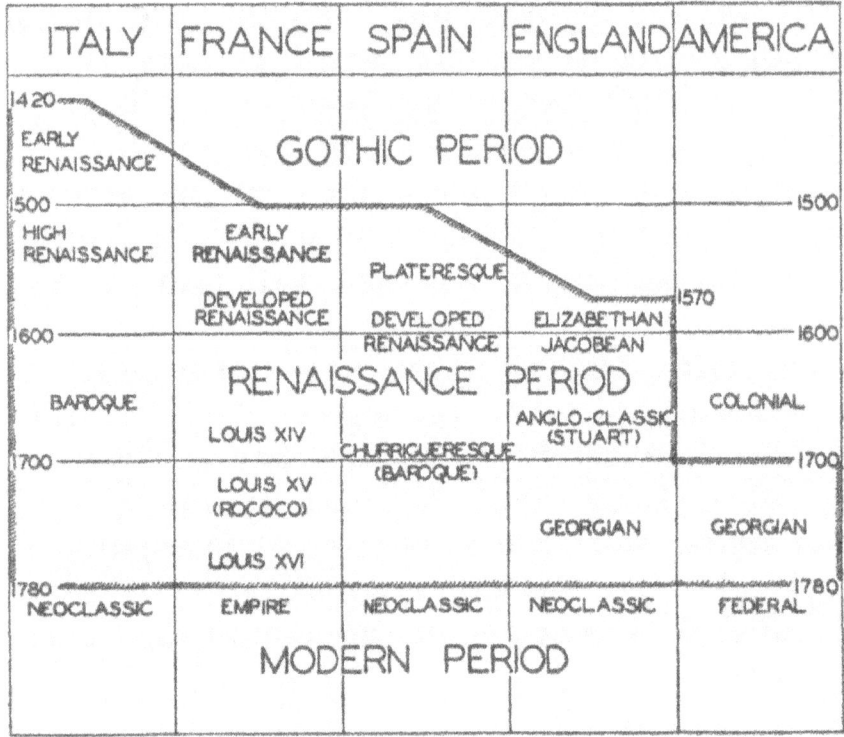

Figure 9.1 "Chart of major European styles of the Renaissance period," from Hugh
   Morrison, *Early American Architecture: From the First Settlements to the
   National Period* (1952).

Integrating the architectural and the national, Morrison produced a matrix of style, period, and region which served as the structure for a narrative that, despite including the colonies of Spain and France, focused chiefly on the English colonies during the colonial period. This emphasis on British America was so naturalized that these colonies were sub-divided by region without being labelled as English or British. Not only were these colonies English, they also were implicitly Protestant, for they subsumed the Protestant Swedes and Dutch within the borders of Anglo-America while the Catholic "others" of Spain and France were situated on the other side of seemingly impermeable double vertical lines. Hoban was included among the eight individual architects that defined the Federal Period, yet while his Irish origins were noted, Ireland itself had no place in Morrison's work.[7]

While Morrison's survey identified origins, architectural and national, the project took on its own Anglo-American dimensions when, the following year, the British architectural historian John Summerson published his classic *History of Architecture in Britain, 1530–1830*.[8] The 1993 edition opens with a map marking the survey's territory. Solid black lines delineate Britain while Ireland, a ghostly presence, appears in dashed outline with only the city of Dublin identified [map 9.1].

Summerson, describing Dublin's eighteenth century architecture as the product of an "alien aristocracy," subsequently subsumed its monuments under English architecture, with the Irish Parliament and the Dublin Exchange appended to chapters on English Palladianism and English Neo-Classicism, respectively.[9] There were, however, two appendices, one for Scotland before the Act of Union in 1707 and a second devoted to the story of "English Architecture in America." For the latter, Summerson cited Morrison as a principal source. The American appendix, while structurally distinct, nevertheless lacked an American identity, for Summerson opened by stating that "The colonization by Englishmen of the eastern seaboard of North America, in the seventeenth century, had the effect of transplanting English architecture to the new world," and he concluded by declaring that throughout both the colonial and early national periods architecture in America represented "English standards pure and simple." This was equally true for America's colonial, Georgian, and "post-colonial" architecture. Thus, prior to the 1830s, Summerson declared, American architecture was nothing more than "a remote provincial outcrop of the English school."[10] Accordingly, the architects of the Federal Period, including the Irishman Hoban, were credited only with the transplantation of English architecture to America.

Summerson's survey subsequently served as a primary building block for later historians, including the Yale trained William Pierson who published his influential survey in 1970. Pierson, while rejecting Summerson's depiction of America as a mere appendage of England, nevertheless considered England to be the ground against which to identify "aspects of American building . . . most closely related to the formation and growth of American society."[11] While stating that "four great European nations" were engaged in American colonization,

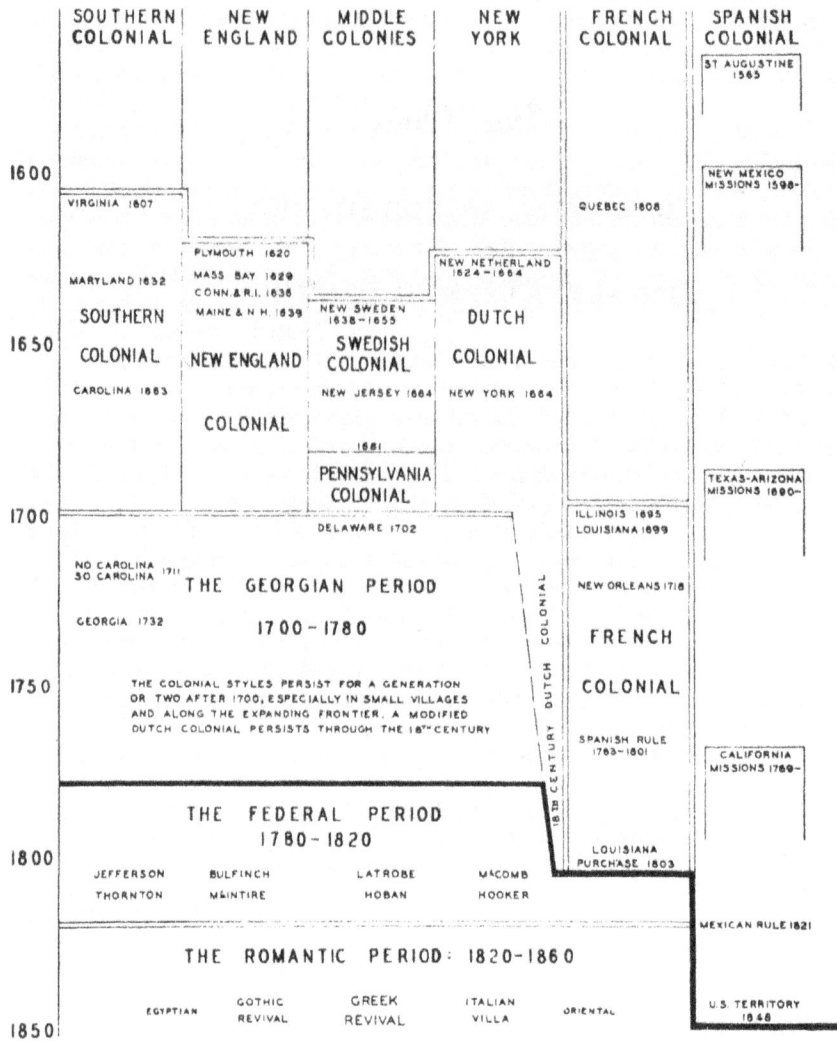

Figure 9.2 "Chart of the chief periods and styles of American architecture to 1860," from Hugh Morrison, *Early American Architecture: From the First Settlements to the National Period* (1952).

nevertheless Pierson stressed that "By far the most important were the English."[12] Thus it was only natural, he continued, that "our major attention . . . will be directed toward the English colonies, and . . . the English architectural background, from which the early colonists took their inspiration."[13] This English background was provided almost entirely by Summerson.[14] However,

Map 9.1 Key map, from John Summerson, *Architecture in Britain, 1530–1830* (1993).

Source: Reprinted with permission of Yale University Press.

Pierson went well beyond Summerson in defining these early American colonists. They were not just English, but "Protestant and middle class."[15] These men not only brought about a revolution but also "ultimately formed the basis of the new nation."[16] This construction of a white, Anglo, Protestant, middle-class America did not originate with Pierson. It can be found in the work of the influential Yale historian and so-called father of American colonial history, Charles McLean Andrews.[17] As early as 1912, Andrews sought to recast the perspective on early America and "to deal with the colonies . . . from the vantage ground of their origin."[18] For despite the presence of Spain, France, and Holland in the New World, Andrews argued that "to the scholar there is only one point of observation, that of the mother country," as it was from "England alone" that "we trace our descent as a nation."[19]

Surveying colonial demographics, Andrews included the Protestant "Scotch-Irish" but not Irish Catholics. His chief source was C. K. Bolton's *Scotch Irish Pioneers in Ulster and America* (Boston, 1910), which claimed to be the first "systematic treatment of the beginning of a migration of settlers of Scotch and English descent from the north of Ireland to the New

Figure 9.3 "Condover Hall, Shropshire, England, 1598" from page 19 in William Pierson, Jr., *American Buildings and their Architects*, Vol. 1, "The Colonial and Neoclassical Styles" (1970): Future Publishing Ltd. The same image of Condover Hall appears on page 72 in John Summerson's *Architecture in Britain, 1530–1830*.

World."[20] Not only did Bolton's work aim to integrate and elevate the role of Ulster Presbyterians during the colonial period, it sought to distinguish these Protestant immigrants from the influx of Irish Catholics.[21] Drawing his historiographical borders along sectarian lines, Andrews admitted only these Ulster emigrants into colonial history – a group that supposedly preserved their "pure" Scottish or English blood even while residing in Ireland. In fact, Andrews later declared these arrivals "were not Irish at all except that they came from the north of Ireland."[22] Andrews admitted there were a few hundred "Celts" in the colonies, mostly indentured servants, but, he continued, "There is no doubt that indentured servants in general made very poor laborers. The Irish Roman Catholics especially were feared and disliked and were not bought if others could be obtained."[23] Published amid contentious debates on immigration, when advocates of strict limits sought to keep out "undesirable" populations, Andrews's characterization of a largely homogeneous Protestant foundation for the nation functioned as a rear-facing projection in the service of present-day political considerations.[24] However, though these Protestant "Scotch-Irish" were recognized as an integral element of eighteenth-century America, they were relegated entirely to the western frontier, a back-country wilderness without civilization.[25] As a result, they could not contribute anything to American culture that could be classified as "Architecture" – at least not according to art historical criteria.[26] Therefore, with Ireland situated securely beyond the borders of architectural history, Pierson began the "pre-history" of his American survey with the origin story of Western architecture, tracing his tale from the Parthenon in Athens to the very same English Prodigy Houses that opened Summerson's *Architecture in Britain* [figure 9.3]. These Elizabethan Prodigy Houses, immense monuments to courtly aristocracy for which there is no real American equivalent, nevertheless served as the starting point for American architectural history. For, Pierson states, it is "against this background . . . in the mother country . . . [that] we will develop our story of American architecture."[27] In forging this first trans-Atlantic connection, Pierson passed over Ireland entirely.

Rather than English Prodigy Houses, however, Pierson could have begun with Irish Plantations. The material was certainly available at the time he was writing. As early as 1907, on the 300-year anniversary of Jamestown, Edward Potts Cheyney, a professor of history at the University of Pennsylvania and a future president of the American Historical Association, published "Some English Conditions Surrounding the Settlement of Virginia" in the *American Historical Review*. Noting that, for Americans, "the settlement of Jamestown presents itself as something unique, the birth of the nation, the first scene in the drama of American history," Cheyney concluded that "the closest analogy" for American colonization was "the plantation of Ireland."[28] Beyond the striking simultaneity of dates, Cheyney identified numerous individuals involved in the colonization of both Ireland and America, while identifying links between the earliest colonizers of British America

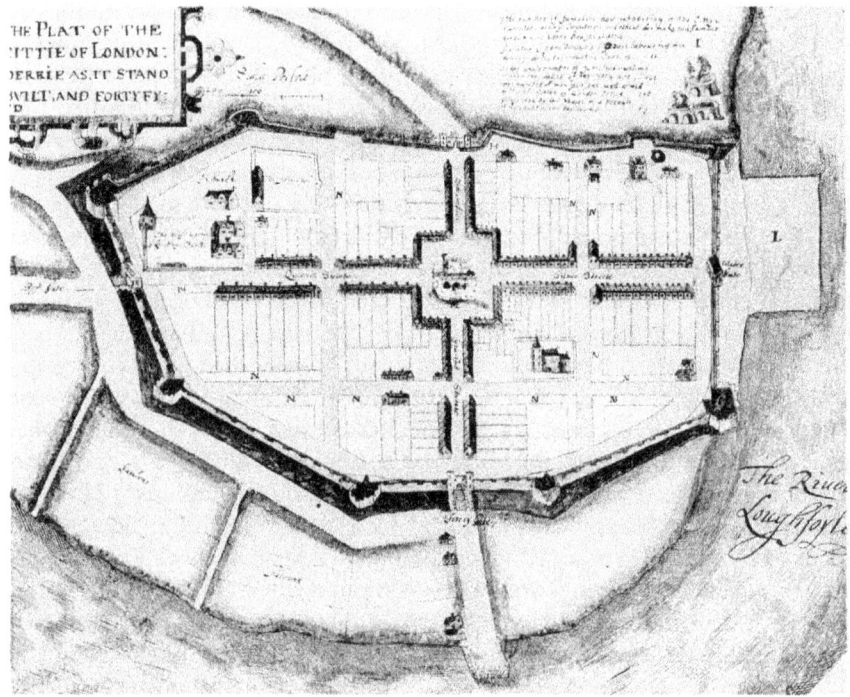

Figure 9.4 "Londonderry in 1622" by Thomas Raven, from Anthony Garvan, *Architecture and Town Planning in Connecticut* (1951).

and the Plantations of Munster and Ulster.[29] By 1934, despite his continued insistence on an Anglo-centric perspective, even Andrews had included the Irish Plantations in his monumental four-volume *Colonial Period of American History*.[30] In fact, these Irish connections had already been introduced into architectural history by Anthony Garvan, in a work published almost twenty years before Pierson's survey. Garvan's award-winning *Architecture and Town Planning in Connecticut* included Thomas Raven's 1622 map of Londonderry and depictions of Irish "bawns," and drew correspondences between them and the earliest settlements of both Jamestown, Virginia, and Connecticut [figures 9.4, 9.5, 9.6, 9.7].[31]

Garvan's interest in Irish-American ties was not purely academic, it ran in the family. His grandfather, Patrick, an immigrant from Co. Cork, had served on the Executive Council of the American-Irish Historical Society (AIHS) alongside the likes of Dr. Thomas Addis Emmet, grandson of the United Irishman and great nephew of the Irish nationalist martyr Robert Emmet. The AIHS, formed in 1897 to recover Irish contributions to early American history that the New England historians had ignored, was not purely local in orientation.[32] Rather, it was perceived as part of a larger, trans-national battle between "Anglo-Saxons" and "Celts." Anthony Garvan's father, Francis,

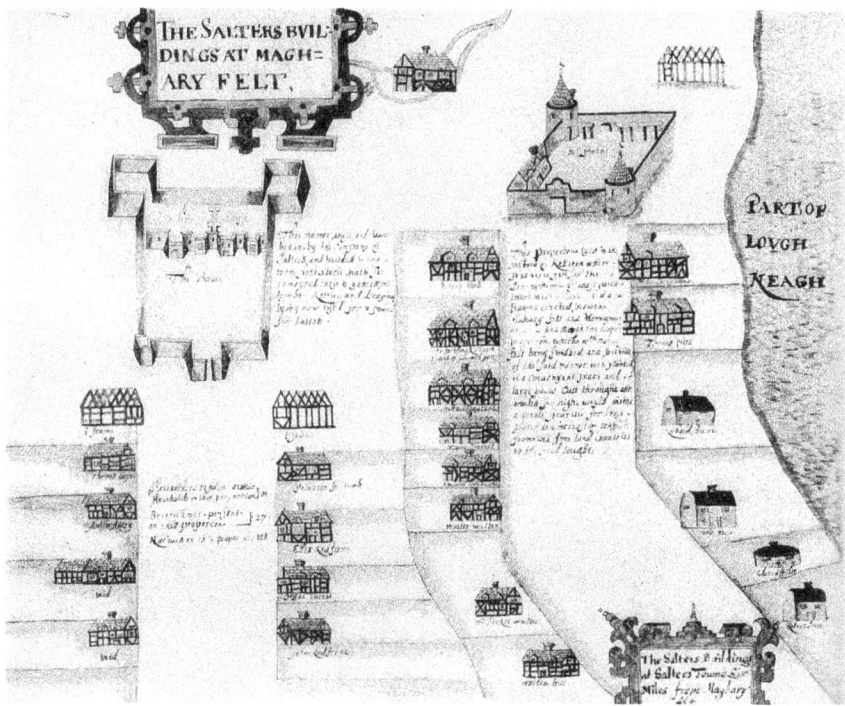

Figure 9.5 "English houses in Ulster," from Anthony Garvan, *Architecture and Town Planning in Connecticut* (1951).

a lawyer and graduate of Yale, later donated the family's collection of over 2,000 books related to Ireland to his *alma mater*, where it was intended as the foundation for an Irish collection.[33] Anthony Garvan and William Pierson would overlap slightly at Yale, and both would go on to earn PhDs there, in 1948 and 1949, respectively.[34] Whether or not Pierson knew Garvan personally, he was certainly aware of his book, for Pierson cited it in an endnote on page 462:

> For the actual methods of planning see: Anthony N. B. Garvan, *Architecture and Town Planning in Connecticut. . .* Garvan makes the interesting suggestion that the method of planning used in the colonization of Ireland during the first quarter of the seventeenth century may have set a direct precedent for the New England towns.[35]

Nevertheless, Ireland remained firmly lodged in the endnotes, situated securely beyond the borders of American architectural history.[36]

Returning to the curious case of James Hoban first encountered in Roos, we find Pierson again emphasizing English connections while erasing Irish

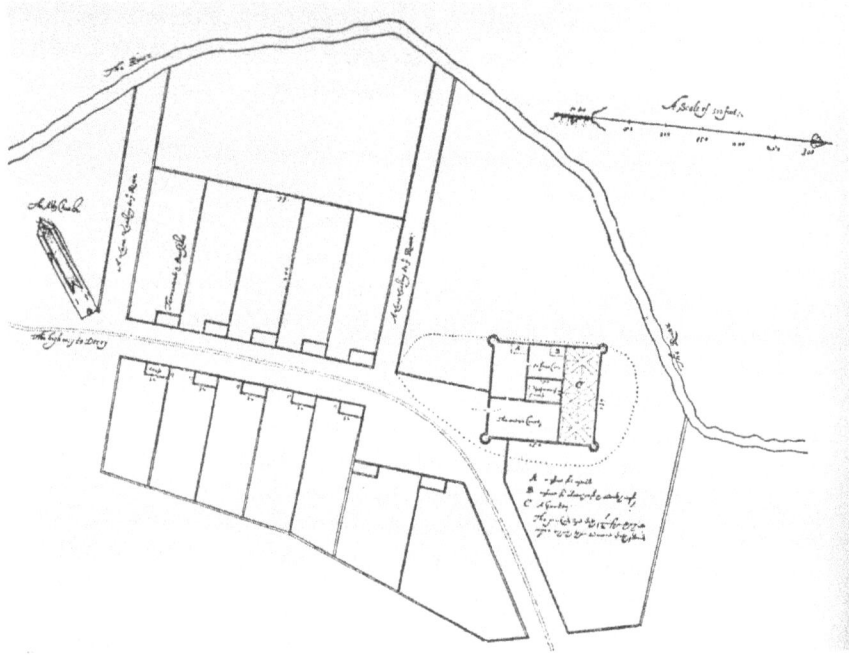

Figure 9.6 "Plan of Macosquin" from Anthony Garvan, *Architecture and Town Planning in Connecticut* (1951).

roots. Hoban's place in the American canon relies solely on his design for the President's House, or White House, in Washington DC, a work that Pierson describes as "a typical mid-eighteenth century English mansion such as those so generously illustrated by Gibbs [figure 9.8]."[37]

Like Morrison, Pierson recognized Hoban as an "Irish-born architect," yet once again Ireland is entirely absent while the White House, due to the Gibbs attribution, is effectively "Anglicized." David Handlin, expanding on Pierson, states in *American Architecture* (1985):

> The commission for the White House went to an Irish-born architect, James Hoban. . . . His scheme was derived from a design by James Gibbs. As such, it was English in inspiration and detail, with little to suggest that it was the residence of the president of a new democratic nation.[38]

Mark Gelernter later expressed the same view in *A History of American Architecture* (1999).[39] A more recent survey finds irony, *not* in the attribution of an English design to an Irishman, but because "the two most important and symbolic buildings created for a radically new government [William Thornton's Capital and Hoban's President's House] were highly conservative

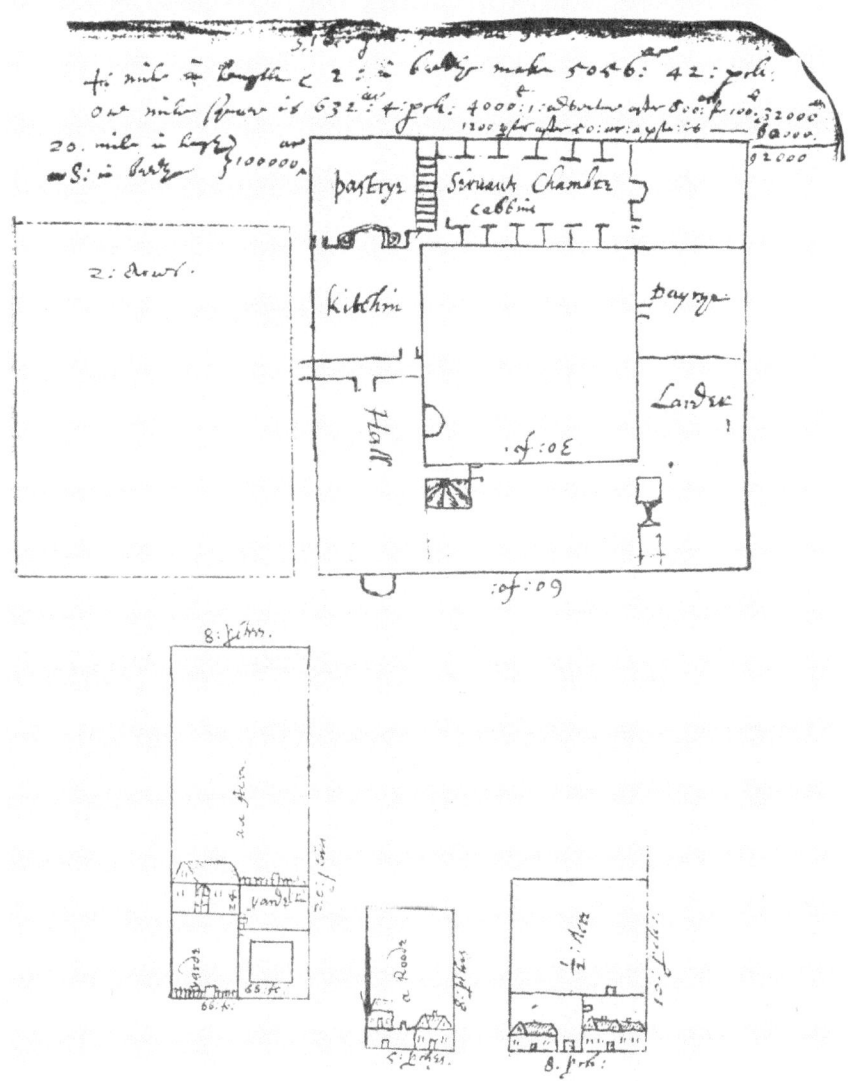

Figure 9.7 "Sketch of bawn and home lots, Winthrop Diary" from Anthony Garvan, *Architecture and Town Planning in Connecticut* (1951). John Winthrop the Younger, son of the founder of the Massachusetts Bay Colony, was born in England and had attended Trinity College in Dublin before following his father to America. He later founded Saybrook and New London in the Connecticut Colony, eventually serving as Connecticut's Governor.

in design and adhered closely to the traditions of English Georgian architecture."[40] There is no questioning of the Gibbs attribution, and admittedly it fit neatly into the well-established Anglo-American framework for early

FIGURE 284. *James Hoban. Design for the President's House, Washington, D.C., original drawing, 1792.*

FIGURE 285. *James Gibbs. Design for a house.*

Figure 9.8 Comparative images of the Hoban and Gibbs elevations. Illustrations on page 399 from William H. Pierson, Jr., *American Buildings and their Architects*, v. 1, The Colonial and Neoclassical Styles (Garden City, NY: Doubleday & Co., 1970).

American architecture, even if the attribution of an English design to an Irish immigrant severed the trans-Atlantic ties that supposedly linked immigrants to their homeland, a condition deemed "natural" when directed at emigrants from England. In Hoban's case, however, his homeland mattered not at all. Furthermore, as Hoban's design was cast as derivative, a copy of an English original, and since Gibbs's publication of 1728 was over 60 years old at the time of Hoban's design, the White House has been characterized by

HOBAN'S DESIGN FOR THE FACADE OF THE PRESIDENT'S HOUSE, ACCEPTED AND FOLLOWED IN THE
BUILDING OF THE WHITE HOUSE

Figure 9.9 "Hoban's design for the façade of the President's House, accepted and
followed in the building of the White House," from Fiske Kimball, "The
Genesis of the White House," *Century Magazine* (February 1918).

architectural historians as old-fashioned and conservative. Consequently, it
has been marginalized by the historiographical imperative that emphasizes
works illustrative of the so-called progress of architecture, with its focus on
the new and innovative. This may account for why the White House has been
omitted entirely in some American surveys, thereby eliminating the survey's
one link to Ireland in the process.[41]

What remains unexamined is the original source of the Gibbs attribution,
for it did not originate with Pierson. Rather, it was first advanced by the
Boston-born "father" of American architectural history, Fiske Kimball, in
"The Genesis of the White House," published in the February, 1918, issue
of the *Century Magazine*.[42] Kimball's identification of Gibbs as the source of
Hoban's design was explicitly intended to refute the widely held belief that
the White House was modeled on an Irish edifice, specifically the Dublin residence of the Duke of Leinster.[43] The derivation from Leinster House had been
noted as early as 1806, and again in 1817, by Hoban's contemporary and
competitor, the English-born émigré architect Benjamin Henry Latrobe.[44] In
fact, the identification of Leinster House as Hoban's source had been consistently repeated over the previous century in numerous works for the general
public.[45] Even in 1918, with the US finally engaged in WWI, John Faris's
Historic Shrines of America, a work addressed to American patriots, opened
its section on the White House by stating: "When, in 1792, James Hoban
suggested . . . the Executive Mansion be modelled after the palace of the Duke
of Leinster in Dublin, his proposition was accepted."[46] Kimball sought to
rewrite this history. His decision to publish in the *Century*, one of the most
widely read magazines of the day, reflected a desire to reach a mass audience rather than architectural professionals, previously his stated preference.[47]
However, lacking any documentary evidence as to the source of Hoban's

design, Kimball's revisionism rested solely on his own formal analysis, from which he concluded, "the White House was not copied from Leinster House, as has been believed, but, like many other American buildings of the time, was modeled on a design of Gibbs."[48] The design Kimball cited, illustrated in plates 52 and 53 of Gibbs's *Book of Architecture*, was an unbuilt "design for a Gentleman's house" intended for Hertfordshire, England [figures 9.9, 9.10, 9.11].[49]

On closer inspection, however, Kimball's formal reading was both flawed and misleading, and has been thoroughly discredited by Desmond Guinness. Most damning was the fact that Hoban's winning competition entry depicted a three-story building though there is no three-story elevation in Gibbs.[50] Guinness also identified other Irish works, including Newcomen Bank with its "oval office," as potential sources for elements of Hoban's design. Furthermore, Hoban's likely sourcebook was Pool and Cash's *Views of Dublin* (Dublin, 1780), rather than Gibbs's *Book of Architecture* [figure 9.12].[51]

Yet solely on the strength of Kimball's personal authority, he was able to read an Anglicized Gibbs into the historiographical record while simultaneously erasing all traces of Ireland. In effect, Kimball successfully provided an English, rather than an Irish, ancestry for the singular symbol of the American Presidency, and by extension the nation.

Still, other questions remain: Would Hoban really have chosen an English, rather than an Irish, source for his design? Would he have worked in

THE ENTRANCE FRONT OF LEINSTER HOUSE, DUBLIN

Figure 9.10 "The entrance front of Leinster House, Dublin" from Fiske Kimball, "The Genesis of the White House," *Century Magazine* (February 1918).

JAMES GIBBS'S DESIGN FOR A GENTLEMAN'S HOUSE. THE MODEL FOR THE WHITE HOUSE

Figure 9.11 "James Gibbs's design for a Gentleman's House. The model for the White House," from Fiske Kimball, "The Genesis of the White House," *Century Magazine* (February 1918).

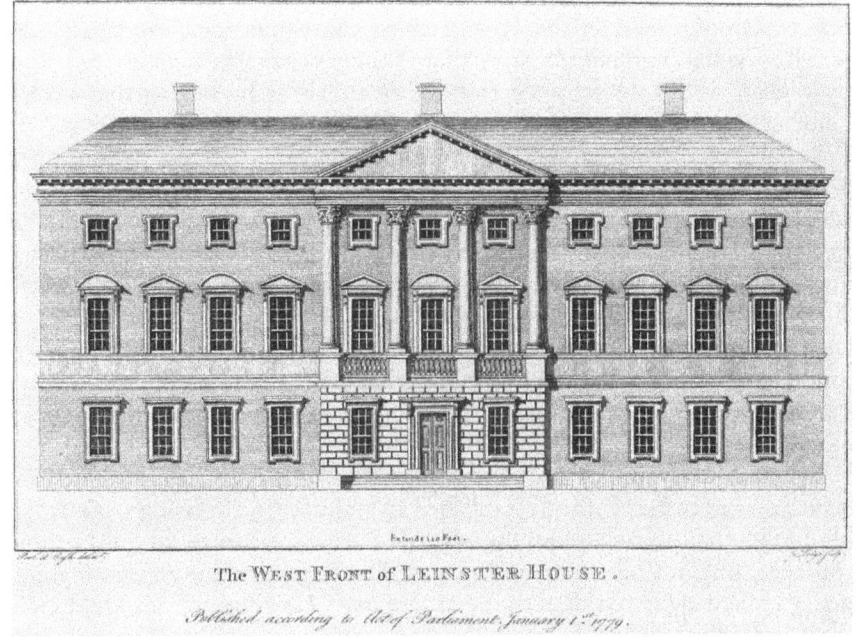

The WEST FRONT of LEINSTER HOUSE.

Published according to Act of Parliament, January 1.st 1779.

Figure 9.12 "The West Front of Leinster House," from Robert Pool and John Cash, *Views of the Most Remarkable Public Buildings, Monuments and Other Edifices in the City of Dublin* (Dublin: J. Williams, 1780).

a conservative English Georgian tradition, or selected a work identified as a home for an English gentleman? In what context should we interpret Hoban's work? And what evidence might shed light on his intentions? Unlike his contemporary Latrobe, who left a voluminous archive, Hoban's papers were destroyed by fire in the late nineteenth century.[52] What we know, therefore, is limited.[53] From what we *do* know, however, any English connections would be highly unlikely. Born in Co. Kilkenney to a Catholic family, Hoban was raised on the Cuffe estate, Desart Court, a work attributed to the Irish architect of the Parliament in Dublin, Edward Lovett Pearce.[54] Trained at the architectural drawing school of the Dublin Society under the Irish architect Thomas Ivory, Hoban later worked for Ivory on important commissions in Dublin, including Newcomen Bank, before emigrating to Philadelphia in March, 1785. He arrived in the city less than a year after another émigré from Dublin, the Catholic political radical Mathew Carey, publisher of Dublin's *Volunteer's Journal*. Once in America, Carey set out to continue his publishing ventures by establishing the *Pennsylvania Evening Herald*, and it was in Mathew Carey's *Evening Herald* that Hoban placed an ad shortly after his arrival promoting not only his architectural services, but also his Dublin background.[55] Far from being an architectural backwater, or a mere "province" of England, Dublin's architecture in the 1780s competed with that of London and, in the eyes of some contemporaries, even surpassed it. The English agriculturalist Arthur Young began his widely read *Tour in Ireland* (1780), undertaken from 1776 to 1778, by stating that Dublin "much exceeded my expectations; the public buildings are magnificent," the Irish Parliament was "grand, . . . much beyond that heap of confusion at Westminster," while the Duke of Leinster's house was "a very large stone edifice, the front simple but elegant."[56] Young also singled out the Dublin Exchange, Trinity College, Lord Charlemont's house in Dublin and his "banqueting room" at Marino for high praise. George Washington, who would later become a friend and correspondent of Young's, purchased a copy of his *Tour in Ireland* two years before Hoban's arrival.[57] Furthermore, it was through Hoban's Irish-American networks, themselves tied to Washington, that he attained success as an architect, first in Charleston, then in the new national capitol.[58]

In Charleston, Hoban went into business with another Irish Catholic from Kilkenny, Pierce Purcell, and established an architectural drawing school there not unlike that of the Dublin Society.[59] He helped organize several Catholic churches, one in Charleston and two in Washington, with one employing a priest Hoban recruited directly from Dublin.[60] He educated his children at the new Georgetown College, established by Bishop (later Archbishop) John Carroll, whose family was of Irish origin. Hoban also established the Washington Artillery in the 1790s, a unit of the capitol city's newly established Volunteers. One historian has noted the unit's peculiarly Irish composition:

> Its captain was James Hoban, the architect, who certainly needs no introduction to readers of Washington history. A glance at the names of some of the other members . . . suggests the Gaelic nature of its personnel. Irish Volunteer units were a commonplace 50 years later; this is the earliest example.[61]

Though it remains unknown if Hoban participated in the Volunteer movement in Dublin, it is not inconceivable that his Irish-American Volunteers could be read as a trans-Atlantic transplantation of an Irish original. Furthermore, as an elected member of the Washington City Council, a position Hoban held from its creation through the end of his life, he served the needs of his constituents, including the numerous Irish immigrants who provided labour for the city's building and infrastructure projects.[62] In fact, Hoban went even further to aid his countrymen, founding the Society of the Sons of Erin in order to provide them with housing, food, and medical services.[63] Such was his loyalty to his fellow countrymen that Hoban, appointed supervisor of all the new city's public works in 1798, was accused by some disgruntled workers of hiring "Irish vagabonds" over trained local workmen.[64] Furthermore, as an early speculator in Washington real estate, Hoban was successful enough to leave a sizable estate, an achievement that eluded many of his contemporaries.[65] His success perhaps owed something to his familiarity with speculative building practices learned in Dublin.

Nor did Hoban forget his homeland. In 1826, Hoban can be found at a meeting of the Friends of Civil and Religious Liberty alongside George Washington Parke Custis, the adopted son of George Washington, as well as the exiled United Irishman William Sampson, who spoke by special invitation.[66] Over forty years after leaving Ireland, Hoban's interest in his "mother country" had not dimmed. The Friends, meeting to support Catholic emancipation in Ireland, simultaneously displayed their antipathy to England. Custis opened with an *Invocation to Ireland*, wishing "Health and success to the Emerald Isle! . . . May she soon be relieved from the Lion's grasp," and closed with "Erin and Liberty, Erin go bragh."[67] Following Sampson's speech, a resolution was passed to form a committee, to which Hoban was named, to draft a statement supporting Catholic emancipation in Ireland in the name of civil and religious liberty.[68] Acknowledging the close ties between Ireland and America during the American Revolution, and referencing the Rights of Man, the meeting produced an "Address to the people of Ireland" supporting Ireland's analogous quest for freedom and prosperity.[69]

Hoban's interest in Ireland was passed on to his son, James Hoban, Jr., a District Attorney in Washington, who published *Gems of Irish Eloquence* in 1841.[70] The timing coincided with the revival of Daniel O'Connell's Repeal Association in Ireland, which sought to undo the 1801 Act of Union with Britain. More than a mere collection of speeches notable for their rhetorical form, their content served as a forceful endorsement of Irish nationalism. The younger Hoban noted that "in our latter day [Ireland] has emerged, in some degree, from the abasement to which a cowardly tyranny had consigned her, and . . . aspires with a boldness, promising success, to the dignity of her ancient national independence," while the speeches were selected so "that they might revive recollections, and retrace the course of recent history."[71] Tellingly, it opened with Robert Emmet's "Speech from the Dock," followed by those of Sampson's mentor, the lawyer John Philpot Curran, as well as speeches by Theobald Wolfe Tone, Henry Grattan, and Henry Flood. It seems fair to suppose, given all the above, that James Hoban derived his design for the President's House not only from Irish sources, but that he also associated that design with his native land, a "mother county" separate and apart from, even opposed to, England. Furthermore, it seems apparent that Hoban's American works call for an Irish context against which to read them, a context excluded by the boundaries imposed by an "Anglo-American" historiographical tradition.

There is yet another context to consider, that of Kimball's interpretive intervention. Kimball likely composed his "Genesis of the White House" in late 1917, after the United States entered the war on the side of Britain.[72] Many Irish-Americans had resisted this Anglo-American alliance and had called for American neutrality, while the anti-war German- and Irish-Americans caused pro-war forces in the United States to view them as disloyal, even treasonable. Kimball's former Dean at Harvard, Herbert Langford Warren, was among the most ardent Anglophiles in Boston, a city that was certainly full of them. Born, raised, and educated in England, Warren had established the architecture program at Harvard and was personally responsible for the course in architectural history, the core of Harvard's curriculum. When Britain declared war in 1914, Warren became a leading member of the American Rights League, the Citizens League, and the "National Committee for America," all groups dedicated to promoting America's entry into the war on the side of England.[73] In 1915, Warren argued, in a letter to the editor of *The Nation*:

> Our whole American political and social thought – the very institutions of this country which German-Americans profess to support . . . – are English in origin and in essence. Without Runnymeade and Lewes and Marston Moor there would have been no Bunker Hill, no Saratoga, nor Yorktown.[74]

In a private letter to his brother, Warren also expressed the belief that Boston would be better off if the Irish could be kept out.[75] Though not a committed Anglophile like his teacher, Kimball was Warren's star student.[76] Other Anglophiles in Boston included architects R. Clipston Sturgis, a Harvard graduate and recent president of the American Institute of Architects who had personal and professional ties to England, and Ralph Adams Cram, a leading practitioner, teacher at Harvard and MIT, and enthusiastic champion of America's "Anglo-Saxon" heritage.

Kimball, awarded Harvard's first Sachs fellowship for "Research toward a History of American Architecture Especially the Period 1776–1825," spent the academic year 1916–1917 in Washington.[77] By then, associations with Dublin had changed radically from the 1780s. Following the Easter Rising in Dublin in 1916, Nora Connolly, daughter of the recently executed James Connolly, visited Boston in July to tell her father's story before a large and sympathetic audience. In December, Hannah Sheehy Skeffington arrived in the United States for a year and a half long tour. In January 1917, she stood before a crowd of over 3,000 at Boston's Faneuil Hall where, under the auspices of the Friends of Irish Freedom, she described the "Irish revolt" and fatal shooting of her husband in Dublin by British soldiers.[78] Invited by students to speak at Harvard, its strongly pro-British President A. Lawrence Lowell unsuccessfully attempted to cancel Sheehy Skeffington's appearance on the grounds that her "propaganda" was pro-Irish, though the pro-British propagandist Ian Beith Hay addressed Harvard audiences multiple times during the same period.[79] In the war of words for hearts and minds, Ireland's case was argued not just in Boston but throughout the United States. In 1917, Shane Leslie's *The Irish Issue in Its American Aspect* called for a reconsideration of relations between Ireland, England, and America, and Leslie invoked Hoban's design as part of his argument:

> Certain it is that the Friendly Sons of St. Patrick raised a "Liberty Loan" for Washington. And when it came to peace, it was on the farm of an Irish Carroll that the White House was erected on the model of Leinster House in Dublin.[80]

Between April and June, 1917, both *The New York World* and the New York *Evening Post* ran multi-part series on the "Irish Question," including opinions on Lloyd George's recently proposed Irish Convention, at a time when it seemed that the "Irish Question" presented the main stumbling block to Anglo-American wartime co-operation.[81] Boston's Irish Catholic Mayor, James Michael Curley, asserted that the Irish Convention was an insult to the intelligence of Irish people, especially given England's long history of broken promises.[82] Curley's vocal support for Irish nationalists complicated his bid for re-election that fall, leaving him battered by charges of disloyalty from his local opponents. The editor of *The* [Boston] *Hibernian* characterized the mayoral contest of 1917 as "a fight between the Irish and anti-Irish forces" in Boston.[83] In September 1917, the front page of *The New York Times* reported the discovery of a "German plot" involving New York Judge Daniel Cohalan and the editor of *The Gaelic-American,* John Devoy.[84] This was followed by an article reporting that Boston's Clan-Na-Gael were voicing renewed defiance of England and unwavering support for Cohalan and Devoy.[85] Across the Atlantic, Sinn Féin's meeting at Mansion House in Dublin that October, attended by over 1,700 delegates, proved they were now "by far the largest body of Irish Nationalists."[86] Weeks later, Boston's Mayor Curley lost his bid for re-election.

And it was at precisely this moment that Kimball, a native of Boston, two-time Harvard graduate, protégé of Herbert Langford Warren, and aspiring member of Boston's Protestant elite, penned his article attributing the source of the White House to an obscure design for an English country house by the London-based Gibbs, rather than an Irish Catholic emigrant's version of a famous building in Dublin. Thus, with a single historiographical stroke,

Kimball replaced an Irish with an English association while simultaneously substituting an Anglo-American for an Irish-American origin story.[87] In fact, there are many other Irish elements in American architectural history, though disciplinary and historiographical boundaries obscure the Irish connections. These works range across borders imposed by geographies, typologies, periods, national imaginaries, and essentialist identities. They include forts and garrisons, land surveys, town plans, domestic dwellings, churches, civic buildings, and monuments. It is only with the erasure of historiographical borders that Ireland ultimately emerges.

Notes

1 For an overview of trans-Atlantic "Anglo-Saxonism" during this period see Paul A. Kramer, 'Empires, Exceptions, and Anglo-Saxons: Race and Rule between the British and United States Empires, 1880–1910', *The Journal of American History* 88 (2002), pp. 1315–1353.
2 See Fiske Kimball, *Domestic Architecture of the American Colonies and of the Early Republic* (New York, 1922); Lewis Mumford, *Sticks and Stones, a Study of American Architecture and Civilization* (New York, 1924); Talbot Hamlin, *The American Spirit in Architecture*, v. 13 of Yale's Pageant of America series (New York, 1926); and Fiske Kimball, *American Architecture* (New York, 1928).
3 Frank J. Roos, Jr., *Writings on Early American Architecture, An Annotated List of Books and Articles on Architecture Constructed before 1860 in the Eastern Half of the United States* (Columbus, OH, 1943), p. 16.
4 Roos, *Writings on Early American Architecture*, p. 4.
5 Roos, *Writings on Early American Architecture*, p. 160. Roos cites two articles by M.I.J. Griffin as sources for Hoban: 'Irish Builders of the White House', *Journal of the American-Irish Historical Society* 7 (1907) and 'James Hoban, the Architect and Builder of the White house', *American Catholic Historical Researches* 3 (1907), pp. 35–52.
6 Hugh Morrison, *Early American Architecture, From the First Colonial Settlements to the National Period* (New York, repr. 1966). First published in 1952.
7 Morrison, *Early American Architecture*, p. 566.
8 John Summerson, *Architecture in Britain, 1530–1830*, Pelican History of Art series (New Haven, 1993). Originally published in 1953.
9 Summerson, *Architecture in Britain, 1530–1830*, pp. 11, 350, 412.
10 Summerson, *Architecture in Britain, 1530–1830*, pp. 512–513.
11 William H. Pierson, Jr., *American Buildings and Their Architects*, vol. 1, The Colonial and Neoclassical Styles (Garden City, NY, 1970), p. 21.
12 Pierson, *American Buildings and Their Architects*, vol. 1, p. 14.
13 Pierson, *American Buildings and Their Architects*, vol. 1, p. 14.
14 Pierson, *American Buildings and Their Architects*, vol. 1, p. 461, n. 1.4. Pierson states: "Although I have used numerous sources for my information about English architecture, I have relied primarily on Sir John Summerson's splendid work, *Architecture in Britain, 1530–1830*, 4th rev. ed. (Penguin Books, 1963). This comprehensive and original volume is one of the Pelican History of Art series and is the finest general development of English architecture available." Pierson, *American Buildings and Their Architects*, vol. 1, p. 461, n. 1.4.
15 Pierson, *American Buildings and Their Architects*, vol. 1, p. 14.
16 Pierson, *American Buildings and Their Architects*, vol. 1, p. 14.
17 For Andrews' stature within the historical profession and his contribution to American colonial historiography see Richard R. Johnson, 'Charles McLean Andrews

and the Invention of American Colonial History', *William and Mary Quarterly* 43 (1986), pp. 519–541; Leonard W. Labaree, 'Charles McLean Andrews: Historian, 1863–1943', *William and Mary Quarterly* 1 (1944), pp. 3–14.

18 Charles McLean Andrews, *The Colonial Period* (New York, 1912), p. vi.

19 Andrews, *The Colonial Period*, pp. vii, 9–10.

20 Charles Knowles Bolton, *Scotch Irish Pioneers in Ulster and America* (Boston, 1910), p. iii.

21 Bolton, *Scotch Irish Pioneers in Ulster and America*, p. 7.

22 Charles McLean Andrews, *Colonial Folkways, A Chronicle of American Life in the Reign of the Georges,* Chronicle of America series, textbook edition (New Haven, 1919), p. 9.

23 Andrews, *Colonial Folkways*, pp. 17, 187.

24 Among the new class of "undesirable" immigrants were Italian Roman Catholics, Eastern European Slavs, and Russian Jews. In *Colonial Folkways*, published five years before passage of the restrictive National Origins Act, a part of the Johnson-Reed Immigration Act of 1924 which established quotas based on nationality, Andrews wrote, "the process of fusion made little progress during the years of dependence under the British Crown . . . and the thousands of immigrants, arriving yearly from the Old World and adding new varieties to the race types already present, rendered assimilation more difficult." Andrews, *Colonial Folkways*, pp. 1–2. In addition to Bolton, Andrews cited Henry Jones Ford's *The Scotch Irish in America* (Princeton, NJ, 1915). The other recognized "racial elements" of the colonial period, French Huguenots, Germans, Swedes, and Scots, were represented by L.J. Fosdick, *The French Blood in America* (New York, 1906); A.B. Faust, *The German Element in the United States* (New York, 1909); L.F. Bittinger, *The Germans in Colonial Times* (Philadelphia, 1901); Amandus Johnson, *Swedish Settlements on the Delaware* (Philadelphia, 1911); and J.P. Maclean, *An Historical Account of the Settlements of Scotch Highlanders in America* (Cleveland, 1900).

25 Andrews, *The Colonial Period* (1912), pp. 101–102, 162, 209–210; Andrews, *Colonial Folkways* (1919), pp. 6, 13, 16.

26 A separate field was established in order to include works that fall outside of the art historical tradition, the Vernacular Architecture Forum, which set itself in opposition to high-style definitions of "Architecture" and instead took everyday buildings as their focus. Billing itself as an interdisciplinary organization, the VAF explicitly draws from the fields of history, architectural history, geography, anthropology, sociology, landscape history, historic preservation, and material culture studies, but not from art history. See https://www.vernaculararchitecture-forum.org/

27 Pierson, *American Buildings and Their Architects*, vol. 1, pp. 20–21.

28 Edward Potts Cheyney, 'Some English Conditions Surrounding the Settlement of Virginia', *American Historical Review* 12 (1907), p. 514.

29 Cheyney, 'Some English Conditions Surrounding the Settlement of Virginia', pp. 515–522.

30 Charles McLean Andrews, *The Colonial Period of American History*, vol. 1, The Settlements (New Haven: Yale University Press and London: Oxford University Press, 1954), pp. xiv, 68–76. First published in 1934.

31 Anthony Garvan's *Architecture and Town Planning in Connecticut* (New Haven, 1951) won the American Society of Architectural Historians' Alice Davis Hitchcock Award in 1951, the third year it was awarded, for "the most distinguished work of scholarship in the history of architecture published by a North American scholar." For Garvan's discussion of the connection to Ulster see pp. 30–44.

32 Among the targets of the AIHS were the Harvard-trained historians John Fiske and Henry Cabot Lodge, the latter being the Congressional Representative, and

later Senator, of Massachusetts. Both Fiske and Lodge were active in immigration restriction efforts.

33 This donation, made in 1931 while Pierson was at Yale, was overshadowed by a prior Garvan donation – a "remarkable" collection of early American decorative arts that Pierson had studied during his coursework and which had earned Francis Garvan high praise from Yale for his patriotic "Americanism." See 'The Garvan Collection of Books on Ireland', *Yale University Library Gazette* 4 (1932), pp. 45–46; 'F. P. Garvan Presents Irish Books to Yale', *The New York Times*, 28 January 1933. E.Y.M., 'Francis Patrick Garvan: 1875–1937', *Bulletin of the Associates in Fine Arts at Yale University* 8 (1938), p. 35. Pierson's graduate study included a course based on the Garvan Collection. According to Pierson, "There was a wonderful course that was offered at Yale in the graduate school, called Pots and Pans, which was taught by Johnny Phillips, who was, of course, the curator of the Garvan Collection . . . It was a very elegant course." Transcript, "Oral history interview with William H. Pierson, 1981 March 11–1982 January 14," Archives of American Art, Smithsonian Institution. [00:42:05]

34 William Pierson matriculated in 1930, earning a B.A. in 1934 and an M.A. in 1936. Anthony Garvan earned a B.A. in 1939 and an M.A. in 1942.

35 Pierson, *American Buildings and Their Architects*, vol. 1, p. 462 n. 2.17.

36 Unlike Pierson, who had been formally trained in the methods of art history, the historical archaeologist Ivor Noël Hume cited Garvan in 1979, and referenced the influence of Ireland on seventeenth century American settlements. Hume included the "Plan of the proposed Anglo-Irish settlement of Macosquin in Ulster's County Londonderry. Ca. 1610" from Garvan's *Architecture and Town Planning in Colonial Connecticut* [figure 9.6], while crediting his visit to Ulster, along with the works of Garvan and John Reps, for providing the missing data necessary for a reconstruction of the Martin's Hundred plantation in Virginia. Hume goes on to say that this "Irish connection" was valid not only in terms of village design, but throughout every facet of contemporary colonial life. . . . Lessons learned in Ireland during the Elizabethan years were learned and digested by British settlement planners in London, and along with a lesser degree of American experience, were packaged in London into colonizing kits . . . [and] given to would-be colonists before they got on the boat. It made no difference where they got off; what they did, and what they had to do it with, remained the same." See Ivor Noël Hume, *Martin's Hundred* (Charlottesville, VA, 1995), pp. 234–239. First published in 1979.

37 Pierson, *American Buildings and Their Architects*, vol. 1, p. 399.

38 David P. Handlin, *American Architecture*, 2nd ed., World of Art series (London, 2004), p. 66.

39 The entry states: "The Irish immigrant architect James Hoban proposed a traditional English country house design for the President's House, largely based on Gibbs." Mark Gelernter, *A History of American Architecture: Buildings in Their Cultural and Technological Context* (Hanover, NH, 1999), p. 112.

40 Leland M. Roth and Amanda C. Roth Clark, *American Architecture: A History*, 2nd ed. (Boulder, CO, 2016), p. 120.

41 See, for example, James Marston Fitch, *American Building, the Forces That Shape It* (Boston, 1947). The early republic is covered in a section entitled "The Roman Idiom: Instrument of Progress," with an emphasis on Thomas Jefferson's inspiration, derived from Revolutionary France, as well as the engineering achievements of Hoban's competitor Benjamin Henry Latrobe. A more recent survey omitting Hoban's work entirely is Michael Lewis, *American Art and Architecture,* World of Art series (London, 2006).

42 Fiske Kimball, 'The Genesis of the White House', *Century Magazine* (February 1918), pp. 523–528. Kimball repeated the same claim in *Domestic*

Architecture of the American Colonies and of the Early Republic (Mineola, NY, 1950), originally published in 1922 by Charles Scribner's Sons, under the auspices of the Metropolitan Museum of Art's Committee on Educational Work. *Domestic Architecture,* still a standard reference today, was based on a series of lectures given by Kimball at New York's Metropolitan Museum of Art in 1920, four years prior to the opening of the museum's American Wing.

43 Kimball, 'Genesis', pp. 525–526.

44 For the quotes from Benjamin Henry Latrobe on the Duke of Leinster's mansion in Dublin as the source of Hoban's design for the White House see William Ryan and Desmond Guinness, *The White House, An Architectural History* (New York, 1980), pp. 68–69.

45 For references to Leinster House as the model for Hoban's design see David Baillie Warden, *A Chorographical and Statistical Description of the District of Columbia* (Paris, 1816), p. 36; George Alfred Townsend, *Washington, Outside and Inside* (Hartford, CT and Chicago, IL, 1874), p. 548; Rufus Rockwell Wilson, *Washington the Capital City and It's Part in the History of the Nation,* vol. 1 (Philadelphia and London, 1901), p. 27; Harriet Earhart Monroe, *Washington, Its Sights and Sounds* (New York and London, 1903), p. 166; Esther Singleton, *The Story of the White House,* vol. 1 (New York, 1907), p. 6. The reference to Leinster House remained in 1933, as *Washington Past and Present, A History* states: "This White House was modeled after the palace of the Duke of Leinster, at Dublin, Ireland; it is a building admirable in proportion and detail, and although minor changes have been made in the interior from time to time, the exterior was considered of such excellence that it has been allowed to keep its original form . . ." Appleton P. Clark, Jr., 'The History of Architecture in Washington', in John Clagett Proctor, LL.M. (ed.), *Washington Past and Present, A History* (New York, 1933), p. 496.

46 John T. Faris, *Historic Shrines of America, Being the Story of One Hundred and Twenty Historic Buildings and the Pioneers Who Made Them Notable* (New York, 1918), p. 230.

47 Kimball had previously published reviews in the Chicago magazine *The Dial*, but recently expressed a preference for publishing in professional journals. In June, 1915, Kimball wrote to Charles H. Whitaker, editor of the *Journal of the American Institute of Architects*: "I should be particularly glad if the paper could appear in the Institute journal rather than elsewhere, for I have hoped that by the method employed in it we might encourage more accurate and fundamental studies of our early monuments to replace the loose jumble of tradition and probability which fills too much of the writing on the subject." Quoted in Lauren Weiss Bricker, 'The Writings of Fiske Kimball: A Synthesis of Architectural History and Practice', *Studies in the History of Art* 35, Symposium Papers 19: The Architectural Historian in America (1990), p. 218.

48 Kimball, 'Genesis', p. 526.

49 Kimball, 'Genesis', p. 526. The house, as described by Gibbs, was intended for Edward Rolt, Esq. to be built in Seacomb Park, Hertfordshire. The house was to be built of brick, with Portland stone used only for the ornamentation, unlike the design for the White House and Leinster House, which are both designed to be entirely of stone. Furthermore, the design for an English country house differs from the urban setting of Leinster House, whereas the Dublin context mirrored the President's House in the new federal city of Washington. In addition, while Gibbs's design had never been built, Leinster House was not only extant but widely admired, thereby meeting one of Thomas Jefferson's criteria, that "for the President's house, I should prefer the celebrated fronts of modern buildings, which have received appropriation of all good judges." See the letter from Thomas Jefferson to Major L'Enfant, 1791, quoted in Kimball, 'Genesis', p. 523.

50 See Chapter Seven, 'The Ancestry of Hoban's Design', in William Ryan and Desmond Guinness (eds.), *The White House: An Architectural History* (New York, 1980), pp. 68–84. The two-story design came about from revisions made after Hoban's initial submission in collaboration with George Washington. See Guinness, p. 68.

51 Robert Pool and John Cash, *Views of the Most Remarkable Public Buildings, Monuments and Other Edifices in the City of Dublin* (Dublin, 1780). Dedicated to the Dublin Society, where Pool and Cash as well as Hoban were students, their plates were exhibited alongside Hoban's drawing "Brackets, Stairs, and Roofs, &c." which won the Dublin Society's Duke of Leinster Medal in 1780.

52 For the classic biography of Latrobe see Talbot Hamlin, *Benjamin Henry Latrobe* (New York, 1955). See also Guinness.

53 A recent publication by the White House Historical Association attempts to address some aspects of this lacuna. See Stewart D. McLauren, ed., *James Hoban, Designer and Builder of the White House* (Washington, DC, 2021).

54 For Hoban see William Seale, *The President's House: A History*, vol. 1 (New York, 1986), pp. 39–49. For Desart Court's attribution to Pearce see the *Dictionary of Irish Architects 1720–1940*, https://www.dia.ie/works/view/13450/building/CO.+KILKENNY,+DESART+COURT

55 Mathew Carey left Dublin in September 1784, arriving in Philadelphia in November. James Hoban left Dublin in March 1785. On Carey see Maurice J. Bric, 'Mathew Carey, Ireland, and the "Empire for Liberty" in America', *Early American Studies* 11 (2013), pp. 403–430; David A. Wilson, *United Irishmen, United States: Immigrant Radicals in the Early Republic* (Ithaca, 1998); and Nicholas M. Wolf and Benjamin Bankhurst, 'Introduction: Mathew Carey, Ireland, and the Politics of Transatlantic Debate', *Éire-Ireland* 50 (2015), pp. 133–137. Hoban's ad reads in full: "Any Gentleman who wishes to build in an elegant style, may hear of a person properly calculated for that purpose, who can execute the joining and carpenter's business in the modern taste, equal to any now done in the city of Dublin. – A specimen of his drawing to be seen, in which he flatters himself he can please, having received different premiums from the Dublin Society. Commands, directed to James Hoban, at the Printers hereof, shall be duly attended to. – May 17, 1785." *Pennsylvania Evening Herald*, 28 May 1785.

56 Arthur Young, *A Tour in Ireland; with General Observations on the Present State of That Kingdom, Made in the Years 1776, 1777, and 1778, and Brought Down to the End of 1779*, vol. 1 (Dublin, 1780), pp. 1–2.

57 Kevin J. Hayes, *George Washington: A Life in Books* (New York, 2017), p. 190; 'To George Washington from Arthur Young, 7 January 1786', *Founders Online*, National Archives, https://founders.archives.gov/documents/Washington/04-03-02-0425. Original source: *The Papers of George Washington*, Confederation Series, vol. 3, *19 May 1785–31 March 1786*, W.W. Abbot (ed.) (Charlottesville, VA, 1994), pp. 498–500.

58 Among Hoban's most influential supporters were two immigrants from Ireland, South Carolina Senator Pierce Butler and his friend Judge Aedanus Burke, both of Charleston and Philadelphia, and both personal friends of George Washington. Burke contributed one of the letters recommending Hoban for the White House commission. See Guinness, pp. 32–33. For Butler and Burke, see Terry W. Lipscomb, *The Letters of Pierce Butler 1790–1794, Nation Building and Enterprise in the New American Republic* (Columbia, SC, 2007); and John C. Meleney, *The Public Life of Aedanus Burke, Revolutionary Republican in Post-Revolutionary South Carolina* (Columbia, SC, 1989).

59 William H. Warner, *At Peace with All Their Neighbors, Catholics and Catholicism in the National Capital, 1787–1860* (Washington, DC, 1994), p. 130.

60 Seale, *The President's House: A History*, vol. 1, p. 57. See also Warner, *At Peace with All Their Neighbors*, pp. 100, 109–110.

61 Frederick P. Todd, 'The Militia and Volunteers of the District of Columbia 1783–1820', *Records of the Columbia Historical Society, Washington, DC 50* (1948/1950), p. 410.

62 Warner, *At Peace with All Their Neighbors*, pp. 135–136.

63 https://www.whitehousehistory.org/hoban-and-irish-washington-1790–1831. David Bailie Warden, an exiled United Irishman, wrote that "Nearly one half of the population of Washington is of Irish origin. The laboring class is chiefly Irish, and many of them have no acquaintance with the English language. They cut the canal, made, and repaired the streets, and executed most of the manual labour of the city." To this, a footnote was added that stated, "In one of the streets of Washington we observed a sign-board with the following inscription: 'Peter Rodgers, saddler, from the green fields of Erin and tyranny, to the green streets of Washington and liberty . . .' – It appears that this saddler is a native of Cork, from which he was banished at the age of seventy-five, for no other reason, as he states, than that of having worn a '*green coloured coat*,' and vented sighs for his '*dear native country*.'" See David Bailie Warden, *A Statistical, Political, and Historical Account of the United States of North America, from the Period of their First Colonization to the Present Day*, vol. 3 (Edinburgh and Philadelphia, 1819), p. 192.

64 Seale, *The President's House: A History*, vol. 1, p. 75.

65 Warner, *A Statistical, Political, and Historical Account*, p. 136.

66 *Proceedings of a Meeting of the Friends of Civil & Religious Liberty, residing in the District of Columbia, assembled at the City Hall in Washington City . . . arranged and published by John Boyle, secretary of the meeting* (Washington, 1826), p. 7. Sampson, an Anglican lawyer from Derry, assisted John Philpot Curran in his defence of United Irishmen in Ireland. Following his arrival in New York in 1806 Sampson successfully defended the confessional privilege of Catholics, which he published as *The Catholic Question in America* (New York, 1813).

67 *Proceedings*, p. 6.

68 *Proceedings*, pp. 14, 16. The full committee included George Washington Parke Custis, William Sampson, Rev. Robert Little, Thomas Carbery, James Hoban, Alexander Kerr, Henry Whetcroft, George Sweeny, Dr. William Jones, James McCleary, Robert Barry, Thomas H. Howland, Col. Isaac Roberdeau, Maj. Christopher Van De Venter, and Edmond Brooke.

69 *Proceedings*, pp. 17–26.

70 James Hoban, Jr., the future District Attorney, would have been eighteen years old in 1826, and he very likely attended the meeting of the Friends of Civil & Religious Liberty with his father. William Sampson had relocated from New York, where he had a law practice with Thomas Addis Emmet, to Washington in 1826, along with his daughter and son-in-law, William Theobald Wolfe Tone, son of the United Irishman.

71 James Hoban, Jr., *Gems of Irish Eloquence, Wit and Anecdote* (Baltimore, 1841), p. ix.

72 Kimball's article appeared in the February 1918 issue of the *Century*. If, as Lauren Bricker asserts, Kimball produced his chapter on American architecture for his *History of Architecture* sometime in 1917, he had not yet made the Gibbs attribution, as his description of the White House refers to it only as an example of the southern tendency to use a portico of tall columns on the front elevation.

See Fiske Kimball and George Edgell, *A History of Architecture* (New York and London, 1918), p. 548.

73 See R. Clipston Sturgis, 'Herbert Langford Warren', *The Journal of the American Institute of Architects* 5 (1917), pp. 352–353; Morton Prince, 'Herbert Langford Warren', *The Journal of the American Institute of Architects* 5 (1917), pp. 353–355.

74 H. Langford Warren, 'The English Tradition', *The Nation* 100 (1915), p. 468.

75 Maureen Meister, *Architecture and the Arts and Crafts Movement in Boston: Harvard's H. Langford Warren* (Hanover, NH, 2003), p. 29.

76 Upon Warren's death in the summer of 1917, Kimball took on the responsibility of completing Warren's *The Foundations of Classic Architecture*, which was published by Macmillan in 1919.

77 *Reports of the President and the Treasurer of Harvard College, 1916–1917* (Cambridge, MA, 1918), p. 91. See also Bricker, 'The Writings of Fiske Kimball', p. 218.

78 'Mrs. Skeffington at Faneuil Hall', *The Sacred Heart Review*, 20 January 1917, p. 83. For an account of her American tour see Hannah Sheehy-Skeffington, *Impressions of Sinn Fein in America* (Dublin, 1919).

79 Sheehy-Skeffington, *Impressions of Sinn Fein in America*, p. 12; 'Captain Ian Hay Beith', *The Harvard Crimson*, 11 December 1916, https://www.thecrimson.com/article/1916/12/11/captain-ian-hay-beith-pfresh-from/; 'Two Sides to a Question', *The Harvard Crimson*, 1 February 1917, https://www.thecrimson.com/article/1917/2/1/two-sides-to-a-question-pthe/; 'Capt. Beith in Union', *The Harvard Crimson*, 9 February 1917, https://www.thecrimson.com/article/1917/2/9/capt-beith-in-union-pcaptain-ian/; 'Major Beith to Speak Sunday, Will Give Address to Law and Graduate Students', *The Harvard Crimson*, 9 November 1917, https://www.thecrimson.com/article/1917/11/9/major-beith-to-speak-sunday-pmajor/. For a defence of Sheehy-Skeffington's speech at Harvard see the *Harvard Alumni Bulletin* 19(17), 25 January 1917, pp. 321–322 and 333–334.

80 Shane Leslie, *The Irish Issue in Its American Aspect, a Contribution to the Settlement of Anglo-American Relations during and after the Great War* (New York, 1917), p. 8.

81 *American Opinion on the Irish Question*, reprinted from *The New York World* (New York, 1917) and *The Irish Convention, as proposed by Premier David Lloyd George. The opinions of prominent Americans of Irish blood*, reprinted from the *New York Evening Post* by the Friends of Irish Freedom (New York, 1917). See also Francis M. Carroll, *America and the Making of an Independent Ireland* (New York, 2021), esp. chapter two, 'America, the War Crisis, and the Irish Problem, 1916–1918', pp. 13–35; and Alan J. Ward, *Ireland and Anglo-American Relations, 1899–1921* (London, 1964), pp. 148–149.

82 James Curley, 'Boston's Mayor Wants No Irish Convention', 7 June 1917, reprinted in *The Irish Convention*, p. 34.

83 *The Hibernian*, 13 December, 1917, Martin Lomasney Scrapbook [microfilm], vol. 26, Massachusetts Historical Society. Quoted in James J. Connolly, *The Triumph of Ethnic Progressivism: Urban Political Culture in Boston, 1900-1925* (Cambridge, MA, 1998), pp. 159–160.

84 'Cohalan and Other Irish Leaders Named in New Expose of German Plots; Von Igel Papers Bared Wide Conspiracy. Justice in Role of Advisor. Cohalan Said to Have Suggested Air Raids on England. Devoy Aid of Casement. Editor of Gaelic-American Agent for German Funds Sent to Irish Rebel. Bomb Offer by Viereck. Committee on Public Information Gives Out Startling Chain of Official Evidence', *The New York Times*, 23 September 1917, pp. 1, 6.

85 'Boston Clan-Na-Gael Thanks Cohalan, Urges Him and Devoy to Keep Up the Fight – Assails Wilson Administration', *The New York Times*, 26 September 1917, p. 4.

86 Editorial of the *Irish Independent*, quoted in Mark Duncan, 'Between Armed Rebellion and Democratic Revolution'; published in *Century Ireland* (July 2017). https://www.rte.ie/centuryireland/images/uploads/content/Ed_105_The_Irish_Question_in_1917_MD_CENTURY_IRELAND_JULY_2017.pdf.

87 Due to the closure of archives during the pandemic, Kimball's papers could not be accessed. It is hoped that further research can soon be conducted on this material.

10 Protestant Demographic Dynamics in early Twentieth Century Ireland, 1901–26

Barry Keane

> Thus, the great age of dispersal began long before the 'troubles', a euphemism popular with the Anglo-Irish to describe the more violent revolutionary period of 1920–23, which has traditionally been seen as the catalyst for this process.[1]

Beginning in 2017, Donald Wood, Robin Bury and Professor Brian Walker have launched a concerted challenge to separate research by David Fitzpatrick, Andy Bielenberg, John Regan and the current author.[2] This research had shown Peter Hart's claim that a 34% native Protestant population collapse was mostly caused by ethnic violence in 1921–23, directed at 'undesirables', could not be sustained by the evidence.[3] This chapter responds to the challenge.[4] Using the manuscripts of the 1901 and 1911 census, it reconstructs the 1901–11 Protestant population dynamics before addressing specific elements of the decline from 1901 to 1926. It shows that Protestant religious demographics were structurally and regionally different to the majority Catholic population long before the revolution.[5] The evidence also illustrates that the revolutionary period slightly accelerated long-term demographic trends in the south and west while the greatest increase in the rate of population loss was actually in Leinster.[6]

In 2012, my 'Ethnic Cleansing?' article concluded that far from Hart's claimed Protestant population collapse in county Cork from 1921–23 'the surprising thing was not how many left but how many remained'.[7] Analysing West Cork Methodist records in 2013, David Fitzpatrick executed a dramatic *volte face* and abandoned this key plank of 'his lamented former [Hart] student's' thesis concluding that Irish minorities were good at keeping themselves 'warm in cold houses'. He observed,

> The spectre of Protestant extermination has distracted debate about revolutionary Ireland for too long and should be laid to rest.

Published shortly after, Andy Bielenberg's detailed, influential and long delayed '*Exodus*' article suggested that enforced departures accounted for an estimated maximum of 16,000 people or 15% of the Free State area's decline.

DOI: 10.4324/9781032691886-10

More recently, John Regan demonstrated conclusively that Hart based his demographic claims on serious errors in his statistics.[8]

All these articles demonstrate the demographic changes were not chiefly driven by the revolution, but many scholars remain unconvinced.[9] Echoing Hart's key demographic argument, the challenge suggests that, as there was little difference in denominational demographics before 1911, the revolutionary years must have driven this dramatic exodus.[10] Professor Walker, for example, believes that 'critical for the movement of the vast majority of these people was violence arising from a number of political, economic, religious, sectarian factors which forced large numbers [40,000] to leave'.[11] These claims are based on Wood's statistical analysis and as these have been published in *Southern Irish Loyalism*, they deserve close attention and review.[12] While all agree the exceptional 1911–26 decline was driven by: harsh economic conditions, British military withdrawal, Great War losses, the 1919 flu epidemic and revolutionary violence, there is no agreement about the relative weight of each. The evidence presented here will allow scholars to refine their analysis of these questions and help weight them correctly, possibly for the first time.

The Protestant Population of the Future Free State, 1911

The uneven distribution of the Protestant population in Ireland had little changed since the seventeenth century. Most Protestants lived in Ulster. The province held almost equal amounts of Catholics, Presbyterians and Anglicans – and all denominations had a similar demographic profile. However, Catholics were in the majority in Ulster's rural south and west, while Protestant denominations had a majority in the urban north and east.

Out of the 327,000 Protestants in what became the Free State (FS), only Leinster had a significant Protestant population.[13] In the FS, Protestants were generally wealthier, usually connected with the British administration and more urbanised than Catholics.[14] In most of Munster and Connacht, Protestants were concentrated in the cities or around British military bases. In rural areas, they were a small (often tiny) minority.

Across the island, 81% of Catholics lived in their birth county. Only 57% of the Church of Ireland and 49% of Methodists did. In the FS, the figures were Church of Ireland 61%, Methodists 55% and Catholics 84%. County-born Church of Ireland fell below 50% in Clare, Galway, Westmeath and Meath, all of which had high rates of decline in 1911–26.[15] So, while few Catholics (or Ulster Protestants) migrated from their birth county to elsewhere in Ireland, in many western counties, Protestants were only there for work.[16] Unsurprisingly, in the north-west, county-born Church of Ireland exceeded 70% in five counties while Methodists exceeded 80% in Donegal, Tyrone and Fermanagh.[17] The cities had high in-migration levels. Antrim (Belfast) stands out with only 38% 'natives' of either main denomination.

Country of birth	Total	RC	CI	CE	Pres	Meth	Total2	Tot. Protestant	NI Protestant	Rest of Ireland
England	74782	19057	16551	26561	3607	3170	68946	49889	14959	34930
Scotland	34115	9417	4872	1530	12897	948	29664	20247	13527	6720
America	9675	9456	783	74	829	128	11270	1814	1137	672
India	3617	1557	1027	646	176	68	3474	1917	547	1370
Wales	2693	766	621	616	169	222	2394	1628	374	1254
Russia	1977	13	15	4	12	1	45	32	19	15
Australia	1004	474	276	66	162	32	1010	536	250	286
France	941	477	119	33	33	7	669	192	56	136
Germany	847	264	177	41	52	12	546	282	84	198
Canada	818	230	260	73	161	38	762	532	279	253
Total	130469	41711	24701	29644	18098	4626	118780	77069	31232	45834

Figure 10.1 Top 10 non-local birthplaces, 1911.[22]

The 1911 Church of England population was concentrated in Antrim, Down and Dublin (43%). Connacht on the other hand had 2% and these were mostly military.[18] Overall, the non-Irish born were mostly Protestant.[19] Outside future Northern Ireland, these imperial-born Protestants numbered almost 45,000.[20] Another 5,525 Church of England were born in the FS.[21] Most FS imperial-born Heads of Household were government. If the British government left, would any of these groups remain?

Demographic Trends, 1901–26

While the FS Protestant population declined by 106,000 in 1911–26, detailed and localised analysis of demographic trends before the revolution question the sudden exodus theory. Wood, for example, states the increased differential between the Church of Ireland over 45 and the national figure, from 3.4% in 1911 to 7.5% in 1926 shows emigration was more important than low fertility between those years. His figures are correct. However, does the evidence support his conclusion?

In fact, by 1901, Church of Ireland agedness already exceeded both the national and Catholic figures and accelerated rapidly through 1901–11. This cannot be a result of revolutionary violence. After all, if Church of Ireland ageing had merely increased at the 1901–11 rate, the outcome would have been 34.16% (1.43% less) which is statistically insignificant.[23]

This article also extends R. E. Kennedy's 1973 analysis of the different religious age profiles from 1926–71 back to 1901.[24] In contrast to the Catholic rate, the percentage of Church of Ireland aged 0–14 declines from 27% to 25% in 1901–11 and then to 23% in 1911–26. This trend is slower in 1911–26 than 1901–11, so this needs explanation if revolutionary violence drove the young out of Ireland.

Over 45	National	Church of Ireland	Methodist	Presbyterian	Catholic
1901	23.58	25.89	-	-	23.8
1911	25.8	29.2	21.2	25.9	25.8
1926	27.5	35.6	34.4	34.7	28

Figure 10.2 Irish Free State area main denominations over forty-five, 1901–26.

Source: Copyright belongs to the author.

Catholic	1901	1911	1926	1936	1946	1961	*Protestant*	1901 CI (Meth)	1911 CI (Meth)	1926 (Meth)	1936	1946	1961
0-14	30	30	30	28	28	32	0-14	27 (25)	25 (25)	23 (23)	19	20	21
15-64	58	61	61	63	62	57	15-64	58 (63)	64 (63)	65 (69)	68	64	61
65+	12	10	9	9	10	11	65+	15 (10)	9 (12)	12 (9)	13	16	18

Figure 10.3 Irish Free State area main denominations by age group, 1901–61.

Source: Copyright belongs to the author.

The census data also shows an increasing dearth of Protestant children the further south and west you go.[25] While a greater percentage of the Church of Ireland were married, they had fewer children per marriage across Ireland.[26] Catholic children per wife was 5.7 and Church of Ireland 4.9.[27] In the FS Church of Ireland, fertility was 4.63 while Catholics had 5.5 children.

In parts of the south-west, Protestant women had even fewer children.[28] If wives who had no children, or did not answer the question, are included, the Church of Ireland rate drops to 3.8, and for Catholics 4.8.[29] Equally, the percentage of single females over 45, especially in the south and west, was higher among the Church of Ireland. In Cork, the percentage was 14% while the Roman Catholic equivalent was 6.5%. Kerry figures were 10.2% and 4.7%. This compounded the degree of Protestant infertility, which also implies a natural decrease.[30]

The 1911 population pyramid confirms the decline in the percentage of children begins before 1901 and this proves the Church of Ireland age profile would have increased by 1926 no matter what. Students of Japanese demography, whose population is expected to decline from 126 million in 2000 to 104 million by 2050 due to increasing agedness, low fertility and very low immigration would recognise this as evidence of a rapidly contracting native Church of Ireland population.[31] As failing fertility was a significant cause of population decline before 1911, this challenges Wood's claim that before '1922, low fertility was not the major cause of natural decease among Southern Irish Protestants'.[32]

It was also possible to construct a very crude denominational birth rate from the 1901 and 1911 censes.

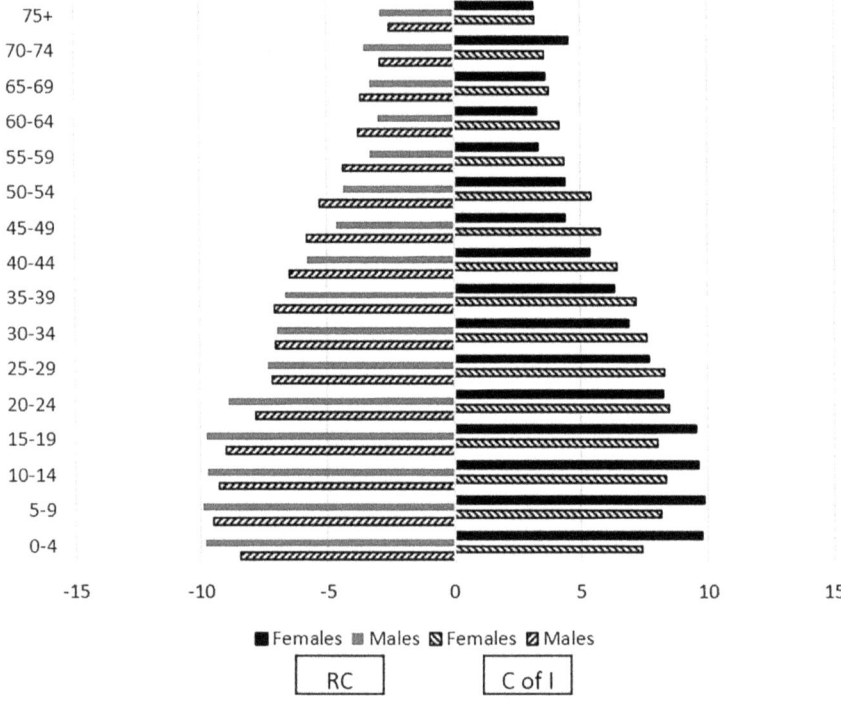

Figure 10.4 Irish Free State area population pyramid of Catholic and Church of Ireland, 1911.

Source: Copyright belongs to the author.

Island-wide there was no difference between Catholics and the Church
of Ireland (19.1 births per 1,000). Excluding future Northern Ireland, the
Church of Ireland birth rate drops to approximately 16 in both 1901 and 1911
while the Catholic does not.[33] Sexton and O'Leary identified post-revolution
FS Church of Ireland birth rates as 'extremely low by any standards' (13 per
1,000), so this pre-revolutionary differential is significant.[34] Of course, deaths
have to exceed births for a natural decrease, but this cannot be established by
denomination before 1926. However, while the 1911 national death rate was
16.6, Connaught (14.0) was lowest with Leinster (18.5) highest.[35] As most
Protestants lived in Leinster, we can infer that the population was close to, or
already suffering, natural decrease. If Wood's claimed death rate of seventeen
is correct, then natural decrease is proved by 1911.[36]

Regional variations become clearer when 1901 and 1911 child-woman
ratios (CWR) are also reconstructed.[37] The 1911 Church of Ireland CWR was
1:35, Catholic 1:47 and Church of England 1:52. This confirms Kennedy's

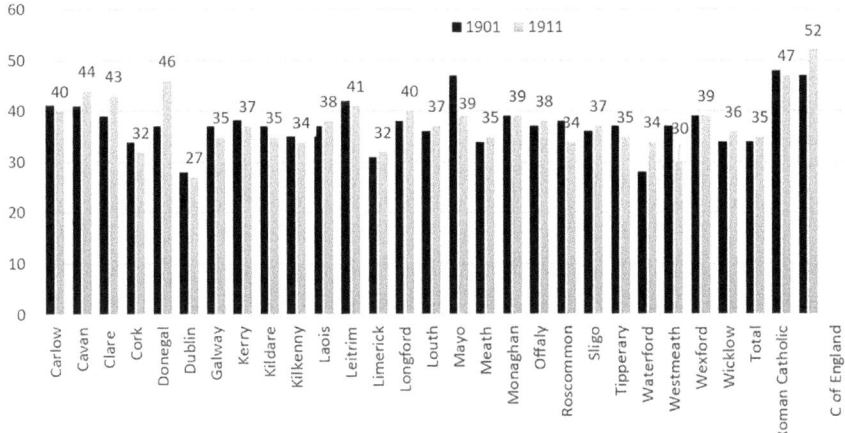

Figure 10.5 Irish Free State area Church of Ireland child-woman ratio by county, 1901 and 1911.

Source: Copyright belongs to the author.

belief that pre-revolution FS Protestant fertility was 60–75% of Catholic.[38] Furthermore, Fitzpatrick's inference that Munster Church of Ireland women produced 30% less children than the north is correct.[39] Wood suggests Protestant urbanisation is the cause of this and points to lower English (36) and the Dublin Catholic CWR (39) to support this. Meanwhile, Church of England mothers were having three children for every two Church of Ireland without any obvious reason for this other than 'lost' children through mixed-marriage or extra use of contraception by the Church of Ireland. Yet, the Church of Ireland CWR for Dublin (27) is lower than the Dublin Catholic ratio, which negates this argument.[40]

The accelerating fertility decline is most obvious locally. In twelve sample counties, the ratio of under 20's to adult females declined from 116 in 1901 to 100 in 1911 and 87 in 1926.[41]

Again, the decline was steeper in 1901–11 than 1911–26. Kerry, Mayo and Sligo, for example, all had ratios above 132 in 1901, but ten years later, this had fallen by 30.

The core cause of this apparent infertility may be due to mixed marriage rates. While the overall 1911 inter-church marriage rate was 1%, this had a far greater effect on the minority than the majority. Fernihough, O Grada and Walsh state 'in Munster, for example, mixed marriage represented around fourteen percent of the marriages in which one spouse was an O[ther] D[enomination] at the start of the 20th century'.[42] If 14% of Protestant marriages resulted in 'Catholic' children, this would partially explain lower Protestant fecundity from 1891.[43] Citing O'Leary's inference that 'the proportion of native-born Protestants marrying Catholics in the Republic of Ireland rose from 6.1 percent before 1926 to 33.5 percent in 1962–66', they conclude that this is the main reason for the twentieth-century decline.[44] Being blunt, *Ne Temere* had a far more dramatic effect on Protestant decline than the rifles of the IRA.[45]

Ne Temere style marriages are evident in an analysis of eight hundred English-born Dublin Episcopalian fathers in 1911.[46] While less than 3% (21) married Irish-born Protestants, 8% (65) married Catholics. Fifty-nine of these had only Catholic children, four had only C. of E. and two followed their parent's religion.[47] As Martin Maguire established this in 1993, it is not new information, but it confirms its impact as early as 1911.[48]

Cohort Depletion, 1901–26

Using cohort survival/depletion analysis, Wood correctly demonstrates emigration was the likely cause of much greater Protestant decline than Catholic in 1911–26.[49] He does not examine the period before 1911. Using his methodology, the tables show male Protestant Episcopalian figures from 1901–26, and the overall depletion for the FS from 1891–26.[50] Church of Ireland depletion for those born in 1887 was 27.8% between 1901 and 1911.[51] The 1892 Church of Ireland cohort declined by 13%.[52] The 1926 Free State census shows Protestant Episcopalian male depletion for the equivalent cohorts (born in 1902 and 1907) was 36% and 28%.[53] Excluding the 1911 Church of England, who wildly distort the figures, the 1902 cohort would be 29% and the 1907 cohort 16%. The similarities are obvious.[54] The whole population declines were 21.3% and 6.9%. In both census periods, Church of Ireland depletion was 8–10% greater.[55] This again suggests the two communities had diverged before the storms unleashed by the Great War and Easter 1916.

Episcopalian	Born after 1901	PE	Tot CI	Tot CE	% Change	Born after 1911	PE	Tot CI	Tot CE	% Change	Born after 1926	PE	% Change
0-4	1897	10477	9188	1289	N/A	1907	9825	8423	1402	N/A	1922	5607	N/A
5-9	1892	11156	9960	1196	N/A	1902	9656	8754	902	N/A	1917	6307	N/A
10-14	1887	11543	10603	940	N/A	1897	9752	9034	718	-6.9 (CE) -1.6 (CI)	1912	7022	N/A
15-19	1882	14256	8789	5467	N/A	1892	12023	8668	3355	+180 (CE) -12.97 (CI)	1907	7027	-28.47 -16.57 CI
20-24	1877	15849	9097	6752	N/A	1887	14,264	7653	6611	+603 (CE) -27.8 (CI)	1902	6172	-36.08 -29.49 CI
Totals	N/A	63281	47637	15644	N/A	N/A	55520	42532	12988	N/A	N/A	N/A	N/A

Figure 10.6 Irish Free State Episcopalian cohort depletion, 1901–26.

Source: Copyright belongs to the author.

National (26 County) Cohort depletion	Born after	1891	Born after	1901	Born after	1911	Born after	1926
0-4	1887	174082	1897	158058	1907	156887	1922	146173
0-5	1882	192978	1892	164732	1902	157597	1917	144764
9-14	1877	211384	1887	17157 -1.43	1897	154182 -2.45%	1912	150814
15-19	1872	209297	1882	174937 -9.06	1892	155523 -5.59%	1907	146047 -6.9%
20-24	1867	169659	1877	163595 -22.06	1887	141288 -18.83%	1902	124047 -21.3%

Figure 10.7 Irish Free State area total cohort depletion, 1891–26.

Source: Copyright belongs to the author.

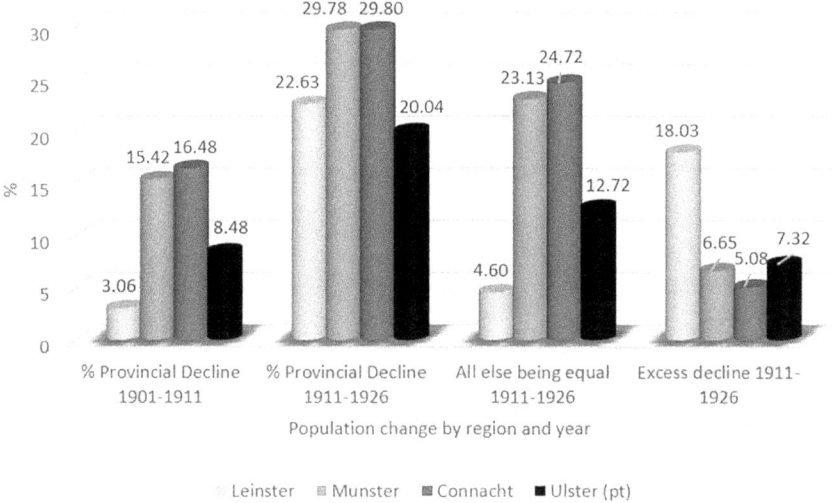

Figure 10.8 Irish Free State area Church of Ireland 'excess' population change, 1901–26.

Source: Copyright belongs to the author.

Leinster Catches Up with the South and West 1911–26

What actually happened in 1911–26 is Leinster, where 65% of Protestants lived, suffered a sudden dramatic Church of Ireland decline. Again, this has not been properly examined.[56] So, in the area with the lowest IRA membership, and where there are few claims of attempts 'to exterminate or drive away all Protestants in the area', the population decline increases from 3% to 22% in fifteen years.[57] Munster and Connacht were already suffering high rates of decline by 1911, and while the rate doubled, this was only a little in excess of what might have been expected in fifteen years without the demographic

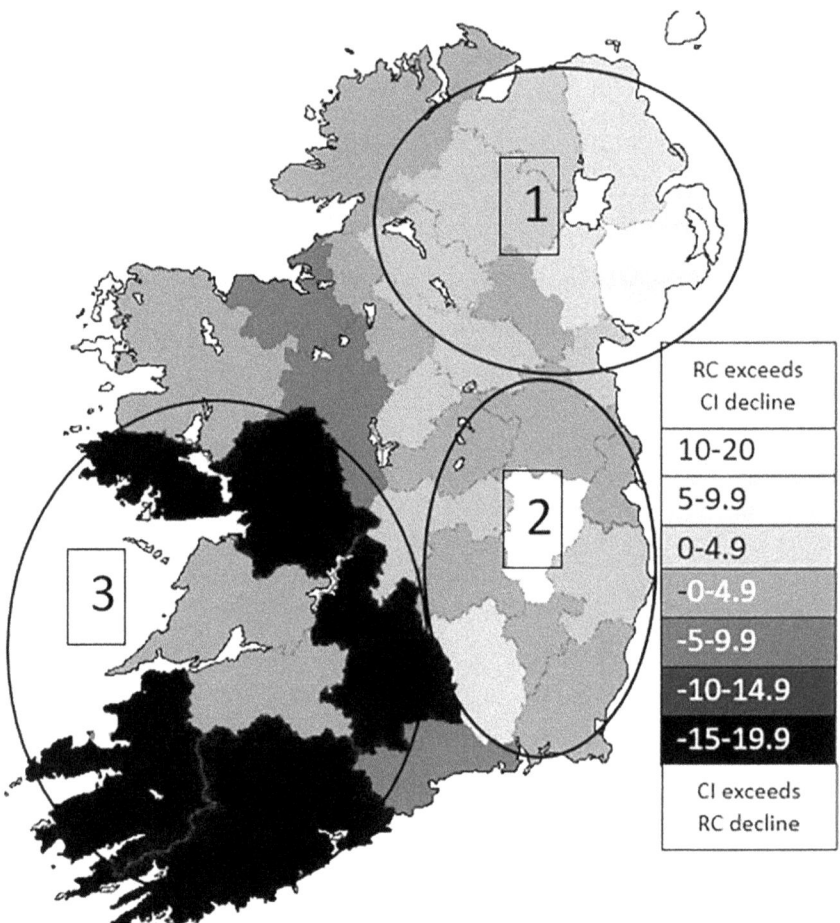

Map 10.1 Irish FS area Catholic versus Church of Ireland 'excess' population change,
        1901–11.

Source: Copyright belongs to the author.

crises in 1911–26.[58] The four charts provide the detailed evidence of this.[59]
And we know from Martin Maguire's research that working-class Dublin suffered dramatic decline, the reasons for which he identifies as mainly
economic.

Conclusion

This chapter establishes the true situation in Ireland for the Protestant denominations before the revolution and demonstrates the demographic dynamics
that drove decline in the early years of the twentieth century.

The map shows Protestant decline 'in excess' of Catholic decline in the decade before the revolutionary period. Three Protestant Irelands can be identified. These had very different dynamics. These are:

1. In the north, all religions were similar in population structure. That being said there was a long-term migration into Belfast, which denuded the west of the young, fit and presumably virile.
2. In Leinster, all religions declined marginally before the revolution with a drift towards Dublin and its hinterland. English Protestants (14.3%) 'propped-up' the Church of Ireland providing potential partners for native Protestant girls in Dublin and those living around the British Army bases. Kildare is an outlier with a substantial increase, but extra soldiers in the Curragh barracks mainly account for this.
3. In the south and west, native Protestant decline significantly exceeded Catholic from 1901 to 1911. In Galway, for example, Catholics declined by 5% and the Church of Ireland by 21% in 1901–11.[60] Here non-natives made up a substantial part of the Protestant population. In Munster, for example, the Church of England population (19.1%) clustered around the large military barracks in Cork, South Tipperary, and Limerick.[61] Elsewhere Protestants were rare except in places like West Cork.[62]

All the evidence show the native Irish Protestant population was failing at a faster rate than Catholics in the FS by 1911. In the south and west harsh economic conditions and changes in land structure drove substantial emigration for all religions. While the Catholic population coped better with these problems by higher in-marriage fertility, minority religions would have faced difficulty in the event of any population shock. During 1911–26, they faced five: the Great War and post-war recession, the influenza epidemic, the impact of *Ne Temere*, the revolution and the British government withdrawal. Most detailed research on the topic shows the revolution accelerated a long established trend.[63] There was no sudden native Protestant exodus as claimed by Bury, Wood, Walker and previously Hart.

Notes

1 T.A.M. Dooley, *Burning the Big House the Story of the Irish Country House in a Time of War and Revolution* (London: Yale University Press, 2022), p. 15. Professor Dooley's lucid and cogent analysis should be required reading for any scholar of this topic.
2 This paper summarises the much more detailed information presented to the 33rd Conference of Irish Historians. The original paper is available from me on request.
3 For Hart's theory, see R. English and G.S. Walker, *Unionism in Modern Ireland: New Perspectives on Politics and Culture* (Houndmills, Basingstoke, Hampshire: Macmillan Press, 1996), p. 93; See also P. Hart, *The I.R.A. and Its Enemies: Violence and Community in Cork, 1916–1923* (Oxford: Clarendon Press, 1999); P. Hart, 'Class, Community and the Irish Republican Army in Cork, 1917–1923',

in P. O'Flanagan and C.G. Buttimer (eds.), *Cork, History & Society: Interdisciplinary Essays on the History of an Irish County*, The Irish County History & Society Series, 6 (Cork: Geography Publications, 1993), pp. 963–985.

4 I would like to thank Ian Dalton and Henry O'Keeffe for their helpful comments and suggestions on earlier versions of this article.

5 The methodology and structure are similar to my 2012 'Ethnic Cleansing'. B. Keane, 'Ethnic Cleansing? Protestant Decline in West Cork between 1911 and 1926', *History Ireland* 20:2 (2012), pp. 35–38.

6 All scholars of this topic concede this method is fraught with difficulty and discrepancies, but in this case, it provides a reasonable degree of certainty as it examines the entire population through the manuscript census. As the printed version of both the 1901 and 1911 census are available at *Histpop* these were used to test the accuracy of the online results.

7 Hart makes a similar point but there is a 30 percent difference between both sets of figures; B. Keane, 'Ethnic Cleansing?'; For a summary and analysis of Hart's use of the term ethnic cleansing see B. Keane, 'Peter Hart and Ethnic Cleansing', *History Ireland* 20 (2012), p. 14.

8 A. Bielenberg, 'Exodus: The Emigration of Southern Irish Protestants during the Irish War of Independence and the Civil War', *Past & Present* (2013), pp. 199–233; D. Fitzpatrick, 'The Spectre of "Ethnic Cleansing" in Revolutionary Ireland', in *Descendancy: Irish Protestant Histories since 1795* (Cambridge: Cambridge University Press, 2014), pp. 181–240; J.M. Regan, '"All the Nightmare Images of Ethnic Conflict in the Twentieth Century Are Here": Erroneous Statistical Proofs and the Search for Ethnic Violence in Revolutionary Ireland, 1917–1923', *Nations and Nationalism* 28(1) (2022), pp. 322–340, https://doi.org/10.1111/nana.12783

9 Ignoring, for example, the fact David Fitzpatrick was analysing a census of an entire West Cork community, some reviewers of *Descendancy* did not accept his extrapolation for all Protestants from the small West Cork Methodist population E. Biagini, 'Descendancy Review: The Decline of Irish Protestantism', *c* (2015), https://www.historyireland.com/20th-century-contemporary-history/peter-hart-and-ethnic-cleansing-2/ (accessed 29 September 2021); The reviews also ignore Table 9.1, p. 291 of *Descendancy* which shows that the Methodist decline in West Cork was 23% between 1911–20 and 11% between 1920–26, meaning that the annual rate of decline was less in the latter period than the earlier.

10 D. Wood, 'Episode 10-Revisiting Protestant Decline in Ireland, 1911–1926', *Southern Irish Loyalism in Context* (2017); R. Bury, *Buried Lives: The Protestants of Southern Ireland* (Dublin: The History Press, 2017); B.M. Walker, 'Southern Protestant Voices during the Irish War of Independence and Civil War, National University of Ireland at Maynooth', *Southern Irish Loyalism in Context*, https://anchor.fm/southern-irish-loyalism-in-context/episodes/Episode-21-Panel-6a-Southern-protestant-voices-during-the-Irish-War-of-Independence-and-Civil-War-reports-from-Church-of-Ireland-synods-Prof-Brian-M-Walker-e2ll7r (accessed 27 March 2020); See also B.M. Walker, *Irish History Matters*, pp. 215–222 & B.M. Walker, 'Southern Protestant Experiences in the Irish Revolution: Reports from Church of Ireland Synods', in Jonathan S. Lofft and T.P. Power (eds.), *Trauma and Survival in the Contemporary Church: Historical Responses in the Anglican Tradition* (Newcastle on Tyne: Cambridge Scholars Publishing, 2021), pp. 135–136.

11 Walker, 'Southern Protestant Voices' at 35.00 Minutes, See also Walker, 'Southern Protestant Experiences in the Irish Revolution', p. 135 where he questions Bishop Dowse's address to the 1923 Cork diocesan who stated that the population had declined by 8% during the violence. Walker ignores the previous sentence where Dowse is reported as saying that he had gone to considerable trouble to collect

the information. Evidence, which I recently discovered in the 1922 volume of the Cork, Cloyne and Ross Church of Ireland Visitation Books held in the Representative Church Body Library, proves both the amount of effort Bishop Dowse went to and that his 8% figure is correct. In a contribution to the 2022 West Cork History festival, Walker reduced this to 30,000 without explanation.

12 D. Wood, 'Protestant Population Decline in Southern Ireland, 1911–1926', in B. Hughes and C. Morrissey (eds.), *Southern Irish Loyalism, 1912–1949* (Liverpool: Liverpool University Press, 2020), pp. 27–47. Being anecdotal and because he uses Wood's statistics B.M. Walker's work is not discussed here other than in Fn. 11; Similarly, Bury's analysis is substantially based on Wood's statistics except for his statement that 'Killaloe diocese 'had declined by two-thirds from its Victorian heyday' to 5,876 by summer 1921'. However, the 1911 census shows that the C of I population in the diocese was 9,222 in 1901 and 7,592 in 1911 showing only a slight increase in decline (17.7–22.6%) in the traumatic decade 1911–21.

13 For simplicity, the 26 county area which became the Free State in 1922 is referred to as the FS

14 Urban Protestants 49%: Catholics 29%; the entire island had 35.5% urban Protestants with Protestants Episcopalians making up. 19% of these, 13.5% Presbyterian, 2% Methodist, and 2% other. All percentages, unless otherwise stated, are abstracted from the 1901 & 1911 manuscript and published censes of Ireland

15 See B. Keane, 'The Boundaries of Protestant Sex before 1916: Abstracts from the 1901 and 1911 Census Data', Paper presented to the 33rd Conference of Irish Historians, a rough draft of which is available on Academai.edu (2021), https://www.academia.edu/48989176/The_boundaries_of_Protestant_Sex_in_Ireland_before_1916 (accessed 12 January 2023).

16 In twenty-one counties Catholic out-migration to elsewhere in Ireland was under 20%. In Clare, Ireland's least Protestant county, male heads of household occupations included government 20%, domestic service 12%, the clergy 7% and landlordism 10%. The pattern is similar in Galway. The equivalent Catholic figures were a fraction of this in both counties.

17 *Census of Ireland: General Report* (1911), Table 125, pp. 222–224; See also Wood, 'Protestant Population Decline', p. 17.

18 The enumerators were required to ask specific denominations rather than general terms like Anglican or Episcopalian. These were Roman Catholic, Church of England, Church of Scotland, Church of Ireland, Presbyterians, Methodists, Independent, Baptists, Society of Friends/Quaker, Jew and Other. Other includes misspelled denomination names, minor denominations and general terms like Protestant Episcopalian or Anglican. Any analysis should be cross-checked with the published census material.

19 While the table, abstracted from the online census is internally coherent it does not match Table 75 of the General Report, 1911, which reported 90,217 born in England and Wales with 38,486 born in Scotland across Ireland. This discrepancy can be resolved by working through the approximate 100,000 Catholics, 64,000 Church of Ireland, 4,900 Church of England, 64,000 Presbyterians, 13,000 Methodists, 1,580 Baptists, 2,000 Society of Friends listed with 'other' birthplaces (people, for example who stated the precise place rather than the county or country as required). With the exception of Cork & Kerry (50% overseas), that is not attempted here as it is too much work for little extra information; See also Ireland Census 1911 General Report Table 75.

20 England, Scotland, Wales, India, Canada, Australia. It should also be noted the 4,969 Church of England recorded under 'Other place of birth' 2,753 lived in the future Free State, of whom more than 80% were imperial.

21 Many of these were actually children of misreported Church of England families by the RIC constables who did the enumeration.
22 Slight discrepancies between the figures presented here and those of David Fitzpatrick, *The Americanisation of Ireland, 1841–1925: Migration and Settlement* (Cambridge, 2019) are explained by different counting methods.
23 There are minor differences between the percentages presented here and in *Southern Loyalism*, p. 30 due to counting discrepancies either by Mr. Woods or me but the key point remains valid.
24 R.E. Kennedy, *The Irish: Emigration, Marriage and Fertility* (Berkley: University of California Press, 1973).
25 In contrast, and concurring with Ó Grada, the 'lost' border counties showed little difference between religions in 1911. Colm Ó Grada, 'Did Ulster Catholics always Have Larger Families?', *Irish Economic and Social History* 12 (1985), pp. 79–88; A.C. Hepburn, 'Catholics in Northern Ireland', in *Minorities in History: Papers Read before the Thirteenth Irish Conference of Historians at the New University of Ulster, 1977* (London, 1979), pp. 84–101.
26 Church of Ireland 49%: Catholics 45%. It would be better to include Methodists and Presbyterians in every set of statistics but generally Church of Ireland demographics suffice.
27 The method used here is to add up all married women who had between 1 and 20 children and divide this into the total of children. The all island figures Roman Catholics 363782 married, 300,122 with born children, 1,704,500 children. 1,704,500/300,122 = 5.67. The published figure for the average number of children was 4.12 across the island.
28 In particular counties: Clare had an average of 5.9 Catholic children while Church of Ireland wives had 4.3 children; Cork was 5.67 Catholic and 4.6 Church of Ireland; Leitrim 5.6 Catholic 5.0 Church of Ireland; Kilkenny 5.37 Catholic 4.8 Church of Ireland; Wexford 5.12 Catholic 4.62. Church of Ireland.
29 This excludes single women as the rate of extra marital births was very small for all religions.
30 Abstracted from the 1911 census; See also Keane, 'Ethnic Cleansing'.
31 United Nations, *Replacement Migration: Is It a Solution to Declining and Ageing Populations?* (New York: United Nations, 2002), https://www.un.org/en/development/desa/population/publications/pdf/ageing/replacement-chap4-jp.pdf) (accessed 29 August 2021).
32 Donald Wood, 'Revisiting Protestant Decline in Southern Ireland, 1911–26', https://podtail.com/en/podcast/southern-irish-loyalism-in-context/episode-10-panel-3a-revisiting-protestant-decline-/ (accessed 29 August 2021); In Wood, *Protestant Population Decline in Southern Ireland*, p. 31 this is changed to 'As Sexton and O'Leary pointed out, the changes that so distorted twentieth-century Protestant demographics did not occur until after 1911' but the note he references presents no evidence before 1911 as Sexton and O'Leary do not examine this; Sexton and O'Leary, *Building Trust in Ireland: Studies Commissioned by the Forum for Peace and Reconciliation* (Belfast, 1996); Bury, *Buried Lives*, p. 19.
33 The birth rate was established by manually counting all children under 1 recorded in the census and dividing this by the total population.
34 Sexton and O'Leary, *Building Peace in Ireland*.
35 See Table 14: Ireland; Census; General Report; 1911: The recorded death-rates for the four provinces are as follows: Connaught, 14.0; Munster, 15.7; Ulster, 16.8; and Leinster; 18.5 per 1,000 of the population: NISRA, https://www.nisra.gov.uk/sites/nisra.gov.uk/files/publications/1911.pdf (accessed 28 August 2021).
36 Wood, *Protestant Population Decline in Southern Ireland*, p. 40; if the differential between birth and death rates remained the same 1,000 people would have reduced to 990 in ten years without any other factor.

37 Child-woman ratio divides the number of children between 0–4 by the number of women of child-bearing age usually 15–49 sometimes 15–44. Wood, *Protestant Population Decline in Southern Ireland*, p. 38 misrepresents my evidence to claim it shows a stable Church of Ireland fertility rate before the revolution but ignores how low it is. This table actually confirms and extends Sexton and O'Leary's analysis of low fertility back to 1901. Methodist fertility was equally low.

38 Kennedy, *The Irish*, Table 40 on P. 117 shows that the Protestant [Church of Ireland, Presbyterian, Methodist & Baptist] CWR in 1926 was 66% of the Catholic one. The 1911 pattern also holds true for 1901.

39 D. Fitzpatrick, 'Protestant Depopulation and the Irish Revolution', *IHS* 38(152) (2013), pp. 643–670; See also Kurt Bowen, *Protestants in a Catholic State: Ireland's Privileged Minority* (Montreal, 1983), pp. 20–40 especially Tables 3 & 4 pp. 28–29.

40 Wood, 'Protestant Decline', p. 34.

41 This follows David Fitzpatrick's methodology. The selected counties represent a good cross-section of the southern counties. Dublin (1901 89, 1911, 81 1926, 67), Kilkenny (106, 95, 95), Carlow (117, 110, 101), Wexford (107, 101, 85), Mayo (132, 103, 85), Sligo (132, 103, 85), Roscommon (126, 105, 87), Meath (103, 92, 84), Westmeath (110, 101, 99), Longford (125, 116, 84), Cork (109, 88, 79) & Kerry (137, 112, 90).

42 A. Fernihough, C. Ó Gráda, and B.M. Walsh, 'Intermarriage in a Divided Society: Ireland a Century Ago', *Explorations in Economic History* 56 (2015), pp. 1–14.

43 This was copper fastened by the *Ne Temere* decree in 1908, which required 'valid' mixed marriages to be conducted by a Catholic priest.

44 R. O'Leary, 'Change in the Rate and Pattern of Religious Intermarriage in the Republic of Ireland', *Economic and Social Review* 30(2) (1999), pp. 119–132; See especially p. 126.

45 *Ne Temere* actually required Roman Catholics be married by a Roman Catholic priest. It makes no mention of children's education. *Exsequendo Nunc* of 1782 stipulated that children of mixed marriages should be raised as Catholics. To marry a Catholic, the local Catholic bishop had to give a dispensation after a written pledge was received from the non-Catholic not to interfere with the raising of the children in the 'true faith'. As this was combined with a 50% conversion rate for the non-Catholic partner until the 1960's this would also have implications for long term denominational survival.

46 Abstracted from the online census and cross-checked, where possible, with marriage certificates at https://www.irishgenealogy.ie/en/ (accessed 12 October 2021). It proved impractical to attempt this analysis for the Church of Ireland.

47 Among 100 English-born (out of 1,044) Catholic fathers, one Baptist wife had Catholic children and one Catholic father had a Church of Ireland family.

48 Abstracted from the 1911 census; M. Maguire, 'A Socio-economic Analysis of the Dublin Protestant Working Class 1870–1926', *Irish Economic and Social History* 20 (1993).

49 This method examines the depletion rate between census intervals for a group of individuals. The usual cohort interval is five years and each group is tracked through the following censes. If the depletion is greater than the expected population loss as a result of deaths then the extra people must have emigrated. See also Sexton and O'Leary, *Building Peace in Ireland*.

50 Data abstracted from 1911 *Census* & Saorstat Éireann, *Census*, 1926, vol. 5, Table 1. The 1901 and 1911 figures were cross-checked against the published versions of the census. The detailed research for females it is not presented as the male charts sufficiently demonstrate the point without increasing clutter.

51 The Church of England is excluded from this figure as, for example, this was a distorting 603% (military) increase for 20–24 years in 1911.

52 For females, the figures are a 15.56% decrease among Church of Ireland and a 93% increase among Church of England.
53 For females, the figures are 35% and 28%.
54 Female 1902 cohort depletion was also 29% while the 1907 cohort was 17%.
55 If the population dynamics of the main minority denominations are mirrored by the small religions then it is reasonable to surmise that these saw similar declines and increases. Whether or which, the minority religions were too tiny to make any significant difference to the overall figures; B. Keane, 'The Church of Ireland Decline in County Cork 1911–1926', *Chimera; The UCC Geographical Society Journal* 2 (1986), pp. 53–59; See also B. Keane, 'The Decline of the Protestant Population in County Cork between 1911 and 1926-abstracts from the 1911 and 1926 census-originally written in 2011', https://sites.google.com/site/protestant-cork191136/ (accessed 29 August 2021).
56 A rare exception is S. Ferran Glenfield, 'The Protestant Population of South-East Leinster, 1834–1981' (M. Litt. thesis, University of Dublin, 1993) & S. Ferran Glenfield, 'Church Going: An Empirical Approach to Nominalism among Anglicans in the Republic of Ireland' (Thesis, University of Warwick, 2015).
57 See B. Keane, 'Peter Hart and Ethnic Cleansing', *History Ireland* 20(3) (2012) for the use of '*exterminate or drive away all Protestants in the area*' by Hart.
58 See also Bielenberg, 'Exodus: The Emigration of Southern Irish Protestants', p. 223.
59 Again in an effort to 'strip out' non-native Protestants only the Church of Ireland is counted, but it holds true for the other Protestant denominations, particularly the Methodists.
60 Ireland, Census 1901 & 1911; Preliminary Report, Table II, Religious Profession by county and sex.
61 In Connacht the Church of England represented a much smaller 6%.
62 Even in the West Cork parliamentary constituency Protestant decline between 1901 & 1911 was 14% while Catholic decrease was 8%. The excess is 6%. In the next fifteen years the excess in the equivalent area was 10%. There is little or no change in the rate.
63 There are, of course minor nuances. Some of the recent body of literature includes P. McGarty, *Leitrim: The Irish Revolution, 1912–1923* (Dublin, 2020). T. Wilson, 'The Strange Death of Loyalist Monaghan, 1912–1921', in S. Pašeta and R.F. Foster (eds.), *Uncertain Futures: Essays about the Irish Past for Roy Foster* (Oxford, 2016); B. Hughes, 'Defying the IRA? Intimidation, Coercion, and Communities during the Irish Revolution' (2017), http://oapen.org/download?type=document&docid=626393m, p. 202; D.P.B. Fitzpatrick, *Politics and Irish Life, 1913–1921: Provincial Experience of War and Revolution* (Cork, 1998); S.M. Carolan, 'Cavan Protestants in an Age of Upheaval, 1919–22' (Thesis submitted to National University of Ireland, Maynooth, 2012), http://eprints.maynoothuniversity.ie/5301/1/Sandra_M_Carolan_20140805110750.pdf (accessed 29 August 2021); Gemma Clark, *Everyday Violence in the Irish Civil War* (Cambridge, 2014) and *Irish Times*, 18 September 2017; Michael Farry, *The Aftermath of Revolution: Sligo 1921–23* (Dublin, 2000); Padraig Deignan, *The Protestant Community in Sligo, 1914–49* (Dublin, 2010). See also J. Regan, '"All the Nightmare Images of Ethnic Conflict in the Twentieth Century Are Here": Erroneous Statistical Proofs and the Search for Ethnic Violence in Revolutionary Ireland, 1917–1923', in *Nations & Nationalism* (Oxford, 2021), pp. 1–19.

11 The Day-to-Day Effects of Partition

Cormac Moore

In June 1947, the *Times Pictorial* supplement of *The Irish Times* featured an article entitled 'One Town – in Two States'. It looked at the town of Pettigo which straddles the border between Donegal in Ireland and Fermanagh in Northern Ireland; and featured many images of how the town was affected by partition. The River Termon that runs through it acts as the boundary line between both jurisdictions. With the creation of the border in 1921, and particularly with the imposition of customs barriers in 1923, the day-to-day effects of partition were keenly felt by residents of the town, residents from both sides of the border. As the *Times Pictorial* article illustrated, cigarettes were cheaper on the Donegal side, whilst sugar was cheaper in Fermanagh. Protestant children from Fermanagh still crossed the river to get to school, while many went the other way at night where closing times in pubs were later. If you wanted to catch a train, which you could do so in Pettigo until 1957, you needed to go to the Donegal side of the town, regardless of which side of the border you lived on.[1] Crossing the border often meant lengthy delays for customs checks on both sides of the border. While people, like those in Pettigo, living directly on the boundary line, experienced the most profound changes to their daily lives with the onset of partition, the division of Ireland impacted on everyone and every organisation on the island.

The partition of Ireland coincided with 'prolonged periods of economic stagnation and decline' for both Irish jurisdictions.[2] During the inter-war period, economic depression prevailed, forcing thousands into unemployment and emigration. Northern Ireland was hard hit by recessions in its traditional industries; shipbuilding, linen and agriculture. For the linen industry, 'this decline was permanent'.[3] There was little effort to co-operate economically with each other during this period. Iterations of Sinn Féin introduced measures that guaranteed a divergence between both jurisdictions on trade, with its Belfast Boycott campaign from 1920 and the Irish Free State's introduction of customs barriers in 1923.

The expulsion of Catholic workers from shipyards and other places of work in the summer of 1920, and the sectarian violence that accompanied it, saw Sinn Féin make one of its first decisions directly relating to the north,

DOI: 10.4324/9781032691886-11

when it started a boycott. Dáil Éireann imposed a boycott 'of goods from Belfast and a withdrawal of funds from Belfast-based banks'.[4] In reality, the boycott soon extended to other businesses and farming and beyond Belfast too. Many saw it as an anti-partitionist move, a way to show that Northern Ireland could not survive without the rest of Ireland.

The boycott involved members of the IRA intercepting and destroying products that originated in the north-east and southern traders were banned from doing business with their northern counterparts. To prevent goods from entering regions, trains were also raided by the IRA. Sinn Féin claimed the boycott was achieving results. Many wholesale firms declared they were badly hit, losing 75 per cent of their trade outside of Ulster. Northern sales-people on the road frequently returned with no orders.[5] Joseph MacDonagh, the boycott director, boasted that 'except in Antrim and Down it was impossible for a Belfast merchant to sell as much as a bootlace in any other part of Ireland'.[6] Ulster traders responded by forming a group, the Ulster Traders' Defence Association, to impose a counter boycott. Ulster people were urged not to buy any southern goods; clothing, meat, butter, biscuits, furniture, stout and whiskey.[7]

With the start of the civil war in the south, the enforcement of the boycott became more uneven and sporadic than it had been before, eventually petering out. It's legacy of driving a psychological wedge between north and south continued far longer. Economically, the boycott had a negative impact on trade in Belfast and other areas in the north of Ireland. In all probability, Belfast trade with the south never recovered to its pre-boycott level, halved by 1924.[8] The boycott also had a negative economic effect on those imposing it, resulting in goods costing more to the consumer and diminished profits for traders.[9] Northern-based banks such as Ulster Bank, Northern Bank and Belfast Bank saw business reduced with deposits down and some sub-branches having to close in the south. The Belfast Bank lost one-fifth of its deposits outside of Northern Ireland and decided to close all its southern branches in 1923.[10] The boycott had minimal impact on its three main industries though; agriculture, shipbuilding, and linen, as they mainly supplied to international markets. Sinn Féin member and Ulster-born Protestant Ernest Blythe claimed the 'boycott would threaten the northern ship-building industry no more than a summer shower would threaten Cave Hill'.[11]

Whilst its economic effects to hamper trade in Belfast met with mixed results, the boycott's aim to unify Ireland was an unmitigated disaster. It resulted in further psychological and physical divisions between north and south, some that had never existed before. Another step by the Irish Free State government in March 1923 had arguably the biggest impact in cementing partition, the imposition of customs duties on imported goods. The creation of a customs barrier was key in translating partition into a reality. It did so in a bid to achieve fiscal independence from Britain and to generate revenue for the exchequer. It was also an attempt to apply economic pressure on the nascent Northern Ireland jurisdiction.[12] In announcing the imposition, the Free State government stated that 'pending a decision as to the future boundary line, a temporary frontier will be placed along the boundary line between the six Northern and twenty-six Southern counties'.[13] The temporary frontier on imported goods lasted for over seventy years, only rescinded due to the introduction of the Single Market throughout the European Union in 1993.

The decision to introduce customs barriers was announced in late February 1923 to be enacted just weeks later, on 1 April, leaving very little time for people and businesses to prepare. The arrangements were agreed between the Free State government and the British government, not the northern administration who had no control over customs and excise. In practical terms, the importing and exporting of merchandise across the border was prohibited except through designated routes and at designated times. Stations were open for the clearance of merchandise between 9am and 5pm daily, except on Sundays.[14] Cross-border roads were designated as 'authorized', 'concession' or 'unauthorized/unapproved'. Many 'unapproved' roads were earmarked for closure. Some roads, using explosives, were 'cratered' and made impassable.[15] Every railway line crossing the border was approved for importation and exportation of merchandise. Although there was free movement of people across the border, those who crossed had their person and personal effects examined to prevent smuggling.[16]

There was widespread disapproval of the decision north and south, particularly from those closest to the border. It was generally felt that the new customs barrier would lead to an increased cost of living for consumers, considerable confusion and lengthy delays in the handling of traffic. The Northern Ireland prime minister James Craig called for the Free State to postpone for all time a customs barrier, claiming,

> Those in the South who proposed to erect that barrier wall, and not the North, would be responsible for partition. There was no such thing as partition if they had not a Customs barrier between the North and the South.[17]

As 1 April drew closer, the physical signs of the new measures began to appear. Declaration forms were issued at railway stations. Proclamations appeared in newspapers, signs and posters displayed in prominent places. Construction began on customs huts and stations along the border, many of them temporary in nature, initially.[18] As well as being April Fool's Day, 1 April 1923 was Easter Sunday, the day the new customs barriers came into operation. Traffic was light, little disruption was caused by the new measures. A man who declared he had nothing to declare in Dundalk was subsequently found to have in his possession a box of one hundred cigarettes. He was duly warned of the grave nature of his offence and told not to do it again. Another merchant caused some amusement when he had to undo a bale of lady's underwear in front of passing onlookers.[19] Once the Easter break was over, the real effects of the customs barrier began to be realised.

The new arrangement led to increased congestion at ports and border controls, with goods awaiting clearance, leading to heavy loses and disruption to businesses. It did result in the closure of some border companies reliant on cross-border trade. The consequences of the new measures were most keenly felt by the border counties, Donegal economically cut-off from Derry, Down from Louth.[20] Although both jurisdictions opted for a relatively open border, with no barbed-wire entanglement to seal the frontier, it severely curtailed the movements of residents along the border. Railway services suffered considerable disruptions with some lines zigzagging the border on numerous occasions, customs examinations expected for each crossing. A train running from Clones to Cavan crossed the border six times in eight miles. Common-sense soon prevailed and it was decided to curb the examinations to just the first point of entry beyond the border.[21]

The trade barriers introduced in 1923 had a negative impact on trade between north and south but less than popular perceptions have contended. Trade had always been more reliant on east-west trade (Britain) rather than north-south trade.[22] Border counties and towns were more effected than others, though. Those counties and towns grew less than they should have historically because of the border.[23] Undoubtedly, the introduction of the customs barrier helped to cement partition. Up to this point, partition was seen by many as just an administrative burden, it hardly impacted on the daily lives of people. The introduction of customs barriers made it tangible, made it real. Movement and trade were now curtailed across the border, impeding long established economic and social ties. It formalised the border, making it easy for the boundary commission to retain the status quo in 1925.

Businesses, trade associations and charities were all impacted by the partition of Ireland. In Cormac Ó Grada and Brendan M. Walsh's study of the economic impact of the border in 2006, 'Did (and Does) the Irish Border Matter?' they claim 'it did, but less than popular perceptions imply'.[24] The largest industry in Ireland, agriculture, had worked effectively under an all-Ireland agriculture department before partition. Even though the department was divided, responsibility for fisheries and the administration of the Diseases of Animals Acts were reserved for the Council of Ireland under the Government of Ireland Act 1920.[25] The department was a particularly complex one, making it extremely difficult to divide. Before partition, the Department of Agriculture and Technical Instruction branches included; Agricultural; Technical Instruction; Statistics and Intelligence; Accounts; Transit and Markets; Veterinary; Fisheries; and Agricultural Wages Board.[26] According to the department, there were examples where 'the staffs are not interchangeable, in some instances consisting of one specialist only'.[27] By and large problems were overcome and both departments, north and south, did learn to cooperate with each other in areas of common interest, such as disease control. In a rare occurrence, both agriculture ministers, Edward Archdale from Northern Ireland and Patrick Horgan from the Free State, met in 1926 to discuss areas of common concern.[28]

A peculiar aspect of partition in Ireland, compared to other divided juris-dictions, is the number of organisations who have chosen to ignore it. Many business, trade and charity groups formed before 1921 remained all-Ireland bodies, including unionist-leaning ones. There was no compunction or obli-gation for most organisations to follow suit once the new international fron-tier was created with the partition of Ireland. With the confusing nature of partition, the uncertainty surrounding its viability, it is little wonder that most bodies remained all-Ireland entities. Retaining all-Ireland structures was also a feature within many sporting bodies, trade unions and religious organisations.[29]

By drawing a line and creating a physical border spanning almost 300 miles, some of the most challenging issues faced by both jurisdictions after partition related to infrastructure and service-based issues. Even after 1925, when many believed the border area was settled, concerns relating to the railway infrastructure, the territorial ownership of bodies of water, and the postal services demonstrated the uncertain and confusing nature of partition. The complexity of the railway infrastructure and ownership within Ireland was compounded dramatically by the creation of a border. Five railway com-panies were directly affected by the new border by serving both sides of it.[30] This was further exacerbated by the Free State's decision to impose a customs barrier in 1923. Both Irish governments agreed in 1924 that the Free State would legislate for railway companies based solely in the Free State territory and the northern government would not look to amalgamate railway compa-nies in Northern Ireland with British ones.[31]

Cross-border cooperation was harder won on the issue of fishing rights on Lough and River Foyle. Disputes over fishing on the Foyle spanned for three decades after partition. The disputes showed the haphazard way in which the border was drawn up. No boundary was delimited at any point for either Lough Foyle or Lough Carlingford.[32] Nobody knew where the border line was on various waterways straddling the border as a result.

The postal services were, like the railways, a reserved service under the Government of Ireland Act 1920. With the Anglo-Irish Treaty overriding the Government of Ireland Act for the twenty-six counties, the Irish Free State took control of its postal services whilst the Imperial parliament in Westminster retained control of the postal services for Northern Ireland. The northern government found it very hard to assert its independence from the rest of Ireland on the issue of postal services. Its dependence on cooperating with the Free State included; residents in border areas in the north being reli-ant on Free State post offices to deliver their mail;[33] sensitive mail for security forces being routed through Free State post offices;[34] and mail from Britain being delivered via the Holyhead-Dún Laoghaire route to different locales in Northern Ireland.[35]

The impact of partition on the infrastructure of the island of Ireland and the services that had served it on an all-Ireland basis beforehand showed the scale of the changes needed to create a border. The confusion and uncertainty that such a cleavage caused was aptly demonstrated by the effects it had on railways, fisheries and postal services. This was further amplified by the different political statuses of both Irish jurisdictions. Customs, practices and services had to be changed overnight to accommodate two political jurisdictions instead of one. In some instances, where economic sense prevailed, as with postal routes and the Erne hydro-electric scheme, it was possible to achieve co-operation between both entities, eventually.[36] In other cases, the psychological partition was too difficult to overcome, with both jurisdictions growing further and further apart from each other.

Arguably, nothing demonstrated the complexity of creating a jurisdiction from scratch, more so than the law. Under the Government of Ireland Act 1920, the judiciary of Ireland was divided into two judiciaries, north and south. There was also a counter system of justice in place, the Republican or Dáil Courts, when Ireland was partitioned. While the Free State was presented with most aspects of a functioning legal system, Northern Ireland was faced with the gargantuan task of creating a whole new justice system for a new entity.

The person chosen to be the first Lord Chief Justice of Northern Ireland was a Catholic, Sir Denis Henry. While Henry was a Catholic, he was not a nationalist, holding a truly unique position by being a Catholic Ulster Unionist MP before he was appointed as Lord Chief Justice.[37] He was faced with the unenviable task of ensuring the judiciary and official appointments as well as a functioning justice system were in place. He also had to secure a building as a courthouse. The government purchased the site of the old potato market, and it was here that the new law courts opened in 1933. For the 12 years before the permanent courthouse was built, it was necessary to use temporary accommodation. The Antrim County Courthouse on the Crumlin Road in Belfast was chosen as the best option available at the time.[38]

The Government of Ireland Act 1920 had practically severed the Bar of Ireland into two bodies but 'all the then existing Members of the Bar had the right of Audience in both areas of Ireland preserved to them'.[39] One of those was Frances Kyle, the first woman to be called to the Irish bar in November 1921. Kyle was immediately followed by Averill Deverell on the same day. Both women made headlines around the world for being the first women to be called to the Bar in Britain or Ireland.[40] That day was also the first call of a divided Irish Bar. Kyle, originally from Belfast, pursued her professional career in Northern Ireland, while Deverell, from Greystones in county Wicklow, pursued her career in the south.[41] Kyle, like all other students from Northern Ireland at the time, still had to study at King's Inns in Dublin to qualify as a barrister. This arrangement continued until 1925. Reconciling two distinct political and judicial entities under the King's Inns umbrella proved difficult and strains started to show. The northern committee of King's Inns was irked that some in the south were exempt from taking examinations for war service, as the war service in question was, 'in some instances, in the forces opposed to the crown'.[42] Those exempted included Kevin O'Higgins, justice minister in the Free State. King's Inns ignored the northern committee's threats to leave and even inflamed the situation by proposing that Irish should be a compulsory language for a call to the Irish bar.[43] The northern bar decided to sever connections and subsequently established an Inns of Court of Northern Ireland, which was inaugurated at the Belfast law courts on 11 January 1926.[44] The main common link between both Irish justice systems was now broken.

The spectre of partition posed vast problems and some opportunities for the Catholic Church and the main Protestant denominations. With the partition of Ireland, the Catholic Church saw itself receiving the best and worst of outcomes with the creation of both jurisdictions. It went on to exert huge control over the Irish Free State on the one hand and became the main voice for the significant but powerless minority in Northern Ireland on the other. There was never a question of the Catholic Church dividing itself along partitionist lines. It remained an all-Ireland body.[45] The Primate of all-Ireland was the Archbishop of Armagh and as a body the whole hierarchy in Ireland met regularly.[46] In fact, of all organisations that were all-Ireland bodies before partition, religious ones had the highest number that remained so after partition.[47]

With the partitioning of Ireland, the three main Protestant churches retained their all-Ireland structures. In 1920, the Primate of the Church of Ireland Charles Frederick D'Arcy emphatically declared that he did not believe that the creation of an administrative boundary would lead to a corresponding division in the church. 'If it did, it would be proof of a very feeble flickering life in the Church'.[48] Even though the majority of Church of Ireland members resided in Northern Ireland, the machinery of the church remained largely based in the south.[49] Due to the major constitutional changes that affected the island of Ireland in the early 1920s, a new legal foundation needed to be created for the Irish Methodist Church to be able to continue as an all-Ireland body. Bills were passed in the Irish Free State and in Northern Ireland in 1928, 'this Methodist Church Act of 1928 was the first instance in which the two parliaments acted identically and simultaneously' allowing the Methodist Church to continue its work throughout the whole island.[50] The one religion in Ireland that saw the greatest institutional changes due to partition was Judaism. It was no longer organised on an all-Ireland basis.[51]

Both Northern Ireland and the Irish Free State were able to show greater scope for separate expressions of how education was to be run in a divided rather than a united country. Such separate expressions were clearly demonstrated in the very different approaches taken on education within both jurisdictions. Whereas Northern Ireland, with Lord Londonderry as Minister of Education, introduced wide-ranging changes that essentially sought to democratise education,[52] the south imposed minimal structural reforms but fundamentally changed the education system in its attempt to Gaelicise

Ireland.[53] The divergence in paths was also clearly illustrated by the obstructionist tactics of the south who refused to recognise the northern jurisdiction, and the failure of both entities to co-operate on areas of common interest such as teacher training and examinations.[54]

The Labour movement was also faced with many challenges when the country was partitioned. The movement included a divergent group of people who had to operate under enormous sectarian and political pressures. Belfast labour candidates who ran as independents in the 1921 election to the Northern Ireland parliament folded their campaign once loyalists prevented them from holding an election rally in the Ulster Hall.[55] The Irish labour movement was not a homogenous group. With many Protestants and Catholics, unionists and nationalists, as well as socialist internationalists, a delicate juggling act was required within the political party and the trade unions after the onset of partition. The labour movement in the north sought to avoid contention and remain united by focusing on labour and trade union issues, on wages and conditions for workers. With 'a mainly Protestant, anti-Unionist leadership and a mainly Protestant, Unionist membership, mutually dependent for their bread and butter, but otherwise at odds, they found themselves walking a tight line between their organisational interests and the politics of their members'.[56] The issues of social reform kept them united. With such divergent views on partition, the topic was avoided as often as possible.

The Irish Trades Union Congress (ITUC) remained an all-Ireland body, primarily because there was no feasible alternative in the north and there was little interest in forming an Ulster Trades Union Congress.[57] William O'Brien, general secretary of the Irish Transport and General Workers Union, emphasised in 1925 'the fact that the working class in Ireland recognises no political or geographical border. Partition prevails almost exclusively in the political sphere'.[58] Recognising that its trade unions and members based in Northern Ireland needed to be treated differently, a Northern Ireland committee of the ITUC was established to speak 'for all trade unions in the north and all trade unionists'.[59] The Labour movement achieved partial union, particularly within trade unionism, by clinging to core interests within the movement and by offering a large degree of autonomy to northern labour activists. The political partition of the island posed problems for all sporting bodies in Ireland too.

The border forced all sports to look at their internal governance structures. Unlike in soccer and athletics and cycling, most Irish governing bodies managed to maintain unity through considerable compromise as issues of political symbolism were tailored to accommodate diverse political and cultural interests.[60] There was a readiness from many sporting bodies to incorporate inoffensive and neutral flags, anthems and emblems such as the four provinces flag, to maintain unity. Great efforts were also made to democratise the internal governance structures of those sports. Most sports that remained united also did not have the identity issues faced by sports like soccer.[61] Sports such as rugby, hockey, cricket, tennis and bowls were primarily the preserve of Protestants from the upper classes of society. The GAA as a pan-nationalist association dominated by Catholics, did little to encourage Protestant and unionist membership. Soccer, like athletics and cycling, had to cater for different religions and classes which contributed to divisions within those sports.

This chapter argues that matters of state policy impacted on people and the organisations they were involved in. There was a lot more complexity, ambiguity and flexibility during this period than simplistic narratives of the past recall. By focusing on the 'lived experience' of people and organisations at the time, one can see that the political and legal partition of Ireland was not followed by a social and cultural partition.[62] Given the piecemeal and haphazard implementation of partition, it was only natural that there would be 'a myriad of reactions, counter-reactions, and interactions' from people and organisations.[63] Generally, the northern government gave no clear political direction on what path organisations themselves should take once Ireland was partitioned. Although the northern government sought as little cooperation with the Irish Free State as possible, an anomalous position existed whereby unionist politicians such as Thomas Moles and John Andrews sought as much divergence politically between the north and the south on the one hand, and actively sought unity in sport on the other. Overall, organisations in Ireland were not subsumed by the 'iron grip of the nation state' and generally chose to pursue their own path in the interests of their members, in pursuit of their own local interests.[64]

Notes

1 *Irish Times Pictorial*, 7 June 1947, pp. 1 and 16.
2 Robert Lynch, *The Partition of Ireland 1918–1925* (Cambridge, 2019), p. 125.
3 David S. Johnson, 'The Economic History of Ireland between the Wars', *Irish Economic and Social History* 1 (1974), p. 58.
4 Terence A.M. Dooley, 'From the Belfast Boycott to the Boundary Commission: Fears and Hopes in County Monaghan, 1920–26', *Clogher Record* 15 (1994), p. 90.
5 *Freemans Journal*, 1 February 1921, p. 3.
6 David S. Johnson, 'The Belfast Boycott, 1920–1922', in J.M. Goldstrom and L.A. Clarkson (eds.), *Irish Population, Economy, and Society: Essays in Honour of the Late K.H. Connell* (Oxford, 1981), p. 293.
7 Belfast: PRONI: COM/62/2/7: 'Boycott – Ulster Traders Defence Association, correspondence and notices concerning the boycott of Northern Ireland goods – 1922', May 1922.
8 Johnson, 'The Belfast Boycott', p. 306.
9 Belfast: PRONI: D1022/2/8: 'Trade Boycott', including memorandum by Clark and a copy of a Sinn Fein decree, 14 November 1921.
10 Johnson, 'The Belfast Boycott', pp. 298 and 299.
11 Dublin: UCD Archives: Ernest Blythe Papers: P24/70: 'Policy in Regard to the North-East', 9 August 1922.

12 Belfast: PRONI: D921/4/5/1: 'Newspaper Clippings and Printed Booklets – IF "ULSTER" CONTRACTS OUT: The Economic Case against Partition', Undated.
13 Donal Hall, 'Partition and County Louth', *Journal of the County Louth Archaeological and Historically Society* 27 (2010), p. 262.
14 London: The National Archives of the U.K. (hereafter TNA): HO 267/49: 'Customs & Excise', March 1923.
15 Peter Leary, 'A House Divided: the Murrays of the Border and the Rise and Decline of a Small Irish House', *History Workshop Journal* 86 (July 2018), p. 280.
16 London: TNA: HO 267/49: 'Customs & Excise', March 1923.
17 The *Times*, 3 March 1923, p. 12.
18 See, for example, *Irish Times*, 28 March 1923, p. 5.
19 *Irish Times*, 2 April 1923, p. 5.
20 The *Times*, 13 September 1923, p. 11.
21 Catherine Nash, Bryonie Reid and Brian Graham, *Partitioned Lives: The Irish Borderlands* (Surrey, 2013), p. 32.
22 Cormac O. Grada and Brendan M. Walsh, 'Did (and Does) the Irish Border Matter?', Institute for British-Irish Studies (Working Paper No. 60, 2006), p. 24.
23 Grada and Walsh, 'Did (and Does) the Irish Border Matter?', p. 22.
24 Grada and Walsh, 'Did (and Does) the Irish Border Matter?', p. 24.
25 Mary E. Daly, *The First Department: A History of the Department of Agriculture* (Dublin, 2002), p. 95.
26 Belfast: PRONI: AUS/2/18: 'Copies of Reports to Dublin Castle by Departments in response to circular regarding administrative changes necessitated by Government of Ireland Act 1920: Department of Agriculture and Technical Instruction for Ireland 1921', 20 and 26 January 1921.
27 Belfast: PRONI: AUS/2/18: 'Copies of Reports to Dublin Castle by Departments in response to circular regarding administrative changes necessitated by Government of Ireland Act 1920: Department of Agriculture and Technical Instruction for Ireland 1921', 20 and 26 January 1921.
28 *Irish Times*, 22 January 1926, p. 7.
29 See Cormac Moore, *Birth of the Border* (Kildare, 2019) for details on how groups reacted to the partition of Ireland.
30 Michael H.C. Baker, *Irish Railways since 1916* (London, 1972), p. 35.
31 London: TNA: HO 267/16: 'Imperial Secretary's Department Northern Ireland – Railways, Northern Ireland – Rail Merger Plan Between Great Britain, Northern Ireland and the Irish Free State', 1 August 1923; *Ulster Herald*, 12 January 1924, p. 5.
32 Kieran Rankin, 'The Creation and Consolidation of the Irish Border', Institute for British-Irish Studies (Working Paper No. 48, 2005), p. 25.
33 Belfast: PRONI: COM/21/21: 'Partition: Representations Calling for the Establishment of a new Post Office on the Northern Ireland side of the Border at Belcoo, Co. Fermanagh', 1922–1924.
34 Belfast: PRONI: COM/21/28: 'Partition: Request from the Inspector General of the RUC that Mail Directed to the Ulster Special Constabulary stationed at Urney, Co. Tyrone Should not be Delivered via Clady Railway Station in the Irish Free State', 1923–1924.
35 See Claire Fitzpatrick, 'Partition, Postal Services and Ulster unionist Politics 1921–27', *International Journal of Regional and Local History* 11 (2016), pp. 31–50.
36 For an analysis of the Erne hydro-electric scheme, see Michael Kennedy, 'The Realms of Practical Politics: North-South Co-operation on the Erne Hydro-Electric Scheme, 1942–57', Institute for British-Irish Studies (Working Paper 25, 2006).

37 Éamon Phoenix, 'Catholic Unionism: A Case Study: Sir Denis Stanislaus Henry (1864–1925)', in Oliver P. Rafferty (ed.), *Irish Catholic Identities* (Manchester, 2013), p. 292.

38 Lord Carswell, 'Founding a Legal System: The Early Judiciary of Northern Ireland', in Felix M. Larkin and Norma M. Dawson (eds.), *Lawyers, the Law and History: Irish Legal History Society Discourses and Other Papers, 2005–2011* (Dublin, 2013), p. 19.

39 George H. Smith, *Sketch of The Supreme Court of Judicature of Northern Ireland: From Its Establishment under the Imperial Act of 1920 down to the Present Time* (Belfast, 1926), p. 46.

40 *Cork Examiner*, 2 November 1921, p. 8.

41 W.N. Osborough, 'Landmarks in the History of King's Inns', in Kenneth Ferguson (ed.), *King's Inn Barristers 1868–2004* (Dublin, 2005), p. 31.

42 Anthony R. Hart, 'King's Inns and the Foundation of the Inn of Court of Northern Ireland: The Northern Perspective', in Larkin and Dawson (eds.), *Lawyers, the Law and History*, p. 201.

43 Smith, *Sketch of The Supreme Court of Judicature of Northern Ireland*, p. 56.

44 Osborough, 'Landmarks in the History of King's Inns', p. 32.

45 Oliver Rafferty, 'The Catholic Church and Partition, 1918–22', *Irish Studies Review* 5 (2007), p. 16.

46 Mary Harris, *The Catholic Church and the Foundation of the Irish State* (Cork, 1993), p. 6.

47 John Whyte, 'The Permeability of the United Kingdom – Irish Border: A Preliminary Reconnaissance', *Administration* 31 (1983), p. 300.

48 *Church of Ireland Gazette*, 2 July 1920, p. 422.

49 Robert B. McDowell, *The Church of Ireland 1869–1969* (London, 1975), p. 111.

50 R. Lee Cole, *History of Methodism in Ireland* (Belfast, 1960), p. 114.

51 Dermot Keogh, *Jews in Twentieth-Century Ireland: Refugees, Anti-Semitism and the Holocaust* (Cork, 1998).

52 Neil C. Fleming, 'Lord Londonderry & Education Reform in 1920s Northern Ireland', *History Ireland* 9(1) (Spring 2001), pp. 36–39.

53 Gearóid Ó Tuathaigh, 'The Irish State and Language Policy', *Fortnight* No. 316, Supplement: The Future of Irish (April 1993), p. 4.

54 Moore, *Birth of the Border*, pp. 173–176.

55 Emmet O'Connor, *A Labour History of Ireland 1824–2000* (Dublin, 2011), p. 93.

56 O'Connor, *A Labour History of Ireland 1824–2000*, p. 188.

57 Charles McCarthy, *Trade Unions in Ireland 1894–1960* (Dublin, 1977), p. 316.

58 *Fermanagh Herald*, 8 August 1925, p. 3.

59 McCarthy, *Trade Unions in Ireland*, p. 314.

60 Moore, *Birth of the Border*, pp. 210–228.

61 Cormac Moore, *The Irish Soccer Split* (Cork, 2015).

62 Peter Leary, *Unapproved Routes: Histories of the Irish Border, 1922–1972* (Oxford, 2016), p. 27.

63 Paul Readman, Cynthia Radding, and Chad Bryant, 'Introduction: Borderlands in a Global Perspective', in Paul Readman, Cynthia Radding, and Chad Bryant (eds.), *Borderlands in World History, 1700–1914* (Hampshire, 2014), p. 3.

64 Readman, Radding, and Bryant, 'Introduction: Borderlands in a Global Perspective', p. 12.

12 Within an Imaginary Border

The 'Protestant Free State' in Independent Ireland

Ian d'Alton

The Northern Ireland 1998 Good Friday Agreement was predicated upon the idea that political and cultural allegiances could be largely self-determined. That concept was not new. Rebecca Bennette argues that German Catholics – following unification in 1871 – responded to Bismarck's *Kulturkampf* by asserting an idea of a distinctive national singularity that ran side-by-side with the 'official' version.[1] French Protestantism exhibited – and still exhibits – similar characteristics.[2] After the Great War fractured the empires within which peoplehoods often co-existed, the new smaller states found that they were faced with the same issues.[3] This was an age of myriad stockaded communities. One such was that of the southern Irish unionists. Deprived of a political raison d'etre after Irish independence, they used their tribal connectivity, mainly denominational, to conjure up a version of the new Irish Free State that provided comfort, continuity and a concordance with their sense of identity. In parallel to the official one, it was in many respects an amalgam of Britain and Ireland, a sort of 'Brireland' – a 'Protestant Free State'. This chapter examines its characteristics and argues that, in contrast to a representation of southern loyalism as rootless and disaggregated, it was a significant important and positive element in ushering southern Protestantism relatively safely through the thickets of the 'Catholic State'.

In 1911, Protestants numbered about 311,000 in the area that was to become the Irish Free State.[4] Overwhelmingly Anglican [Church of Ireland], their spread throughout the general population was uneven, with a proportion of 21 percent in Dublin but only 4 percent in the west.[5] Dublin and Cork cities possessed not only substantial professional and entrepreneurial classes but also a Protestant working-class, most evident in the capital.[6] Prosperous farmers, shopkeepers and small businessmen formed a significant component of the Protestant community.[7] A busy if narrow intelligentsia was centred in the Church of Ireland and Trinity College. The ghosts of the Anglo-Irish gentry hovered over all – a minor proportion of the Protestant population, but still contributing a large part of the noise, especially through the medium of memoir and fiction.

DOI: 10.4324/9781032691886-12

This peoplehood formed a socio-economic elite. In 1926, accounting for only 7 percent of the population, it had well over 50 percent of the bankers, 40 percent of the lawyers and 20 percent of the doctors.[8] Around a fifth of managerial positions and large farms were still in Protestant hands.[9] Shops, firms and professional people in the smaller towns were economically significant in the lives of their local areas.[10] In contrast, Protestants accounted for only 3 percent of agricultural labourers – their voices, and those of other poorer Protestants, only occasionally break the cover of non-elite silence.[11]

What apparently happened to Protestant demography in the revolutionary period was a constant background hum to notions of contemporary identity and community trajectory. Voluntary and involuntary migration; the departures of military families, civil servants and police after 1922; some small Great War casualties; and the ongoing secular effects of mixed marriages, late marriage and small families all played a part in the decline in numbers by a third between the censuses of 1911 and 1926.[12] A lively historical debate has largely revolved around the extent to which Protestants were driven out in the revolutionary period, complicated by the essential unknowingness of the personal and familial impetuses for migration.[13] The different experiences of the Protestant communities in north and south were particularly marked.[14] In Northern Ireland, the overall Protestant population increased both in absolute and relative terms – 'for while antagonistic forces have driven many of our people out of Southern Ireland, we are holding our own in the north' as the archbishop of Armagh expressed it.[15] The apocalyptic vision of two demographers (*c.* 1946) saw the Church of Ireland 'becoming a Church of the North with a Southern appendix' and that 'the awareness of all Ireland as its environment and the consciousness of the Anglo-Irish cultural tradition might weaken it almost to the point of extinction'.[16]

All this was unsettling. Around and after the revolution, it seemed that many southern Protestants did not now know what they were; or, indeed, what others expected them to be. In contrarian Protestant essayist Hubert Butler's formulation, they were 'nobody's children'.[17] For Irish Protestants, their place in the new state was essentially determined by the majority's indulgence which could not always be taken for granted, exemplified by the *Leader* newspaper in April 1944 querulously complaining that 'Protestants cannot understand that this is a Catholic country'.[18]

But religious beliefs aside, the new regime was not entirely uncongenial. In significant respects, this innately conservative and relatively prosperous people found it not too difficult to go with the Irish Free State's flow.[19] For tax-paying Protestants, the state turned out to be fiscally orthodox. Protectionism suited its family businesses. Its cultural conservatism chimed with those who didn't necessarily want to divorce, limit their family's size by artificial means or expose their servants to licentious literature. Like many Catholics, Protestants were condemnatory of socialism and suspicious of statism – one instance was the *Church of Ireland Gazette*'s characterisation of the 1951 mother-and-child scheme as 'communist interference in the family'.[20] Controversialists like poet W.B. Yeats, Robert Smyllie, editor of *The Irish Times*, and essayist Hubert Butler were often dangerously ahead of those they claimed to represent.[21]

Above all, in the light of their experiences during the War of Independence and the Civil War, Protestants appreciated the state as a guarantor of law and order.[22] In 1924, the provost of Trinity College expressed himself well pleased with the Free State government; in 1936 *The Irish Times* was moved to write that 'On many points of policy we agree, more or less cordially, with Mr de Valera'.[23] On the surface at any rate, Protestants accepted the new dispensation. Almost before the ink had dried on the Treaty a Dublin cleric asserted that 'we must be loyal as a matter of principle'.[24] The Presbyterians too acquiesced in the new state – albeit on the basis that 'liberty and honesty and good-will rule'.[25] The extent to which all this exhortatory carefulness reflected what was really boiling in the breasts of the ex-southern unionists is open to question. It might have been more a matter of prudence, of safeguarding their privileges, than any heartfelt Damascene conversion.[26]

Thus, an elaborate choreography found Protestants avoiding confrontation, while official Ireland did not want to drive a relatively well-educated and prosperous community away, taking its talents and its money with it and giving priceless ammunition to 'I-told-you-so' Northern Ireland unionists. It helped that Irish society was quite homogenous, with few ethnic or linguistic barriers. Contracting out of the state apparatus entirely – as Estonia allowed its minority German population to do in the field of education in the early 1920s – was never really a serious option.[27] A defined political Protestantism only manifested itself in the border counties of Donegal, Cavan and Monaghan in the inter-war years – and even there, superglued to the rest of Ulster by the Orange Order, it was principally about the social psychology of a huddled community tantalisingly outside the glow.[28]

But if they did want to engage, where, and how, were the limits set? When Dublin Castle was handed over to the Provisional Government in January 1922 the *Church of Ireland Gazette* urged Protestants to realise 'no less than by the majority, that they are an integral part of the State'.[29] In 1933, one cleric remarked of the Church of Ireland that 'her sons and daughters have taken part in everything that concerns the welfare of the country, and their only wish has been that a larger share should come into their hands'.[30] The problem with *that* was it suggested participation in the same Ireland that Catholics inhabited; Protestant gain might come at the expense of Catholic loss. It also carried the rather patronising implication that Protestants could run Ireland better. In her private correspondence, writer Edith Somerville certainly thought so; in 1920 her fictional landlord Dan Palliser wondered about his fellow rural district councillors: 'How, with materials such as these, was he, or anyone else, to build Jerusalem in Ireland's green and pleasant land?'[31] And while many individual Protestants[32] worked on in the new administration, the *Gazette*'s call in late December 1921 for southern loyalists to be brought more generally into the provisional government – on the grounds that they were patriotic and it could do with their business and financial expertise – was not taken up.[33]

An identity set solely by reference to the official Irish Free State carried with it the unacceptable odour of a specifically Catholic nationalism. The challenge posed by this was articulated by Kate Alcock, the fictional feisty Protestant heroine in Lennox Robinson's 1926 play *The Big House*: 'Ireland is not more theirs than ours . . . we've spent so much time sympathetically seeing theirs that we've lost sight of our own'.[34] Catholic transcendental nationalism, whether through ignorance or design, found it difficult to comprehend an Irishness that involved notions of cultural Britishness, but a strong spatial identity with their particular part of the island; political wariness, but active economic engagement; a sense of moral individualism but a tribal religiosity; and a utilitarian approach to patriotism.[35] So: the question was, how could *their* Free State be *our* Free State as well?

The hidden empathy that southern Protestantism had with certain aspects of the official polity offers one answer. Colin Reid has a striking phrase about the Protestant nationalist Stephen Gwynn, in that he was '. . . dominated by . . . pursuit of an imagined Ireland'.[36] Borrowing this then, one way the minority could come to terms with the contemporary was to conceptualise a more congenial Ireland, a 'Protestant Free State', an alternative universe side-by-side with the Catholic one. This would not be a west Britain, nor a nostalgic never-was Ireland constructed by the Anglo-Irish writers. It was a parallel entity that worked in the contemporary, minimising points of contact with the world that, in novelist Elizabeth Bowen's words, 'lay alongside ours but never touched'[37] but which *could* touch it, and take from it, whenever necessary or desirable.

This Protestant Free State requires careful examination to find evidence of its existence; clues are often minute and fleeting. Take the Irish Senate, for instance. One of its original purposes was to provide a voice for the Protestant minority, which it did – but Protestant senators are occasionally found in effect having private debates amongst themselves about their Ireland – one particular example was on the outbreak of war in September 1939, between Protestant senators (most supported neutrality, but one wanted Ireland to declare itself on the Allied side).[38]

The basic premises underpinning the Protestant Free State were constitutional, social, patriotic, moral and imperial. The principal constitutional pillar on which it rested was the Irish Free State as a Dominion, an Irish constitutional monarchy, a symbolic continuum from the previous regime. As the 1922 constitution put it, 'A Legislature is hereby created, to be known as the Oireachtas. It shall consist of the King and two Houses'.[39] This was *the* vital bridge between old and new. That constitution enabled Protestants to engage in the comforting fiction that they were still living some sort of twilight British royalist world. Curtseying to Tim Healy as Governor-General was not quite the same as to the countess of Aberdeen, but it was better than to nobody.[40]

The Free State passport had a 6-penny consular stamp in Irish, but it was still His Britannic Majesty that requested that the bearer pass freely.

Spontaneous renderings of *God Save the King* at the Armistice Day remembrances in the Phoenix Park in 1931 and 1950 were rare public manifestations of loyalty usually kept close to the chest.[41] If public royalism had to keep its head down, it could demonstrate a louder voice in Protestant privacy, as in 1935 on the silver jubilee of King George V, when Bishop Godfrey Day of Ossory ordered special services to be held in his churches; and Sir Jack Leslie – still describing himself as Lord Lieutenant of Monaghan – organised a loyal address from the Protestants of the county.[42]

The declaration of the republic in 1948 tested this Protestant view of itself. On the coming into force of the Republic of Ireland Act, the *Church of Ireland Gazette* contented itself with a rather sour reference to Bishop Kerr's polemical book *The Independence of the Celtic Church in Ireland*, noting the Papal Bulls that had 'energetically' ceded Ireland to Norman kings.[43] *The Irish Times* was angry and sad; but it encouraged its Protestant readership to be 'unconditionally loyal' to the new republic.[44] Crystallised in the Church of Ireland having to decide on what to do about prayers for the King in its services, there was a rearguard action against change. Anglicanism is rather good at muddling through and the Church more or less slipped into praying for 'our Rulers' rather than the King.[45] But 1949 did not herald a clean break. Thus, King George VI's death in 1952 was marked by services in Cashel Cathedral and St Finn Barre's Cork, while Limerick Mothers' Union said prayers.[46] As Nora Robertson put it in 1960, 'In respecting new loyalties it had not seemed incumbent upon us to throw our old ones overboard'.[47]

Symbols came to bear an inordinate importance. The availability of appeals to the Privy Council, Irish representative peers in the House of Lords, and the investiture of the Prince of Wales and the royal dukes of Gloucester and York as Knights of St Patrick in 1927, 1934 and 1936 respectively had little practical significance; but they mattered.[48] The urban architecture was still reassuringly Protestant. Even many post boxes, although now painted green again, still had their royal ciphers.[49] Dublin continued, pro-rata, to have nearly twice as many streets called after Queen Victoria as had London.[50] Even as stamps and coins – Yeats's 'silent ambassadors of national taste' – were issued by the Free State in 1928, a substantial amount of British currency still circulated.[51] In the coded freemasonry of Protestant conversation *Dún Laoghaire* was still Kingstown, *Cobh* Queenstown, O'Connell Street Sackville Street and *Port Laoise* Maryborough. Clubs and professional bodies still had royal prefixes. Flying the Union Flag – as Trinity College continued to do until at least 1939 – may have been provocative, but it was not illegitimate.[52]

The self-contained nature of superior Protestant social and economic corporatism allowed the delusion to foster that there *was* a Protestant State. 'Expert at keeping themselves warm in cold houses',[53] Protestantism to an extent became an internal diaspora, a manifestation of Neal Ascherson's 'inner emigration'.[54] It withdrew into self-imposed apartheid and economic, social and spatial ghettos,[55] driven by class considerations and the *Ne temere* decree, writing letters to themselves in the *Times* and the *Church of Ireland Gazette*. Sectarian job advertising kept Catholic and Protestant economic and social systems apart right up to the 1970s – a Church of Ireland employment bureau was in operation after 1925, and in 1944, the Dawson Employment Bureau for 'employers and unemployed members of the Church of Ireland' was advertised in the *Gazette*.[56] Operating a Lilliputian *civitas*, synods and parish vestries aped parliamentary and local government. Wider public service could be undertaken in the governance of denominational hospitals, schools and a university. The mortal danger represented by mixed marriages was countered by an extensive Protestant network of church 'socials' and dances, further underpinned by a cat's-cradle of church and charitable bodies to create coherence, place and a sense of civic society.[57] The structure was economically underpinned by Protestant firms and farms. In all this, it was quite possible to live a Protestant life and die a Protestant death without much troubling the other side. This suited the other side, too – segregation was actively encouraged by the Catholic church. Protestants could have *their* Free State if they wanted, where they could be identified, contained and corralled.

Protestant Free State patriotism manifested itself in an attachment to 'home' rather than nation – 'the physical precincts were . . . central to identity'.[58] The Irish gentry were exemplars of this attitude, increasingly 'turned to geography in the attempt at patriotization'.[59] Passionate attachment to their 'Big Houses' is seen in Lady Gregory's devotion to Coole, Edith Somerville's embrace of Drishane and Elizabeth Bowen's desperate quest to keep Bowen's Court going in the 1950s. And in fiction, too: Kate Alcock defines *her* allegiance as 'I believe in Ballydonal, it's my life, it's my faith, it's my country'.[60]

The Protestant Free State increasingly represented itself as possessing a true, independent Irishness with moral purity and exemplary behaviour, floating above and outside temporal trivialities and constitutional conundrums. As the *Gazette* wrote in 1922:[61]

> Our conception of national freedom is not a thing of oaths or formulae. It is a state of mind in which every citizen, being himself free to hold whatever opinions his conscience may dictate to him, grants the same rights to his neighbours of all classes and all creeds.

Archbishop Gregg's words in 1932 reflected that in the ecclesiastical sphere:

> Today the Church of Ireland turns neither to Windsor nor to Rome for the appointment of its bishops . . . It is an Irish, self-governing organization, as free from the interference of Britain or of the Vatican as the Celtic Church in the days of Columba.[62]

This 'Irishness' had a moral rather than a political or national vision; Anglicans were to 'serve the highest interests of the nation, and . . . uplift its standards of character and conduct'.[63] It could be gentle; the vision of the bishop of Limerick in 1944 was of Protestantism as precept – 'To set our own house in order, to live hopefully in it in neighbourly fashion, to express a method of living valuable to the State'.[64] It could be angry and smug, a holding of the lesser nation to account; Gregg's novelist daughter puts vicious words into a fictional Protestant heroine quarrelling with a Catholic republican in the 1930s, where the lady savagely suggests that 'you need people like us to keep you sane'.[65]

This conception of Protestantism as a moral power had obvious attractions for a community bereft of the political variety. It also spoke to the evangelical and missionary streak in Irish Protestantism. Darting out now and again from the circled wagons, the nation could be snatched back to righteousness. On the ground, this manifested in such as a strong opposition to gambling, for instance. The Catholic Free State had no particular problem, somewhat borne out by the fact that the Irish Hospitals Sweepstake (established in 1930) was the first in 150 pages of advertisements in Saorstát Éireann's 1932 *Official Handbook*. Protestant hospitals were reluctant to take the Devil's money; and on one occasion, the Church of Ireland Board of Education even protested to the Irish Department of Education about examination questions that included calculating odds.[66]

Finally, mirroring that of the official one, the Protestant Free State had an outward-looking perspective. Riding on the back of a 'global citizenship' provided by Ireland's association with the Empire was another way to bypass the new dispensation. Facilitated by an open travel area with Britain and a shared cultural heritage Protestants could still move back and forth on the hyphen between Anglo and Irish, serving in the British military and the wider Imperial service. Gaelicisation was seen as the principal threat to this form of global citizenship – if successful, wrote one cleric, 'it means . . . goodbye to the modern world'.[67] But Protestant reactions to the language issue were complex and often contradictory. What exercised them was utility and compulsion, not enmity to the language per se – at a Church of Ireland Dublin conference to mark the 1500th anniversary of St Patrick's reputed landing in Ireland a session was wholly in Irish – 'very well attended, especially by young people', and printed in the official report.[68]

That conference did not exhibit a Protestant sullen nostalgia for things past. Ways were looked for to connect to the contemporary. The 'Protestant Patrician state', an enthusiasm fuelled by a desire to counter celebrations of the Eucharistic Congress, emphasised the Church's place in the new Ireland. With dubious ecclesiastical history (later comprehensively debunked), the Church of Ireland asserted its pre-Reformation credentials, retrofitting St Patrick into Irish history as a sort of proto-Protestant. Skipping over the inconveniences of plantations and penal laws, Archbishop Gregg could claim implausibly but sincerely that the Church of Ireland was 'the most Irish thing there is in Ireland'.[69] Here, in contrast to what the literary record might indicate, is a dynamic identity, a 'meme', a form of cultural evolution that sees ideas behave in much the same way as mutating genes.[70] In Joe Ruane's and David Butler's phrase about southern Protestants, 'the uncertainty and complexity of their status may itself shape that experience'.[71] It did.

The minority had no future as 'ex-unionists' with nowhere to look but in the rear mirror. But as 'Protestants' they could chart the road ahead. A generational change facilitated this. From independence, Protestants developed a believable contemporary reality for themselves, based on a defined ethnicity and sense of purpose.[72] In terms of southern Protestants' developing sense of identity, this held considerable significance since it was one which was referenced to themselves – they had ownership of it. That ethnicity – manifested in the Protestant Free State – subsides gradually like a slow puncture through to the 1960s when the Other became less alien and 'Catholics became Protestants', as Roy Foster has economically, if rather provocatively, put it.[73] From the mid-sixties, too, there's an increasing sense of the primacy of the secular in society, as the imagined Protestant Free State – a comfort in harder times – slowly conflates with the Catholic one, and the 'border' between the Catholic and Protestant versions of the State gradually disappears. Whilst not exhibiting the heroic view and knowledge of their history that, for instance, French Protestants had (and this may have been to their advantage),[74] southern Irish Protestants lived an internally legitimate and mainly positive story in independent Ireland. If we seek an explanation of why, in essence, the southern Irish Protestant journey was able to take place with relatively little trauma and dislocation when compared with the fate of other dominant minorities in Europe – and, indeed, with that other politico-religious minority on this island, the Northern Catholics – this is one explanation of how it happened. If being politically British was no longer possible, and the Irish Catholic Free State was uncongenial for cultural, class and sectarian reasons, then the only option left if Protestants wanted to stay in their homeland (and, like Catholics, most did) was a liveable-in *Protestant* Free State. And if it facilitated the strange, but relatively calm, death of unionist Ireland, that was all to the good.

Notes

1 O. Heilbronner, 'From Ghetto to Ghetto: The Place of German Catholic Society in Recent Historiography', *Journal of Modern History* 72(2) (2000), pp. 464–465; R. Bennette, *Fighting for the Soul of Germany: The Catholic Struggle for Inclusion after Unification* (Cambridge, MA, 2012), pp. 187–194.

2 J. Ruane, 'Majority-minority Conflicts and Their Resolution: Protestant Minorities in France and in Ireland', *Nationalism and Ethnic Politics* 12(3–4) (2006), pp. 509–532; J. Ruane, 'Ethnicity, Religion and Peoplehood: Protestants in France and in Ireland', *Ethnopolitics* 9(1) (2010), pp. 121–135.

3 See J. Coakley, 'Independence Movements and National Minorities: Some Parallels in the European Experience', *European Journal of Political Research* 8(2) (1980), pp. 215–247; T. Wilson, 'Ghost Provinces, Mislaid Minorities: The Experience of Southern Ireland and Prussian Poland Compared, 1918–23', *Irish Studies in International Affairs* 13 (2002), pp. 61–86; T. Wilson, *Frontiers of Violence: Conflict and Identity in Ulster and Upper Silesia, 1918–1922* (Oxford, 2010).

4 Irish 'Protestants' are generally defined as including members of the Church of Ireland [Anglicans], Methodists, Presbyterians, and some minor Christian denominations. Anglicans comprised about 80% of the Free State Protestant population, compared to less than 50% in Northern Ireland.

5 R.B. McDowell, *Crisis and Decline: The Fate of the Southern Unionists* (Dublin, 1997), p. 4.

6 M. Maguire, 'The Dublin Protestant Working Class, 1870–1932: Economy, Society, Politics' (Unpublished MA thesis, University College Dublin, 1990); M. Maguire, 'The Organisation and Activism of Dublin's Protestant Working Class, 1883–1935', *IHS* 29(113) (May 1994), pp. 65–87.

7 M. Maguire, 'The Church of Ireland and the Problem of the Protestant Working-class of Dublin, 1870s–1930s', in A. Ford, J. McGuire, and K. Milne (eds.), *As by Law Established: The Church of Ireland since the Reformation* (Dublin, 1995), p. 202; Saorstát Éireann, *Census of Population, 1926*, X, *General Report* (Dublin, 1934) (P. 1242), pp. 49–50.

8 McDowell, *Crisis and Decline*, p. 5; Saorstát Éireann, *Census of Population, 1926*, X, *General Report,* pp. 54–55.

9 Saorstát Éireann, *Census of Population, 1926*, X, *General Report,* pp. 50–52; R.B. McDowell, *The Church of Ireland, 1869–1969* (London, 1975), pp. 121–122.

10 K. Bowen, *Protestants in a Catholic State: Ireland's Privileged Minority* (Montreal, 1983), pp. 83–87.

11 H. Crawford, *Outside the Glow: Protestants and Irishness in Independent Ireland* (Dublin, 2010); D. Nuttall, *Different and the Same: A Folk History of the Protestants of Independent Ireland* (Dublin, 2020).

12 Saorstát Éireann, *Census of Population, 1926*, X, *General Report,* pp. 46–47.

13 For representative discussions of population trends between 1911 and 1926 see McDowell, *Church of Ireland*, pp. 119–123; A. Bielenberg, 'Exodus: The Emigration of Southern Irish Protestants during the Irish War of Independence and the Civil War', *Past and Present* 218 (February 2013), pp. 223, 230–231; D. Fitzpatrick, 'Protestant Depopulation and the Irish Revolution', *IHS* 38(152) (2013), pp. 643–670; D. Wood, 'Protestant Population Decline in Southern Ireland, 1911–26', in B. Hughes and C. Morrissey (eds.), *Southern Irish Loyalism, 1912–1949* (Liverpool, 2020), pp. 27–48.

14 C.F. D'Arcy, *The Adventures of a Bishop. A Phase of Irish Life: A Personal and Historical Narrative* (London, 1934), p. 245. It was specifically noted by the bishop of Killaloe as late as 1932 – '. . . perils which peculiarly beset us outside Ulster, of reduced and reducing numbers . . .' – W. Bell and N. Emerson (eds.), *The Church of Ireland A.D. 432–1932. The Report of the Church of Ireland Conference held in Dublin, 11th-14th October, 1932, to which is Appended an Account of the Commemoration by the Church of Ireland of the 1500ᵗʰ Anniversary of the Landing of St. Patrick in Ireland* (Dublin, 1932), p. 14. [Hereafter *The Church of Ireland A.D. 432–1932*].

15 Government of Northern Ireland, *Census of Population of Northern Ireland 1926. General Report* (Belfast, 1929), li, table xxviii; D'Arcy, *The Adventures of a Bishop*, p. 245.

16 R. McDermott and D. Webb, *Irish Protestantism Today and Tomorrow. A Demographic Study* (Dublin, n.d.), p. 23.

17 H. Butler, *Escape from the Anthill* (Mullingar, 1985), p. 148.

18 *Leader,* 22 April 1944.

19 Butler, *Escape from the Anthill*, pp. 114–121.

20 P. Semple, 'Previous Generations Would Be Astounded at Attitudes to Churches in Ireland Today', *Irish Times*, 18 November 2014.

21 L. Pilkington, 'Religion and the Celtic Tiger: The Cultural Legacies of Anti-Catholicism in Ireland', in P. Kirby, L. Gibbons, and M. Cronin (eds.), *Reinventing Ireland: Culture, Society, and the Global Economy* (London, 2002), pp. 125–133; D. Ó Corráin, *Rendering to God and Caesar: The Irish Churches and the Two States in Ireland, 1949–73* (Manchester, 2006), pp. 97–99; R. Foster, *The Irish Story* (London, 2001), p. 190.

22 C. O'Halloran, *Partition and the Limits of Irish Nationalism* (Dublin, 1987), pp. 79–85; 'Toryism in Trinity by the Editor', *Bell* 8(3) (1944), p. 186.

23 *Irish Times,* 11 April 1924; T. Brown, *The Irish Times. 150 Years of Excellence* (London, 2015), p. 138.

24 Revd T. Drury – *Church of Ireland Gazette* [hereafter *CoIG*], 16 December 1921.

25 J. Mooney, 1922 Minutes of the General Committee of the Presbyterian Association, vol. 1918–1930 – archives of the Abbey Presbyterian Church Dublin; also reported in *Irish Times*, 17 January 1922.

26 Letter from C.M. Gibbon, *Irish Times*, 27 May 1922.

27 Revd D. Hall, Protestant Primary School Manager – Letter in *Irish Times,* 9 December 1926.

28 See T. Wilson, 'The Strange Death of Loyalist Monaghan, 1919–21', in S. Paseta (ed.), *Uncertain Futures. Essays about the Past for Roy Foster* (Oxford, 2016), pp. 174–187; D. Fitzpatrick, *Descendancy: Irish Protestant Histories since 1795* (Cambridge, 2014), pp. 49–51.

29 *CoIG*, 6 January 1922.

30 C.A. Webster, 'The Church since Disestablishment', in W.A. Philips (ed.), *History of the Church of Ireland from the Earliest Times to the Present Day*, vol. 3 (Oxford, 1933), p. 422.

31 E.Œ. Somerville, *An Enthusiast* (London, 1921), pp. 65–67.

32 For a prominent example: Gordon Campbell, later the second Lord Glenavy, head of the Department of Industry and Commerce from 1922 to 1932 – J.J. Lee, *Ireland 1912–1985: Politics and Society* (Cambridge, 1989), pp. 120–124; *Irish Times*, 1 August 1963; P. Campbell, *My Life and Easy Times* (London, 1988), pp. 280–282.

33 *CoIG*, 30 December 1921; P. Buckland, *Irish Unionism I: The Anglo-Irish and the New Ireland 1885 to 1922* (Dublin, 1972), pp. 288–290.

34 L. Robinson, 'The Big House', in C. Murray (ed.), *Selected Plays Lennox Robinson* (Gerrard's Cross, 1982), p. 196.

35 The historian Lecky had put it thus – 'I have never looked upon Home Rule as a question between Protestant and Catholic. It is a question between honesty and dishonesty, between loyalty and treason, between individual freedom and organised tyranny and outrage' – quoted in McDowell, *Crisis and Decline*, p. 2.

36 C. Reid, *The Lost Ireland of Stephen Gwynn: Irish Constitutional Nationalism and Cultural Politics, 1864–1950* (Manchester, 2011), p. 245.

37 E. Bowen, *Bowen's Court & Seven Winters* (London, 1984) – *Seven Winters*, p. 48.

38 Seanad Debates, 2 September 1939 at https://www.oireachtas.ie/en/debates/debate/seanad/1939-09-02/3/ (accessed 1 December 2021).

39 https://www.irishstatutebook.ie/eli/1922/act/1/enacted/en/print (accessed 30 November 2021); E. Stephens, 'The Constitution', in Saorstát Éireann (ed.), *Official Handbook* (Dublin, 1932), pp. 77–78.

40 McDowell, *Crisis and Decline*, p. 170.
41 *Irish Times*, 15 November 1950; McDowell, *Crisis and Decline*, p. 170.
42 Leslie's message of condolence to Queen Mary, 25 January 1936 – Leslie papers, MS 49,495/2/39, NLI; R. Hartford, *Godfrey Day, Missionary, Pastor and Primate* (Dublin, Cork, 1940), pp. 116–117.
43 *CoIG*, 22 April 1949.
44 *Irish Times*, 20 April 1949.
45 M. Moffitt, 'This "Rotten Little Republic": Protestant Identity and the "State Prayers" Controversy, 1948–9', in I. d'Alton and I. Milne (eds.), *Protestant and Irish: The Minority's Search for Place in Independent Ireland* (Cork, 2019), pp. 82–98; Ó Corráin, *Rendering to God and Caesar*, pp. 12–19.
46 *CoIG*, 14 May 1937, 22 February 1952.
47 N. Robertson, *Crowned Harp: Memories of the Last Years of the Crown in Ireland* (Dublin, 1960), p. 9.
48 P. Galloway, *The Most Illustrious Order: The Order of St Patrick and its Knights* (London, 1999), p. 100; T. Mohr, 'The Privy Council Appeal as a Minority Safeguard for the Protestant Community of the Irish Free State, 1922–1935', *Northern Ireland Legal Quarterly* 63(3) (2012), pp. 365–395.
49 UK postboxes were green until the 1880s, when they were painted red.
50 Derived, by the author, from gazetteers of London and Dublin in 1925.
51 T. Mohr, 'The Political Significance of the Coinage of the Irish Free State', *Irish Studies Review* 23(4) (2015), pp. 451–479.
52 See *Leader*, 19 November 1927.
53 Quoted in R. Foster, 'Feeling the Squeeze' [A review essay of Fitzpatrick, *Descendancy*], *Dublin Review of Books* 66 (April 2015), http://www.drb.ie/essays/feeling-the-squeeze?utm_medium=email&utm_campaign=The+Dublin+Review+of+Books+April+2015&utm_content=The+Dublin+Review+of+Books+April+2015+CID_84befcf6ad218db24c2e4199f6e56593&utm_source=Email%20marketing%20software&utm_term=Feeling%20the%20Squeeze (accessed 1 December 2021).
54 N. Ascherson, 'Communist Dropouts', *New York Review of Books*, 13 August 1970.
55 N. Allen, *George Russell (Æ) and the New Ireland, 1905–30* (Dublin, 2003), pp. 141–232; I. d'Alton, '"In a Comity of Cultures" – the Rise and Fall of *The Irish Statesman*, 1919–1930', in F. Larkin and M. O'Brien (eds.), *Periodicals and Journalism in Twentieth Century Ireland* (Dublin, 2014), pp. 112–115.
56 N. Meehan, 'Shorthand for Protestants: Sectarian Advertising in the *Irish Times*', *History Ireland* 17(5) (September/October 2009), pp. 46–49.
57 See the Dean of Christ Church on 'Social Service' – *The Church of Ireland A.D. 432–1932*, pp. 186–190; M. Maguire, 'The Organisation and Activism of Dublin's Protestant Working Class', pp. 77–87; C. O'Connor, '"My Mother Wouldn't Have Been as Hurt": Women and Inter-church Marriage in Wexford, 1945–65', in d'Alton and Milne (eds.), *Protestant and Irish*, pp. 229–245.
58 O. MacDonagh, *States of Mind: A Study of the Anglo-Irish Conflict, 1780–1980* (London, 1983), p. 28.
59 D. Kiberd, *Inventing Ireland* (London, 1996), p. 107.
60 Murray, *Selected Plays*, p. 197.
61 *CoIG*, 6 January 1922.
62 *The Church of Ireland A.D. 432–1932*, pp. 235–236; *Irish Independent*, 14 October 1932 reported it as '. . . The Church turned neither to *London* nor to Rome for the appointment of its bishops' [my italics].
63 *The Church of Ireland, A.D. 432–1932*, p. 239.
64 *Bell*, 8(3) (1944), p. 228.

65 B. Fitzgerald, *We Are Besieged* (Bantry, 2011), p. 234.
66 Church of Ireland Board of Education, minutes 7 December 1948 – MS 2/1, Representative Church Body Library, Dublin.
67 Revd C.B. Armstrong, headmaster of St Columba's – *The Church of Ireland A.D. 432–1932*, p. 223.
68 The subject was the Bible and the Book of Common Prayer in Irish – marrying Protestantism and a contemporary issue, the language, but largely ignoring the proselytising impetus behind it – *The Church of Ireland A.D. 432–1932*, pp. 147–166.
69 *The Church of Ireland A.D. 432–1932*, p. 235.
70 R. Dawkins, *The Blind Watchmaker* (London, 1991), pp. 157–158.
71 J. Ruane and D. Butler, 'Southern Irish Protestants: An Example of De-ethnicisation?', *Nations and Nationalism* 13 (2007), p. 619.
72 Ruane, 'Ethnicity, Religion and Peoplehood', pp. 121–135; J. Coakley, 'Religion, Ethnic Identity and the Protestant Minority in the Republic', in W. Crotty and D. Schmitt (eds.), *Ireland and the Politics of Change* (London, 1998), p. 102.
73 R. Foster, *Luck and the Irish* (London, 2007), pp. 37–66.
74 Ruane, 'Ethnicity, Religion and Peoplehood', p. 126.

13 Fault Lines of Trade Union Disunity, 1922–1939

Gerard Hanley

The advent of independent Ireland in 1922 did not occasion a blossoming of Irish trade unionism. If anything, the 1920s and 1930s witnessed the growth of internecine union rivalry, destructive personal animosities among trade union and labour leaders, and a breach between Irish and British-based unions. The weakness of the movement's organisational structures and the personal enmity among some senior trade union leaders gravely damaged the movement in the 1920s and 1930s. The multiplicity of trade unions in Ireland fragmented the movement and led to inter-union rivalry with individual unions competing for small groups of workers of the same class. This rivalry was akin to tribalism where trade unionists expressed loyalty to their own unions rather than to a national movement. The causes of disunity after independence have received relatively little academic attention.[1] This chapter considers three significant causes of division – organisational weakness and structures ill-fitted for their intended purpose, fractious leadership feuds and a damaging civil war between Irish and British-based unions. The latter has been an unlighted aspect of labour history in Britain and Ireland. Secondly, this chapter departs from the established narrative which locates disunity in the 1930s. Instead, it traces the roots of the aforementioned causes of division to 1922. These fault lines compounded one another with the result that in the Irish context, the prospect of a thriving labour movement was always remote.

Organisational Weaknesses

A fundamental shortcoming of the Irish trade union movement was the structure of the Irish Trade Union Congress (ITUC), the Irish-based governing body established in 1894. In establishing the ITUC, Irish trade unions simply replicated the British model. This unthinking importation proved in Emmet O'Connor's words 'a delusion that blithely ignored the vast differences in economy, employment structure, and politics between both countries, it split the urban from the rural movement, widened the breach between artisans and labourers, and depoliticised a generation of trade unionists'.[2] Consequently, the organisational structures of the ITUC were not designed to cater

DOI: 10.4324/9781032691886-13

for the needs and demands of Irish workers. William O'Brien, a dominant figure in the Irish labour movement, recalled that the ITUC did little except pass the same resolutions year after year 'and nothing much resulted from it'.[3] Fundamentally, the role and authority of congress were uncertain.

The structural inadequacy of the ITUC was exacerbated by a decision in 1912 to establish a political wing. Five years later, the organisation's new name – the Irish Labour Party and Trade Union Congress – symbolised the greater importance attached to the political dimension of the organisation, even though this was not the intention of the revised constitution presented to the 1918 annual congress.[4] In a letter to affiliated unions, the national executive maintained that the purpose of the new constitution was 'to provide machinery for organising the political branch of the Labour Movement while keeping it subordinate to the Industrial branch'. The political work was to supplement but not supplant trade union activities which 'will always be predominant'.[5] The combination of political and industrial sides of the labour movement in a conjoint body proved incongruous and militated against the efficient organisation of both wings.[6] It belied an unsettled relationship between the political and industrial sections within congress. Over time, that relationship became increasingly fraught.

It was soon apparent to many trade unionists that industrial affairs were not receiving adequate attention within congress. At the 1922 congress, the Irish Women Workers' Union (IWWU) submitted a resolution to appoint a special committee to deal only with industrial matters.[7] Louie Bennett, joint secretary of the IWWU, noted that several complaints had been raised in congress of 'too much talk about politics'.[8] The ensuing debate on the resolution indicated strong divisions between delegates predisposed to political affairs and those who griped that industrial matters had been relegated to a distant second position. At the behest of congress, the IWWU agreed to withdraw the resolution on the basis that the incoming national executive would consider the possibility of appointing a sub-committee to address industrial affairs. Bennett stressed the importance of reform and, with extraordinary prescience, warned her colleagues that 'some preparations [must be] made for the difficulties that are facing us tomorrow'.[9] At the 1923 congress, the IWWU again withdrew a similar resolution following agreement by congress that the matter would be considered at a special congress in March 1924.[10] But at that gathering, a resolution in the name of the IWWU for a special committee devoted to industrial matters was once again stymied. Thomas Johnson, ILP&TUC secretary and leader of the Labour Party, moved a counter resolution on behalf of the national executive to increase that body from fourteen to seventeen and thereby allowing the work of the executive to be sub-divided.[11] Johnson insisted that it was impossible to make a distinction between social and political questions. His resolution effectively sabotaged the IWWU resolution which was lost by thirty-nine votes to eighteen, while Johnson's motion was carried on a show of hands.[12] The issue resurfaced at the 1924 congress but not in the form of a resolution. When discussion of an amendment put forward by the Irish Engineering Industrial Union (IEIU) to a resolution regarding inter-union rivalry was cut short by congress, IEIU delegates walked out in protest.[13] A spokesperson explained that the IEIU protest arose when attempts 'to get an expression of opinion from Congress on industrial policy' failed due to the inordinate amount of time which had been devoted to political matters.[14]

The discontent between the industrial and political wings was not unidirectional. In its report to congress in 1925, the national executive drew attention to the unsatisfactory level of political support received by the Labour Party from trade union branches.[15] Buoyed up by its success in the 1925 local elections, the Labour Party maintained that the time was ripe for a concerted effort to build up an effective political organisation. However, it could not rely, as it had in the past, merely on the support of trade unionists.[16] This raised the spectre of the committed 'political activists' within the ILP&TUC fighting for an even greater share of the congress stage, a move which further antagonised the committed trade unionists within the organisation. Notably, the national executive's report questioned whether the constitution, which had only been adopted in 1918, was 'out-of-date' and did not afford 'sufficient prominence to the political side of the movement'. The report concluded that the incoming national executive should review the entire situation in relation to political work.[17] This was an overt attempt by the executive to steer a more political course, but in so doing, it created the conditions for a counterproductive power struggle between the political and industrial sections of congress.

In January 1926, R. J. P. Mortished, congress assistant secretary, maintained that he did not foresee a separation of the political and industrial sides of the labour movement 'for a considerable time to come'.[18] Nonetheless, separation was central to a motion on reorganisation moved by the national executive at the 1926 congress.[19] The trouncing of Labour at the September 1927 general election, when the party lost nine of its twenty-two Dáil seats including that of Johnson, prompted a renewed focus on the organisation of the labour movement, in general, and of its political element, in particular.[20] By the time of the 1929 congress, 'political activists' within the movement had decided to take charge of organisational reform. In effect this amounted to a separation of the two distinct elements within the ILP&TUC that had existed since 1914. It was belatedly realised that trade unions in Ireland were ineffective instruments for political activity.[21] William Norton, a member of the national executive and a future leader of the Labour Party, promoted the creation of autonomous political and trade union bodies. Only in this way could Labour garner more votes. Norton moved a motion on autonomy at the 1929 congress.[22] The debate on the resolution emphasised the need to develop the political side of the movement, as opposed to the industrial side. This appeared to be at odds with the case presented by the IWWU at the 1922 congress which argued the need for the better development of the industrial side.

Despite the often rancorous debate since 1922, the plan for separation met with wide approval when the special conference convened in Dublin on 28 February 1930.[23] Yet, as Charles McCarthy notes acutely, 'in the division of the labour movement in 1930. . . the trade union organisation was the remnant'.[24] While the separation ultimately came about to promote the development of the Labour Party, there was scant reference in the report of the special conference of what, if any, advantages autonomy might bestow on the trade unions.[25] The separation did not, in the short-term, improve the fortunes of the Labour Party which only succeeded in having seven of its thirty-three candidates elected to Dáil Éireann in 1932 when Éamon de Valera's Fianna Fáil party took office for the first time.[26] When the ITUC stood alone, without the Labour Party, at the 36th annual congress in August 1930 the problems bedevilling the trade unions – inter-union disputes, the multiplicity of unions and the status of British-based unions – remained as before.

Destructive Personal Enmities

A second potent source of division among Irish trade unions was the bitter personal dispute between Jim Larkin and William O'Brien, the foremost trade union leaders of the time and the subject of several studies.[27] The Liverpool-born Larkin founded the ITGWU in 1908 and played a leading role in the Dublin lockout of 1913–1914 after which he departed for the United States. On his return to Ireland in 1923 he fought an unsuccessful legal battle to regain control of the ITGWU, the largest union in Ireland, from O'Brien who dominated that body from 1918 until his retirement in 1946. When Larkin was expelled from the ITGWU in March 1924, he established the rival Workers' Union of Ireland (WUI). Larkin and O'Brien were arrogant, self-centred and implacable enemies. For over twenty years, the development and reform of the wider trade union movement was stunted by their unrelenting enmity which only ended with Larkin's death in 1947.[28] Furthermore, the power struggle dispute sullied labour's reputation in the mind of employers, politicians and the public. The Larkin-O'Brien enmity and the subsequent split in the ITGWU are central to explaining the weakness of the trade union movement.

Trouble was expected when Larkin returned to Ireland in April 1923 and reprised his role as ITGWU general secretary. The timing of his homecoming was not propitious. Labour had polled exceptionally well in the June 1922 general election when seventeen of its eighteen candidates were returned at a time when union membership was increasing. The ITGWU had flourished during Larkin's eight-year absence. Some leading trade unionists questioned Larkin's motives and feared his potential to cause dissention and undermine the gains made by the labour movement.[29] A second fear was that discontented elements within the labour movement might utilise Larkin's 'wild bull methods' to pursue their own minority agendas.[30] The Dublin Trade Council (DTC) under P.T. Daly was a case in point. Throughout the 1920s it represented itself as Larkinite and communistic and fought against the ILP&TUC under O'Brien. Within weeks of Larkin's return, relations with O'Brien had collapsed. An argument between them on 30 May 1923 regarding the purpose of Larkin's visit to the United States in 1914 occasioned an irrevocable breakdown. An enraged Larkin declared that that he could no longer work with O'Brien. A split in the ranks of the ITGWU was inevitable. At a meeting of no. 1 branch on 5 June in the La Scala Theatre, Dublin, attended by some 2,500 members, Larkin denounced O'Brien and demanded his resignation from the union's national executive.[31] With little support among union members outside Dublin, Larkin undertook an unsuccessful tour of union branches across the country. His disruptive tactics triggered a raft of correspondence from provincial branches. A common theme was the view that Larkin's move was driven by ego rather than policy and that it amounted to an attack on themselves as trade unionists as much as the executive.[32] O'Brien's ambition for power and portrayal of himself as the true heir of Connolly revealed an ego as inflated as Larkin's. Both men shared unattractive traits: they were autocratic, insensitive and difficult to work with. But unlike Larkin, O'Brien was scrupulously organised and, crucially, enjoyed the support of an overwhelming majority of the ITGWU's national executive.[33] Larkin was expelled from the ITGWU on 14 March 1924 following a raft of special delegate conferences, legal actions and counteractions.[34] O'Brien later recalled that the breach with Larkin in 1923/4 'caused unprecedented dissension, turmoil and bitterness in the Irish labour movement'.[35]

The establishment in June 1924 of the WUI by the Larkin family, with 'Big Jim' as its general secretary, poisoned trade unionism in Ireland for the next two decades. Some 16,000 members of the ITGWU, mainly in Dublin, defected.[36] The reverberations of this struggle were not only felt by the labour movement, but also by workers, employers and the general public. Many of the trade disputes over the following decade, particularly in the Dublin area, had little to do with disagreements between employers and workers but were generally the result of turf wars between the ITGWU and the WUI. Inter-union disputes broke out in the construction industry, the docks, theatres and cinemas, and the bakery trade. Both the WUI and ITGWU sought exclusive trade union rights in various employments and the methods adopted to force one union's domination over the other, but mostly on the part of the WUI, included, according to an ITGWU annual report, 'bullying, terrorism, physical violence . . . and intimidation'.[37] In a statement to the press in September 1924, the national executive of the ILP&TUC provided a damning predict on the inter-union civil war:

> Workmen lost wages, businesses were dislocated . . . tradesmen not connected with the dispute were disemployed, and no material advantage was even hoped for – certainly was not attained – while the moral damage to trade unionism in loss of strength and prestige is incalculable. No

good cause was served by these disastrous strikes, their only use seems to have been to pander to the vainglory of individuals desirous of making a show of power.[38]

According to one 'leading' but unnamed contemporaneous trade unionist, the disputes had the potential to bring about not only social and industrial chaos but also widespread anarchy.[39] An editorial in *The Irish Times* on 19 November 1924 attributed much of the blame for the paralysis of industry in Dublin to Larkin and it feared that Dublin would face economic ruin as business was diverted to Belfast.[40]

A Dáil debate on unemployment in October 1924 noted that 'unnecessary strikes', which had 'dragged on for weeks and months', were caused by a lack of unity within the labour movement and contributed to high levels of unemployment.[41] Many employers became exasperated at the impact of inter-union squabbling on their businesses. In July 1925, the Coal Merchants' Association locked out ITGWU and WUI workers until a satisfactory guarantee was obtained that all men employed in the coal yards would work together amicably, regardless of their union affiliation. This action was supported by the Dublin Employers' Federation.[42] In November 1924, Dublin employers decided to pursue a policy of dismissing any employee who refused to perform legitimate duties. The press generally attributed blame to Larkin who was accused by one newspaper as pursuing 'labour terrorism'.[43] Larkin's biographers have variously described his behaviour at this time as 'unpredictable' and 'self-destructive egomania'.[44]

While the ITGWU was the main target of Larkin's 'wrecking policy', the ILP&TUC was equally concerned about the danger he posed for Irish trade unionism. In September 1924 the national executive issued a manifesto revealingly titled: 'A Call for Unity'. This deplored 'disunity in the ranks of Labour' and supported the stance of the ITGWU by denouncing Larkin's 'disruptive tactics'.[45] Such strong words were futile because the WUI was not affiliated to congress. Predictably, an attempt by the WUI to affiliate in 1934 was opposed by the ITGWU. O'Brien accused Larkin of waging war on the labour movement for more than eleven years and declared that 'no employer, or combination of employers, has ever inflicted upon the labour movement the damage which James Larkin is directly responsible for'.[46] Despite the historical evidence of Larkin's unbalanced personality, egotism and the damage he inflicted on Irish trade unionism, an iconic perception of him has endured as the ultimate trade unionist and defender of workers' rights.

The problems which Larkin presented for the labour movement forced the ILP&TUC to realise its own helplessness but it was too weak to confront its shortcomings. Its strength and courage seemed to be sapped by the independence of its affiliated organisations and their respective leaders. Much of the disunity within trade unionism could be attributed to the self-interests of some of its leaders. One congress delegate noted that unity is apparent 'among the working class at the bottom, [but] not so much amongst the Trade Union figures at the top'.[47] A remove between top and base was reflected regularly in correspondence between rural-based trade union secretaries and their Dublin-based national executives. One rural ITGWU branch secretary described his colleagues at headquarters as 'unapproachable "Brass-hats" whose 'idle words' were 'nothing short of empty bauble, arrant humbug, sheer make-believe, catchy sob-stuff, childish and pathetic clap-trap'.[48] This chasm between local officials and headquarters staff was often the cause of both local officials and union members forming new alliances, more often than not with Larkin's WUI. At the 1924 ILP&TUC congress, Luke Clancy, the president, found it difficult to accept that a movement which had been known for 'its determination, its unity of purpose, and its high idealism could, within the space of a year, be torn asunder by sectional feuds'.[49] The subtle subtext of Clancy's address was that change was necessary within the labour movement to resolve differences and remove misunderstandings. He discreetly questioned the quality and suitability of trade union leaders by suggesting that if the highest interests of the movement are to be pursued and maintained then 'the best and most courageous men and women in the Movement must be elected to positions where they will advise and guide . . . and they must be ever assured of the confidence, co-operation and loyalty of those who elect them'.[50] Clancy called on delegates to give the executive their undivided support to enable it to pursue 'a strong open policy . . . to save the Irish Labour Movement from destruction'.[51] What that policy was or might be was not addressed.

Anglophobic Nationalism

If organisational shortcomings and a civil war between Larkin and O'Brien were not sufficient obstacles, inter-union disharmony between Irish and British-based trade unions further exacerbated the situation. Before the Irish Revolution of 1912 to 1923, the Irish labour movement saw itself as having a common purpose and, to some degree, a shared structure with its fraternal trade unionists in Britain. That breadth of outlook narrowed during the Irish struggle for independence which saw the greening of the labour movement. In addition, after 1922, the jurisdictional environment was more complex with new governments in Dublin and Belfast. Some Irish trade unionists believed that the position of British or amalgamated trade unions in Ireland was compromised by the fact that they were affiliated to both the British and Irish TUCs. A nationalist fervour was evident at the 1922 congress, the first since Irish independence. James Carr, representing the Limerick United Trades and Labour Council, moved a resolution that 'all Irish workers should be catered for by Irish Unions'. He claimed that by 'listening to two voices' the Irish labour movement was weakened.[52] The implication was that the ILP&TUC should not permit the affiliation of trade unions registered in another country. At this time, twenty-one trade unions affiliated to congress, with a combined membership of 100,000, had headquarters in Ireland, whereas another seventeen with a membership of over 46,000 were based in Britain.[53] Carr's motion was vigorously opposed by the British-based unions. For example, the Railway Clerks' Association disparaged it as 'a green resolution from green people'.[54] In the event, the motion was withdrawn but the sentiment underlying it did not dissipate.

Although congress did not call on British trade unions to withdraw from Ireland, some of its decisions revealed an adverse disposition towards them. To prevent the growth of maverick unions and the fragmentation of the movement, congress operated a policy of discouraging 'break-away' unions by refusing them affiliation. Anglo-Irish divisions tested the integrity of that practice. In 1921, some members of the Amalgamated Society of Woodworkers (ASW) withdrew to form the rival Irish National Union of Woodworkers (INUW). Taking advantage of congress's changed attitude towards amalgamated unions the INUW applied for affiliation at the end of the 1920s. This was opposed vigorously by the ASW which threatened to withdraw from congress if the INUW was admitted.[55] Not only did the ASW have a long tradition in Ireland, but its 7,000 members dwarfed the 500 in the INUW. The cause of the INUW was championed by William O'Brien and Helena Molony, the republican, trade unionist and feminist. When the INUW affiliated in May 1931, the ASW promptly withdrew.[56] Three years later, the ASW had been coaxed to return, largely because its Irish members had remained steadfastly loyal to the Society, but the INUW remained affiliated.[57] There was a growing belief among the leaders of Irish-based trade unions that the days of British unions in Ireland were numbered, and that their demise should be hurried along in the national interest. The most influential advocate of this view was William O'Brien as leader of the ITGWU. His motivations were an amalgam of nationalism and naked personal ambition. While a rising sense of nationalism among Irish trade union members should not be discounted, nationalist sentiment was stoked deliberately by the trade union leadership.

By 1933, the ITGWU had successfully enticed 'whole sections and branches' of British unions 'numbering hundreds' into its membership. and it became clear that its intention was to target the membership of British unions 'until the entire wage-earning class in Ireland was organised and controlled entirely from within Ireland'.[58] In November 1933, a large advertisement appeared in the national press under the heading: 'An Irish Union for Irish Tramway Men' along with details of a meeting to be held in Dublin on 13 November aimed at encouraging members of British unions to join an Irish union. All of the speakers were ITGWU officials or 'ITGWU' Senators and TDs.[59] This strategy was not aimed solely at workers in the DUTC. Protest meetings 'against the formation of an English union' were organised in many Irish towns where workers were members of British unions.[60] By April 1934, the ATGWU had lost 420 members in the DUTC, though 1,576 remained. The ATGWU was convinced that prominent members were induced financially to encourage other members to defect to the ITGWU and that these

actions were supported by the six 'ITGWU TDs'. Sam Kyle, the Irish secretary of the ATGWU, described a toxic atmosphere which gave rise to an
'extremely bitter national feeling'.[61] The ATGWU's London-based general
secretary, Ernest Bevin, one of the greatest British trade union leaders of the
twentieth century and stalwart of the Labour Party, confided in Kyle that
nothing would give him 'greater joy than to hear from you that you have
cleared the Irish Transport Union out of the Dublin Tramways, even if it does
mean paying a price'.[62]

A sense of Anglophobia was evident in the utterances of Irish trade unionists in the 1930s with amalgamated unions referred to as 'British unions',
'British-controlled unions', 'English organisations' and 'foreign controlled'
unions. This unsavoury tone was the antithesis of trade union comradeship and
fraternity. Delegates from the amalgamated trade unions naturally objected to
such 'spurious patriotism' at congress.[63] Crucially, O'Brien turned a deaf ear
to calls for fraternal reconciliation and was determined to drive a deep wedge
between Irish and British-based unions. At congress in 1933, he declared: 'We
are a separate and distinct nationality. We believe we know what the Labour
movement stands for in this country'.[64] Later that year, in an address in Dungarvan he suggested that the most useful service British unions could render
to Irish workers was to 'leave them alone'.[65] Bevin believed that the ITGWU
was 'racially' motivated in its attempt to undermine the ATGWU. He was
determined not to allow it 'to be broken by people with ulterior motives'.[66] To
this end, the council of the TGWU granted as much autonomy to the ATGWU
as possible 'to try and create in the minds of the members that, in effect, their
business is being handled by an Irish Executive'.[67]

An unexpected result of the Irish-British rivalry within congress was that
it reenergised the focus and resolve of the amalgamated unions in the face
of growing trade union nationalism. Their Irish members had possessed a
traditional loyalty to these unions which had never displayed any evidence
of 'trade union colonialism'.[68] Some of the amalgamated unions, such as the
ASW, accused congress of 'disorganising' Irish workers while the National
Union of Railwaymen, another British-based union, declared that nationalism and patriotism were irrelevant because union organisation stood for the
'emancipation of the working class'.[69] In addition to demanding equal protection under congress rules, the amalgamated unions steadily increased the
number of their delegates.[70] This had significant implications for the future of
the Irish trade union movement over the following decade.

The increased incidence of trade disputes during the 1930s had the potential to damage not only the trade union movement, but also Irish industry
and the wider economy. Between 1929 and 1938, a total of 941 disputes
involving 95,569 workers took place and caused the loss of 3,346,000 working days.[71] Notably, the number of trade disputes increased significantly
between 1932 and 1937. This was a product of the marked expansion, albeit
from a pitifully low base, of industrial activity in Ireland. Between 1935 and

1938, almost one-quarter of disputes lasted for an average of six to ten days, while twenty-two per cent were in excess of thirty days.[72] A report prepared by the Department of Industry and Commerce on inter-union trade disputes from 1932 to 1941 identified a total of thirty-six such disputes during this ten-year period.[73] However, another detailed report on industrial disputes in the 1930s identified 'trade union questions' as having been the cause of forty-six disputes during the four-year period between 1935 and 1938 when 48,615 working days were lost.[74] The report writer wondered if there are too many trade unions in Ireland. He also called for the introduction of an arbitration scheme which would focus on the prevention of strikes and work stoppages rather than having to find a solution to resolve individual strikes.[75]

A strike in the Dublin transportation services in 1935, which the ITGWU described as the most stubbornly fought in twenty years, exhausted public and government tolerance of trade union behaviour. The strike lasted eleven weeks and came to an end on 17 May 1935. It had involved almost 3,000 workers, who were members of either the ITGWU or the ATGWU.[76] To the dismay of the general public and the government, the strike, which commenced over the dismissal of a worker, was soon transformed into a demand for a wage increase. It had a devastating effect on Dublin businesses and seriously inconvenienced the general public. Although not an inter-union dispute, below the surface the bitter conflict between the Irish and British-based trade unions smouldered. Their mutual animosity was temporarily held in check for the duration of this protracted dispute with the DUTC.[77] Both unions feared losing members to the other and were poised to appropriate as many as possible should an opportune moment arise. In the aftermath of the dispute open hostilities between the unions resumed.[78] Union and national rivalries had as much to do with the strike as any economic causes and, as Alan Bullock reveals, Bevin was determined not to collapse the dispute 'if only to show that the ATGWU could be as militant as its Irish rival'.[79]

In March 1935, Helena Molony, the IWWU representative on the national executive and its delegate to congress, warned her executive colleagues of the damage being inflicted on the trade union movement by the DUTC strike. She called for an examination of the matter at the earliest possible opportunity so as to bring an end to internecine quarrelling and disunity.[80] The appeal captured the attention of her national executive colleagues and at the 1935 congress held in Derry, the national executive advised delegates that

the time has arrived when a more orderly state of affairs should be called into existence amongst the existing Trade Unions to prevent any further disruption into warring competitive sections . . . The National Executive feel a duty devolves on them to call attention to the disintegrating circumstances which are manifesting themselves in the Trade Union Movement throughout the country leading to an absence of harmony and unity.[81]

The national executive proposed far-reaching recommendations designed to discourage house unions (unions controlled by employers), break-away unions caused by a grievance against existing unions and inter-union rivalry. The main objective was to arrest the fragmentation of trade unionism and to present 'a solid unified union front' to the industrially organised employers.[82] There was no mistaking a grave sense of concern for the future.

As 1935 progressed, inter-union disputes, internal labour divisions and differences, and demarcation strikes had escalated to such a degree that the credibility and integrity of the ITUC was at stake. The DUTC strike prompted the government to intervene as Fianna Fáil TDs became increasingly vociferous in their demands for action against unions.[83] Eventually, this led to the introduction of Trade Union Acts in 1941 and 1942 which regulated trade unions and other bodies such as employer organisations. In these perilous circumstances, the national executive held a special trade union conference on 25 April 1936 at which delegates directed the executive to establish a commission to inquire into and report on trade union reform.[84] The national executive called for 'a vast organisational improvement' and noted that the commission might occasion 'a complete turning point in the life of the Trade Union Movement'.[85] This proved wishful thinking. The attempted reform foundered.

The rivalry between Irish and British-based unions led to the creation of the Congress of Irish Unions in 1945 which represented most of the Irish-based unions, including the ITGWU. All of the British unions remained with the ITUC. Such a deep and self-inflicted wound underlined the weakness of the Irish labour movement. This unfortunate state of affairs persisted until 1959 when both congresses reunited to become the Irish Congress of Trade Unions.[86] Only then did the opposition of Irish and British unions to one another abate.

Conclusion

There has been a tendency in the historiography to identify the 1930s as the decade of disunity and division within the Irish labour and trade union movement. The present article argues that the roots of this disharmony can be found in the immediate aftermath of Irish independence in 1922. The hopes and promises with which labour entered independent Ireland were hollowed out by three factors, largely of its own making: a flawed organisational structure, destructive personal enmities and the rise of a misplaced Anglophobic nationalism within trade unionism. Congress demonstrated that as an organisation it was spectacularly ill-prepared for independence. For over two decades, it lacked the ability to strengthen and develop its structures or to make any significant contribution to improving and developing labour relations and supporting machinery. Fundamentally, the conjoining of a political party and a trade union within congress stunted the development of both. This occasioned unseemly divisions as each bloc vied for control. A weak and ineffectual congress could not address a raft of interunion disputes during the late 1920s and 1930s. These were intensified by the unrelenting personal war waged by the two big beasts of the Irish labour movement. Both Larkin and O'Brien knowingly placed their vendetta above the interests of the broader labour movement. This had two detrimental consequences. First, it inhibited the development of the movement in the 1920s when political space and opportunity existed for the Labour Party prior to the establishment of Fianna Fáil. Second, it hindered the reform of trade unionism and delayed the introduction of much-needed labour relations procedures and machinery. The antagonism towards British-based unions emerged in 1922. It was partly a consequence of the separatist nationalism that had led to the establishment of the Irish Free State but it was also partly the result of political opportunism by Fianna Fáil and, in particular, by William O'Brien. He cast aside the fraternal bonds of trade unionism and engaged in a second trade union civil war with Ernest Bevin and the ATGWU. Like all civil wars, the damage was pervasive. The weakness of the labour movement in independent Ireland bore testament to that.

Notes

1 The standard accounts are Charles McCarthy, *Trade Unions in Ireland, 1894–1960* (Dublin, 1977); Donal Nevin (ed.), *Trade Unions and Change in Irish Society* (Dublin, 1980); Donal Nevin (ed.), *Trade Union Century* (Dublin, 1994). The period before 1914 has been examined in Emmet O'Connor, 'Problems of Reform in the Irish Trades Union Congress, 1894–1914', *Historical Studies in Industrial Relations* 23(24) (2007), pp. 37–59.
2 Emmet O'Connor, *A Labour History of Ireland, 1824–2000* (Dublin, 2011), p. 65.
3 National Library of Ireland (hereafter NLI): William O'Brien Papers: MS 15,704/7/10, undated article by O'Brien, 'British and Irish Labour'.
4 Donal Nevin, 'Decades of Dissension and Divisions, 1923–1959', in Nevin (ed.), *Trade Union Century*, pp. 85–86.
5 *ILP&TUC Annual Report* (1918), pp. 129–130.
6 Nevin, 'Decades of Dissension', p. 86.
7 *ILP&TUC Annual Report* (1922), p. 201.
8 *ILP&TUC Annual Report* (1922), p. 201.
9 *ILP&TUC Annual Report* (1922), pp. 208–209.
10 *ILP&TUC Annual Report* (1923), p. 101.
11 *ILP&TUC Special Congress Report* (1924), p. 49.
12 *ILP&TUC Special Congress Report* (1924), pp. 52–57.
13 *ILP&TUC Annual Report* (1924), p. 182.
14 *ILP&TUC Annual Report* (1924), p. 201.
15 *ILP&TUC Annual Report* (1925), p. 30.
16 *ILP&TUC Annual Report* (1925), p. 30; Niamh Puirséil, *The Irish Labour Party, 1922–1973* (Dublin, 2007), p. 21.
17 *ILP&TUC Annual Report* (1925), pp. 30–31.
18 Mortished, 'Trade Union Organisation in Ireland', p. 227.
19 *ILP&TUC Annual Report* (1926), p. 152.
20 Puirséil, *Irish Labour Party*, pp. 26, 30.
21 Arthur Mitchell, *Labour in Irish Politics, 1890–1913: The Irish Labour Movement in an Age of Revolution* (Dublin, 1974), p. 280.

22 Puirséil, *Irish Labour Party*, p. 30; *ILP&TUC Annual Report* (1929), pp. 106–107. On Norton, see Lawrence William White, 'Norton, William Joseph ('Bill')', in James McGuire and James Quinn (eds.), *Dictionary of Irish Biography* (Cambridge, 2009) (accessed 21 May 2019).
23 Puirséil, *Irish Labour Party*, p. 31.
24 McCarthy, *Trade Unions*, p. 92.
25 *ILP&TUC Annual Report* (1930), pp. 124–138.
26 Puirséil, *Irish Labour Party*, p. 37.
27 Larkin has attracted far more historical attention than O'Brien in numerous articles and monographs ranging from early biographical studies such as Emmet Larkin, *James Larkin: Irish Labour Leader, 1876–1947* (London, 1965) to the most recent treatment by Emmet O'Connor, *Big Jim Larkin: Hero or Wrecker?* (Dublin, 2015). The fullest coverage of O'Brien is Thomas J. Morrissey, *William O'Brien, 1881–1968: Socialist, Republican, Dáil Deputy, Editor, and Trade Union Leader* (Dublin, 2007).
28 Nevin, 'Decades of Dissension', p. 95.
29 Puirséil, *Irish Labour Party*, p. 12.
30 Dublin: NLI: O'Brien Papers: MS 13,961/4/9, 'Thomas MacPartlin to O'Brien', May 1923.
31 Dublin: NLI: O'Brien Papers: MS 15,679/6/27, 'O'Brien to editor of the Irish Times', 20 March 1956.
32 Dublin: NLI: ITGWU Papers: MS 27,062 (1), correspondence in relation to submitting Larkin dispute to a delegate conference; Emmet O'Connor, *Big Jim Larkin*, p. 221.
33 Morrissey, *William O'Brien*, p. 232; Nevin, 'Decades of Dissention', p. 95; O'Connor, *Big Jim Larkin*, p. 246.
34 Dublin: NLI: ITGWU Papers: MS 27,071 (5), 'ITGWU Annual Report', 1924; 'IL&PTUC Annual Report', 1923, p. 43; Nevin, 'Decades of Dissention', p. 90.
35 Dublin: NLI: O'Brien papers: MS 15,679/6/27, 'O'Brien to editor of the *Irish Times*', 20 March 1956.
36 O'Connor, *Labour History*, pp. 130–131; Nevin, 'Decades of Dissention', p. 90.
37 NLI: ITGWU Papers: MS 27,071(5), 'ITGWU Annual Report', 1924.
38 *Irish Independent*, 27 September 1924.
39 *Freeman's Journal and Irish Independent*, 25 June 1924.
40 *Irish Times*, 19 November 1924.
41 *Dáil Éireann Debates*, 9, 30 October 1924, pp. 476–480.
42 O'Connor, *Big Jim*, p. 244; Morrissey, *William O'Brien*, p. 229.
43 *Freeman's Journal*, 25 November 1924.
44 Donal Nevin, *James Larkin: Lion of the Fold* (Dublin, 1998), p. 76; O'Connor, *Big Jim Larkin*, p. 325.
45 *ILP&TUC Annual Report* (1925), pp. 33–37; NLI: ITGWU Papers: MS 27,071(5), 'ITGWU Annual Report', 1924.
46 Dublin: NLI: O'Brien Papers: MS 15,677/20, 'O'Brien to P.T. Daly (Dublin trade union council)', September 1934.
47 W.H. Threadoold, delegate from the Associated Blacksmiths, Forge and Smithy Workers, speaking at 1946 Congress, see *ITUC Annual Report* (1946), p. 156.
48 Dublin: NLI: William O'Brien Papers: MS 15,676/1/93, 'T. Bourke (secretary Westport Quay Branch ITGWU) to O'Brien', 21 November 1930.
49 *ILP&TUC Annual Report* (1924), p. 118.
50 *ILP&TUC Annual Report* (1924), pp. 119–120.
51 *ILP&TUC Annual Report* (1924), p. 175.
52 *ILP&TUC Annual Report* (1922), pp. 239–240.
53 Mortished, 'Trade Union Organisation in Ireland', pp. 214–215.

54 *ILP&TUC Annual Report* (1922), p. 240, comments by J.T. O'Farrell, Railway Clerks' Association.
55 McCarthy, *Trade Unions*, p. 121A.
56 National Archives of Ireland (hereafter NAI): ITUC and Labour Party Minutes, ICTU Box 100, G4/82/38, 'Minutes of ITUC national executive meeting', 8 May 1931 and 29 April 1932.
57 Dublin: NAI: ITUC and Labour Party minutes, Book C, Box 100, G4/82/38, 'Minutes of ITUC national executive meeting', 10 November 1933; McCarthy, *Trade Unions*, pp. 123–127.
58 Dublin: NLI: ITGWU Papers, MS 27,085(6), 'Annual Report for 1933'; ITGWU Papers, MS 27,085(11), 'Report of Proceedings of ITGWU annual conference 1934'.
59 *Irish Independent*, 9 November 1933.
60 University of Warwick, Modern Records Centre (hereafter UWMRC): TGWU Papers: MSS 126/TG/64/1/4, 'Poster advertising protest meeting against an English Union', November 1933.
61 Coventry: UWMRC: TGWU Papers: MSS 126/TG/64/1/4, 'Kyle to Bevin', 17 April 1934 and 19 November 1934.
62 Coventry: UWMRC: TGWU Papers: MSS 126/TG/64/1/4, 'Kyle to Bevin', 17 April 1934 and 19 November 1934, 'Bevin to Kyle', 1 May 1934.
63 *ITUC Annual Report* (1933), pp. 125–127.
64 *ITUC Annual Report* (1933), p. 132.
65 Dublin: NLI: William O'Brien Papers: MS 15,676 (1), 'Speech by O'Brien to workers in Dungarvan', 6 October 1933; Morrissey, *William O'Brien*, pp. 267–268.
66 Coventry: UWMRC: TGWU papers: MSS 126/TG/64/1/4, 'Bevin to Kyle', 15 November 1933.
67 Coventry: UWMRC: TGWU papers: MSS 126/TG/64/1/4, 'Memorandum of meeting between the general secretary and representatives of the TGWU general executive council and a deputation from Area 11 Committee ATGWU', 10 October 1933.
68 McCarthy, *Trade Unions*, pp. 127–128.
69 Allen, *Fianna Fáil*, p. 60.
70 *ITUC Annual Report* (1934), p. 122; McCarthy, *Trade Unions*, pp. 126–128.
71 Dublin: UCDA: Seán MacEntee Papers: P67/229(14), Presidential address by C.P. McCarthy to the Commerce Society of Cork University College on 'Industrial disputes and wage levels in Éire', 11 March 1940.
72 Dublin: UCDA: Seán MacEntee Papers: P67/229(14), Presidential address by C.P. McCarthy to the Commerce Society of Cork University College on 'Industrial disputes and wage levels in Éire', 11 March 1940.
73 Dublin: UCDA: MacEntee papers: P67/239(15), Report by the Dept. of Industry and Commerce in connection with 'Trade disputes in Ireland arising out of inter-union differences since 1932'.
74 Dublin: UCDA: Seán MacEntee Papers: P67/229(14), Presidential address by C.P. McCarthy to the Commerce Society of Cork University College on 'Industrial disputes and wage levels in Éire', 11 March 1940.
75 Dublin: UCDA: Seán MacEntee Papers: P67/229(14), Presidential address by C.P. McCarthy to the Commerce Society of Cork University College on 'Industrial disputes and wage levels in Éire', 11 March 1940.
76 *Irish Independent*, 18 May 1935.
77 Bill McCamley, *The Role of the Rank and File in the 1935 Dublin Tram and Bus Strike* (Dublin, 1981), p. 1.
78 McCamley, *The Role of the Rank and File*, p. 21.
79 Alan Bullock, *The Life and Times of Ernest Bevin: Volume 1, Trade Union Leader, 1881–1940* (London, 1960), p. 18.

80 Dublin: NAI, ITUC and Labour Party Minutes 1923–1935, Book C, Box 100, G4/82/38, Minutes of ITUC resident committee, 5 April 1935.
81 *ITUC Annual Report (1935)*, p. 65.
82 *ITUC Annual Report (1935)*, pp. 65–66.
83 Allen, *Fianna Fáil*, p. 49.
84 *ITUC Annual Report (1939)*, pp. 44–45.
85 ITUC Annual report (1936), p. 46.
86 Nevin, 'Decades of Dissension', pp. 94–96.

14 'A Peripatetic University for Catholic Social Activists'

John Hayes and the International Origins of Muintir na Tire's 'Rural Weeks'

Barry Sheppard

'This social device is correctly claimed to be Irish-made by Irish people for Irish needs'.[1] These were the words of Stephen Rynne, writer, rural activist, and biographer of Canon John Martin Hayes on the late cleric's informal assemblies, the 'Fireside Chat'. These assemblies, where the ordinary rural man could have his voice heard on whatever was pressing on his mind, took place during Hayes's organisation's rural gatherings, the Rural Week. If the Fireside Chat was uniquely Irish, the surroundings which enveloped it were not. The organisation which Hayes had founded in May of 1931, Muintir na Tire (the People of the Land, hereafter MNT),[2] a mainstay of twentieth century rural Ireland had strong European origins. Initially formed as a rural co-operative parent body for commodity producers, the movement, stifled by lack of growth, soon transitioned to a broader vocationalist community development organisation. Despite a seemingly sharp change in direction, its focus was largely the same, the uplift of Ireland's rural people and to make life on the land productive and attractive.

Hayes's concern for the plight of rural people was largely driven by his traumatic early life experiences during the Land War. Born in Murroe, Co Limerick on 11 November 1887, Hayes arrived into a family in turmoil, exiled for five years from their home, the victims of landlord and bailiff eviction (it would be almost thirteen years before they returned). Finding solace in a hut erected by the Land League, these years in exile became the family 'saga',[3] moulding the young family member's political leanings and forever tying them to the land struggle. This early upheaval also anchored Hayes to the plight of the small farmer and rural labourer. Clearly a product of rural Ireland, Hayes was nonetheless much more than the rustic 'good sagart',[4] an image which often followed him in later life.

The image of Hayes as a simple rural priest has obscured his rich cosmopolitanism, the result of many years living in both Paris and Liverpool where he absorbed much of the intellectual and cultural influences those cities had to offer. A five-year period studying in Paris's Irish College (1907–1912) introduced Hayes to European Catholic social thought, as well as a broad selection of Catholic social movements which had become embedded throughout much of Western Europe. This period did much to direct the later life of the

DOI: 10.4324/9781032691886-14

young student, when he brought the lessons of rural Catholic Europe back to Ireland. Similarly, his first mission after ordination (1915–1924) offered much in terms of socio-religious ideas which he brought back to his beloved rural homeland. This time he was sent to the Parish of Mount Carmel on the banks of the Mersey in Liverpool where he witnessed much upheaval, a consequence of the Irish revolution.

It was France, however, which exercised the most influence over the young Hayes as he studied in the city's famed Irish College. Seeking a cultural education alongside his religious studies, Hayes surreptitiously ventured beyond the walls of the College to learn the language and soak up as much of the cultural influences which were laid before him.[5] Living in the City of Light, Hayes could also not escape, even if he wanted to the influence of French cultural Catholicism. Despite having taken a significant blow with the 1905 Law on the Separation of the Churches and the State,[6] Cultural Catholicism had witnessed an 'astounding' reawakening in the country.[7] Hayes was swept up in the atmosphere of defiant piety, particularly during the beatification celebrations of St Joan of Arc in 1909. An evangelised Hayes wrote enthusiastically to his family in Limerick, rhapsodising about the life-changing impact of the celebrations, and wondering if the like would ever be seen in Ireland.[8]

During his time in Paris, the fallout from the Law of Separation had brought with it much conflict, with areas of urban France becoming hotbeds of anti-clericalism. Often spilling over into violence, Hayes had witnessed street fighting first-hand.[9] Rural France, while not escaping the 'instability and polarization' of the time,[10] had maintained a strong Catholic cultural character with a 'more 'active' and 'social' form of Catholicism' and offered Hayes a sanctuary of sorts.[11] Given his upbringing in the Irish countryside, periodic retreats to the familiarity of rural terrain is unsurprising. It was a vital outlet which he took full advantage of, touring the countryside and observing rural practices.[12] At least partially driving this more proactive Catholicism which prevailed in rural France were sodality organisations inspired by several notable lay intellectuals who would soon become globally renowned in Catholic circles. Figures such as Count Albert de Mun and François-René de La Tour du Pin, along with Henri Lorin, the first president of the *Semaines Sociales de France*, made up three 'of the principal proponents of social Catholicism in France'.[13]

De Mun was of particular importance, having been a central figure in Catholic social endeavour since the 1870s.[14] The inspiration behind several important Catholic organisations which flourished in the country, his influence could be found in *Oeuvre des Cercles* (the Catholic Workingmen's Clubs), and the *Association Catholique de la Jeunesse Française* (ACJF), which like MNT in Ireland were concerned with the 'rural exodus'.[15] Another important organisation which evolved from the ACJF, the *Jeunesse Agricole Chrétienne* (JAC), became prevalent in many parts of rural France, focusing on the future of rural youth.[16] Hayes spoke of the importance of both the ACJF and the JAC in a 1934 radio address as his own organisation gathered steam, noting that he wished to see the triumph of the JAC 're-echo' in rural Ireland.[17]

Another of the triumvirate which drove French social Catholicism, and which would have a considerable impact upon Hayes was the 'veteran' Henri Lorin.[18] Lorin's journey began in de Mun's *Oeuvre des Cercles*,[19] where he gained much experience and insight into the problems facing French society. From here he went on, in 1904 with Marius Gonin and Adéodat Boissard,[20] to establish the movement which had the most long-lasting influence on John Hayes, the *Semaines Sociales* or social weeks of France. The *Semaines*, which was to quickly spread across France and beyond, was conceived as a sort of migratory popular university for social research. In one city after another, year by year, it would enable the leading Catholic experts on social and economic questions to instruct serious students as well as large popular audiences, in short one-week courses.[21] Travelling each year to a different location, the *Semaines* attempted 'to visit all corners of France',[22] bringing social Catholicism's message with it. The format, simple and transferrable was noted as a 'perambulating, yearly university for the study of social questions'.[23] According to Moon, the popular yearly travelling university 'represented a continuation of the movement inaugurated by de Mun and La Tour du Pin' in the late 1800s.[24]

It is apparent that Hayes absorbed much of this proactive Catholic culture from his time in France. In fact, he made a series of journeys back to the country after his ordination where he temporarily worked in a rural French parish.[25] Yet, he was not alone in paying attention to French Catholicism. The French 'travelling university' had been reported on in Irish newspapers as early as 1906,[26] long before Hayes adopted the model in the 1930s. By 1920 as the *Semaines* model spread far beyond France's borders, the *Anglo-Celt* newspaper marvelled at the movement which had spread 'to Holland, Spain, Italy, Poland, Belgium, and Switzerland, and, finally, to South America, everywhere meeting with great success'.[27] The *Drogheda Independent* in late 1925 also noted the international success of the movement and asked its readers 'cannot something on these lines be done in Ireland'?[28] And while some comparisons were made in the mid-1920s between Ireland's Catholic Truth Conference and the French *Semaines Sociales*,[29] it would not be until the 1930s with the introduction of MNT's Rural Weekends and Rural Weeks that the connection would truly be made.

The Beginning

In MNT's official *Handbook* of 1941, a decade after the organisation was founded, Fr Hayes recalled the origins and early development of the rural organisation in an article entitled 'The Beginning'. Noting the importance of gathering people together to discuss rural Ireland's problems, Hayes recalled his quest of discovering what had been done to bring rural people together in other countries. Citing the influence of the 'Semaines Rurales' or Rural Weeks of France, he noted how 'the people of the countryside came together and fraternised, got to know each other' attending exhibitions and lectures.[30] This format, which Hayes had clearly found to be the best example which would

best serve MNT's needs would be central to their annual programme until the
end of the 1960s when it was replaced with an annual conference format.

In the existing literature on MNT, there is seemingly conflicting terminol-
ogy used when it comes to the intellectual lineage of MNT's Rural Weeks,
with the terms 'Semaines Sociales' and 'Semaines Rurales' both employed.
This point needs some clarification. Devereux, in his 1991 study of MNT's
anti-urbanism cites the 'Semaine Sociale' of rural France as important to the
organisation's development.[31] Whereas Mary Kenny, in *Goodbye to Catholic
Ireland*, writes of the influence of the 'Semaines Rurales'.[32] Indeed, there are
many references to both in other parts of the literature,[33] which may give
rise to some confusion. Both terms, however, are correct as the *Semaines
Sociales* and *Semaines Rurales* were effectively branches of the same movement, one having evolved from the other a matter of years after the main
group's foundation.

Jean Terrel's 1923 work on the French *Semaines Sociales* clearly demonstrates that the *Rurales* evolved from the main social week early in its
existence while remaining ideologically connected to the parent stem. Arguing that rural matters were always prevalent in the *Semaines Sociales* from
its beginning in 1904, Terrel contends that to address rural issues properly,
some modification in the movement's approach was needed which would
shift the focus squarely to French rural life. This, it is argued, was an easy
transition, given the original *Semaines Sociales* long-standing concern for
rural people. The first attempts at a specific *Semaine Rurales* were made in
Lyon in 1912, followed by Besançon, near the border with Switzerland.[34]
Despite some minor adjustments from the original gatherings, the ethos and
message remained constant.

The *Semaines* model was enormously successful from its inception in
1904. However, as Parker Moon shows, a similar format to the *Semaines*
had been in use by German Catholics during the 1890s.[35] It was, however, in
France where the format found a widespread receptive audience, becoming
an institution in the country's Catholic social movement. Moon shows that
the model quickly found some success in Belgium (another nation Hayes borrowed much from),[36] which held its first 'agricultural week' in 1905, with a
labour week inaugurated from 1908. The Dutch instituted their own 'social
week' at Utrecht in 1906, followed by Spain and Italy which launched theirs
in 1907. Further afield, Poland established similar conferences at Warsaw,
Przemysl, and Poznań, while Luxemburg, Switzerland, Austria and others
developed similar institutions in these years.[37] Furthermore, it was not long
before the idea crossed the Atlantic to the Americas,[38] including a hugely successful French-Canadian version which was established in 1920.[39]

Interestingly, the Canadian branch, the *Semaine Sociale du Canada*, was
viewed not as a variation, but as a direct descendant. In a report on the inaugural Canadian *Semaines* in 1920, a letter from the General Commission of
the French *Semaines Sociales* was read, acknowledging kinship and stating,
'where could she feel closer to its origins than at home, than in the country

which still remains "New France"'?[40] From the outset, the Canadian version of the gathering shared the same concerns with the plight of rural people as the parent movement, sounding alarm at the cityward trend.[41] The gathering also demonstrated a paternalistic trait in its concerns for rural people which it shared with the plethora of international Catholic social groups which had emerged in the original's wake, including MNT.[42]

Interestingly, early *Semaine Sociale du Canada* gatherings noted Ireland as an important country alongside Belgium, Holland, and France for advancing a form of confessional collectivism which was compatible with *Semaines* goals.[43] The reality was somewhat different, however, as Ireland at this stage was far off the European pace when it came to social Catholicism and the type of gathering that was now expanding across the globe. Why then was this the case? Cahill and O'Leary both argue that European countries where Catholic social endeavours had thrived had not faced the same pressing social and political questions Ireland had. European countries had not been preoccupied with questions of national independence or the energy-sapping 'land question'. Nor had they to deal with the legacy of the penal laws which had forced the Irish Church to focus on the not inconsiderable task of the reconstruction of its institutions.[44] Nevertheless, Ireland's late bloom of social Catholicism began, according to Whyte in the 1930s with the emergence of MNT,[45] as Irish Catholic social groups redressed the balance, bringing the state in line with its Western European neighbours and co-religionists.

That MNT had initially emerged as a rural co-operative movement did not mean that it was not driven by Catholic values. Leo XIII's 1891 encyclical, *Rerum Novarum* was integral to MNT's understanding of how society should be.[46] As the movement evolved from a rural co-operative to a community movement based on vocational principles, so too did its embrace of Catholic social teaching. A week after the organisation's launch on 15 May 1931 Pope Pius XI published *Quadragesimo Anno* (On Reconstruction of the Social Order), which dealt with, among other issues, the principle of subsidiarity, the principle of occupational organisation, and social justice and social charity.[47] *Quadragesimo Anno's* publication changed Hayes's thinking about 'how rural interests might best be organised',[48] leading to a new approach which reflected the up-to-date teaching. It was in this new era that the *Semaines*-style gatherings became more important as they offered the chance to gauge a variety of opinions in rural Ireland and to bring people from different strands of society together in line with papal instruction.

Irish Rural Weeks

Initially, Hayes believed that the week-long format which had become successful throughout many parts of Europe was too long for Irish needs and that a shortened version would suffice.[49] Labelling it as an 'experiment', the first *Semaines*-style gathering took place in the Cistercian Monastery, Roscrea in November 1933 as a 'Rural Weekend'. Like its well-established European counterparts, the experimental gathering saw a wide cross-section of rural society come together, 'priests, professional people, big farmers and small farmers, highly cherished Protestants and the elusive farm labourers' laying the work for the Rural Weeks which were to follow.[50]

The truncated version of the *Semaines Sociales* in Ireland proved very successful, with much favourable newspaper coverage. Key to the success of this new venture was Fr Edward J. Coyne, a noted expert in European Catholic social movements,[51] and steadfast ally of Fr Hayes. Coyne's clerical career was illustrious; holding positions in several important European Catholic institutions,[52] he brought some much-needed experience to this first gathering. In his account of the first 'Rural Weekend' for the *Irish Monthly*, Coyne stated that while the gathering as a 'new departure' for Ireland, it was not an entirely new endeavour, as its origins were to be found on mainland Europe.[53]

Press coverage of this 'new departure' for Ireland also drew attention to the model's European origins. The *Tipperary Star*, one of the first titles to give its support to MNT, stated 'it is based on a similar practice in France where farmers and labourers from miles around gather together at Colleges and like institutions for week-ends to discuss economic problems as they affect rural interests'.[54] Building quickly on the success of and interest in this first 'Weekend', ten more were held over the period 1933 to 1937, when the organisation began its week-long format, known as 'the Rural Week'. From the beginning, however, domestic matters were placed alongside international rural life, with issues impacting Belgium, Holland, Italy, and the Baltic regions up for discussion.[55] Toner, commenting upon the success of the endeavour, stated that it 'aroused the interest of the thinking men' as to the future of the organisation.[56] It was a future which would increasingly bring the organisation closer to its European origins, as well as developing new international alliances.

The year of 1937 proved an important period in the development of MNT and its own gatherings. That year was the launch of its first Parish guild in the new era, and as noted above, it was the first week-long event in the organisation's history (although the 'Weekends' would continue to be held). Hosted at Coláiste Deuglán, Ardmore, Co Waterford, the first week-long gathering exceeded all expectations and drew a larger cross-section of Irish life together than before. Farmers, teachers, young people, doctors, clergy, and businessmen descended upon Ardmore to discuss pressing matters, including rural electrification and water improvement for farmhouses.[57] The successful experiment in bringing various walks of life together saw MNT look outward, beyond Ireland's borders for their next Rural Week. In 1938, the event was again staged at Ardmore. However, at this year's event, MNT, partly with an eye on the deteriorating political situation across Europe, decided to bring together leading rural and intellectual figures from across the continent to speak at the organisation's first 'International Day'.

International matters had been addressed from the very first Rural Weekend in 1932, so it made much sense to carry down this route with the establishment of a dedicated day to international rural matters. In doing so, the organisation was continuing a tradition established by the French *Semaines Sociales* which had a pronounced international element from its early days.[58] A small, but significant array of international speakers was assembled by Hayes, who had relentlessly worked throughout the year to entice people to the landmark event. Representatives from Belgium, France, Italy, Portugal, and Britain took up invitations to speak at the event,[59] with national newspapers, demonstrating their continued interest in the organisation, exclaiming that 'Europe Comes to Ardmore'.[60]

Building upon the modest successes of the first International Day, the organisation widened the net for the sequel in August of 1939, welcoming delegates from France, Italy, the United States, New Zealand, Germany, and Belgium.[61] With war in Europe on the horizon, the atmosphere in Galway was tense, and ill-feeling among the international delegates prevailed, with many refusing to fraternise with one another.[62] The content of some of the delegates' speeches also caused much rancour. German representative, Helmut Clissmann, head of the German Academic Exchange organisation (DAAD) in Ireland,[63] was offered a stinging rebuke by chair Liam de Roiste in his concluding remarks, taking aim at the country's ruling Nazi party.[64] The Italian delegation fared little better, with their domestic politics and excursions into Abyssinia criticised by the Irish in attendance.[65] Hayes, while visibly dismayed by the acrimony on display,[66] found some comfort in the attendance of Monsignor Luigi Ligutti, the rural pioneer from the National Catholic Rural Life Conference (NCRLC) in the United States. Ligutti was one of the most famous priests of the period,[67] and would become an important friend to Hayes and MNT in the decades ahead.[68]

Social Order Summer School

It is important to acknowledge that while Hayes and the MNT hierarchy pathed the way for community change and rural development based upon European examples, others within the state were also looking to the same sources of inspiration. Notable Irish clergy such as Fr Coyne and Fr Edward Cahill, another figure who had close associations with Hayes,[69] played an important role in bringing European ideas to Ireland. Cahill had noted in his 1932 *Framework of a Christian State*, the power of the *Semaines* movement and its potential in Ireland.[70] The Social Order Summer School, an initiative driven by Coyne[71] and which had much input from Cahill's *An Rioghacht*,[72] was hosted at Clongowes Wood between 1935 and 1939 and took the same continental 'social week' format.[73] Tackling many of the same topics which MNT engaged in at their rural gatherings,[74] it too acknowledged its transnational origins by extending fraternal greetings to the *Semaine Sociale de France*.[75] Not only this, it acknowledged the kinship and shared goals it had with MNT, with Coyne noting the Rural Week and claiming Hayes's organisation was energetically tackling the same issues the Summer School was.[76]

International Rural Community

Whereas the Social Order Summer School ground to a halt in 1939, along with Hayes's 'International Day' ambitions, the Rural Weeks would continue. The onset of war a mere matter of days after the conclusion of 1939's Rural Week saw MNT members lamenting the disintegration of international relations and the collapse into conflict of what they viewed as the 'international family'.[77] Undeterred, the organisation with Hayes at the helm persisted with their internationalist outlook, bringing important international rural figures to Ireland to speak with MNT audiences at Rural Weeks and Weekends at the war's end, including Ligutti who returned on numerous occasions.[78] Indeed, Ligutti would invite Hayes to speak at his own organisation's inaugural 'International Day' gathering in Ohio in 1949.[79]

MNT's flagship event continued until 1969 and expanded its international themes beyond the initial 'International Day'. The event grew steadily year by year, showcasing an impressive diversity of speakers and attendees. The impressive array of international delegates at the 1962 gathering, for example, was commented upon by the *Catholic News Service* feed. The publication also, importantly, highlighted the potential for the spread of MNT's ideas in other nations:

> Among the 300 delegates to the Rural Week was a group of 12 students from Swansea University in Wales who came to Ireland for field work with Muintir na Tire's guilds. Other students, who come from Iran, Thailand, Indonesia, Sierra Leone, Jamaica, British Guiana, Nigeria and Malaya, said Muintir na Tire's ideas could be applied to their own countries' rural problems.[80]

That so many countries were represented by the early 1960s, several years after the death of MNT's founder was viewed as testament to Hayes's life's work. Certainly, in the wake of a successful 1963 Rural Week in the Franciscan College, Gormanstown, it was noted that the organisation was only building upon the foundation stone which Hayes had laid,[81] demonstrating that his shadow still loomed large over the organisation.

Conclusion

The intellectual origins of MNT's Rural Weeks are indisputable. Emerging from the vibrant French social Catholic movement of the early twentieth century, the gathering found receptive audiences across the European continent and beyond in a short number of years. While it is unclear when Hayes first encountered the *Semaines* gatherings, he had submerged himself in French life and culture, accumulating an advanced working knowledge of the French social movement. His first forays into bringing this model of forum into Ireland were tentative, experimenting first with weekend gatherings before progressing to full weeks a short number of years later. What was apparent from the outset was that these gatherings in rural Ireland would incorporate international themes to complement their international origins. As the organisation developed, particularly in the post-war years, the example borrowed from continental Europe was now being viewed as a platform for furthering Catholic social ideas internationally, carrying on the early transnational traditions.

Notes

1 Stephen Rynne, *Father John Hayes, Founder of Muintir na Tire, The People of the Land* (Dublin, 1960), p. 115; Marie-Emmanuelle Chessel, 'From Duties to Rights: Revisiting the 'Social Catholics' in Twentieth Century France' in *French History*. 33 (2019), pp. 587–605.
2 *Muintir na Tire Rule Book* (Dublin, 1931) (N.A.I., Muintir na Tire General File, TAOIS/S 10816).
3 Rynne, *Father John Hayes*, p. 102.
4 *Nenagh Guardian*, 23 January 1932.
5 Rynne, *Father John Hayes*, p. 41.
6 Herman T. Salton, 'France's Other Enlightenment: Laïcité, Politics and the Role of Religion in French Law', *Journal of Politics and Law* 5(4) (2012), pp. 30–41.
7 Brenna Moore. *Sacred Dread: Raïssa Maritain, the Allure of Suffering, and the French Catholic Revival 1905–1944* (Notre Dame, 2012), p. 3.
8 Rynne, *Father John Hayes*, pp. 39–40.
9 Ralph Gibson, *A Social History of French Catholicism 1789–1914* (London, 1989), pp. 270–271, Rynne, *Father John Hayes*, p. 43.
10 Neil McWilliam, 'Monuments, Martyrdom, and the Politics of Religion in the French Third Republic', *The Art Bulletin* 77(2) (June 1995), pp. 186–206.
11 M.C. Cleary, 'The Plough and the Cross: Peasant Unions in South-Western France', *The Agricultural History Review* 30(2) (1982), pp. 127–136.
12 Rynne, *Father John Hayes*, pp. 41–42, Mark Tierney, *The Story of Muintir na Tire 1931–2001, The First Seventy Years* (Tipperary, 2004), p. 4.
13 C.J.T. Talar, 'An Americanist in Paris: The Early Career of the Abbé Félix Klein', in Derek C. Hatch and Timothy R. Gabrielli (eds.), *Weaving the American Catholic Tapestry, Essays in Honor of William L. Porter* (Oregon, 2017), p. 114.
14 Parker Thomas Moon, 'The Social Catholic Movement in France under the Third Republic', *The Catholic Historical Review* 7(1) (April 1921), pp. 24–34.
15 Cleary, 'The Plough and the Cross', p. 131.
16 Vincent Flauraud, 'La JAC [Jeunesse agricole catholique] dans le Massif central méridional (Aveyron, Cantal) des années 1930 aux années 1960' (PhD, Université Aix Marseille, 2003), p. 32.
17 Transcript of John Hayes Speech on Irish Radio, 11 April 1934 (N.U.I.G., John Hayes Papers, P134/12/1/2/2), p. 2.
18 Peter Bernardi, 'Social Modernism: The Case of the Semaine Sociales', in Darrell Jodock (ed.), *Catholicism Contending with Modernity: Roman Catholic Modernism and Anti-Modernism in Historical Context* (Cambridge, 2000), p. 279.
19 Parker Thomas Moon, *The Labor Problem and the Social Catholic Movement in France: A Study in the History of Social Politics* (New York, 1921), p. 320.
20 John McManners, *Church and State in France, 1870–1914* (London, 1972), p. 111.
21 Moon, *The Labor Problem*, p. 341.
22 Guido Erreygers, 'On The Interpretation of Potron's Equations as Translations of The Social Doctrine of the Church', *Rivista Internazionale di Scienze Sociali* (Aprile–Giugno 2014), pp. 161–178.

23 Maurice Blondel, *The Letter on Apologetics, and History and Dogma/Texts Pre-sented and Translated by Alexander Dru and Illtyd Trethowan* (London, 1964), p. 39.
24 Moon, *The Labor Problem*, p. 341.
25 *The Nationalist (Tipperary)*, 3 July 1940.
26 *Belfast News Letter*, 1 August 1906.
27 *Anglo-Celt*, 12 June 1920.
28 *Drogheda Independent*, 5 December 1925.
29 *The Nationalist (Tipperary)*, 8 September 1926.
30 John Hayes, 'The Beginning', in *Muintir na Tire Official Handbook 1941* (Tipper-ary, 1941), pp. 43–47.
31 Eoin Devereux, 'Saving Rural Ireland-Muintir na Tire and Its Anti-Urbanism, 1931–1958', *The Canadian Journal of Irish Studies* 17(2) (December 1991), pp. 23–30.
32 Mary Kenny, *Goodbye to Catholic Ireland: How the Irish Lost the Civilization They Created* (Dublin, 2000), p. 151.
33 Raymond O'Connor, Olive McCarthy, and Michael Ward, *Innovation and Change in Irish Credit Unions* (Cork, 2002), p. 28.
34 Jean Terrel, *Les Semaines Sociales* (Paris, 1923), pp. 90–91.
35 Moon, *The Labor Problem*, p. 341.
36 Tierney, *The Story of Muintir na Tire*, p. 25.
37 Moon, *The Labor Problem*, p. 340.
38 *The Catholic News Sheet*, 14 June 1920.
39 Jean-C Falardeau, 'Review of The Social Thought of French Canada as Reflected in the Semaine Sociale, by Sister Marie Agnes of Rome Gaudreau', *The Canadian Historical Review* 27(3) (1946), pp. 315–317.
40 Semaine Sociale du Canada, *Compte rendu des cours et conferences* (Montreal, 1920), p. ix.
41 du Canada, *Compte rendu des cours et conferences*, p. 28, Semaine Sociale du Canada, *'Capital et Travail' Compte rendu des cours et conferences* (Montreal, 1922), p. 163.
42 Devereux, 'Saving Rural Ireland', p. 28.
43 Semaine Sociale du Canada, *Compte rendu des cours et conferences* (Montreal, 1922), p. 42.
44 Don O'Leary, *Vocationalism and Social Catholicism in Twentieth-Century Ire-land* (Dublin, 2000), p. 21., Edward J. Cahill, *The Framework of a Christian State* (Dublin, 1932), p. 262.
45 J.H. Whyte, *Church and State in Modern Ireland 1923–1979* (NJ, 1980), p. 68.
46 Eoin Devereux, 'Class, Community and Conflict: The Case of Muintir na Tire Ltd.', *Tipperary Historical Journal* (1995), pp. 94–102.
47 See Rupert Ederer, *Economics as If God Matters: Over a Century of Papal Teach-ing Addressed to the Economic Order* (Plymouth, 2011).
48 Tony Varley, 'Reviewed Work(s): The Story of Muintir na Tíre 1931–2001 – the First Seventy Years by Mark Tierney', *Journal of the Galway Archaeological and Historical Society* 58 (2006), pp. 197–199.
49 Hayes 'The Beginning', p. 44.
50 Rynne, *Father John Hayes*, p. 113.
51 Lili Zách, 'Catholicism and Anti-Communism: The Reactions of Irish Intel-lectuals to Revolutionary Changes in Hungary (1918–1939)', *Diacronie* 33(1) (March 2018), pp. 1–23, Edward J. Coyne, 'Corporative Organization of Soci-ety', *Studies: An Irish Quarterly Review* 23(90) (June 1934), pp. 185–202.
52 *Irish Examiner*, 27 May 1958.

53 Edward J. Coyne, 'The First Rural Weekend in Ireland', *The Irish Monthly* 62(727) (January 1934), pp. 10–16.
54 *Tipperary Star*, 18 November 1933.
55 *Tipperary Star*, 25 November 1933.
56 Jerome Toner, 'Democracy and the Parish in Ireland', *Blackfriars* 32(371) (February 1951), pp. 65–69.
57 Tierney, *The Story of Muintir na Tire*, p. 50.
58 *Semaine Sociale de France IV Session Amiens* (1907), p. 25.
59 Rynne, *Father John Hayes*, pp. 154–155.
60 *Irish Press*, 31 August 1938.
61 *Irish Examiner*, 12 August 1939.
62 Rynne, *Father John Hayes*, p. 165.
63 Gisela Holfter, 'Ernst Scheyer', in Gisela Holfter (ed.), *German-Speaking Exiles in Ireland 1933–1945* (Amsterdam, 2006), p. 154.
64 Rynne, *Father John Hayes*, p. 163.
65 Rynne, *Father John Hayes*, p. 163.
66 Rynne, *Father John Hayes*, p. 163.
67 Duane A. Schmidt, *Iowa Pride* (Fairfax, 2002), p. 82.
68 Vincent A. Yzermans, *The People I Love: A Biography of Luigi G. Ligutti* (Minnesota, 1976), p. 89.
69 Thomas J. Morrissey, *The Ireland of Edward J. Cahill SJ 1868–1941: A Secular or Christian State* (Dublin, 2006), p. 175.
70 Edward Cahill, *Framework of a Christian State: An Introduction to Social Science* (Dublin, 1932), pp. 268–269.
71 Seán Faughnan, 'The Jesuits and the Drafting of the Irish Constitution of 1937', *Irish Historical Studies* 26(101) (May 1988), pp. 79–102.
72 J. Waldron, 'An Rioghacht (The League of the Kingship of Christ): A Retrospect', *The Irish Monthly* 78(924) (June 1950), pp. 274–280.
73 Kieren Mullarkey, 'Ireland, the Pope and Vocationalism', in Joost Augusteijn (ed.), *Ireland in the 1930s: New Perspectives* (Dublin, 1999), p. 99.
74 Edward J. Coyne, 'The Social Order Summer School', *The Irish Monthly* 65(771) (September 1937), pp. 577–587, *Nenagh Guardian*, 30 July 1938.
75 *Irish Independent*, 18 July 1939.
76 Coyne, 'The Social Order Summer School', p. 586.
77 *The Landmark* 2(8) (August 1945), p. 3.
78 *Irish Examiner*, 20 August 1962.
79 Rynne, *Father John Hayes*, p. 221.
80 *Catholic News Service*, 20 August 1962.
81 *Drogheda Independent*, 24 August 1963.

15 Beyond the Pale? Representations of the Teddy Boy Subculture in Irish Theatre, 1955–1965

Ciara Molloy

Dublin, 12 September 1960. The Lord Mayor, Maurice Dockrell, officially opens the Third Dublin International Theatre Festival at the Mansion House.[1] The Festival will run between 12 and 25 September, and already over 1,200 overseas bookings have been made to see its various productions.[2] During that time, no less than fourteen plays will be performed in theatres throughout the city,[3] and one of those plays, *The Scatterin'*, is predicted to become 'a highlight of the Festival'.[4] Its author is a twenty-seven-year-old playwright named James McKenna, and its subject matter concerns a demonised youth subculture known as the Teddy Boys.

Pulitzer-prize winning author Junot Diaz once claimed that 'if you want to make a human being into a monster, deny them, at the cultural level, any reflection of themselves', and accordingly this chapter examines the reflections of the Teddy Boy subculture through the prism of McKenna's play. This chapter first examines the nature of press coverage surrounding the Teds in 1950s' Ireland, arguing a moral panic repertoire was employed to depict members of the subculture as undesirable folk devils. The second section discusses McKenna's simultaneous reification and challenging of stereotypes surrounding the Teds. The final section considers critical receptions to *The Scatterin'* following both its Dublin and London debuts. Overall, this chapter emphasises how studying the cultural underpinnings of crime and deviance generates an enhanced understanding of the manner by which boundaries of acceptable and non-acceptable behaviour are navigated and negotiated in a particular historical context.

Creating Folk Devils

The Teddy Boys are often described as the first teenage subculture to emerge in post–World War II Britain.[5] Their subcultural style was broadly based on fashions popular during the reign of King Edward VII from 1901 to 1910, and included velvet lapels, string ties, long draped jackets, narrow drainpipe trousers, colourful waistcoats and thick crepe-soled shoes.[6] Initially, the Ted style was designed by Savile Row tailors as the preserve of upper-class

DOI: 10.4324/9781032691886-15

youths,[7] but was soon appropriated by the 'lumpen proletariat' of South London and as a result was construed as a primarily working-class subculture.[8]

There were also strong American influences that underpinned the Ted style. Their hair was frequently combed in a particular manner known as DA (Duck's Ass), mimicking the hairstyles of contemporary teenage icons such as American actor Tony Curtis;[9] their drapes were partially inspired by the Pachucos, a gang of Mexican-American and Chicano youths who wore zoot suits with draped jackets;[10] while their crepe-soled shoes (also known as brothel creepers) were offshoots of the desert or chukka boot worn by soldiers stationed in the deserts of North Africa.[11] Moreover, the jive and the bop were the dancing styles of the Teds and had been introduced by American G.I.s in Britain before the onset of rock 'n' roll music.[12] Therefore, the style and leisure activities of the Teds were the product of an internationalised Anglo-American youth culture.

Stanley Cohen has outlined that during a moral panic, namely a disproportionate reaction to a perceived social crisis, the media draws upon various techniques including symbolisation, sensitisation, dramatisation and escalation to sensationalise and exaggerate the threat posed by a particular group.[13] As the following paragraphs will argue, the Irish press availed of such techniques to represent the Teds not just as nuisances or mere deviants, but as veritable folk devils personifying malign intent linked to violence and delinquency.[14]

The first confirmed sighting of a Teddy Boy in Dublin was on Merrion Row, as reported by the *Cork Examiner* on 23 July 1954.[15] Seán Ó Serbháin, however, had written a month earlier in the *Irish Press* that 'I am told that the species is not unknown in Dublin, though I have never set eyes on one myself', indicating the Teds may have appeared in Dublin as early as June 1954.[16] His zoological account of the Teds as an exotic phenomenon is noteworthy. Initially, Irish newspapers viewed Teddy Boys with amusement, with fashion crime due to their 'eccentric' clothing and hairstyles the only type of criminal activity attributed to them.[17]

Within six months of their Dublin debut, however, public opinion as gauged from newspaper coverage had turned from amusement to wariness. By Christmas 1954, there were hundreds of Teds in Dublin city who travelled in groups, and this collective and identifiable subculture was perceived as highly threatening. Tensions were brewing in the city between the Teds and local managers and doormen of Dublin ballrooms, who had apparently taken the initiative to ban any male in Teddy Boy clothing from entering dances.[18] By September 1955, the Vigilance Committee, established by Archbishop McQuaid to keep an eye on 'Communist activities and other anti-Catholic activities, such as Liberalism',[19] reported that 'the "Teddy Boys" were now excluded from all ballrooms in the city'.[20] Teds had become public enemy number one, their very style of clothing symbolic of delinquency and depravation.

It is worth briefly examining the volume of newspaper coverage surrounding Teds in 1950s and 1960s Ireland.[21] There were two key peaks where concern over Teds was particularly high, namely 1956 and 1959:

The 1956 coverage was partially in response to disturbances at Christ Church Cathedral in Dublin on New Year's Eve 1955 during which bottles and bricks were thrown at members of the Gardaí;[22] Teds were blamed for these delinquent activities. It was by no means clear that Teds were definitely behind these incidents; the *Longford Leader*, for instance, attributed the New Year's Eve disturbances to 'youth of the Teddy Boy class',[23] a vague reference which fails to answer whether actual Teds or merely a group of working-class youths were responsible for the incident.

This negative coverage was further amplified by an episode which occurred on 8 January 1956. Amateur light welterweight champion boxer Harry Perry was stabbed in the neck on Grafton Street when he tried to separate a group of eighteen-year-olds who were fighting.[24] District Justice Henry McCarthy asked Inspector Hurley whether the perpetrators in this incident were wearing Teddy Boy fashions, and Hurley ambiguously replied, 'They had a tendency that way. They had the haircut'.[25] Despite Hurley's unclear answer, the perpetrators were nevertheless represented by the press as Teddy Boys. They were depicted as pathologically deviant and calls for harsher criminal justice responses to the subculture particularly emanated from provincial sections of

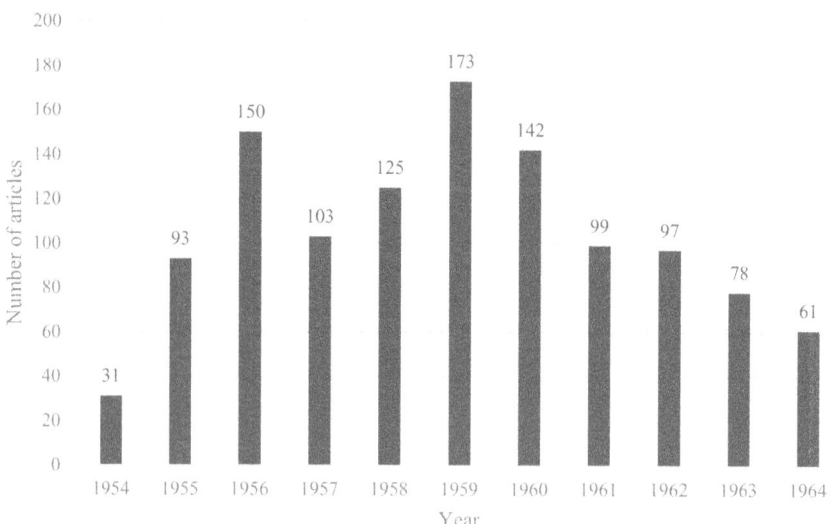

Figure 15.1 Volume of newspaper articles referring to "Teddy Boy(s)" in Irish Newspaper Archives, 1954–1964

Source: Copyright belongs to the author.

the press, who perhaps feared the subculture would further spread beyond the pale (both literally and figuratively).[26]

Throughout 1956, there were also disturbances associated with the screening of the film *Rock Around the Clock* (described as the Teds' 'very own movie')[27] starring Bill Haley and His Comets. The first such disturbance took place at the Star Cinema in Crumlin in July 1956, and the *Evening Herald* dramatically reported that a gang of Teddy Boys threw missiles such as bottles, smashed exit signs, and ripped arm covers off seats. Teenagers jived between cinema aisles and further screenings of the film were cancelled. Yet the supposedly riotous element of this event was undermined by the fact that although nine Gardaí were on duty at the time, no arrests were made.[28] This either represented a profound failure by Gardaí to apprehend clearly identifiable members of a (purportedly) delinquent subculture in a confined space; or, more likely, suggests that the disturbances as reported by the newspaper were exaggerated and not serious enough to warrant the initiation of formal criminal justice measures.

The subculture enjoyed a further resurgence towards the end of the 1950s. In 1959, Ireland was in the grips of an apparent crime wave with 17,865 indictable offences recorded (an 8% increase compared to the previous year).[29] At a press conference held in Garda headquarters regarding these crime figures, Commissioner Daniel Costigan argued that 'there was no serious Teddy boy problem' in Ireland compared to Britain.[30] Nevertheless, Costigan's allusion to the Teds indicates they were considered (in the minds of the public at least) as one of the primary causes of rising crime levels.

Gardaí in Limerick and Dublin were reportedly attacked by Teds in July and August 1959 respectively, which further emphasised their seemingly violent tendencies.[31] International events also sensitised such negative representations, with Irish newspapers dedicating significant levels of coverage to incidents of juvenile delinquency committed by Teds in Russia,[32] Italy,[33] Portugal[34] and Yugoslavia.[35] On Christmas Eve 1959, the so-called Teddy Boy riots took place in Dublin, whereby around 200 youths were involved in clashes with the Gardaí on O'Connell Street. Left-over vegetables from the Moore Street market were among the projectiles flung at the Gardaí, who responded by drawing their batons (their heavy-handed tactics serving to further escalate the incident).[36] Over forty people were reportedly injured during the riots.[37] Many of the youth involved in these riots were university students, who had seemingly started the incident by throwing squibs on the roadway.[38] In the Dáil however, Minister for Justice Oscar Traynor described their involvement as 'the innocent actions of students who were facing their holidays', whereas the Teddy Boy 'scoundrels' tried to 'cash in' on these innocent activities by starting a riot.[39] The behaviour of the middle and upper class university students which incited the riots was excused, while the working-class Teds who appeared to play a reactive role were blamed for the entire affair.

Overall, through use of a moral panic repertoire which symbolised Edwardian clothing as troublesome, dramatised the activities of the Teds, and was sensitised by international episodes of juvenile crime, the press solidified the subculture's association with violence and delinquency. Furthermore, the violent police reaction to the 'Teddy Boy riots' as outlined above further escalated conflict and cemented the folk devil status of the Teds in the eyes of the public. It was during the backdrop of this second peak of the Teddy Boy phenomenon that a young playwright named James McKenna wrote a play about members of the subculture called *The Scatterin'*.

Enter Stage Left: *The Scatterin'*

James McKenna was from a working-class background, born in Dublin and raised in Kilcoole Co. Wicklow, and enjoyed a vibrant career as a sculptor, poet and playwright. His play *The Scatterin'* – which was marketed by Alan Simpson and Carolyn Swift of the Pike Theatre as a 'Rock 'n' Ballad Fantasy' due to its inclusion of rock 'n' roll music as well as traditional Irish ballads[40] – revolves around the lives of six Dublin Teddy Boys, Con, Jemmo, Tony, Patzer, John-John and The Bird. It deals with their frustrations as Dublin working-class youths, their attempted emigration to Birmingham and Jemmo's arrest at the North Wall Quay for stabbing a member of An Garda Síochána. Throughout his play, McKenna engaged in a contradictory depiction of the Teddy Boy subculture; he challenged assumptions surrounding the origins of and societal reaction to the Teds, but fell into conventional stereotypes when describing their internal composition and activities. These variegated representations will be outlined in turn.

In terms of their origins, McKenna viewed the Teds as products of structural forces such as emigration and unemployment, as opposed to contemporary media representations which viewed the Teds as pathologically deviant. For instance, Jemmo claims in the play that 'I've been scroungin' here an' there an' gettin' bits o' jobs. I've been going around for a year now without a bit o' work. I marched with the unemployed crowd';[41] this was ostensibly a reference to The Dublin Unemployed Association which was set up in the 1950s and which engaged in several confrontations with the Gardaí.[42]

This sympathetic depiction of the Teds as products of social inequality accorded with his own personal experience of unemployment and emigration. By the time McKenna wrote *The Scatterin'*, he had already emigrated four times to England in search of employment,[43] much like his Teddy Boy characters. He expressed a lot of resentment for what he felt was his enforced exile and the failure of the Irish state to provide a living for its citizens. In the poem *Oxford Street is Long* (1965), McKenna wrote that 'we saw the Lion retreating / From GPO to Beggar's Bush. / But withal I have no nation [. . .] / And my only consolation is / That / Oxford Street is long'.[44] In other words, Irish independence from British rule did not improve the lives of its citizens who were still forced to emigrate to the land of the former colonial oppressor in order to make a living. In 1973, reflecting on his attitude towards the state in the fifties, McKenna admitted that he was extremely angry and had good reason to be:

> In Government parlance and official cynicism the Mailboat Irish were 'invisible exports'. It is hard to convey the total official non-concern for the Irish people in the fifties . . . we were a nation of demoralised men in gabardines.[45]

Reflecting McKenna's own personal experiences, *The Scatterin'* deals with themes such as social exclusion, emigration and unemployment, and can be interpreted as a critical social commentary on 1950s Irish society. In highlighting these structural origins of the Teddy Boy subculture, McKenna invited sympathy for them and succeeded to some extent in humanising these disenchanted young men.

Regarding societal reaction to the Teds, McKenna allowed a narrative of victimhood to ensconce the Teds, which again contested the prevailing press narrative of Teds as perpetrators. He did this by condemning the violent police reaction towards the subculture. In the play, a policeman grabs Conn by the shoulder and asks him his name – he says 'I'll get your name if I have to beat it out o' you'.[46] Another Garda comments to the Teds: 'There's a low dirty streak in your breed but, be God, we'll knock it out o' ye'.[47] In the final scene of Act I, Conn is violently beaten up by the Gardaí. This is reminiscent of the informal justice dispensed by policemen such as Garda James 'Lugs' Branigan who served in the Liberties in Dublin and frequently came into contact with the Teddy Boys.[48] In this regard, McKenna's play was prophetic for its challenging of the heavy-handedness and lack of accountability of policing in 1950s Ireland, and in doing so he called for a more empathetic approach to this demonised subculture.

Yet while humanising the Teds, McKenna also reified certain stereotypes which surrounded them, such as the subculture's masculine composition. No Teddy Girls appear in McKenna's play, despite the presence of female members of the subculture in 1950s and 1960s Dublin.[49] Indeed, there is a largely negative view of women which permeates the play; Jemmo for instance, describes women as 'brass faced bitches'.[50] A strong female character in the form of Sue Raftery does appear in the play, but her presence is mainly used to highlight themes such as romance and sexuality. For instance, when asked why she is emigrating to Birmingham, Sue responds that she is 'tired of men who never seem to know what they want'.[51] It seems that frustration with spinsterhood, rather than the desire to achieve self-actualisation or broaden her horizons, underpins Sue's motives. This undermines McKenna's supposed feminist credentials,[52] and reaffirms the position of women as second-class citizens in 1950s Ireland.

Another aspect in which McKenna's play upholds contemporary stereotypes surrounding the Teds is in relation to their activities. The play cul-
minates with the stabbing of a policeman by Jemmo, who is later captured
and hanged for his crime. Granted, there were some isolated incidents of
knife crime associated with Irish Teds in the 1950s, such as the stabbing
of Harry Perry as outlined in Section I, but in general, stabbing incidents
by Teddy Boys were more common internationally (particularly in England
and New Zealand).[53] Indeed, as Holohan has argued, the Irish Teds were
'more style than substance' in the sense that they adopted the clothing but
not necessarily the behaviour of their English counterparts.[54] In spite of this,
McKenna largely upheld the perceived violent behaviour and nature of the
Teds. Jemmo's justification for the stabbing of a policeman is noteworthy. He
claims that 'no, it wasn't a great thing; but I'm not sorry. It was somethin''
though. The only thing I've ever done in all me life . . . I was born when all
the shootin' an' shoutin' was over'.[55] This may be interpreted as McKenna's
criticism of the legacy of the revolutionary generation. To engage in such acts
of violence and aggression was to partake of this revolutionary generation,
to prove one's worth as a man, and to gain a sense of achievement and status.
Jemmo's espousal of violence, McKenna implies, was a result of adherence
rather than opposition to societal norms and values.

This simultaneous challenging and reification of stereotypes surrounding
the Teds throughout *The Scatterin'* initially appears contradictory, but in
reality, such contradictions serve one purpose, namely to demonstrate that
the Teds were products of the society in which they lived. The vices of the
Teds so demonised by the media, such as the glorification of violence, were
simply manifestations of underlying virtues expressed by society. Society
overall emerges from McKenna's play as hypocritical, because in spite of
its condemnation of the Teds, it was ultimately responsible for giving rise to
structural conditions that catalysed the emergence of the subculture in addition to fuelling its activities.

Critical Receptions

At this point, it is useful to consider the critical receptions that greeted *The
Scatterin'*. With regard to its Dublin debut at the 1960 Theatre Festival, from
the outset the technical aspects of the play were negatively received by crit-
ics. The music, under the direction of A.J. Potter, was described as 'effective, if at times not only off beat but off key'[56] while Des Hickey described
McKenna's dialogue as 'not brilliant and his poetry no better than pastiche
O'Casey'.[57] The second Act, in which the Teds sit around a campfire in the
Dublin Mountains and drink bottles of stout while pondering the mysteries
of life, the universe and everything, was particularly criticised as disparate.[58]
Further criticism was proffered on the basis that 'the action is allowed to
halt too frequently', 'too much freedom is given to the actors',[59] it lacked a
proper storyline[60] and often delivery of lines was unconvincing.[61] According

to Thomas Kilroy, although the play was considered to be 'the outstanding production of the festival', it failed 'to offer the experience of great drama to the audience'.[62] Rather its strengths lay in its social commentary and its humanising of the 'Dublin delinquent',[63] and it is these social and emotional values which emanate most strongly from contemporary reviews.

Granted, there were minor criticisms raised regarding McKenna's challenging of norms surrounding Catholicism, deference to authority and appropriate use of language. On the opening night, an audience member yelled 'keep religion out of it' when one of the Teds onstage insulted nuns.[64] The *Irish Independent* further added that 'a false note was struck too in that vivid brutal incident involving the Gardaí',[65] a reference to the assault perpetrated on Conn in Act I.[66] Apart from these minor criticisms, the biting social commentary which McKenna engaged in was mostly lauded. Des Hickey, reviewer with the *Sunday Independent*, described the play as 'the most lambasting thing in the Irish theatre since Behan' for its criticisms of the establishment and the Gardaí.[67] *The Irish Times* claimed that the play 'burns as no other play about Dublin people has since O'Casey was born'.[68] These parallels with O'Casey and Behan placed McKenna in line as an inheritor of a working-class literary tradition. The audience could resonate with its messages and seemingly embraced its verbal onslaught of the political establishment, even if opinions on the merits of criticising the Gardaí were divided.

Yet what resonated most strongly with critics was the play's raw energy and emotional power. The *Irish Independent* described it as 'a sprawling, vital, vivid, theatrical, tour de force'[69] while P. Ó Conchúir noted that 'there is lively meaning in it, anger and wildness, tears and fights, and it is rare we get this type of food in theatres in this country'.[70] There was a danger, however, that much of this emotional value stemmed from the musical and dance numbers in the play rather than its content. Indeed, this danger was actualised when Methuen & Co. Ltd Publishers refused to publish *The Scatterin'* in book format in 1960 on the grounds that it would not have 'many readers as a published text, for the reason that a great deal of its attraction lies in the dance and the spectacle'.[71] It was perceived as appealing to audiences on the grounds of carnivalesque entertainment as a piece of 'irrational fun',[72] which was perhaps inevitable following the Pike Theatre's decision to categorise it as a fantasy musical. This was incongruent with the critical social commentary that McKenna sought to convey.

Following its success in the 1960 Festival, *The Scatterin'* ran for five weeks in the Theatre Royal in Stratford East in London starting from 2 April 1962.[73] It was an East End debut rather than a West End one, but nonetheless a significant achievement for a first-time playwright. Alan Simpson produced the play in London alongside Oscar Lewenstein,[74] but the reception of the play by London critics was nothing short of disastrous. The technical shortcomings of the play were emphasised to a large extent by London critics. Bernard Levin of the *Daily Express* memorably wrote that 'the play is so disjointed that I think my hip has come out in sympathy'[75] while David Nathan in the

Daily Herald described it as 'two hours of unrelieved keening'.[76] Granted, Robert Muller of the *Daily Mail* designated it 'an enjoyable, unfinished rough and tumble', though sarcastically added that McKenna 'does not permit such decadent things as character development, construction or a plot to get between us and his play'.[77] In many ways, such reviews were perhaps to be expected – emotional and social values had carried the play on a wave of success in Dublin, but with little sense of attachment to the content or setting of the play, London audiences were less likely to overlook its various technical flaws.

Pure entertainment as opposed to hard-hitting social criticism was expected by London audiences from Irish plays,[78] and *The Scatterin'* was no exception. The *Yorkshire Post* wrote in its review that 'being Irishmen, it is natural for them to pour out their feelings of resentment, hate, love and superstition in song or in story form'.[79] The musical genre of the play was seen as innovative in Dublin, but in London was used as a basis for reinforcing racial prejudices against Irish people. Stage Irishry was expected; insightful social commentary was not. Ironically, it seems McKenna's play fell victim to the same type of stereotypical attitudes that he had (partially) attempted to challenge in relation to the Teds, albeit on a racial rather than a cultural level.

Coda

Overall, this chapter considered representations of the Teddy Boy subculture in 1950s Ireland through the lens of James McKenna's debut play *The Scatterin'*. It delineated the Irish press' deployment of a moral panic repertoire to portray the Teds as contemporary folk devils and outlined the seemingly contradictory reification and challenging of such stereotypes through McKenna's play while also considering the critical receptions which greeted *The Scatterin'* both in Dublin and London.

There are a host of intriguing dichotomies which emerge throughout McKenna's play. These dichotomies surface in relation to the values held by a subculture and dominant culture; between perceptions and realities of deviance; between agency and structure; and between the margins and mainstream. But perhaps this mass of contradictions is the entire point of the play. McKenna conveys to the audience that these dichotomies often constructed in relation to youth identity, popular culture and deviance are artificial and not necessarily oppositional. Indeed, the overarching message of his play seems to be that the Teddy Boys are no different from the rest of Irish society, because Irish society is just as bad as they are.

Ironically, however, McKenna's negative message also acts as a purveyor of hope. It demonstrates that the line which demarcates acceptable and non-acceptable behaviour – deviance and non-deviance – is ultimately a constructed one. The constructed nature of such a line provides much-needed perspective on crime and deviance, and challenges us to reach across the barricades to seek understanding of phenomena that we are otherwise inclined to demonise and dismiss. Amidst a mass of ostensible contradictions, McKenna communicates that the folk devils we create are nothing more than a distorted reflection of our own image. His message is a timely (and enduring) one.

Notes

1 *Cork Examiner*, 13 September 1960.
2 *Cork Examiner*, 13 September 1960.
3 *Evening Herald*, 13 September 1960, p. 4; *Irish Times*, 27 August 1960.
4 *Irish Independent*, 14 September 1960.
5 Robert Cross, 'The Teddy Boy as Scapegoat', *Doshisha Studies in Language and Culture* i–ii (1988), pp. 236–291, at p. 240.
6 *Irish Press*, 10 May 1954; *Irish Press*, 2 June 1954; *Cork Examiner*, 23 July 1954; *Cork Examiner*, 28 June 1955.
7 Cross, 'The Teddy Boy as Scapegoat', p. 245.
8 Tony Jefferson, 'The Teds: A Political Resurrection', *CCCS Stencilled Paper*, no. 17 (1973).
9 *Irish Press*, 14 March 1955.
10 For further discussion of the zoot suiters, see Luis Alvarez, *The Power of the Zoot: Youth Culture and Resistance during World War II* (Berkeley, 2008).
11 Ray Ferris and Julian Lord, *Teddy Boys: A Concise History* (Preston, 2012), p. 6.
12 Ferris and Lord, *Teddy Boys*, pp. 4–5.
13 Stanley Cohen, *Folk Devils and Moral Panics: The Creation of the Mods and Rockers* (London, 1972).
14 Steven Hayle, 'Folk Devils without Moral Panics: Discovering Concepts in the Sociology of Evil', *International Journal of Criminology and Sociological Theory* vi(2) (2013), pp. 1125–1137.
15 *Cork Examiner*, 23 July 1954. For further discussion of the Teds in an Irish context, see Carole Holohan, *Reframing Irish Youth in the Sixties* (Liverpool, 2018); Eleanor O'Leary, *Youth and Popular Culture in 1950s Ireland* (London, 2018); Kevin Kearns, *The Legendary "Lugs" Branigan: Ireland's Most famed Garda* (Dublin, 2015).
16 *Irish Press*, 2 June 1954.
17 *Irish Press*, 2 June 1954; *Irish Press*, 28 September 1956.
18 *Evening Herald*, 11 December 1954.
19 '"V" Committee – Establishment and minutes of meetings 1954–59' (Dublin Diocesan Archives [D.D.A.], Communists AB8/B/XXIII/1).
20 'Minutes of the "V" Committee, held on Monday 24 September 1955' (D.D.A., Communists AB8/B/XXIII/13/1).
21 These newspaper articles were searched from 1 January to 31 December of each year using the keywords "Teddy Boy" and "Teddy Boys". Interestingly, there was a prominent racehorse called 'Teddy Boy' during this period (perhaps indicative of the cultural permeation of the Teddy Boy subculture to various spheres of Irish society) and therefore the search was carried with the exclusion of the terms 'horse' and 'racing'.
22 *Longford Leader*, 7 January 1956.
23 *Longford Leader*, 7 January 1956.
24 *Cork Examiner*, 10 January 1956; *Nationalist and Leinster Times*, 14 January 1956.

25 *Irish Times*, 21 January 1956.
26 *Longford Leader*, 7 January 1956; *Nationalist and Leinster Times*, 14 January 1956; *Connacht Sentinel*, 17 January 1956.
27 Bernard Neary, *Lugs: The Life and Times of Jim Branigan* (Dublin, 1985), p. 56.
28 *Evening Herald*, 31 July 1956.
29 Garda Commissioner, *Report of the Commissioner of an Garda Síochána on Crime for the Year Ended 30 September 1959* (Dublin: 1959), p. 2.
30 *Evening Herald*, 1 May 1959.
31 *Nenagh Guardian*, 4 July 1959; *Evening Herald*, 10 August 1959.
32 *Irish Independent*, 16 September 1959.
33 *Evening Herald*, 20 August 1959.
34 *Irish Press*, 13 October 1959.
35 *Evening Herald*, 12 November 1959.
36 *Cork Examiner*, 28 December 1959.
37 *Fermanagh Herald*, 9 January 1960.
38 *Cork Examiner*, 28 December 1959; *Connacht Tribune*, 2 January 1960; *Westmeath Examiner*, 9 January 1960.
39 *Dáil Éireann deb.*, clxxix, 376 (11 February 1960).
40 *Irish Times*, 25 August 1960; 'Letter from Carolyn Swift to Claud Cockburn, 30 November 1959' (T.C.D. MS, Pike Theatre Papers, 10813 400/1).
41 'The Scatterin' prompt copy', p. 45 (T.C.D. MS, Pike Theatre Papers, 10813 13/1).
42 Neary, *Lugs*, p. 46.
43 *Sunday Independent*, 18 November 1973.
44 James McKenna, *Poems* (Dublin, 1973), p. 21.
45 *Sunday Independent*, 18 November 1973.
46 'The Scatterin' prompt copy', p. 17 (T.C.D. MS, Pike Theatre Papers, 10813 13/1).
47 'The Scatterin' prompt copy', p. 18.
48 Neary, *Lugs*; Kearns, *The Legendary "Lugs"*.
49 In their *City Newsreel* broadcast on 29 November 1954, Raidió Éireann held an interview with Teddy Boys and Teddy Girls in Dublin city; *Evening Herald*, 2 December 1954. Unfortunately, a record of this interview no longer survives in the RTÉ Archives.
50 'The Scatterin' prompt copy', p. 7 (T.C.D. MS, Pike Theatre Papers, 10813 13/1).
51 'The Scatterin' prompt copy', p. 38.
52 Michael Pierse (ed.), *A History of Irish Working-class Writing* (Cambridge, 2018), p. 33.
53 In Britain, on 2 July 1953 a youth called John Beckley was stabbed on Clapham Common in south London following a fight between four local youths and a group of Teds known as the Plough Boys. Michael Davies was sentenced to death for Beckley's murder, though his sentence was later commuted to life imprisonment; Clifford Williamson, 'The Ted Scare', *Revue Francaise de Civilisation Britannique* xix(1) (2014), pp. 49–66; Tony Parker, *The Plough Boy* (London, 2013). In New Zealand, what was dubbed by the Irish press as the 'Teddy Boy Café' murder trial took place in Auckland in October 1955. A twenty-one-year-old Teddy Boy and Belfast emigrant named Albert Lawrence Black was tried and convicted for the murder of twenty-year-old Alan Jacques in Ye Olde Barn café in Auckland. Black was executed on 5 December 1955; *Belfast Telegraph*, 18 October 1955; *Cork Examiner*, 20 October 1955; *Irish Press*, 21 October 1955; *Cork Examiner*, 17 November 1955; for a fictional account of the case, see Fiona Kidman, *This Mortal Boy* (London, 2019).
54 Holohan, *Reframing Irish Youth*, p. 75. Though it is entirely possible (and indeed likely) that the extent of violence of English Teds was exaggerated by the contemporary press.

55 'The Scatterin' prompt copy', p. 44 (T.C.D. MS, Pike Theatre Papers, 10813 13/1). For discussion of the impact of the revolutionary generation on young men in 1930s and 1940s Ireland, see Bryce Evans, '"How will we kill the evening?"': "degeneracy" and "second generation" male adolescence in independent Ireland', in Catherine Cox and Susannah Riordan (eds.), *Adolescence in Modern Irish History* (Basingstoke, 2015), pp 151–175.

56 *Irish Press*, 14 September 1960.

57 *Sunday Independent*, 18 September 1960.

58 L.S. Tuathail agus P. Ó Conchúir, 'Féile drámaíochta agus scannán', *Comhar* xix(11) (1960), pp. 24–26, at p. 28. Translated by the author.

59 Tuathail agus Ó Conchúir, 'Féile drámaíochta agus Scannán', p. 28.

60 Niall Montgomery, 'The Scatterin', *Development* xxvi (1960), pp. 38–39, at p. 39.

61 *Hibernia*, 23 September 1960.

62 Thomas Kilroy, 'Dublin International Theatre Festival: The New Irish Plays', *The Furrow* xi(10) (1960), pp. 679–683, at p. 680.

63 Kilroy, 'Dublin International Theatre Festival', p. 681.

64 *The Observer*, 18 September 1960 (T.C.D. MS. Pike Theatre Papers, 10813 388a/20); *Evening Herald*, 14 September 1960; *Evening Herald*, 5 December 1973. The scene that caused such insult to this single theatregoer was presumably in Act I, when Jemmo described the convents as 'woman factories' that 'stuff their little brains with all sorts o' slop about the sanctity of woman and the wonder of womanhood'; 'The Scatterin' prompt copy', p. 7 (T.C.D. MS, Pike Theatre Papers, 10813 13/1).

65 *Irish Independent*, 14 September 1960.

66 'The Scatterin' prompt copy', p. 18 (T.C.D. MS, Pike Theatre Papers, 10813 13/1).

67 *Sunday Independent*, 18 September 1960.

68 *Irish Times*, 14 September 1960.

69 *Irish Independent*, 14 September 1960.

70 Tuathail agus Ó Conchúir, 'Féile drámaíochta agus scannán', p. 28.

71 'Letter from John Cullen of Methuen & Co Ltd Publishers to Alan Simpson, 24 November 1960' (T.C.D. MS, Pike Theatre Papers, 10813 400/60).

72 Montgomery, 'The Scatterin', p. 39.

73 Desmond Egan and Niamh Hoare (eds.), *James McKenna: A Catalogue* (Newbridge, 2005), p. 16.

74 *Daily Mail*, 3 April 1962 (T.C.D. MS, Pike Theatre Papers, 10813 389).

75 *Daily Express*, 3 April 1962 (T.C.D. MS, Pike Theatre Papers, 10813 389).

76 *Daily Herald*, 3 April 1962 (T.C.D. MS, Pike Theatre Papers, 10813 389); see also *Evening Herald*, 30 April 1962.

77 *Daily Mail*, 3 April 1962 (T.C.D. MS, Pike Theatre Papers, 10813 389).

78 *Irish Times*, 4 April 1962.

79 *Yorkshire Post*, 3 April 1962 (T.C.D. MS, Pike Theatre Papers, 10813 389).

16 Politics and the Praxis of Power

The Political Establishment and the Talented Young in Post–World War II Ireland

Tomás Finn

Speaking at his Fine Gael party's Ard Fheis in 1958, John A. Costello proclaimed that 'the challenge to Irish democracy must be met [by] the talented young'.[1] Given criticisms of apathy, political indifference and 'aloof neutrality'[2] Costello and others had directed specifically at Donal Barrington, the future Supreme Court Justice and other members of the intellectual society, *Tuairim*[3] and more generally at the younger generation, the process by which Ireland and its political parties would be modernised from the 1950s to the 1970s was far from straightforward. How then did the political establishment and in particular Fianna Fáil and Fine Gael come to accept that the emerging generation should have a greater voice in the governance of their country. This was in part a response to increasing demands from younger people and a recognition of the need of political parties to attract new members and to seek support from this, an emerging electorate, but also an attempt to limit, direct or control the impact of a more radical youth. The gradual acceptance that youth needed their own platforms whether it be different forums in Universities and in youth political organisations so as to be better able to articulate their needs and seek to influence public policy and public opinion reflected the transformation Ireland underwent in these decades. This, the process whereby politics and political parties were modernised and the younger generation gained a voice therein is key to the emergence of modern Ireland.

That the main political parties' engagement with the younger generation was to an increasing extent driven by their relative electoral fortunes from the late 1950s is not a surprise. An early attempt by Fianna Fáil to generate interest among the youth in 1955 with the existence of the Kevin Barry (combined Universities) branch in Dublin did not come to much with the branch having to be revived in 1963.[4] Speaking at the earlier meeting of the need for a reorganisation of the party and new policies, Seán Lemass, once he became Taoiseach, was to the fore of moves towards a more open economy and society. The new Taoiseach spoke in 1959 with confidence about the new era and 'new spirit' that was in evidence especially among young people in the country.[5] Pointing to different voluntary organisations such as *Tuairim*,

DOI: 10.4324/9781032691886-16

the European Council and Muintir na Tíre, Lemass argued that it was not important as to whether such organisations and the government agreed with one another or not but that they continue to attract 'public goodwill and support'. He maintained that they represented the 'desire of the people . . . to have a direct share in the great work of national development'. While Lemass did not elaborate here on youth political parties, his speech was far removed from the treatment the subject received from others such as Senator Joseph Connolly. In 1953, in his pamphlet, *How does she stand?: An appeal to Young Ireland*, Connolly, a former friend of Eamon de Valera, appealed to those young men and women of 'reasonable intelligence, good character and a reasonable sense of what is right and wrong' to become involved in politics;[6] in a similar vein, Fine Gael's John A. Costello called in 1959 on 'real patriotic effort' from all people. Costello urged 'those with convictions or those with beliefs in certain policies which they consider to be right' to join political parties. If they do not 'actively challenge those with the wrong policies the wrong policies will continue to do their damage and take their toll, and the responsibility will be chiefly on those who shirked or feared the fight, and allowed the good causes to go undefended'.[7] Where Connolly differed from Costello and indeed Lemass was in the remedies needed to resolve Ireland's social and economic ills. Connolly's argument for a 'restoration of the old spirit of Sinn Féin and Irish Ireland' was one that was hardly likely to entice the younger generation into politics.

It was the Fine Gael party which was at this stage to the fore of both criticising the youth as well as calling for their increased engagement in politics. Having, at the 1954 General Election come to within 15 seats of the perennially dominant Fianna Fáil party, the party began to address shortcomings in its organisation and the lack of attractive policies following its defeat at the 1957 election. That, as previously noted, it would be John A. Costello, the Taoiseach during the two inter-party governments in the post World War II period, who would oversee such moves, was not on the face of it, obvious. A traditionalist on social and moral questions, Costello's belligerent style as well as his oratorical skills were reflected in different speeches, particularly at his party's Ard Fheiseanna. Whereas in 1954, he expressed confidence and satisfaction at the 'growing numbers of young people'[8] interested in the party, this as is evident in the result at the 1957 election was short-lived. While he continued in 1958 to express 'pride' in the party's success in gaining support from the younger generation, Costello went on to accuse the 'younger people of ability and education', who through 'cynicism' and by remaining 'aloof' from politics, 'cowardly' left a 'vacuum'. This, he claimed, 'has already done much to bring nearer the unhappy day when violent, irresponsible or self-seeking men may finally secure the power with which they could do such damage'.[9] A reference to the continuing IRA border campaign and a clear indictment of those who choose not to join political parties, Costello's speeches softened the following year when he argued that 'younger people always have had a welcome' in Fine Gael and that they would have 'a full share in the direction of policy and the control of the party'.[10]

Given Costello, with a busy legal career, was a part-time politician for much of his life, his commitment to this is questionable. And yet as Taoiseach, he recognised the need to open up the economy as the country moved away from protectionism towards free trade and after the 1957 election, when Fine Gael found itself out of government, he oversaw the establishment of a Research and Information Centre, led by the new generation in his son, Declan and T. F. O'Higgins. While the centre anticipated future debates within Fine Gael on the *Just Society* policy,[11] John A. Costello argued in 1960 in a letter to James Dillon the then party leader that Fine Gael needed to move to the left before claiming that it 'could never become a Socialist Party'. Urging Dillon to act, he again expressed the need for young people to have an 'effective voice' in the party and be 'freely permitted to express their views'. He went on to claim that 'if the Fine Gael party were to survive it can only do so by attracting the younger people in the country'.[12] Early hopes that this would come to fruition, that Fine Gael had, by recruiting the 'intelligent youth', gained a decisive advantage over Fianna Fáil, were reflected in the 'young lions' of the party's Central branch running for election for local government in 1960 and the establishment of a Fine Gael National Youth Council in 1961.[13] The following year, 1962, a UCD branch was established and party leader James Dillon opened the first social event of the Cork Fine Gael youth group, advising 'young people to approach the actual work of politics with enthusiasm'.[14] Warning against cynicism, Dillon, however, as leader did little to facilitate increased engagement from the younger generation and indeed his policy approach was heavily criticised by Fine Gael's Vincent Browne.[15] Debates over the party's future policy direction went hand in hand with criticism of the side-lining of the voice of the youth as divisions became increasingly public as the decade progressed.

The University sector was for much of the 1960s the focus of student activity. In terms of political parties, Fianna Fáil leader and then Taoiseach, Seán Lemass' appeal for 'younger persons to enter politics'[16] had been the impetus for Costello to take a practical step towards the creation of youth political groups in Fine Gael. Following a meeting with young students at University College Dublin, Costello argued in a memorandum in most likely late 1959 for a Fine Gael branch to be established in that university. Given the links the party had with UCD,[17] it was unsurprising that the party's most active student branch was within this college. Difficulties in identifying what its primary activities would be and how to recruit members led Costello to claim that if the UCD authorities did not allow a branch to be registered as a student association, it could then include members from Trinity.[18] While Michael Tierney was still UCD president, no student political clubs were granted permission to meet within the University[19] so students from all universities would attend meetings usually in a hotel in the city centre, thus effectively side stepping the need to be recognised by their University.

In 1966, Jeremiah Hogan, Tierney's successor as president, finally allowed the three main political parties, Fine Gael, Fianna Fáil and Labour, to hold meetings within the university, with each of them having stands during their university's Fresher's week.[20] This both reflected the increased interest among students in politics but also helped the parties attract more members. The following year, 1967, University College Cork granted recognition of the political parties on condition among other things that the parties were registered by the Oireachtas, that they only have three meetings a year and that they would not receive funding from the college.[21] University College Galway seems to be the exception having as of 1968 not granted permission for political parties to exist within that college.[22] Student protests became more prevalent in response with Labour being involved in one in Galway with the Vietnam War being its subject and another in UCC when the British Ambassador spoke at a meeting of the college's Political Discussion Group.[23] Northern Ireland, including the banning of the Sinn Féin Republican clubs, was the theme of this protest. When considering whether to recognise this party, the Dublin Universities differed in their approach with Trinity choosing to recognise them as the Republican Club's constitution claimed that it were not affiliated to a political party. On the other hand, UCD took the contrary position that only branches of political parties registered at the Oireachtas would be recognised and allowed exist.[24] This was one cause of the 1968 'Gentle Revolution' where radical students demanded a greater democratisation and other reforms with regard to the running of the University. More generally, it reflected a leftward shift in student opinion as domestic and international issues such as housing, Northern Ireland, the war in Vietnam and Apartheid in South Africa increasingly impressed on the student mind.

It was the UCD branch of Fine Gael which strongly advocated that the party adopt a more progressive agenda by fully committing to the *Just Society* policy. Arguing for greater state intervention in the pursuit of an end to social and economic inequality, the document was the subject of divisions between liberal and more conservative elements of the party. From 1965 through to 1968, Vincent Browne called for greater equality in *Quo Vadis*, the Fine Gael Youth publication[25] before going on to lead the student campaign for the party to change its name to Fine Gael: the Social Democratic party.[26] Ahead of the party's Ard Fheis in 1968, Browne in an article in the *Irish Times* contrasted the 'impatience and irritation . . . of the younger section with the lethargy, equivocation and torpor of the Oireachtas party'.[27] Sponsored by nine branches, Browne proceeded to propose the motion for a name change before the party at the Mansion House where it received strong support before Gerry Sweetman, a conservative TD, effectively ended the debate. Somewhat optimistically, the significance of the episode according to *The Irish Times* was that the 'Youth and students had . . . revived Fine Gael'.[28] Described as the 'liveliest political conference seen in Dublin in 30 years', much of this was due to the student and youth branches. Not all members of the Fine Gael party, however, valued or agreed with this energy and activism.

This was also true of Fianna Fáil's UCD branch. In practical terms, the relative quiescence did not matter as the branch remained the most successful with more members than both Fine Gael and Labour.[29] Highlights for FF's UCD branch included its secretary having the honour at the annual Arbour Hill commemoration of reading for the first time the 1916 Proclamation in Irish and English and newly elected TD Gerry Collins receiving a heroes' welcome when returning to speak to the society after his successful by-election.[30] Where the branch did not during the 1960s challenge the party's leadership in the same way as the youth wings of Fine Gael did theirs, the students in Fianna Fáil were not immune to the changing climate. Examples include an article in Ógra the combined University's branch's publication advocating that worker's representatives should be included on the boards of publicly owned firms and one member arguing for the opening up of diplomatic relations with the Soviet Union.[31] More controversial for the party was the Arms trial and the fallout with a significant number of the Galway students branch resigning and the Fianna Fáil Youth movement disbanding in protest at the treatment that they believed Gerry Boland was receiving at the time.[32] Particular displeasure was aimed at Erskine Childers, the then Tánaiste's comments in Galway that it was the IRA's actions that provoked a change of strategy by the British Army with Boland's new political grouping Aontacht Éireann claiming this is what provoked the students' resignation from the branch.[33]

What happened to the politically active after leaving college was a question increasingly placed on the agenda. Newly elected Fine Gael TD, Garret FitzGerald, for one, advocated in 1969 greater engagement with the youth. Echoing what John A. Costello said at the start of the decade, FitzGerald claimed it was 'vitally important that the voice of young people should be heard in Leinster House'.[34] From the viewpoint of the youth, the 1972 referendum, which lowered the voting age from 21 to 18, only added to calls for the political parties to establish youth wings. Fianna Fáil's decision to exclude younger voters from the 1973 election meant that those aged between 18 and 25 could not vote until the 1977 election.[35] The Union of Students in Ireland went so far as to accuse Fianna Fáil of a 'serious abuse of power'.[36] And yet once defeated in the 1973 election, the party addressed any such conception, targeting the youth vote in 1977. Fianna Fáil in 1975 was the first party to establish a youth national conference with the theme 'looking to the future'.[37] Having rejected the creation of a youth wing throughout the 1960s, the party was the first to set one up, namely Ógra Fianna Fáil. That same year, 1975, Fine Gael decided not to create one.[38] The paradox then was that Fine Gael would not establish a youth wing until 1978 even though it had, at least according to its own members but also as claimed in an analysis in 1973 of the branches in Trinity,[39] had for the most part the more vibrant youth members. Part of the reason for this hesitancy was it seems a caution and fear as to the role such a body could play in dissenting from party policy. The experience of, however, being out of government was critical to an increasing interest in the youth of Ireland. That and the fact that Garret FitzGerald became party leader following their defeat in the 1977 election resulted in the establishment of a youth movement finally in the following year with Labour Youth following in 1979. To the fore of FitzGerald's mind was the need to capture the youth vote and the youth movement was key to partly realising this objective. This was of course all part of a greater strategy in terms of reorganising and modernising the party that would see it come to within five seats of Fianna Fáil at the November 1982 election.

During the 1960s and 1970s, young people become an increasingly prominent part of the national debate as the main political parties recognised the value of the youth vote. This reflected the greater role young people played in the economic life of the country as well as through events such as the commemoration of the 1916 Rising and as one unsuccessful and another successful Presidential candidate, namely T. F. O'Higgins and Erskine Childers sought to define their Presidency as one in which youth would have a central place. The reality did not always match the discourse as in truth youth represented a subordinate part in the priorities of the political parties. And yet efforts were made to ensure that the voice of the youth was represented and included in national debates. The transformation in how politicians engaged with the younger generation from the 1950s through to the 1970s is an important marker of the modernisation of Ireland. This transition from when few thought of them to one where they formed a social and political category in of themselves is a notable development. While Fine Gael was to the fore in attempts to harness their voice, Fianna Fáil's greater professionalism meant it was usually more effective in capturing their vote. Despite the challenges, the more radical voices represented to the political establishment and they did at different times generate controversy which needed to be managed or controlled, youth and the younger generation did not significantly differ in the way they allocated their votes or articulated their preferences from their elders. As the younger generation entered the world of work and many married young and had their own families, it was not surprising that their preferences in many ways accorded with those of the older generation as in truth many of them faced similar challenges in their lives. This was reflected in the relative strengths of the youth wings of the political parties with Labour youth University parties generally not having much support. Nevertheless, it is also true that the youth's support for left-wing and more liberal values did have an impact as Ireland moved closer to the European mainstream during the 1960s and 1970s. The impetus the youth gave to the *Just Society* proposals or Garret FitzGerald's liberal constitutional crusade or indeed Fianna Fáil's success at the 1977 general election is difficult to measure but present for all that. What can be said is that the form political youth bodies took illustrates that the political establishment recognised the importance of youth even if their voice was not always heard.

Notes

1 UCD Archives, John A. Costello Papers, P190/315, Text of the address given by Mr. John A. Costello, S. C., T. D., Leader of the Opposition at the Fine Gael Ard Fheis on 5 February 1958, pp. 7 & 13. For more on Costello, see David McCullough, *The Reluctant Taoiseach: A biography of John A. Costello* (Dublin, 2012).
2 *Irish Times*, 6 February 1958.
3 Tomás Finn, *Tuairim, Intellectual Debate and Policy Formulation: Rethinking Ireland, 1954–75* (Manchester, 2012); Tomás Finn, '"Towards a Better Ireland": Donal Barrington and the Irish Constitution', in Laura Cahillane, James Gallen, and Tom Hickey (eds.), *Judges, Politics and the Irish Constitution* (Manchester, 2017), pp. 217–233.
4 *Irish Times*, 27 April 1955, 9 March 1963.
5 Dáil Éireann Debate, vol. 176, col 1577, 'Committee on Finance – vote 3, Department of Taoiseach', 21 July 1959. For more on Seán Lemass and his engagement with *Tuairim* see Finn, *Tuairim, intellectual debate and policy formulation* and more generally among others on Lemass, see John Horgan, *Seán Lemass: Enigmatic Patriot* (Dublin, 1997).
6 Joseph Connolly, *How Does She Stand? An Appeal to Young Ireland* (Dublin, 1953), pp. 60, 14.
7 UCD Archives, John A. Costello Papers, P190/758 (7), Text of the address given by Mr. John A. Costello, S. C., T. D., Leader of the Opposition at the Fine Gael Ard Fheis on 11 February 1959; UCD Archives, John A. Costello Papers, P190/315, Text of the address given by John. A. Costello, on 5 February 1958.
8 UCD Archives, John A. Costello Papers, P190/298, Text of the address given by John. A. Costello on 17 February 1954.
9 UCD Archives, John A. Costello Papers, P190/315, Text of the address given by John. A. Costello on 5 February 1958.
10 UCD Archives, John A. Costello Papers, P190/758 (7), Text of the address given by Mr. John. A. Costello, S. C., T. D., Leader of the Opposition at the Fine Gael Ard Fheis on 11 February 1959.
11 Ciara Meehan, *A Just Society for Ireland, 1964–1987* (London, 2013).
12 UCD Archives, John A. Costello Papers, P190/340 (2), letter from Costello to James Dillon, 13 January 1960. For more on Dillon see Maurice Manning, *James Dillon: A Biography* (Dublin,1999).
13 *Irish Times*, 22 October 1959, 18 June 1960, 26 June 1961, 25 July 1961, 2 April 1962.
14 *Irish Times*, 8 November, 2 April 1962.
15 *Irish Times*, 22 February 1965.
16 UCD Archives, John A. Costello Papers, P190/266, Memorandum, no date. [c. a. 1959].
17 Donal McCartney, *UCD: A National Life: The History of University College Dublin* (Dublin, 1999), p. 185.
18 UCD Archives, John A. Costello Papers, P190/266, Memorandum, no date. [c. a. 1959].
19 *Irish Independent*, 27 May 1968.
20 *Irish Press*, 14 October 1966.
21 *Irish Examiner*, 14 November 1967.
22 *Irish Press*, 22 March 1969.
23 Carole Holohan, *Reframing Irish Youth in the Sixties* (Liverpool, 2018), p. 52; *Irish Examiner*, 23 November 1967.
24 *Irish Press*, 19 April 1968.

25 *Irish Times*, 13 September 1965, 22 March 1967. According to the *Irish Times*, 1965 was also the year the party's Youth Group published the first issue of its newspaper, *The Citizen*. *Quo Vadis* appeared on two occasions, later being integrated into *The Citizen*.
26 *Irish Times*, 4 November 1965; Meehan, *A Just Society*, p. 77.
27 *Irish Times*, 14 May 1968.
28 *Irish Times*, 15 May 1968.
29 Holohan, *Reframing Irish Youth*, p. 56.
30 *Irish Times*, 27 March, 22 November 1967.
31 *Irish Times*, 26 February 1968. Also *Irish Times*, 22 March, 4 April 1967.
32 *Irish Times*, 8 May 1971. For more on the Arms trial see for example Dermot Keogh, *Jack Lynch: A Biography* (Dublin, 2008).
33 *Irish Times*, 19 February 1972.
34 *Irish Times*, 26 January 1969. See Garret FitzGerald, *All in a Life: An Autobiography* (Dublin: Gill and Macmillan, 1991).
35 Holohan, *Reframing Irish Youth*, p. 57.
36 *Irish Times*, 23 February 1973.
37 *Irish Times*, 23 February 1973.
38 *Irish Times*, 27 March 1975.
39 *Irish Times*, 11 April 1973. While a lively branch, Fine Gael had only established it in Trinity in 1972.

17 'To Hell or to Connaught'

Margaret Thatcher, Northern Ireland and the Prospect of Repartition, 1979–1990[*]

Stephen Kelly

I will never be prepared to walk out and let the terrorists win.

[Margaret Thatcher, 28 June 1988][1]

Introduction

Margaret Thatcher's attitude to the prospect of repartition and the redrawing of the boundary of Northern Ireland, including the mass transfer of Northern Catholics to the Republic of Ireland, during her period as prime minister of the UK[2] from 1979 to 1990 is analysed in this chapter.[3] Despite being repeatedly informed by her leading civil servants and ministerial colleagues that repartition had the potential to ignite a full scale civil war in Northern Ireland, to borrow former secretary of state for Northern Ireland Douglas Hurd's diagnosis,[4] it is argued that Thatcher harboured a long held misconception that the redrawing of the boundary between the Republic of Ireland and Northern Ireland would greatly improve cross-border security and diminish the threat posed by Irish Republican paramilitaries.[5]

Thatcher's rather naïve interpretation of the repartition question merely reinforced the perception amongst those who worked close to her of her general ignorance of the subject of Northern Ireland. Far too often, Thatcher demonstrated a certain 'primitiveness' towards the prospect of repartition and more generally the UK government's Northern Ireland policy, regularly overwhelmed by the complexities of the subject that confronted her, to borrow Sir David Goodall's description[6] (Goodall held the post of deputy under-secretary of state to the Foreign Office, 1984–1987).[7] As I have argued elsewhere, throughout Thatcher's premiership, Northern Ireland always felt like an 'annoying distraction', a sideshow to more urgent socio-economic issues, including her obsession with reducing rampant inflation and how to temper the power of the trade unions.[8] In as much as Thatcher had little interest in agriculture, the arts, sports and transport, Northern Ireland was not an area of party or government policy that she was naturally drawn towards. As a result, the subject 'rarely featured high on *her* list of political priorities nor was it a topic which she ever truly understood'.[9]

DOI: 10.4324/9781032691886-17

In fact, Thatcher's relationship with Northern Ireland is associated most with personal experiences of loss, a sense of hopelessness and perpetual paramilitary violence. On the eve of entering government in 1979, she suffered the devastating loss of Airey Neave, her shadow secretary of state for Northern Ireland from 1975 to 1979, murdered by the Irish National Liberation Army (INLA) in March of that year. Five years later, PIRA came within inches of assassinating Thatcher at the Conservative Party conference in Brighton in October of 1984. In July of 1989, Thatcher experienced further tragedy and personal loss following the callous assassination by the PIRA of her close friend and political ally Ian Gow. In fact, Thatcher's sympathies were generally kept for the hundreds of British soldiers and members of the Royal Ulster Constabulary (RUC) and associated security forces who lost their lives during her time in office. In her own words, she despaired at having to send 'young boys over [to Northern Ireland] to their deaths'.[10]

It should, therefore, come as no surprise to learn that security policy always remained 'the single most important policy' in relation to Thatcher's Northern Ireland policy.[11] She was obsessed with security policy, channelling much of her energy and thinking vis-a-vis Northern Ireland on how to tackle paramilitary violence, chiefly Irish Republican terrorism. It is partly because of her prioritizing security policy over political initiatives for Northern Ireland that she quickly gained a reputation as an inflexible militarist. Her 'no surrender' attitude was confirmed by her refusal to concede 'political status' during the 1981 Republican hunger-strike, during which time Bobby Sands and a further nine prisoners died. 'From this time forward', to use Thatcher's words, 'I became the [P]IRA's top target for assassination'.[12]

Thatcher's prioritizing of security policy over confronting the political realities of day-to-day life in Northern Ireland naturally impacted on her attitude towards Northern Catholics and more broadly Irish Nationalism. Throughout her premiership, as a staunch unionist dedicated to persevering the constitutional link between Great Britain and Northern Ireland, Thatcher deeply resented many Northern Catholics' rejection of their British identify and nationality. In holding such strong beliefs Thatcher thus fostered a point of view (that she never completely abandoned) that those Northern Catholics who did not wish to remain under British rule should be relocated to the Republic of Ireland.

As is analyzed below, in January 1984, Thatcher raised the prospect of the transfer of Northern Catholics to the Republic of Ireland. As David Goodall recounted 'the Irish', Thatcher was reported as saying, 'were used to large scale movements of population. Only recently there had been a population transfer of that kind'. At this point, Goodall noted that 'the silence around the fire became transfused with simple bafflement'. After a pause, he asked whether she could be 'possibility thinking of [Oliver] Cromwell?'. Thatcher confirmed this to be correct. 'Prime Minister', Goodall interjected, 'Cromwell's policy towards Ireland was known as "To Hell or to Connaught" and it left a scar on Anglo-Irish relations which still haven't healed'.[13] Goodall and the others sitting alongside him were genuinely stunned by Thatcher's comments. Goodall could simply not fathom that Thatcher, as head of the UK government, would revive the memory of Oliver Cromwell, 'dubbed the butcher of Ireland', and encourage tens of thousands of Catholics to leave Northern Ireland for the Republic of Ireland (during the Cromwellian war in Ireland, 1649–1653, Cromwell's forces forcefully evicted thousands of Catholics from Ulster).

Such episodes confirmed Thatcher's often confused and occasionally ignorant attitude to Northern Ireland. Despite repeated interjections from her leading civil servants and ministerial colleagues that such a policy may in fact lead to a full-scale civil war, not to mention be interpreted as an act of ethnic cleansing, she routinely brought up the perceived merits of repartition.

There is 'No Tidy Dividing Line': The Origins of Thatcher's Attitude to Repartition, 1979–1984

Thatcher always found the Irish border and the prospect of repartition a conundrum. Throughout her premiership, she occasionally brought up the prospect of repartitioning Northern Ireland and of authorizing the adjustment of the Irish border to accommodate the transfer of Northern Catholics to the Republic of Ireland. Charles Moore, Thatcher's official biographer, suggests that at arriving at this understanding, Thatcher had in her mind the Irish Boundary Commission Agreement of 1925,[14] which under the terms of the Anglo-Irish Treaty of 1921 was established to 'determine whether areas with a large Catholic population should be transferred to the Irish Free State'.[15]

Whether Thatcher did, in fact, even know about the IBCA, never mind use it as a template for her own thinking about the subject, is unclear. However, what is clear, in supporting this proposition, Thatcher was under the misguided belief that this would help to improve the security situation, specifically cross-border security along the border between the Republic of Ireland and Northern Ireland. Repeatedly, she had to be reminded that there was 'no tidy dividing line' between the intertwining Catholic and Protestant communities, including in Belfast and Londonderry, to quote Douglas Hurd.[16]

In his memoir, Hurd recalled with frustration how Thatcher tended to begin 'from square one' each time there was a meeting to consider Northern Ireland policy.

> I do not know how many times she began a conversation with me by saying that the answer might be to redraw the [North-South] border so as to be rid of areas which were substantially Nationalist and retain a loyal and impregnable Unionist province.

'Repeatedly', Hurd wrote, 'I had to tell her of the tribal map of Belfast hanging in my office at Stormont. Hurd continued:

> The map looked as if an artist had flung pots of orange and green paint haphazardly at the canvas. . . . The intertwining of the communities was hopelessly complex. The same was broadly true of Londonderry, and for four of the six counties of the Province. The term 'ethnic cleansing' was not yet in vogue, but ethnic cleansing on a brutal scale would have been needed if repartition were to have any effect.[17]

Thatcher, however, refused to ditch the repartition proposal. According to Charles Powell, Thatcher's private secretary for foreign affairs, 1983–1990, on another occasion, the British prime minister suggested that if the UK government sanctioned the construction of a new 'straight line border' between Northern Ireland and the Republic of Ireland and 'not one with all those kinks and wiggles in it, it would be easier to defend'.[18] On this occasion, it took the forceful intervention of Sir Robert Armstrong, cabinet secretary, 1979–1987, to dissuade Thatcher of her support for repartition. 'It wasn't as simple as that', he informed his prime minister, 'because the nationalist communities were not all in one place, not all in Fermanagh and Tyrone and South Armagh and so on'.[19]

Yet again, and despite such interventions, Thatcher refused to abandon the prospect of repartition, including the mass transfer of Northern Catholics into the Republic of Ireland. For example, at a late-night meeting at Chequers, in January 1984, convened to discuss Northern Ireland, Thatcher is again recorded as raising the subject of repartition. Apart from Thatcher also in attendance were Sir Geoffrey Howe, secretary of state for foreign and commonwealth affairs, 1983–1989, James Prior, secretary of state for Northern Ireland, 1981–1984, Armstrong and Goodall.

It was simply logical, Thatcher was reported as stating, to encourage Northern Catholics 'who did not wish to remain under British rule' to relocate to the Republic of Ireland. 'Why could we not redraw the Border to exclude predominantly Catholic areas and relieve ourselves of the expense of paying social security to people who did not want to belong to the United Kingdom anyway?', she pondered.[20] Not for the first nor last time it took the forceful intervention of her civil servants to remind Thatcher that this would not solve the problem as Catholic and Protestant communities were 'too intermingled in Border areas', to quote Goodall.[21]

Thatcher seemed unable to drop the prospect of repartition. As Charles Moore has explained, such examples of Thatcher's references to repartition were typical from her general pessimistic outlook towards Northern Ireland. During her often lengthy and distracted frustrated pronouncements about terrorism, she would put forward 'various ideas', including reparation, in the hope of making some progress on Northern Ireland.[22] Indeed, on another occasion, she compared Northern Catholics to Germans in the Sudetenland during the 1930s, 'hardly a point calculated to reassure either side', to quote Richard Vinen.[23]

Such episodes confirmed how difficult Thatcher found it to 'accept at an emotional level the idea that Irish Nationalists could never be brought up to accept the democratic legitimacy of British sovereignty', in the words of Marc Mulholland. She was 'obsessed with the idea of solving the problem by somehow creating a purely British enclave state in Ireland'. In fact, Thatcher's attitude to Northern Catholics demonstrated her inability to 'engage with the unattractive reality that Irish Nationalists were inassimilable to British sovereignty'.[24]

At heart, Thatcher was instinctively a unionist. For this reason, she found it almost impossible to acknowledge that many Catholics in Northern Ireland felt a stronger allegiance to the Republic of Ireland rather than the UK. Northern Ireland was British, as much so as the Falklands, Gibraltar or Hong Kong, she reasoned. Therefore, she could not fathom why many of the Catholic population rejected a British identity and nationality. Thatcher's prejudices were certainly shaped by her detest for Irish Republican violence and her opposition to a united Ireland, which threatened to tear apart the union between Great Britain and Northern Ireland. Consequently, throughout her leadership of the Conservative Party, she never wavered in her commitment to maintaining Northern Ireland's constitutional position within the UK. Above all else, to quote Armstrong, when it came to Northern Ireland's constitutional position within the UK, Thatcher's 'rock was sovereignty'.[25]

Yet, one must tread cautiously when prescribing the label 'unionist' to Thatcher. On an emotional level, Thatcher was primarily an English unionist. As with Scottish and Welsh unionism, she had a limited and defective understanding of Ulster unionism. To paraphrase Richard Finlay, for such a 'committed unionist', Thatcher had a poor understanding of Scottish, Welsh and Irish unionism, failing to grasp the complex historical dynamics that had characterized the development of unionism in these three countries.[26] This stance was particularly true in relation to Northern Ireland. Thatcher never developed a 'feel' for Northern Ireland, including its distinctive culture, history and socio-economic foundations, to quote John Hume, Social Democratic and Labour Party (SDLP) leader, 1979–2001.[27] Indeed, as much as Thatcher knew little about the manufacturing cities and industrial centres of the North of England, Scotland and Wales, Northern Ireland remained an alien place. As such, to borrow David Cannadine's astute description in many ways, Thatcher was 'only prime minister of the south-east of England and the rural constituencies'.[28]

The Proposed 'Radical Re-drawing of the Boundary': Thatcher and the Merit of Repartition, 1984–1987

While the British government under Thatcher never considered repartition as a *viable* policy (irrespective of Thatcher's personal superficial interest in the topic) the subject was at least examined at the highest-level during Thatcher's second term in office, 1983–1987. Declassified British government files from 1984 reveal that Thatcher, together with some of her most senior ministerial colleagues, including Sir Geoffrey Howe and James Prior, debated the merits of repartition and potential changes to the boundary of Northern Ireland.[29] Their interest in the topic stemmed from a briefing paper produced on behalf of the Northern Ireland Office (NIO), in conjunction with research conducted by Dr Paul Compton of Queen's University Belfast.

Dated 6 June 1984, in this paper, Compton opened with the proposition that the partition of Ireland under the terms of the Government of Ireland Act of 1920 (which established two self-governing polities: Northern Ireland and Southern Ireland), was 'necessary' and 'justified' but ultimately 'flawed' by the 'messy way in which it was executed', to borrow the NIO's critique of Compton's analysis.[30] Compton argued that the central cause of the present difficulties in Northern Ireland was it's 'over-bounding' and that closer attention should have been directed towards the geographical distribution of Catholics and Protestants in the region.[31]

Compton thus raised the prospect of redrawing 'the boundary [between the Republic of Ireland and Northern Ireland] now in a way which would produce a more homogenous population in Northern Ireland'. In support of his analysis, Compton used 1971 census figures and 'examined distribution by religion in District Council and Ward areas', although he recognised that not all Catholics favoured a united Ireland.[32]

An important finding of Compton's research was that the then current distribution in Northern Ireland between Catholics and Protestants was 'even more intermingled than at the time of partition in the early 1920s'. As he recorded, 'Even where the Catholics are in a majority there tends to be a substantial Protestant minority'.[33] Consequently, Compton argued that such high levels of intermingling across Northern Ireland 'ruled out a simple realignment separating Roman Catholics from Protestants altogether'.[34]

As a result, Compton turned his attention to examining 'the scope for redrawing the boundary in a way which would achieve significant reduction in the size of the minority [i.e. the Catholic minority]'. He proposed three possible boundary revisions which would significantly reduce the size of Northern Ireland. The most radical of these proposals (labelled Version A) proposed to leave the population of Northern Ireland to just over 1 million, 'of whom 73.5% would be Protestant and 26.5% Roman Catholic'. In the words of the NIO, this 'radical re-drawing of the boundary' would thus involve ceding 'more than half the present area of Northern Ireland' to the Republic of Ireland. In his paper Compton also suggested 'ceding most of the city of Derry' to the Republic of Ireland and effectively establishing a walled ghetto in west Belfast, creating 'a wedge-shaped area in west Belfast' running from Twinbrook to the Divis Flats.[35]

In the final analysis, Compton *rejected* the prospect of redrawing the Northern Ireland boundary. 'Whereas moving half a million people might be the obvious solution for a totalitarian regime', the paper concluded, 'we face problems as regards the spirit and letter of human rights provisions and international opinion'.[36]

On 21 June 1984, Thatcher convened a meeting as No. 10 Downing Street to examine the British government's Northern Ireland policy, including the subject of repartition. Those in attendance included Thatcher's ministerial colleagues, Sir Geoffrey Howe and James Prior, together with Robert Armstrong, David Goodall and Charles Powell. Following a general discussion regarding recent developments in Northern Ireland those in attendance examined the subject of repartition in light of Dr Compton's recent policy paper. After a brief discussion, the minutes record (in a sterile manner) that there was 'agreement that repartition did not offer a way forward'[37] (Thatcher's underlining of this sentence with a straight line signified her approval).[38]

Although one cannot for certain determine why Thatcher and her colleagues rejected the repartition approach, as outlined by Compton, the available circumstantial evidence would strongly suggested that the proposal was viewed as 'silly nonsense', to quote Jeffrey Donaldson speaking in 2014.[39] As Goodall wrote in his diary, 'The idea of a population transfer was not pursued'.[40] Indeed, the current leader of the Democratic Unionist Party perhaps encapsulated perfectly the response from Thatcher and her ministerial and civil servants, alike, on debating the merits of repartition in the context of Compton's policy paper. 'The idea that you could repartition Northern Ireland', Donaldson exclaimed in the same 2014 interview sourced above, 'not only in terms of our land border with the Irish Republic but also internally, with Belfast divided into different legal jurisdictions similar to a mini Berlin, is just bonkers'.[41]

Conclusion

Baroness Thatcher died on 8 April 2013, at the age of eighty-seven, following a stroke. In the rush to mark Thatcher's passing, Fleet Street reflected on the sense of divisiveness that had characterized her political career. *The Mirror* led with the front-page headline, 'The woman who divided a nation'.[42] *I* newspaper carried a similar message with the central headline, 'Thatcher, as divisive in death as she was in life'.[43] In Northern Ireland, Thatcher's passing sparked a bitter debate regarding her legacy. In the Nationalist enclaves of the Bogside of Derry and the Falls Road in west Belfast, large crowds, many of whom were not born during Thatcher's premiership, gathered to drink champagne and to toast her demise.[44] Yet, in working-class Loyalist and middle-class Unionist areas, alike, Thatcher's death was marked with respectful tributes.[45]

How can one best describe Thatcher's legacy in relation to Northern Ireland? In truth, Northern Ireland rarely featured high on her list of political priorities nor was it a topic which she ever truly understood. Deep down, she resented having to commit so much of her energy and time to the subject and was impatient with a situation which did not easily lend itself to a 'rational solution'.[46] On the occasions when Northern Ireland was forced to the top of her agenda security considerations – not political factors – determined her policy stance.

During her premiership, Thatcher occasionally raised the prospect of repartition and the redrawing of the boundary of Northern Ireland, including the mass transfer of Northern Catholics to the Republic of Ireland. This was a vivid example of her naivety on the subject. Despite repeated utterances from prominent Whitehall officials and ministerial colleagues alike, that such a policy might lead to a full-scale civil war in Northern Ireland, Thatcher continued to debate the merits of repartition, particularly during her second term in office.

Thatcher's occasional support for the potential redrawing of the boundary of Northern Ireland was conditioned by her misguided belief that such a policy would invariably improve cross-border security along the Irish border and as a result diminish the threat posed by Irish Republican paramilitaries. Indeed, as we have learned Thatcher was obsessed with terrorism, channelling much of her energy and thinking into how to tackle paramilitary violence. From the beginning of her leadership of the Conservative Party until her retirement fifteen years later, a strong anti-terrorist doggedness permeated her thinking on Northern Ireland. As she recorded in *The Downing Street Years*, 'My policy towards Northern Ireland was always one aimed above all at upholding democracy and the law: it was always therefore determined by whatever I considered at a particular time would help bring better security'.[47]

Thatcher's obsession with Northern Ireland security policy was a critical factor in her decision to sign the Anglo-Irish Agreement (AIA) in November 1985. Under the terms of this Accord, and to the irritation of Ulster Unionists and many within the Conservative Party, Dublin was granted a 'consultative' role in the affairs of Northern Ireland.[48] One of the main reasons why Thatcher decided to sign the AIA, and specifically agree to allocate the Irish government with a 'consultative' role in the affairs of Northern Ireland, was in the hope that such an approach would greatly improve security, by isolating the terrorists and increase cross-border security co-operation between Dublin and London.[49]

However, by the time Thatcher left office in November 1990, her previous contention that the AIA had failed to live up to her expectations on cross-border security matters seemed to have proven accurate. In the words of Graham Goodlad, if judged by the 'criterion Thatcher prized most highly, the improvement of security in Northern Ireland', the AIA 'could scarcely be rated a success. In the three years to the end of 1985 there were 195 deaths as a result of political violence'; in the three years from January 1986 to January 1989, the 'corresponding figure was 247'.[50]

Thatcher's political downfall witnessed a significant shift in the British government's Northern Ireland policy away from the security realm to the political arena, with a recognition that security policies alone could not deliver an end to the violence. This modification in policy was partially driven not only by economic necessity but also in the context of the end of the Cold War and a realisation on behalf of the British government that medium-term political dialogue must take precedence over a long-term aspiration of defeating Irish Republican terrorism. For example, by the turn of the 1990s, the net transfer of exchequer funds to Northern Ireland from the rest of the UK had risen from under £1,250 million in 1979–1980 to approximately £2,500 million in 1991–1992, the 'equivalent', to quote Howe, 'to some £4,500 a year for each of the 530,000 households in Northern Ireland'.[51]

Consequently, under the leadership of John Major, Thatcher's successor as Conservative Party leader and British prime minister, 1990–1997, the British government refocused its energies on establishing political dialogue with the political parties of Northern Ireland and the Irish government. In fact, Thatcher's forced retirement provided an added impetus to the path towards peace in Northern Ireland, which eventually led to the signing of the Belfast Agreement in 1998. As long as she remained British prime minister, the Sinn Féin leadership, under Gerry Adams, found it impossible to convince the PIRA Army Council to announce an unequivocal ceasefire; a prerequisite set down by the British government *before* Sinn Féin was provided with a seat at the negotiation table. As Ed Moloney noted, PIRA supporters would have condemned even 'the suggestion of a deal with Thatcher as surrender' – the 'hatred' between her and the Republican community was 'just too deep'.[52]

In the final analysis, Thatcher's legacy on Northern Ireland is associated with political naivety, frustration and a sense of hopelessness. Apart from the assassination attempt on her own life by the PIRA and the loss of close friends, including Airey Neave and Ian Gow, to acts of Irish Republican terrorism, Thatcher's thinking on Northern Ireland was conditioned by the continued murder of British soldiers, RUC officers and associated members of the security forces, who lost their lives during her premiership. As she exclaimed to taoiseach (Irish prime minister) Charles Haughey during a techy encounter in June 1988: 'I must send more young boys over to their deaths. . . . There is a borderline there but it is not an effective border'.[53] As this quotation demonstrates, even towards the end of her premiership Thatcher continued to harbour a suspicion that the Irish government had deliberately failed to implement promised improvements in cross-border security in the bid to tackle Irish Republican paramilitaries using the Republic of Ireland as a safe haven.

Notes

* A version of this chapter was first presented at the 33rd Irish Conference of Historians, 'Borders and Boundaries: Historical Perspectives', University of Galway, 21 May 2021.
1 Comments by Thatcher. Record of meeting between Thatcher and Charles J. Haughey (Irish prime minister: taoiseach), Hanover, Germany, 28 June 1988. National Archives of Ireland (NAI) Department of the Taoiseach (DT) 2018/68/38.

2 Henceforth, Thatcher is referred to as 'British prime minister' rather than the prime minister of the UK (i.e., the United Kingdom of Great Britain and Northern Ireland).

3 A shorter version of this article was first published in N.C. Fleming and James H. Murphy (eds.), *Ireland and Partition: Contexts and Consequences* (Clemson, 2021). For relevant secondary literature on this subject see Stephen Kelly, 'Margaret Thatcher, Repartition, Cross-border Security and the Irish Border, 1979–1990', pp. 183–204; Diarmaid Ferriter, *The Border: The Legacy of a Century of Anglo-Irish Politics* (London, 2019), p. 106; Graham Goodlad, *Thatcher* (Abington, 2016), p. 155; Liam Kennedy, *Two Ulsters: A Case for Repartition* (Belfast, 1986); Liam Kennedy, 'Repartition', in John McGarry and Brendan O'Leary (eds.), *The Future of Northern Ireland* (Oxford, 1990), pp. 137–161; Charles Moore, *Margaret Thatcher: The Authorized Biography, Vol. 2: Everything She Wants* (London, 2015), pp. 305–306; and Richard Vinen, *Thatcher's Britain: the politics and social upheaval of the 1980s* (London, 2010), pp. 217–218. See also Kelly, *Margaret Thatcher, the Conservative Party and the Northern Ireland conflict, 1975–1990*, p. 2. The research on which this chapter is based consists of hitherto unused and recently declassified primary sources from several archival institutions in Great Britain and Ireland, including the National Archives of the United Kingdom. See department files held by the National Archives of the United Kingdom (TNA): Prime Minister's Office (PM); the Cabinet Office (CAB); the Northern Ireland Office (NIO); and the Foreign and Commonwealth Office (FCO); This article has also utilised personal papers held by Churchill Archives Centre, University of Cambridge, the files of the Departments of Taoiseach and Foreign Affairs at the National Archives of Ireland and the Margaret Thatcher Foundation. See UC CAC: David Goodall manuscript, Misc. 74 and the Margaret Thatcher Papers (THCR) and https://www.margaretthatcher.org/. In particular, the release of declassified British government departmental files related to Thatcher's premiership under the U.K. state's 'twenty-year' rule permits this article to offer a fresh interpretation of the subject matter under investigation.

4 Hurd was secretary of state for Northern Ireland from 1984 to 1985. See Douglas Hurd, *Memoirs* (London, 2004), p. 335.

5 As the title of this article suggests its contents focus on Thatcher's attitude to repartition and Northern Ireland. For a more in-depth study of Thatcher's Northern Ireland policy during her period as leader of the Conservative Party from 1975 to 1990 see Stephen Kelly, *Margaret Thatcher, the Conservative Party and the Northern Ireland Conflict, 1975–1990* (London, 2021).

6 See David Goodall manuscript marked 'Part 1', 'The making of the Anglo-Irish Agreement of 1985 (The Hillsborough Agreement): A personal account', 10. University of Cambridge (UC) Churchill Archives Centre (CAC) Misc. 74.

7 Believed to be 'a deeply reflective and industrious Catholic (Charles Moore even described Goodall as an 'almost saintly Roman Catholic') he was descended from an old Anglo-Irish family in Co. Wexford. In fact, in retirement, he retained a strong emotional bond with Ireland, holding the post of president of the Irish Genealogical Research Society from 1992 to 2012. See Howe, *Conflict of Loyalty*, 415 & Moore, *Margaret Thatcher: The Authorized Biography*, vol. 2, 302. See also Recording of paper, 'A tale of two islands: Anglo-Irish relations from a British perspective', by David Goodall. Delivered as part of the Centre for Contemporary Irish History Seminar Series, 2014–2015 (Trinity College Dublin, 25 March 2015). See https://soundcloud.com/tlrhub/repubics-compared-reflections-on-anglo-indian-irish-relations.

8 Kelly, *Margaret Thatcher, the Conservative Party and the Northern Ireland Conflict, 1975–1990*, p. 2.

9 Kelly, *Margaret Thatcher, the Conservative Party and the Northern Ireland Conflict, 1975–1990*, p. 2.
10 See for example, comments by Thatcher. Record of meeting between Haughey and Thatcher, Hanover, Germany, 28 June 1988. NAI DT 2018/68/38.
11 Kelly, *Margaret Thatcher, the Conservative Party and the Northern Ireland Conflict, 1975–1990*, p. 3.
12 Thatcher, *Margaret Thatcher: The Downing Street Years*, p. 391.
13 See Goodall manuscript, 10. UC CAC Misc. 74.
14 Under Article 12 of the Anglo-Irish Treaty of 1921 the Northern Ireland government retained her existing status, as defined by the provisions of the Government of Ireland Act of 1920. However, Article 12 also made provisions for the establishment of a boundary commission, which would revise the border at a later date. It was not until November 1924, nearly three years after the treaty was signed, that the IBCA began its investigation. Northern Ireland refused to appoint a commissioner, therefore, the British and Dublin governments agreed that London should select a commissioner on behalf of Northern Ireland. The Irish government appointed minister for education, Eóin MacNeill as their representative on the commission, J.R. Fisher assumed the role as Northern Ireland commissioner and Richard Feetham, a South African judge, chaired the proceedings. To the bewilderment of the Dublin government the IBCA recommended a relatively insignificant adjustment of the border, with the transfer of some 130,000 acres and 24,000 people from Northern Ireland to the Free State. The report also envisaged a smaller transfer of land and people from the South to the North. There was outrage and confusion in Dublin and the Irish government's representative Eóin MacNeill promptly resigned from the IBCA. In the end, following retracted negotiations in London, on 3 December 1925, an agreement was reached revoking the powers of Article 12 of the Anglo-Irish Treaty of 1921. The border between Dublin and Belfast, therefore, remained unchanged. For an overview of the IBCA's investigations, see Michael Laffan, *The Partition of Ireland, 1911–1925* (Dundalk, 1983), pp. 99–105.
15 Moore, *Margaret Thatcher: The Authorized Biography*, vol. 2, p. 306*.
16 See comments by Douglas Hurd. Hurd, *Memoirs*, p. 335.
17 Hurd, *Memoirs*, p. 335.
18 Quoted in Ferriter, *The Border*, p. 106.
19 Comments by Armstrong. Quoted in the *Guardian*, 16 June 2001.
20 See Goodall manuscript, 10. UC CAC Misc. 74. See also Moore, *Margaret Thatcher: The Authorized Biography,* vol. 2, pp. 303–304.
21 See Goodall manuscript, 10. UC CAC Misc. 74.
22 Moore, *Margaret Thatcher: The Authorized Biography*, vol. 2, pp. 303–304.
23 Vinen, *Thatcher's Britain*, pp. 217–218.
24 Marc Mulholland, '"Just Another Country"? The Irish Question in the Thatcher Years', in Ben Jackson and Roberts Saunders (eds.), *Making Thatcher's Britain* (Cambridge, 2012), pp. 180–196, 190.
25 Author's interview with Lord Armstrong of Ilminster, 27 October 2015.
26 Richard Finlay, 'Thatcherism, Unionism and Nationalism: A Comparative study of Scotland and Wales', in Jackson and Saunders (eds.), *Making Thatcher's Britain*, pp. 165–179, 165, 168.
27 Comments by John Hume. Record of meeting between Thatcher and Hume, 9 February 1984. NAI DFA 2014/32/1940.
28 See David Cannadine, *Margaret Thatcher: A Life and Legacy* (Oxford, 2017), pp. 58 & 84–85.
29 See record of meeting to discuss Northern Ireland, No. 10 Downing St., 21 June 1984. TNA PREM 19/1286.

30 See NIO paper, 'Repartition', 6 June 1984. TNA PREM 19/1286.
31 See NIO paper, 'Repartition', 6 June 1984. TNA PREM 19/1286.
32 See NIO paper, 'Repartition', 6 June 1984. TNA PREM 19/1286.
33 See NIO paper, 'Repartition', 6 June 1984. TNA PREM 19/1286.
34 See NIO paper, 'Repartition', 6 June 1984. TNA PREM 19/1286.
35 See NIO paper, 'Repartition', 6 June 1984. TNA PREM 19/1286.
36 See Northern Ireland Office paper, 'Repartition', 6 June 1984. TNA PREM 19/1286.
37 See record of meeting to discuss Northern Ireland, No. 10 Downing St., 21 June 1984. TNA PREM 19/1286.
38 Thatcher's general style was to insert comments and marks while digesting the content of a memorandum/policy paper. A wiggly line invariably meant Thatcher's disproval, repeated underscoring of a passage with a straight line signified her approval.
39 Comments by Jeffrey Donaldson. Quoted in the *Belfast Telegraph*, 4 January 2014.
40 See Goodall manuscript, 10. UC CAC Misc. 74.
41 Comments by Jeffrey Donaldson. Quoted in the *Belfast Telegraph*, 4 January 2014.
42 *The Mirror*, 9 April 2013.
43 *I*, 9 April 2013.
44 *The Derry Journal*, 9 April 2013.
45 See https://www.bbc.co.uk/news/uk-northern-ireland–22067370.
46 Goodlad, *Thatcher*, p. 155.
47 Thatcher, *Margaret Thatcher: The Downing Street Years*, p. 384.
48 A copy of the AIA (November 1985) is available from TNA CAB 164/1777.
49 The other four factors were: (a) to neutralise the growing support for Sinn Féin; (b) Thatcher's desire to promote peace, stability and to reconcile the two major traditions in the hope of achieving a devolved government in Northern Ireland; (c) the pressure she experienced from those closest to her, notably Sir Geoffrey Howe and a cabal of senior civil servants under the authority of Robert Armstrong; and lastly (d) a more immediate consideration was her relationship with U.S. president, Ronald Reagan. See Kelly, *Margaret Thatcher, the Conservative Party and the Northern Ireland Conflict, 1975–1990*, pp. 224–226.
50 Goodlad, *Thatcher*, p. 165.
51 See Howe, *Conflict of Loyalty*, p. 412.
52 Ed Moloney, *A Secret History of the IRA* (London, 2003), p. 283.
53 Record of comments by Thatcher. Record of meeting between Haughey and Thatcher, Hanover, Germany, 28 June 1988. NAI DT 2018/68/38.

Index

For Product Safety Concerns and Information please contact our EU
representative GPSR@taylorandfrancis.com
Taylor & Francis Verlag GmbH, Kaufingerstraße 24, 80331 München, Germany

www.ingramcontent.com/pod-product-compliance
Ingram Content Group UK Ltd.
Pitfield, Milton Keynes, MK11 3LW, UK
UKHW020456040925
462578UK00007B/136